Language Rights and the Law in the United States

BILINGUAL EDUCATION AND BILINGUALISM
Series Editors: Professor Colin Baker, *University of Wales, Bangor, Wales, Great Britain*
and Professor Nancy H. Hornberger, *University of Pennsylvania, Philadelphia, USA*

Other Books in the Series
At War With Diversity: US Language Policy in an Age of Anxiety
  James Crawford
Bilingual Education and Social Change
  Rebecca Freeman
Dual Language Education
  Kathryn J. Lindholm-Leary
Foundations of Bilingual Education and Bilingualism
  Colin Baker
Identity and the English Language Learner
  Elaine Mellen Day
An Introductory Reader to the Writings of Jim Cummins
  Colin Baker and Nancy Hornberger (eds)
Language and Literacy Teaching for Indigenous Education: A Bilingual Approach
  Norbert Francis and Jon Reyhner
Language Minority Students in the Mainstream Classroom (2nd Edition)
  Angela L. Carrasquillo and Vivian Rodriguez
Languages in America: A Pluralist View
  Susan J. Dicker
Language, Power and Pedagogy: Bilingual Children in the Crossfire
  Jim Cummins
Language Revitalization Processes and Prospects
  Kendall A. King
Language Socialization in Bilingual and Multilingual Societies
  Robert Bayley and Sandra R. Schecter (eds)
The Languages of Israel: Policy, Ideology and Practice
  Bernard Spolsky and Elana Shohamy
The Native Speaker: Myth and Reality
  Alan Davies
Policy and Practice in Bilingual Education
  O. Garcia and C. Baker (eds)
Power, Prestige and Bilingualism: International Perspectives on Elite Bilingual Education
  Anne-Marie de Mejía
The Sociopolitics of English Language Teaching
  Joan Kelly Hall and William G. Eggington (eds)
Teaching and Learning in Multicultural Schools
  Elizabeth Coelho
World English: A Study of its Development
  Janina Brutt-Griffler

Please contact us for the latest book information:
Multilingual Matters, Frankfurt Lodge, Clevedon Hall,
Victoria Road, Clevedon, BS21 7HH, England
http://www.multilingual-matters.com

BILINGUAL EDUCATION AND BILINGUALISM 40
Series Editors: Colin Baker and Nancy H. Hornberger

Language Rights and the Law in the United States

Finding Our Voices

Sandra Del Valle

MULTILINGUAL MATTERS LTD
Clevedon • Buffalo • Toronto • Sydney

With respect for the past and great hope for the future, this book is dedicated to my parents, Jose and Iris Del Valle, and my two daughters, Emily and Amanda.

Library of Congress Cataloging in Publication Data
Del Valle, Sandra
Language Rights and the Law in the United States: Finding Our Voices/Sandra Del Valle.
Bilingual Education and Bilingualism: 40
Includes bibliographical references and index.
1. Language policy–United States. 2. Linguistic minorities–Legal status, laws, etc.–United States. 3. English language–Political aspects–United States. 4. Civil rights–United States.
I. Title. II. Series.
P119.32.U6 D45 2003
306.44'973–dc21   2002015683

British Library Cataloguing in Publication Data
A catalogue entry for this book is available from the British Library.

ISBN 1-85359-645-0 (hbk)
ISBN 1-85359-658-2 (pbk)

Multilingual Matters Ltd
UK: Frankfurt Lodge, Clevedon Hall, Victoria Road, Clevedon BS21 7HH.
USA: UTP, 2250 Military Road, Tonawanda, NY 14150, USA.
Canada: UTP, 5201 Dufferin Street, North York, Ontario M3H 5T8, Canada.
Australia: Footprint Books, PO Box 418, Church Point, NSW 2103, Australia.

Typeset by Wordworks Ltd.
Printed and bound in Great Britain by the Cromwell Press Ltd.

I am in search of my
mother tongue,
I am in search of the
mother tongue.
American can't hold me,
has always been my second language,
I am, in search. I seek my mother tongue.
More than the sounding of women
it is an understanding,
a knowing about cosmos,
this universe in all our bodies,
earth.

from *Mother Tongues – III*,
by Jacqueline Johnson

Contents

Acknowledgments

Although this book was written by one person, it would not have come to fruition if I were not nurtured and developed by extraordinary and committed individuals: those who inspired me with their dedication to civil rights struggles, to Latinos and to true community empowerment. They have contributed to this book in different ways – some may have read drafts of the manuscript, others may have talked through legal and political issues with me; all of them filled me with a deep sense of justice that I tried to embody in my own life and work. Always, always they helped me find my own voice.

This book is essentially the brain child of Diana Caballero who has been the best kind of friend: an inspiration and a confidant. Her sense of urgency over the plight of Latino children in the US was not only infectious, it was mobilizing. She was the first person who filled me with what became a decade-long commitment to bilingual education, simply by being her own self – uncompromising and passionate. Most importantly, she has always had such confidence in me that I am buoyed above my own self-doubts.

To no lesser extent my other "best" friends, Olga Perez and Iris Morales have been emotional, spiritual and political mentors. Committed to the independence of their own minds, they transcend boundaries of race, class, and gender to reflect what is best in thoughtful, caring human beings. To them I owe the space they helped me create to find my own mind from which all creative acts ultimately flow

I have had the great opportunity to work with some wonderful people at the Puerto Rican Legal Defense and Education Fund. For their encouragement, support and just because they continue doing their work in the toughest of times I thank: Ken Kimerling, Arthur Baer, Nina Perales, Evette Soto-Maldonado, Sara Rios, Marilucy Gonzalez, Foster Maer, Carmen Calderon, Miguel Correa, and Alan Levine. For allowing me to work on this book while also at the Fund, I owe great thanks to our director, Juan A. Figueroa. For what seemed like an endless amount of typing and for keeping a clear head even while they tried to decipher my handwriting, thanks go to Mildred Jurado and Denise Lopez.

There are others outside of the Fund who are passionately committed to language rights, and who are constant sources of inspiration. They are Luis O. Reyes, Juan Cartagena, and Stan Mark.

For reviewing the chapter on employment discrimination, I thank Ed Chen. To the following interns who did research or cite-checking while at the Fund, I also owe a debt of gratitude: Sarah Erving, Monica Berry, Anthony Vargas.

I would also like to thank my editor at Multilingual Matters, Colin Baker, for his great insight and enthusiastic support; his questions and comments forced me to refine my thinking and write a better book than would have been possible without him.

Finally and foremostly, I thank my husband, Larry Drucker. He is my lodestar and touchstone; without him I never would have found the voice with which to write this book.

Sandra Del Valle

Introduction

WHAT IS THIS BOOK ABOUT?

This book is an attempt to provide a comprehensive review of the legal status of minority languages in the US and to place that review within an historical and political context. I use the term "language rights" to refer to the set of laws and policies that regulate the treatment of minority languages and those who use minority, or non-English, languages in the US, the language minority communities themselves. The status of minority languages is reflected in decisions made as to whether a government actively restricts the use of minority languages, whether it accommodates them by, for instance, translating documents and judicial proceedings or whether it nurtures them by, for instance, providing long-term bilingual education programs. Throughout this book, I characterize the US policy toward minority languages as swinging from tolerant to hostile with a pragmatic rather than an idealistic core. From a history of tolerating minority languages in order to enlist the sympathies of recent immigrants for the American Revolution to the blatantly xenophobic repression of the German language during World War I to a kind of grudging acceptance of the presence of minority languages that characterized the late twentieth century, the treatment of minority languages has gone hand-in-hand with the status of language minority communities in the US.

For various reasons, it is important to me to use the rhetoric of "rights" in relation to language. First, it is an acknowledgment that language minorities do have claims on the use of their native languages in public and private places that cannot be easily abridged. Simple recognition of that fact alone can be empowering for language minorities and will also tell the public-at-large that language is itself a political and legal issue that cannot be taken for granted.

Second, language rights in the US are part of the civil rights world, a world where the word "rights" has not only social and political, but also definite legal consequences. In this civil rights realm, rights are ideas and claims that are taken so seriously that they can be, and are, made the subject of legislation, litigation, and Supreme Court pronouncements. Although language rights generally are a relative newcomer to this world, they are one that both advocates and opponents must be prepared to see debated at the highest levels of our government.

This book then is about language rights law. It covers all of the law in this area of which I am aware from the perspective of one who passionately believes that language choice is a fundamental aspect of personhood and ought not to be limited except in extremely narrow situations.

No legal field, whether it is property, contracts, civil rights, or trusts and estates, can ever be extracted from its human element, so a legal work on minority languages is deeply embedded in the human experience. As a work dedicated to the legal dimensions of minority languages in the US, then, this book traces the development of a nation, of its people and of its attitudes toward language minorities. It is also an attempt to flesh out the role of language minorities in the development of our jurisprudence, a virtually un-explored area. The legal stories of these communities in the US are what this book hopes to document.

FOR WHOM IS THIS BOOK WRITTEN?

This book is written for activists, advocates, lawyers and non-lawyers, students, and all those who cannot be easily labeled whose hearts and minds are committed to the struggle for the promotion, preservation and protection of language minority communities in the US. Although I have tried hard to limit the use of *legalese*, the fact that I am a lawyer and that this is a book about law will undoubtedly make the reading harder for some than for others. If I alienate anyone because of the legal nature of the writing, I profoundly apologize, because the cause of language rights is not furthered by the loss of potential advocates. I would, however, ask that readers do use their best efforts to follow the book; I don't think careful readers will be disappointed.

WHY WAS THIS BOOK WRITTEN?

Mostly, this book was written because I felt I had a lot of knowledge about language rights law that would be most useful if shared with as many others as possible. I owe the opportunity to acquire this knowledge to the years I have spent as a lawyer at the Puerto Rican Legal Defense and Education Fund, a not-for-profit organization located in New York City that does a variety of civil rights work but specializes in language rights. While I have engaged in various kinds of work while at the Fund, I know that there is more work to be done than I or the Fund alone can handle and more work that could be done if language minority communities themselves were aware of their rights and could take the work into their own hands. Also, there are many lawyers whom I think would like to help the one or two members of language minority communities who might seek them out, but who simply don't have the base of knowledge necessary to begin helping them in any legal way. This book will help those lawyers help others.

This book was written at a particularly significant historical moment for language minorities. In the US, the question of minority language rights has taken on new resonance because of the explosive growth in immigration over the last decade, with unprecedented numbers of people coming from countries that have little or no tradition of English usage. The early analysis of the results of the 2000 Census took many by surprise when it showed that the Latino population, expected to reach record proportions in 2030, was already changing the face of the nation. The Asian population alone had grown by at least 41%[1] since the last Census taken a decade earlier and the Latino population had grown by 58%.[2] Not surprisingly then, the number of speakers of languages other than English grew at seven times the rate of English-only speakers and the rate of those who do not speak English "well" rose by 48.5%.[3] How the nation responds to these exciting demographic changes remains to be seen. Unfortunately, we have had some indications already that our newest immigrants are not being welcomed wholeheartedly, and that minority language usage will be the framework in which assimilation, acculturation, and nationalism will be debated. Specifically, federal anti-immigrant legislation has been passed, social services that appear to benefit immigrants are being reduced, many states have passed English-only laws, and bilingual education has become a lightning rod political issue rather than a strictly pedagogical matter.

Although I am a lawyer, I am not naive, nor self-indulgent enough to believe that the work that needs to be done is only, or even primarily, legal work. I think the book demonstrates repeatedly that the law is a crude tool for defining or protecting such fundamentally human attributes as language, ethnicity, or even race. Although these have been defined to a great extent in US society by the courts, legal language is the one kind of language that is indeed limited and that can contain only just so much of human experience.

Throughout this book, I point out the political battles that must be waged and the need to engage in very grassroots activity if language minority communities want to see real progress. I do know that having legal rights recognized and explicated in courts of law can be very helpful, but I have also seen those rights reduced to nothing more than mere words on paper because of the lack of a commitment to implementing court orders "on the ground."

Ultimately, this book is a work of advocacy. While I attempt to give an accurate and comprehensive account of language rights law, I do so as an act of arming people with knowledge – legal, political, and historical – whether or not they are language minorities themselves, and/or whether they are also lawyers, advocates, activists or students, so that their work on behalf of language minorities can be done more effectively. With this goal in mind, I critique certain judicial decisions, uncover common legal themes and judicial concerns, and provide recommendations for action and alternative legal paradigms where appropriate.

SECURING A PLACE FOR LANGUAGE RIGHTS IN THE CIVIL RIGHTS WORLD

Another goal for the book is to more firmly establish language rights as a legitimate field of legal study and as another pillar in the civil rights world along with the traditional areas of education, housing and voting rights. Civil rights law was, in a significant sense, born in 1954 with the school desegregation decision, *Brown v. Board of Education*. Civil rights law today still has all the markings of its birth – a negative rights structure that places a premium on remedying past acts of discrimination within a Black–White racial archetype. The many-hued immigrants of today, without a substantial, and sometimes without *any*, history of discrimination in the US, whose primary markers are ethnicity and the arguably mutable characteristic of minority language usage, simply do not fit the traditional civil rights model.

Complicating the task of integrating language rights into the civil rights world is the fact that language rights law, as a distinct field, is still in development. Indeed, some might say that it does not yet exist as a separate legal area. There are only a few Supreme Court decisions relating specifically to the claims made by language minorities, and those that have been made have been decidedly vague about how to analyze language-based claims, so there is little guidance for the lower courts. Basic decisions, like whether language minorities can be treated for constitutional purposes like ethnic minorities, are still undecided even though language minorities have had cases before US courts for at least a hundred years. Still, decisions implicating language rights can be found in a plethora of legal areas from constitutional law to criminal law to consumer law to employment to education and voting; their presence in all legal areas is growing.

In many instances, however, there are few common principles uniting the judicial reasoning and there is an *ad hoc* nature to many decisions as judges scramble to apply established legal principles to a new community, making, what may at least sound like new legal demands. Even in more established areas such as employment law there will be rogue courts that will chafe at the prospect of securing greater rights for language minorities and that make decisions based less on law than on bias. It seems that every set of facts can lead to completely different decisions simply depending upon which court was making the decision at which moment.

Language minorities, then, are a challenge to the civil rights world even as they represent the future into which civil rights law must evolve if it is to survive as an area for progressive lawyering. For there are still great social injustices in the US and intolerable acts of discrimination still take place. They are, however, more subtle than the mandated separation of races that occurred fifty years ago when racial discrimination was tolerated or even encouraged in some communities. Today, discrimination has gone underground, couched in the words of economics or administrative expediency: where a garbage dump is placed, how much financing a school receives, where a neo-natal intensive care unit is sited, all are decisions that can be made with negative consequences for minorities, but are much harder to label as invidious discrimination than were the acts of yesterday. There is little room in the conventional "civil rights box" for these more sophisticated forms of discrimination, and the size of this box is getting smaller and smaller. For this is a nation currently hostile to civil rights generally, and traditionally suspicious of group-rights with their connotations of disparaging free choice and individuality. Our judiciary is one that dislikes second-guessing the decisions of legislators and policymakers. Meanwhile, language minorities who increase in number each day are stepping into the civil rights fray at an historically important moment. Which battles civil rights lawyers choose to fight and how they frame their arguments will help shape civil rights for the future; I contend that the complexities that language minorities bring to this process need to be integral to those considerations.

The fact that language rights law has not yet gelled into a known area of law with its own set of maxims and jurisprudence means only that the language minority community is still coming into its own from the civil rights litigation perspective. Even so there do exist certain cases, well-known amongst civil rights lawyers, that have formed the basis for other language rights decisions and cut across factual and regional variations. Cases like *Meyer v. Nebraska* in the due process field, *Hernandez v. New York* in the equal protection area, *Carmona v. Sheffield,* in the social services field, *Negron v. New York* in criminal justice, *Garcia v. Gloor* in the employment area, and *Puerto Rican Political Action Coalition v. Kusper* in the voting rights area. The cases are important from every perspective – in the development of civil rights law generally; for their impact, either positively or negatively, on language rights activism, and for their reflection of the national temper at an historical moment.

Indeed, this is an important time for language rights law, even if its future is cloudy. The language minority community in the US is growing, and will undoubtedly engage in more litigation, some of which may end up before the Supreme Court. With traditional civil rights law suffering the blows of a conservative federal judiciary over the past decade and the Supreme Court becoming more conservative itself, the resolution of those claims could have negative consequences for language minority communities generally. Still, there are local courts, state courts and circuit courts with progressive judges with politically astute and humane agendas that keep the original civil rights dreams of social equity alive. As with all emerging areas, there are opportunities for creative legal maneuvering for those interested in doing cutting-edge work. Although the shape of the final product is still unknown, more litigation will result in more decisions and, by the middle of the twenty-first century, we may very well have an established and more coherent body of language rights law.

THE CONTENT AND ORGANIZATION OF THE BOOK

This book is organized generally into areas of law in which there have been judicial decisions regarding language rights. All of those areas of which I am aware of case law have been covered, from criminal justice and consumer law to employment and voting rights. Since law is essentially a product of political and social forces, I include chapters on the history of minority languages in the US, and try to integrate as much social and political analysis into the legal discussions as I can without detracting from the legal discussion. My feeling is that language minority communities need to know about all aspects of the struggle over language if they are to understand the nature of these struggles and be able to agitate for themselves.

The book begins with a summary of the historical treatment of minority languages during the period of the nation's formation, and covers the political and legal context of the World War eras. The cases covered in this section are particularly important because the nation was experiencing such a high degree of insecurity about its immigrant background that minority language usage was barely condoned and in the case of the German language clearly repressed. We see some of the most important language rights cases coming out of that period and the contribution made by language rights to the development of equal protection and due process law.

The second chapter brings us to the present in terms of the most recent examples of oppressive language policies with the passage of a host of English-only laws in the states. This chapter also contains an analysis of the popularity of English-only laws and the myths used by their proponents to disparage language rights today. This is an important chapter, particularly because it covers many themes and uncovers biases that are found in many judicial decisions discussed in later chapters.

The third chapter is on citizenship and voting rights, and brings us more formally into the specific areas of language rights law. I begin with the role that English literacy plays in the citizenship process because becoming a citizen is a fundamental experience for many language minorities and reflects a nation's basic conception of itself and what it feels are the characteristics bearing on citizenship. Since there is little law in this area, I have combined the law on citizenship with voting rights, an elemental expression of citizenship.

The fourth chapter concerns language rights in the workplace; this is one of the most developed areas of language rights law and one that we will likely see lead to litigation at the Supreme Court level. The areas covered in this comprehensive chapter include English-only workplace rules, compensation for bilingual employees, accent discrimination, and the duties of labor unions to their language minority members.

Chapter 5 is also very comprehensive, as it covers language in the classroom with all of the debates and litigation surrounding bilingual education included in detail. The historical, legislative, and pedagogical bases for bilingual education are discussed as well as the most recent assaults on bilingual education and the litigation that arose in the late twentieth and early twenty-first centuries in an attempt to protect bilingual education. The chapter also includes recommendations for continued action and agitation for activists interested in continuing the struggle for bilingual education in a hostile climate.

Chapter 6 discusses the specific issue of Native American education and the role that native language repression played in the political oppression of Native

Americans and the federal expansion into Indian-held land. This is a particularly brutal history, but one that all language minorities need to be aware of if they want to know the true nexus between language, politics, and power.

The seventh chapter concerns language in the courtroom context. As with employment, this is a very developed area of law, and notions of equal protection and due process are discussed in depth. The chapter is divided into three parts, with coverage of the criminal justice context on everything from interrogations and searches to plea bargains, trials, and sentencing procedures. Chapter 7 also covers the civil trial context and Immigration and naturalization Service (INS) hearings. There is also an in-depth discussion of the issues raised by bilingual jurors that were the basis for the most recent Supreme Court decision in the language rights arena. The last section of the chapter concerns the treatment of language minorities in prison and the extent and limits of the Eighth Amendment of the US Constitution.

Chapter 8 also looks at due process concerns outside the world of strictly judicial proceedings to one in which many language minorities often come into contact: administrative hearings within the context of governmental services such as public assistance and public housing. The reader will notice the much lower standards of due process protection offered to language minorities in this area, and the judicial unwillingness to require governmental translations of important documents.

The ninth chapter concerns consumer law, and pays close attention to those areas in which language minorities are most likely to be affected: commercial transactions and products liability. The section on commercial transactions will cover those situations in which products such as stoves or refrigerators or even personal loans are negotiated, and the role of language in that process. The section on products liability covers the duty of manufacturers to translate warnings and advisories on products for language minority members of the purchasing public.

The last chapter concerns international law, and is more aspirational than the others. It gives an overview of the role of international law in domestic civil rights litigation and summarizes those international law documents that do offer some protection to linguistic minorities. I acknowledge the limited role that international law plays in judicial thinking on civil rights, but argue for activists to continue to raise possible breaches of international law, regardless of judicial restraint, because of my own belief that the US must be held accountable to international human rights norms.

For the past ten years I have been primarily involved in the struggle over bilingual education in New York City. Bilingual education is given a prominent place in this book undoubtedly because of my deeper knowledge of the area. However, it is a prominence for which I am unapologetic. Viewing language rights generally through the prism of bilingual education has helped keep the focus of my work on the core issue of civil rights work generally and language rights work in particular: respect for minorities. For bilingual education cannot easily be legitimized by reference to the short-term self-interests of the majority. Its true nature must be faced: it demands more than simple toleration of native language usage; it requires nurturing; it demands more than modest accommodations, in the way that bilingual voting ballots do; it cannot be excused as an administrative convenience or economic necessity, in the way that translated governmental documents can be. That bilingual education is currently one of the most unpopular civil rights in the country is not a happenstance. Bilingual education demands that language minorities be accepted *as* language minorities, and not as reflecting the inconvenience of a foreign language that must be and can be eradicated and replaced with the more convenient English language. Indeed, the defense of true bilingual education amounts to a demand that the majority culture give minorities the one most valuable asset that would make litigation unnecessary: respect.

My ultimate hope for this book is that, by making the law accessible, it gives language minority communities one of the tools necessary to demand and achieve that respect for themselves.

Notes

1. The Asian population grew by either 41% or 64% depending upon whether Asians alone are counted or Asians in mixed racial categories are counted. *See* CENSUS 2000 PH C-T-15. GENERAL DEMOGRAPHIC CHARACTERISTICS BY RACE FOR THE UNITED STATES: 2000 Table 4: General Demographic Characteristics for the Asian Population. *Compare to:* US CENSUS BUREAU DP-1 GENERAL POPULATION AND HOUSING CHARACTERISTICS: 1990 Data Set: 1990 Summary Tape File 1 (STF 1)-100 Percent data. Census information can be readily obtained at the Census Bureau's website: www.census.gov

2. *See* US CENSUS BUREAU DP-1 GENERAL POPULATION AND HOUSING CHARACTERISTICS: 1990 Data Set: 1990 Summary Tape File 1 (STF 1)-100 Percent data. *Compare to* US CENSUS BUREAU, THE HISPANIC POPULATION: Census 2000 Brief at 3.

3. *See* US CENSUS P035 AGE BY LANGUAGE SPOKEN AT HOME BY ABILITY TO SPEAK ENGLISH FOR THE POPULATION 5 YEARS AND OVER – Universe: Population 5 Years and Over Data Set: Census 2000 Supplemental Survey Summary Tables.

Chapter 1

A History of Language Rights: Between Tolerance and Hostility

INTRODUCTION

Advocates of English as an official language of the US often argue that it is the sole use of the English language, or at least its sole official use, that has acted as a "glue" to hold our country together since its inception.[1] They argue that immigrants of old did not receive special linguistically accommodating services and that they readily gave up their old customs and languages to happily "melt" into the new American mainstream.[2] The historical record, however, does not support their contentions. Indeed, during what could be seen as the country's most vulnerable stages – it's actual formation – bilingualism and multilingualism were much more prevalent than today amongst the population as a whole, and the use of minority languages was tolerated and officially sanctioned by state and local governments. Rather than leading to any de-stabilization, the use of minority languages helped the government coalesce its disparate peoples around the concept of the US as an entity reflecting democratic principles, a republican form of government and constitutionalism. The sense was that, by reaching out to language-minority communities in their own languages, they would witness the tolerant nature of the government, come to defend it, and support its philosophy and institutions.

Advocates can take much heart from this history, and ought to be aware of its dimensions. However, it cannot be concluded from this historical episode that the US is a minority-language-loving nation. The US, neither on the national nor the state levels, has engaged in the promotion of minority language usage for its own sake. Instead, its policies on language have been practical, assimilation-oriented and tolerant only to the extent necessary. It is probably most accurate to say that the

US tolerated and sustained instances of official multilingualism at certain historical periods because it made good, efficacious sense to do so.

This chapter is divided roughly into thirds. The first third begins with an overview of the nation's language policies at the time of its formation, the period when the nation grew from a group of colonies to its expansion across the west and its colonization of Puerto Rico, from roughly the early 1800s through 1917 when Puerto Rico's residents were granted US citizenship; it then discusses current language issues on the island. By providing this history I hope to ensure that language rights activists can effectively refute arguments that this nation has always been monolingual and that its strength is drawn from that linguistic homogeneity. Also, a review of the debates on minority language usage and its role in determining the fates of different territories still echoes today and reveals the very chauvinistic roots of modern language restrictionists.

The second part of the chapter discusses the growth and uses of the Fourteenth Amendment in language rights cases. This is then shown in "action" in the last third of the chapter, which covers language rights during the World War eras. This period is especially important for language rights advocates because during that time of national anxiety language minorities were viewed with extreme suspicion, and minority languages themselves were targeted for repression and even elimination. It was the World War I era that gave birth to the language rights case *Meyer v. Nebraska*, that would ultimately be decided by the US Supreme Court.

LANGUAGE RIGHTS DURING NATION-FORMATION

State efforts

Thomas Jefferson felt that the states themselves would best reflect the needs of their citizens and protect individual liberties against federal tyranny. Within the context of language rights, this precept was true at least in the nation's early years. The states necessarily had to be responsive to the demands of their citizens and when a powerful language-minority group, like the Germans in Ohio or Pennsylvania, took control of the executive or legislative machinery, their interests were championed. This led to a panoply of language tolerant policies including the public support of bilingual and minority language schools in some of these states.

This section will look a little more closely at these policies in those states where official bi- and multilingualism have had a sustained history.

Ohio and Pennsylvania

When Ohio became a state in 1802 it already was home to a substantial German community who were its first permanent settlers. Not surprisingly, then, the first legislative documents of the state issued in 1772 were printed in German. After 1833, however, the German immigration from Europe grew to "gigantic proportions," and many German language islands were established throughout the state with Cincinnati and Cleveland as favored areas.[3] Although there was no specific mention of the German language in the state's constitution, legislation was repeatedly passed from 1817 through the 1830s that allowed the printing of the state laws in German. By the 1880s, German was so prevalent in the state that Ohio was considered a bilingual state by an outside visitor.[4] This was possible, according to Kloss, because of a continuous and strong presence of German representation in the legislature. The strength of this representation is most noticeable in the attitude of at least one pro-German legislative club founded in 1912. Their mission, the cultivation of the German language and ethos was unabashedly presented:

> To cultivate German ideals, such as the German language, German gymnastics, German songs, and German lectures as well as liberal convictions.... Furthermore it is the objective of this club to work with all honest means toward perfecting the teaching of German in the public schools more and more until it has achieved equal status with English in the curriculum.[5]

Even before bilingual education became the lightning rod for issues of ethnicity and multiculturalism in the twentieth century, publicly supported minority language and bilingual education had existed in the US since the eighteenth century.[6] Most of the efforts to maintain separate minority-language schools supported with public funds were made by Germans in those geographical areas in which they were concentrated.

As with Ohio, from about 1710, Pennsylvania had been home to large numbers of the German community. By 1830, the ethnic Germans comprised one-third of the White population. In these areas, German was the standard language used. As in Ohio, public documents, including the proceedings of the Pennsylvania constitutional convention in 1776, were published in German. Germans achieved political power with the rise of the Jeffersonian party and from 1808 to 1855 every governor of the state was German.

As for the schools, by 1776 the Germans had established a sizeable network of German language schools; the bilingual Franklin College was founded in 1787, and the state superintendent of schools allowed for the public financing of German public schools to be on an equal footing with English language schools. The popularity of German language instruction did not end until the turn of the century.

In the meantime, in the 1837–1838 state constitutional convention, the issue of the language of instruction in public schools became a source of debate. The debate is important, says one law professor because it "demonstrates the lawmakers' sophisticated awareness, at an early time in this nation's history, of the implications of creating constitutional or statutory status for one or another language."[7]

Delegate Barnitz of York County expressed his concern that giving an official imprimatur to the English language would undermine the vitality of minority languages:

> That language carries with it something of authority, by means of its operation in the laws and the regulations of the laws; named unless some special provision is made for the education of the descendants of the German people in the German language, all those who may be in any respect concerned in the admin-

istration of the laws, will be apt to believe that they have discharged the whole duty required of them by the constitution, so soon as they have seen the school law carried into operation in the English language. To my mind, this is a serious difficulty.[8]

Delegate Heister's position, however, ultimately was the successful one; he argued for leaving language choice to the individual and for those with political power to see to it that the legislature protects their interests. He said:

> The German population can have instruction in the German language, if they desire it. They constitute about one-third of the wealth and population of this state, and the legislature, in which body they have themselves their due portion of representatives, will not undertake to exclude them from having instruction in their own language, if they desire to receive it through that medium.[9]

In the end, the state's constitutional amendment made no mention of the language of instruction, and in 1837, the legislature did pass a law that permitted the founding of German language schools as co-equals with English language schools.

California

California has a rich linguistic history reflecting its origins as a Spanish colony, then a Mexican territory, with both Spanish and indigenous populations infusing it with their languages, histories and cultures.

California was under Spanish rule from about 1542 to 1822. From 1810 to 1821, however, the war in Mexico displaced Spanish rule from North America and in 1821 the *californios*, California's residents, were Mexican nationals. Mexicans had a hard time controlling the *californios*, however; between 1831 and 1836 California had eleven different government administrations and an additional three governors were simply ignored by the independent *californios*. Moreover, California was rich with cattle and became a beaver trapper's dream, both luring Yankees from the east and establishing wagon trails through Utah and to the US. In 1846 although the Yankee presence was still a minority, it was growing at a rapid rate, and the US government was becoming increasingly interested in acquiring the territory especially as it would give the nation access to the Pacific.

As California had no military might, it was, in some commentators' minds, a conquest waiting to happen.[10] The conquest happened as a result of the Mexican–American war being fought over Texas. The US was able to take possession of California without firing a shot. The war with Mexico ended in 1848 with the signing of the Treaty of Guadalupe Hidalgo. California became a state in 1850.

The Treaty is an important document for it provided that Mexican citizens who remained within the newly ceded territory for a year after ratification would become US citizens; it also granted certain religious, political and civic rights to the *californios*. The Treaty attempted to protect the language and culture of the native population. By the time the state began drafting its first constitution in 1849, the Gold Rush had driven thousands of Anglos to the area turning the *californios* into minorities virtually overnight and making them into strangers in their own land. Yet respect, or at least empathy, for the conquered and a belief that the Treaty required linguistic tolerance, led to the codification of a bilingual state in the 1849 constitution. The constitution provided that "all laws, decrees, regulations and provisions emanating from any of the three supreme powers of this State, which from their nature require publication, shall be published in English and Spanish."[11] From 1852 to 1863 through a series of legislative enactments, procedures for the translation of the laws into Spanish were adopted.

Despite the generous language of the 1849 constitution, in 1855 English was declared to be the language of instruction in California's schools. The school language laws were meant to serve the later, White, immigrants and only mentioned the right to a "foreign language."[12] Spanish as a foreign language would not even have the cache of French or German until 1913, when it was added to the five living languages that could be taught in the state's schools.[13]

The linguistic rights freely given in the original constitution, however, became a source of great contention by the next constitutional convention in 1878. The arguments from both sides on whether to translate the laws into Spanish were heated, with one delegate arguing that the translation of documents into Spanish was no longer needed since the government was producing hundreds of documents in Spanish-only for "foreigners." Another delegate responded that the native born of California could not be called "foreigners."[14] Yet another delegate argued that the translations were at least morally, if not legally, required under the Treaty of Guadalupe Hidalgo. Delegate Ayers said:

> ... if I am not mistaken, in the treaty of Guadalupe Hidalgo there was an assurance that the natives should continue to enjoy the rights and privileges they did under their former Government, and there was an implied contract that they should be governed as they were before. It was in this spirit that the laws were printed in Spanish ... [i]t would be wrong, it seems to me, for this convention to prevent these people from transacting their local business in their own language. It does no harm to Americans, and I think they should be permitted to do so....[15]

The constitutional provision was passed anyway.[16]

The last official edition of the California laws in Spanish was published in 1878; in 1894 the English-only provision was re-adopted as an amendment to the constitution, and an English language literacy requirement was imposed for eligibility to vote. Despite the official pronouncements to the contrary, minority languages, especially the Spanish language, have continued to be an essential and dynamic ingredient in the character of California.

The role of linguistic diversity in California continues to be an unfortunate source of controversy and contention. The most recent manifestation of California's continuing discomfort in this area is the struggle over bilingual education which came to a heated climax in 1996. This struggle and its implications for the nation are discussed in Chapter 5 on bilingual education.

New Mexico

In 1804 the first Anglos entered New Mexico and by 1821 New Mexico had become part of Mexico. During this time, New Mexico did not enjoy status as a full-fledged member state of Mexico but came close to achieving that status just before the US occupation. As a result of the Mexican-American War, as discussed above, US troops entered the area in 1846 and it became a territory of the US in 1851. In the Treaty of Guadalupe Hidalgo, New Mexico was to become a state "at the proper time." Unlike the gold-rich and Anglo-dominated California, New Mexico would not see that time come until 64 years later, in 1912.[17] That the race and language of the people of New Mexico played a role in the federal government's hesitancy to grant it full statehood is well-documented.

In 1876, both the House and Senate committees on territories recommended statehood for New Mexico. However, the minority report of the House argued that the territory was not yet ready for statehood because the area was settled by "a people nine-tenths of whom speak a foreign tongue, most of whom are illiterate, and the balance with little American literature."[18] The people of New Mexico were described contemptuously as being neither European or Indian: "few are pure-blooded or Castilian, ...the rest being a mixture of Spanish or Mexican and Indian [living in a] condition of ignorance, superstition, and sloth that is unequaled by their Aztec neighbors, the Pueblo Indians."[19]

The domination of Spanish in the territory is obvious – there were few Anglos in New Mexico at the time. Indeed in 1874, 70% of the schools were conducted only in Spanish and 33% were bilingual; only 5% were conducted in English. The 1884 school law for the state stated:

> [e]ach of the voting precincts of a county shall be and constitute a school district in which shall be established one or more schools in which shall be taught orthography, reading, writing, arithmetic, geography, grammar and the history of the United States in either English or Spanish or both, as the directors may determine.[20]

By 1889 the percentages of schools conducted solely in Spanish had decreased, with 30% conducting their instruction in Spanish only and 42% in English only.[21]

Heinz Kloss says that the reason for the repeated refusal to make New Mexico a state was "the unwillingness to create a state in which most of the inhabitants were Spanish-speaking."[22]

> When, for example, in 1902 Congress established a special committee to investigate conditions in the territory, this committee almost completely ignored the economic and social prerequisites for statehood but concentrated almost exclusively on the use of Spanish in the courts, the schools, the families, and in the streets. The committee ascertained that English was still a foreign language for the mass of the population and declared that New Mexico would finally be permitted to become a state if its population, under the impact of domestic in-migration, became roughly acculturated.[23]

In an 1892 House report by the Committee on the Territories, the issue of race and language was directly addressed:

> [o]bjections [regarding 'the character of the population of the Territory'] have been urged against the admission of New Mexico which are not usually brought forward against the admission of other Territories.... It has been asserted that the people of New Mexico are not Americans; that they speak a foreign language and that they have no affinity with American institutions.[24]

The report sought to reassure the Congress on the worthiness of the Territory's statehood by arguing that Spanish was being replaced by English, and that "the people of New Mexico realize that they are a part of the Untied States, and that the English language is the national language, and it is a fixed and definite principle among them all that the English language shall be taught to every child in New Mexico."[25]

Despite the House's efforts, statehood was denied. The issue of the prevalence of Spanish in the territory took on extra vigor the next time statehood was considered in 1902. A republican Senator from Indiana, Albert Jeremiah Beveridge, chaired these hearings and, apparently forgetful of New Mexico's national, linguistic, and cultural heritage, was appalled at the Spanish character of the area. To gather evidence in opposition to the statehood movement, he attached to the record exhibits of legal notices in English and Spanish and hearings lists of criminal indictments showing a preponderance of Spanish surnames.[26] His contention was simple: New Mexico was an area populated by Spanish-speaking criminals, and as such unfit for statehood. The nexus between prejudice and language could not be made more baldly.

The investigation into New Mexico's readiness to become a state and the hearings chaired by Beveridge were precedential in their hostility to the population and in their search for incriminating uses of Spanish. Beveridge equated the prevalent use of Spanish with the foreign-ness of its population and also with its unworthiness to become a state.

During the hearings the term "Mexican" was used to refer to all Hispanics: natives as well as recent immigrants from Mexico itself. Everyone else was referred to as "American." Beveridge would not allow statehood for New Mexico that year, asserting that the "Mexicans " of the Southwest were "unlike us in race, language, and social customs." For Beveridge, statehood would be contingent upon assimilation. It was not until 1910 that there would finally exist just a bare English-speaking majority in New Mexico. Statehood came two years later.

Although Beveridge tried to leave his English-centric imprint on the documents creating the new state, New Mexico as a state continued the tradition of bilingualism that it had forged as a territory. Prior to becoming a state, New Mexico had long published its laws bilingually, writing originally in Spanish and then translating into English. The 1912 constitution, still in effect, contains a recitation of civil rights not to be denied anyone on the basis of their race, color, or ethnic descent, so children of Spanish descent are not to be excluded from public schools or sent to separate public schools. There was even an arguable provision for bilingual education:

> the legislature shall provide for the training of teachers in the normal schools or otherwise so that they may become proficient in both the English and Spanish languages, to qualify them to teach Spanish speaking pupils and students in the public schools and educational institutions of the state, and shall provide proper means and methods to facilitate the teaching of the English language and other branches of learning to such pupils and students.[27]

The constitution also required that all laws passed by the legislature continue to be printed in English and Spanish and put the civil rights of speakers of English and Spanish on an equal footing by providing that:

> the right of any citizen of the State to vote, hold office, or sit upon juries, shall never be restricted, abridged or impaired on account of religion, race, language or color, or inability to speak, read or write the English or Spanish languages except as may be otherwise provided in this constitution.[28]

Bilingual editions of the laws of New Mexico continued to appear until 1949. Spanish continued to be used in the House of Representatives where one-fifth of the salaries paid by the legislature in 1923 went to interpreters and translators.[29] The use of Spanish in the classroom, however, was not wholly supported. As noted earlier, the number of schools teaching only in Spanish dropped dramatically in the ten years after 1874 – no doubt reflecting the pressure on the populace to become a state and show its willingness to assimilate. By 1911 there were complaints that the New Mexico school authorities were outright neglecting the Spanish language in the schools. Kloss states that:

> [w]e may therefore assume that between 1900 and 1912, the year in which statehood was achieved, an almost complete removal of Spanish from the schools took place. It is even possible that this was one of the prerequisites for statehood, as had been the heavy Anglo-American immigration after 1900.[30]

Louisiana

The United States purchased Louisiana from the French in 1803 after a hundred years of French rule and approximately forty years of Spanish rule. Needless to say the area was multilingual, multi-hued and culturally diverse. Until 1830, a majority of Louisiana's population was of French descent. In 1805, while it was still a territory, the schools that existed (presumably private) were bilingual in French and English. Louisiana became a state in 1812, and its first constitution required that all laws, public records of the state and judicial and legislative written proceedings be promulgated in French and English. The subsequent constitutions of 1845, 1852, and 1864 contained similar provisions.

The first school law of the state was passed in 1847 and did not specifically address the language of the schools as much as it regulated the relationship between French and English language schools. This law was clear that the French school could be the only public school of a district and that it should not be considered a special school. The school law of 1870 contained no express language provision, but left the decision about the subjects of instruction to the members of the school board.

It was not until after the Civil War, during which Louisiana was decidedly on the side of the south, that protections for the French language were eliminated from the constitution. The issue arose during the constitutional convention of 1864 when one delegate, Alfred Hills, said:

> I believe the English language is the official language of this country. I believe in a homogenous people, in one language and one system of law, and I believe that the publication of the laws of this State, or the proceedings of any convention, or any English court, in the French language, is a nuisance and ought to be abolished in this state or any other.[31]

The 1864 constitution expressly required that the common schools were to be conducted in English.[32]

When the democrats took control of the state in 1879, however, pro-French provisions were re-inserted in the constitution, although not as strongly as in the 1845 constitution. For instance, although English was again prescribed as the language of instruction in the public schools, in those towns or counties where French was the predominant language, the elementary subjects could also be taught in French provided that no additional expenses were incurred.[33] By 1881, however, it was clear that French would not again have the ascendancy it did before the Civil War; after that year there were no more French editions of the state laws. By 1921, French was seen as superfluous. The 1921 constitution contained no references to the French language and required that all public school instruction be in English.[34]

Puerto Rico

The politics of language is played out nowhere more graphically than in Puerto Rico, where the island's continued intermediate status as neither an official colony of the US nor a recognized state is intricately tied to the place of Spanish on the island. Therefore, it is important in this instance to discuss some of the social and civic features of Puerto Rico in order to contextualize the language debate on the island.

Puerto Rico was one of the territories acquired by the US as a result of the Spanish–American War. A military government was formally installed in 1898 and continued until 1900 when it was replaced by a civil government under the Foraker Act. Brigadier General George W. Davis, who was the military governor the longest, proposed that under the civil government there be only a governor, executive council, and judiciary (all to be appointed), because he felt that "this island ... is not capable of carrying on such a government as Hawaii is able to maintain."[35] Under the Foraker Act, however, Congress approved a mix: an elected house of delegates to be checked by an appointed upper house, which had a majority of Americans, and a governor appointed by the US President who would enjoy veto power.

Under the Foraker Act, those residents of Puerto Rico as of the date of the signing of the Treaty who did not elect to keep their Spanish allegiance and their children were to be "citizens of Puerto Rico and entitled to the protection of the US."[36] This protection, however, gave Puerto Ricans less than what they enjoyed under Spanish rule: they would not have US citizenship nor a vote in the House of Representatives.

In 1917 Congress passed the Jones Act, which granted collective US citizenship to citizens of Puerto Rico who wished. Still, the official status of Puerto Rico with respect to its relationship to the US is unclear; a series of Supreme Court decisions found that it was neither officially incorporated in the US nor could it be described as only a territory.[37] A 1953 United Nations resolution of which the US approved gave some shape to the relations between the island and the US:

> ... in accordance with the spirit of this resolution, the ideals embodied in the United Nations Charter, the traditions of the people of the United States and the political advancement attained by the people of Puerto Rico, due regard would be paid to the will of both the Puerto Rican and American peoples in the conduct of their relations under their present legal statute, and also in the eventuality that either of the parties to the mutually agreed association might desire any change in the terms of the association.[38]

The Foraker Act brought Puerto Rico within the US tariff wall and, as of 1902, Puerto Rico no longer enjoyed any trade protections in its dealings with the US. Free trade with the US gave a great impetus to the production of sugar; land devoted to sugar cane kept multiplying, as did land for tobacco and tobacco exports. The expansion of sugar production was accompanied by a concentration of ownership and control. From 500 little sugar mills producing 125 tons annually per mill in 1897, production went to 20,000 tons from each of 41 mills in 1938. Although there was a "500-acre rule" that prohibited one corporation from accumulating more than 500 acres of land, the law was not enforced. Indeed, 11 of the 41 mills were owned by four American companies that also owned 23.7% of the land; over half of the island's land was devoted to sugar production.[39] Since so much of the land was devoted to sugar production for export, the price for foodstuffs and agricultural products was high. As a result, Puerto Rican workers spent most of their income on food.[40]

Meanwhile, wage earners received low wages even by continental standards, and employment was irregular. Average annual earnings of a sugar worker in 1931 were $169 and after 1941, when New Deal improvements were implemented, the average annual earnings were $269.

Improvements began to be seen under Luis Muñoz Marín who founded the Democratic Peoples Party with the goal of implementing island-wide economic and social reforms. Under Muñoz's rule, the 500-acre rule was finally enforced and illegally-obtained lands were sold or simply given to Puerto Rican workers. Industries were jump-started, and social housing and highway systems, hotels and tourism became important sectors of economic development. From 1940 to 1958, education expenses increased eightfold and income increased almost fivefold.[41]

Muñoz also made significant contributions to the politics of Puerto Rico. He was able to have a law passed that would provide for the popular election of the island's governor, and he became the first one so elected. He also oversaw the creation and adoption of Puerto Rico's constitution of 1952 in which Puerto Rico was declared a commonwealth, a political association, which the United Nations said "respects the individuality and the cultural characteristics of Puerto Rico, maintains the spiritual bonds between Puerto Rico and Latin America."[42] The constitution reads more like the constitution of a state than of a province: Congress cannot annul Puerto Rican laws; the island continues to belong to the US's tariff area, and the US retains a monopoly in foreign policy and military matters. The Resident Commissioner, however, remained a feature with a voice but no vote in the House of Representatives. In return, the island's residents pay no federal taxes. Finally, Puerto Ricans continue as citizens of the US but vote only in the presidential primary elections, and not in the final ones.

Under Spanish rule Puerto Rico had been a poor, neglected colony with little formal education in place. Under US rule improvements were made in schooling and in the economy, but the island was exploited by US mercantilists who were interested in monopolizing their trade and had little interest in learning either the native language or anything about the native culture. Almost immediately, Puerto Rico began to suffer from the kind of linguistic intolerance demonstrated by the White settlers' treatment of Native American languages on the US mainland discussed in Chapter 7. Puerto Rico's name was changed, for a thankfully short time, to *Porto Rico* in order to make it more pronounceable for the Americans. The island was declared bilingual by the military government, although almost none of its inhabitants spoke English and almost all public and private affairs were conducted in Spanish. Dr Victor Clark, President of the Insular Board of Education in 1899 wrote that:

> [an] important fact that must not be overlooked is that a majority of the people of this island do not speak pure Spanish – their language is a patois almost unintelligible to the natives of Barcelona and Madrid. It possesses no literature and little value as an intellectual medium. There is a bare possibility that it will be nearly as easy to educate the people out of their patois into English as it will be to educate then into the elegant tongue of Castile.[43]

Still, the military governor Guy Henry ordered all public school teachers to become proficient in English and instituted an English proficiency test for high school graduation. As with the treatment of Native Americans, the physical colonization of a people was the impetus for the attempted colonization of their language and culture in order to re-make it in the image of the conquerors. The force with which the Puerto Ricans would continue to hold on to their native language, and make attempts to replace it with English into a political issue, certainly could not have been foreseen.

Not surprisingly, the US's first official words concerning education in Puerto Rico stressed the need for teachers who could "teach the American or English language, commencing with the younger children. It is believed that those who can speak English only can accomplish the purpose by object lessons."[44] The focus of the US government's Americanization efforts was the schools. The first US school laws in Puerto Rico had salutary elements: abolishing a fee system, providing for free text books and for a graded school system, and setting requirements for teachers and their salaries. The US, however, attempted to "[transplant] the American school system to Puerto Rico irrespective of conditions differing from those of the states."[45] In the meantime, "the emphasis in the schools was placed on the study of English and on patriotic exercises."[46] Since Puerto Rico had no cadre of English-proficient teachers to teach the children, US-born teachers were to be brought to the island to teach English. The first of these teachers were not generally successful as some were mere adventurers, not trained educators and others, sent to rural areas, got home-sick shortly after arriving and left.

Meanwhile, the Commissioners of education kept changing English language instructional policies in the schools as often as they themselves changed, which was about every two years. One Commissioner was convinced that English needed to be the language of instruction in all subjects except Spanish; the next would institute a policy that the elementary grades would be taught bilingually but with an emphasis on English; still another insisted that all elementary grades would be taught in Spanish and that English would be taught as a subject beginning in the first grade, with increases in the time spent learning English in the seventh and eighth grades.[47] One Commissioner would be under presidential orders that the teaching of English in Puerto Rico proceed "with vigor, purposefulness and devotion, and with the understanding that English is the official language of our country."[48] Another Commissioner would believe that "the Spanish language will not and should not disappear from these schools. It will be a hindrance, not a help to deprive these people of an opportunity to acquire both languages."[49]

While the language policies came and went, the children (presumably for whom these policies were being created) were dropping out of school in droves; so many were gone by the fourth grade that English language instruction before that time was considered by some researchers to be a waste of time, since the students would never go on to use the language within the school system.[50] Yet, the curriculum in the elementary grades was so weighted toward learning English that many basic skills were simply not being taught.

Commentators from the Brookings Institution in Washington DC felt that Puerto Ricans wanted to learn English, although not at the expense of their native tongue. They wrote a report that stated, in part, that "[t]o tens of thousands of the dis-inherited in Puerto Rico a knowledge of [the English] ... language seems to promise –perhaps fallaciously – a better economic future. Popular willingness to make sacrifices for the schools is in some degree due to this pathetic faith."[51]

After more changes in commissioners and consequent changes in policies, the school law of 1969 was passed. That law provides that "[i]nstruction in Spanish and the intensification of the teaching of English as an additional language shall be unalterable standards." The University of Puerto Rico in Rio Piedras, founded as an English-only college, also gave way and switched entirely to Spanish.

The place of Spanish in the civic life of Puerto Rico is unassailable. Officially bilingual, all government documents are available in both English and Spanish – as are services at governmental offices. There is a decided bias towards Spanish and the lower, local courts operate only in Spanish. However, the federal district courts operate only in English, which has given rise to some problems that are discussed in Chapter 7 on jury service.

Nowhere else is language more clearly a potent symbol of nation and culture than in Puerto Rico. Part of this is undoubtedly explained by the heavy-handed approach to the Spanish language that the US has taken since it colonized the island. The increasing economic potency of English on the island has also contributed to a sense that the Puerto Ricans are a "culture under siege."[52] Many felt that:

> the intrusion of English [into Puerto Rico] had the potential for damaging Puerto Rico as a separate identity, and that English was actually destroying the Spanish language .... Supporters of this viewpoint held that Spanish language was also endangered by a number of societal factors: the desire of new members of the middle class to separate themselves from the poverty of their past, the influence of the mass media, the penetration of North American companies onto the island, and the need for a working knowledge of English as a prerequisite for employment.[53]

The continued status of Puerto Rico *vis-à-vis* the US has made the island's language policies into a political football. Those political parties that would like to see Puerto Rico ultimately become a state of the US realize that the island must embrace English more and that English must become a popular language. Those who oppose statehood use the Puerto Rican's love for their language and anxiety about overbearing US policies to garner votes for themselves. All of this came to a head in the 1990s when the Languages Act, which had been passed shortly after the US's takeover of Puerto Rico and which had declared the island bilingual, was changed in 1991 by a law recognizing Spanish as the official language of the island. This maneuver had been orchestrated by the Popular Democratic Party which supports continued commonwealth status.[54] The Statement of Purpose for the bill stated that:

> the dominance of our mother tongue must be first above any other consideration. The Puerto Rican people feel in their souls is that Spanish is their language.... the Spanish language is synonymous with our being. The affirmation of the common language of the people is an affirmation of national personality.[55]

Then in 1993, former Governor Pedro Rossello of the New Progressive Party signed a law making both English and Spanish official languages again. "Rossello regarded this action as a major step toward Puerto Rico becoming the fifty-first state."[56] There was strong opposition to Rossello's actions which was reflected in the November 1993 plebiscite: statehood was rejected by a slight margin: 46% voted for statehood, 48% for continued commonwealth status, and 4% for independence. The continued ambivalence of the Puerto Rican people towards the US was reflected vividly in the plebiscite results of 1998. There, the fifth category, "none of the above" gained the absolute majority with 50.3% of the votes. Statehood came in second with 46.5% of the votes. Usually, there is a close to even split between the "commonwealth" status and statehood, with a small percentage voting for independence. In 1998, however, the commonwealth status had been denigrated to "territorial commonwealth" which the Popular Democratic Party, supporters of the continued commonwealth status, opposed and advocated against. The ploy was successful as it received only 0.1% of the vote and "none of the above" beat the statehood option. "None of the above" was certified as the winner of the status plebiscite.

A case that arose while Puerto Rico hurtled between official bilingualism and official Spanish was the kind that could only have arisen in Puerto Rico – an Anglo teacher dominant only in English sued for discrimination because she could not pass the Spanish-only test needed to obtain her permanent teaching license.[57] After deciding that the case should go to trial the Equal Protection claim, the matter was settled with Puerto Rico's Department of Education issuing Kathy Smothers a teaching license.[58]

In the meantime, *US English*, an organization devoted to working to make English the official language of the nation, was avidly working in Puerto Rico, where it has an office. Misrepresenting the historical and current status of state language laws, a US English spokesmen told Congress:

> we feel it would be badly misleading for the people of Puerto Rico to vote in the plebiscite thinking that any language, other than English, can be the official language of a state in the union. English is the common language of the people of the United States, and one day will be recognized as the official language of government in this country. At that time, we believe that Puerto Rico, as all other states, will follow the laws of the land and accept English as the official language of government.[59]

The language debate in Puerto Rico clearly has many undertones and implications. It brings into bold relief many of the issues that our US courts and policymakers only hint at when language is discussed on the mainland: the issues of hegemony, colonial power, economic status within the island and between the island and the mainland, nationalism, and language as an inseparable element of and a conveyor of culture. All of these stand out so boldly in Puerto Rico because it is such a small island, so economically besieged and overwhelmed by the presence of the US that it holds on to its language with a kind of tenaciousness that seems to border on the desperate. There is a reason for that: US language and culture so permeate the island that it is only a stubborn grasp of the native language that keeps the island from being another bastion of English-language dominance. In 2002, Spanish is still the language of the island, with approximately 20% of the population fluent in English and 98% fluent in Spanish.[60]

THE FOURTEENTH AMENDMENT AND ITS IMPORTANCE TO LANGUAGE RIGHTS CLAIMS

From the First Amendment to the Fourteenth Amendment, the Constitution has had a role in the development of language rights law. The Fourteenth Amendment, however, with its Equal Protection and Due Process Clauses is the constitutional linchpin on which language minorities have traditionally sought to have their rights realized. The Equal Protection Clause is particularly important because it prohibits racial and ethnic discrimination, and its interpretation has set the parameters under which many language rights claims are decided. The World War cases that follow relied upon either the Equal Protection or the Due Process Clauses or both to either validate or dismiss language rights claims. Before the cases are discussed, a brief primer on these two important Clauses follows.

The Fourteenth Amendment

Most language rights cases have primarily involved interpretations of the Fourteenth Amendment. The Equal Protection and Due Process clauses of the Fourteenth Amendment are the two most well-known clauses of a three-clause section which also includes the Privileges or Immunities Clause.

Section 1 of the Fourteenth Amendment states:

All persons born or naturalized in the United States, and subject to the jurisdiction thereof, are citizens if the United States and of the State wherein they reside. No State shall make or enforce any law which shall abridge the privileges or immunities of citizens of the United States; nor shall any State deprive any person of life, liberty or property without due process of law; nor deny to any person within its jurisdiction the equal protection of the laws.

Enacted during Reconstruction and three years after the Thirteenth Amendment prohibiting slavery, the Fourteenth Amendment was clearly an attempt to put the newly freed slaves on as much of an equal footing as possible to White men and to protect them from state actors who would surely seek to undermine the spirit if not the letter of the Thirteenth Amendment. The Due Process and Equal Protection Clauses appear to be limited to functional purposes: the Due Process Clause, as a guarantee of fair procedure and the Equal Protection Clause as "a guarantee of evenhanded administration of the laws, i.e. of equal treatment by courts and law enforcement agencies."[61]

The Privileges or Immunities Clause, called "the forgotten clause" was supposed to be a mirror-image of Article IV §2 of the original Constitution.[62] As such it was arguably meant to protect citizens of the states from any infringement by the states of their rights as federal citizens of the United States. Like the Equal Protection and Due Process Clauses, the Privileges or Immunities Clause was to be an important tool in the struggle between state and federal powers and an attempt by the federal government to hold aberrant states accountable for their treatment of US citizens:

"The mischief to be remedied was not merely slavery and its consequences; but the spirit of the insubordination and disloyalty to the national government which had troubled the country of so many years in some of the states."[63]

Unfortunately in 1872 in the *Slaughterhouse Cases*, the US Supreme Court took a deadly swipe at the Privileges or Immunities Clause, essentially limiting its protections to just a few rights considered to be federal in scope, like the right to assemble or petition for redress of grievances.[64]

Because of the limited scope of the Privileges or Immunities Clause, advocates have had to rely upon the other two Clauses and wrench them from their previously functional purposes to take on the substantive aspects intended for the Privileges or Immunities Clause. This explains the strange life of the Due Process Clause, which while clearly intended to impact "processes," has been used with some success to guarantee substantive rights as in *Meyer v. Nebraska*.[65]

Extending the reach of the Equal Protection Clause

One important question over which there is still considerable controversy is what rights are civil rights; what rights does the Bill of Rights attempt to protect?

Some have ambiguously stated that Congress attempted to guarantee its citizens (or in the case of the Equal Protection and Due Process Clauses, its "persons") the natural rights of "freemen."[66] Chancellor Kent noted that the "inalienable rights" of citizens include the right to personal security, the right to personal liberty and the right to acquire and enjoy property.[67]

What exactly those substantial rights are is still a subject of dispute. The generous, ambiguous and fluid nature of the rights to be protected is important for language rights activists who are presenting a constituency that was only a minor player in the minds of the Original Framers and whose language-based issues the Original Framers were not attempting to address. A fluid understanding of "natural rights" is not only justified by constitutional history, but means that the Constitution is a living document, responsive to the changes in demography, technology, values, and mores.

With the virtual loss of the Privileges or Immunities Clause, the Equal Protection Clause grew to be understood as a "pledge of the protection of equal laws"[68] and not as simply an equal treatment under laws. The Equal Protection Clause is concerned with the "right to equal treatment which demands that every person have the same access to particular protected interests" (such as voting) as everyone else. There is also the right to "treatment as an equal" which "requires that government treat each individual with equal regard as a person" without reference to specific interests.[69] Essentially, the Equal Protection Clause prohibits governmental discrimination on the basis of an individual's race, ancestry, national origin, or ethnicity. Discrimination may be understood as "directed detrimental action, motivated by prejudice and not deserved by the victim"[70]

The growth of the Equal Protection Clause to protect groups and traits not only related to race is an important step for language minorities, but has not yet been fully developed. That the Equal Protection Clause was supposed to protect more than only "Negroes" was made clear in 1880 by the Supreme Court in *Strauder v. West Virginia* where the Court stated:

> If in those States where the colored people constitute a majority of the entire population a law should be enacted excluding all White men from jury service ... we apprehend no one would be heard to claim that it would not be a denial to White men of the equal protection of the laws. Nor if a law should be passed excluding all naturalized Celtic Irishmen, would there be any doubt of its inconsistency with the spirit of the amendment.[71]

This led the way to the Supreme Court's decision invalidating a pattern of discriminatory administration of California's law limiting the operation of wooden laundries in *Yick Wo v. Hopkins*.[72] The 200 laundry owners prohibited from operating their laundries were all Chinese, while 80 non-Chinese laundry owners were not required to abide by the law. The Court found no reason for the discrimination "except hostility to the race and nationality to which the petitioners belong and which in the eye of the law is not justified."[73] The case was not only important for its expansion of the protected groups under the Equal Protection Clause but because the law at issue was not on its face discriminatory but was being enforced principally against Chinese businessmen. The Court stated:

> [t]hough the law itself be fair on its face and impartial in appearance, yet, if it is applied and administered by a public authority with an evil eye and an unequal hand, so as practically to make unjust and illegal discriminations between persons in similar circumstances, material to their rights, the denial of equal justice is still within the prohibition of the Constitution.[74]

Although the Court in *Yick Wo* used the Equal Protection Clause for the benefit of the Chinese, it was still certainly a "race" case. It was not until 1954 that the Supreme Court stated unequivocally that discrimination based on national origin violates the Equal Protection Clause. In *Hernandez v. Texas*,[75] the Supreme Court overturned the conviction of a Mexican-American man who had alleged the systemic exclusion of Mexicans Americans from jury service. The Court found that Mexican Americans were a group that constituted a separate class entitled to the protections of the Equal Protection Clause. Rejecting the argument that the Clause was only meant to protect African Americans, the Court stated:

> [b]ut community prejudices are not static, and from time to time other differences from the community norm may define other groups which need the same protection. Whether such a group exists within a community is a question of fact. When the existence of a distinct class is demonstrated, and it is further shown that the laws, as written or as applied, singled out that class for different treatments not based on some reasonable classification, the guarantees of the Constitution have been violated.[76]

The important but arguably fine distinctions between race, ethnicity, ancestry, and national origin, however, are yet to be worked out by the courts, and the four are often confused or used interchangeably. These distinctions, however, do make a difference in how language claims are treated and can mean the difference between a successful or an unsuccessful litigation strategy. Ancestry can be defined as "ancestral descent or lineage"[77] – essentially from where one's ancestors came. Since we have many ancestors, ancestry can be a rich mix that reflects many different countries. National origin is simple,[78] it means only where one was born but it can also include where one's ancestors have come from. Race can be understood as a "local geographic or global human population distinguished as a more or less distinct group by genetically-transmitted physical characteristics."[79]

Ethnicity is arguably the most complicated. Juan Perea states that:

> ethnicity refers to physical and cultural characteristics that make a social group distinctive, either in group members' eyes or in the view of outsiders. Thus ethnicity consists of a set of ethnic traits that may include, but is not limited to race, national origin, ancestry, language, religion, shared history, traditions, values, and symbols – all of which contribute to a sense of distinctiveness among members of the group.[80]

The reason for judicial confusion is clear: all four labels have aspects that shade into each other. Indeed, a dictionary can barely describe one without reference to the others, and in one dictionary[81] "Germans" (clearly an ethnic group) is given as an example of "race." Such a lack of clarity should argue for the broadest possible protections; for if race is clearly covered under the Equal Protection Clause and what are aspects of ethnicity could also be considered aspects of race, then discriminations based on "ethnic" traits such as accent, surname, and dress ought to be strictly scrutinized.

Modern Equal Protection analysis

The Equal Protection Clause requires examination of two types of situation. One, usually described as *de jure* discrimination, concerns governmental classifications of individuals. Here the Equal Protection Clause is concerned that the government not be involved in invidious discrimination against certain groups of people. The other, usually described as *de facto* discrimination, is concerned with the government's failure to classify; the equal treatment of people situated in such disparate places that treating them the same way results in unequal protection of the laws.

The courts have developed something like a three-tiered test to help them determine whether a state actor is making permissible, governmentally warranted distinctions between individuals or whether it is actually engaged in some kind of impermissible discrimination.

Rational basis review

This is the most deferential form of review developed. The courts here are really just looking for the state to articulate a rational basis for the classifications made;

neither a suspect group nor fundamental rights are at issue; yet governments must still be held to some standards of acceptable, rational behavior. This type of review has often been called essentially a "default," since the courts accept almost any justification proffered. The Constitution, under this analysis, invalidates only that governmental choice that is "clearly wrong, a display of arbitrary power, not an exercise of judgment."[82]

Intermediate or heightened scrutiny

The courts have developed an intermediate level of scrutiny that is usually applied in gender discrimination cases.[83] Courts use other techniques to hold governments more accountable under this standard of review. For instance, the government must articulate its justification for the classification in the litigation challenging it, and the courts have limited the use of afterthought by state actors who try to justify their actions with legitimate rationales that had no real place in the consideration of the legislation.[84] Finally, courts require that the legal scheme under challenge be altered so as to permit rebuttal in individual cases.

Heightened scrutiny has taken on a number of different variations, and has actually been applied to a host of situations where neither the ultra-deferential rational basis review is appropriate, nor are strict formulations of race and ethnicity involved. Intermediate scrutiny is generally triggered under two circumstances.

The first is if important, though not necessarily "fundamental," interests are at stake.[85] Either a significant interference with liberty or a denial of a benefit vital to the individual can trigger intermediate scrutiny.[86]

Second, intermediate scrutiny is triggered if "sensitive, although not necessarily suspect, criteria of classification are employed."[87] So for instance, alienage has been treated as a "partly suspect" class because of aliens' long history of disadvantageous treatment and their ready identifiability.[88]

The strict scrutiny test

The courts will hold governments to a high standard of review in two situations: when a classification "operates to the disadvantage of some suspect class," or when a classification "impinges upon a fundamental right explicitly or implicitly protected by the Constitution."[89] A suspect class is generally a group that is discrete, identifiable, small, and vulnerable to the majority. In addition to African-Americans, Latinos and Asians have also been found to be suspect classes.[90] In order to survive a court's strict scrutiny, the government's reason for the classification must bear a necessary relationship to a compelling governmental interest. Strict scrutiny has often been called "strict in theory and fatal in fact," meaning that the government never gets over the high legal hurdles placed before it.[91]

So the first line of inquiry for a court is whether either a fundamental right or a racial/ethnic discrimination is at issue. Some examples of fundamental rights include voting, candidacy, the exercise of intimate personal choices, and litigation.[92] Interestingly, many aspects of life that we would think are fundamental human rights are not accorded high protection by the federal courts; neither education, housing, social services or employment are considered fundamental constitutional rights. These are treated as "social" issues, the relative worth of which the legislatures are left free to determine.[93]

The ways in which a "suspect" class is defined is critically important for language minorities. Under the Supreme Court test articulated in *US v. Carolene Products*,[94] "discrete and insular" groups are to be afforded protection. The accepted wisdom has been that only immutable, unchangeable characteristics are the hallmark of these protected groups. So racial and ethnic traits, which an individual does not choose and cannot divest himself of, are what mark people as minorities deserving of special protections. Skin color and other physical features, accent and surname have all been treated as immutable characteristics.[95] The central concern here is the rooting out of government action that is tainted by the sort of prejudice "which tends to curtail the operation of those political processes ordinarily to be relied upon to protect minorities in our society."[96]

Discrimination on the basis of race/ethnicity can take many forms. *Yick Wo* was an example of a facially neutral law that was *enforced* in a discriminatory manner. *Hunter v. Erickson*[97] is an example of a benign-looking law that falls most heavily on minorities. There, the court invalidated a city charter amendment providing that the city council could implement no ordinance dealing with racial, religious, or ancestral discrimination in housing without the approval of a majority of the city's voters. The court reasoned that:

> although the law on its face treat[ed] Negro and White, Jew and gentile in an identical manner, the reality [was] that the law's impact [fell] on the minority, for it was those who would obviously benefit from laws barring racial, religious, or ancestral discrimination and thus it was minorities whom the amendment deliberately disadvantaged: "[t]he majority needs no protection against discrimination.... Even more than other forms of disadvantage, hurdles imposed in the political process itself on groups traditionally the subjects of prejudice must therefore be strictly scrutinized, and ordinarily invalidated.[98]

Clearly, laws can be discriminatory on their face as well. Such laws have almost uniformly been struck down.[99] Governments can also take actions that have a discriminatory impact and/or purpose. The role of motive in this analysis has become paramount. In these situations, the law is neutral on its face and appears to be administered in a neutral manner, yet it has a disproportionately negative impact on a protected group, or has a discriminatory purpose.

The Supreme Court, however, has placed a high hurdle for minorities looking for succor under the Equal Protection Clause. One of the most important recent developments in Equal Protection doctrine has been the reading of an *intentional discrimination* requirement into the clause. In *Washington v. Davis*,[100] the Supreme Court held that the crucial issue for equal protection purposes is whether there is sufficient evidence of a discriminatory purpose for the challenged state action. While the disparate impact of a challenged state action on a protected group is one factor that the courts will now look to in determining whether there was an impermissible motive, it is only one factor in a "totality of circumstances" to be considered.

Since *Washington*, there are two extreme situations in which disparate impact alone was used to strike down state action. The *first* situation is when a neutral statute is selectively enforced to such an extreme extent as to constitute a *prima facie* case of discriminatory purpose. Some systematic state behavior must be shown. The classic example of this type of behavior is in the jury-selection process: "[a] purpose to discriminate must be present which may be proven by systematic exclusion of eligible jurymen of the proscribed race or by unequal application of the law to such an extent as to show intentional discrimination."[101]

The Due Process Clause of the Fourteenth Amendment

The Due Process Clauses of the Fourteenth Amendments is concerned that individuals not be deprived of life, liberty or property by the state government, without first having first been accorded some kind of due process. Historically, the courts developed "substantive due process" and "procedural due process" analyses. Substantive due process was really utilized from 1890 to 1937 and *Meyer v. Nebraska* and its progeny discussed below can be understood best as examples of this theory.

Substantive due process analysis was developed at a time when the courts were trying to negotiate a balance between federal and state powers. It had originally seen the state as the ultimate guarantor of individual liberties and rights, and tried to protect the states from unwarranted federal intrusions. The Civil War and Reconstruction, however, made it clear that the individual could have interests that the states were not prepared or willing to protect at all. In attempting to protect the individual, then, from state intrusions into private spheres, the Supreme Court recognized certain circumscribed areas of legitimate state action such as policing, taxing and *eminent domain*.

Procedural due process has its historical origins in "the notion that conditions of personal freedom can be preserved only when there is some institutional check n arbitrary governmental action ..."[102] Under this analysis, the courts look to see whether the right being taken by the government is indeed afforded due process protection, then the court determines exactly how much "process is due." Insignificant or transient entitlements that someone could lose at any moment are not afforded due process protection. By guaranteeing notice and an opportunity to be heard before a substantial loss is suffered, the Clause commands that individuals participate in the decision as to what happens to them.

In determining whether a person has a property interest in something that arises to the level of meriting due process protection, the courts look at whether the right asserted can be found in the constitution or common law or more recently, whether the state has created an expectation in individuals based on state law. So that for instance in *Goldberg v. Kelly*,[103] the Supreme Court held that New York could not terminate public assistance payments to a particular recipient without affording him the opportunity for an evidentiary hearing prior to termination. Justice Brennan noted that in today's society welfare payments are more like an entitlement than a gratuity.

After determining whether an interest is constitutionally protected, the courts look to see what kind of process or how much process is actually due. Although the two questions seem to be analytically distinct, in practice, the weight of the substantive entitlement will often color the level of process required. The dominant approach to procedural due process is more concerned with the minimization of factual error than with expressions of individual dignity. The level of process due really varies according to "specific factual contexts" since "not all situations calling for procedural safeguards call for the same kind of procedure."[104] Within this context, the cost to government in providing for mechanisms to minimize error is balanced against the harm to the individual in being erroneously deprived of that interest.

Due process is nothing, of course, if the individual to be dispossessed of a right is not afforded notice of that possibility and an opportunity to be heard. As will be discussed below, in language rights cases the reasonableness of the notice afforded is a paramount issue. The method chosen to give notice need not lead to actual notice, but must be "reasonably calculated, under all the circumstances, to appraise interested parties of the pendency of the action and afford them an opportunity to present their objections."[105] Due process also requires that there be an opportunity to present every available defense.[106]

LANGUAGE RIGHTS DURING THE WORLD WAR ERAS

In the World War I era, the Supreme Court decided three cases of major importance to language rights and to the evolution of constitutional law generally. Another case briefly discussed arose in the context of World War II and was decided by a Hawaii federal trial court. The wartime nature of the cases is particularly important, for it was in these years that high immigration rates coincided with a growing distrust of foreigners. These two elements resulted in insecurity about the definition of the nation's character; an Anglo, Protestant, northern-European, English-speaking nation were the essential characteristics that had pervaded the national imagination. However, immigration from other European countries, and by people resistant to relinquishing their native language and culture, threatened that perception of iron-clad homogeneity. The World War I era was marked by the national hysterical response to that perceived threat. As often occurs, legislators responded to the national mood by passing, amongst other things, language restrictive legislation that, in an attempt to force conformity of the newest immigrants, sought to blot out languages other than English from usage.

Meyer v. Nebraska [107]

In 1923, the US Supreme Court used the Due Process Clause of the Fourteenth Amendment to strike down language-restrictive legislation that criminalized the use of German in Nebraska, Idaho, and Ohio. The effect of the Supreme Court's decision in *Meyer v. Nebraska* was to place language-minority communities squarely

within the protections of the nation's Constitution and to undermine arguments
that equated English language usage with the rights and responsibilities of full citizenship. Constitutional law scholars, however, cite *Meyer* for its role in expanding
the depth of the Due Process Clause to ensure that families be left to raise their children as they see fit and for adding yet another unenumerated right to the panoply of
rights being "found" by the Court under the Ninth Amendment.[108] Not a word is
mentioned in these traditional texts about the role that the case played, and
continues to play, in the evolving area of language rights. For their part, language
rights advocates today continue to cite *Meyer* as one of the Supreme Court's clearest
statements on the constitutional protections afforded language minorities.

The context

The significance of *Meyer v. Nebraska* cannot be understood without reference to
the political and social context from which it sprang. Between 1820 and 1920,
approximately 7 million Germans immigrated to the United States, comprising 15%
of all immigrants during that period. Between 1850 and 1900, Germans comprised
at least a quarter of all immigrants to the US.[109] Of the 92 million Americans reported
in the 1910 census, 2.5 million were born in Germany, and millions more were the
children and grandchildren of German immigrants.[110]

At first, they settled primarily in "Germantown" Pennsylvania, then they
stretched westward within the state until a whole string of German agricultural
settlements was scattered from upstate New York to New Jersey and from Pennsylvania southward "forming an almost unbroken chain of German-speaking communities" reaching into Georgia.[111] "Germans in the nineteenth century tended to
retain their culture, as their predecessors had done in earlier centuries. The German
language could be heard spoken on the streets of Cincinnati or St Louis, and
German language newspapers appeared daily in fifteen American cities."[112] Not
only were Germans an identifiable ethnic community, they were a powerful and
confident community that took a justifiable pride in a culture that had produced
Beethoven, Schiller, Goethe, and Rilke. The ethnic Germans had political and social
clubs that protected their interests and sought to protect the German language and
culture as well as political leaders in several states. German influence was strong
enough to create and support a large network of German parochial schools where
the preservation of the native language was a dominant feature.

General public perception of the Germans was positive; they were seen as the
"best type of immigrant": law-abiding, patriotic, hard-working, assimilable.[113] Yet
fear of foreigners, even German ones, was still present. Benjamin Franklin
expressed his suspicion of ethnic Germans in words which linked language,
national identity and threats to national safety that are often echoed today:

> Those [Germans] who come hither are generally the most ignorant Stupid Sort
> of their own Nation, and as Ignorance is often attended with credulity when
> Knavery would mislead it, and with Suspicion when Honesty would set it
> right; and as few of the English understand the German language, and so
> cannot address them wither from the Press or the Pulpit, 'tis almost impossible

to remove any prejudices they once entertain .... I remember when they modestly declined intermeddling in our Elections, but now they come in droves, and carry all before them, except in one or two counties; Few of their children in the Country learn English; they import many books from Germany; and of the six of the printing houses in the Province, two are entirely German .... In short unless the stream of their importation could be turned from this to other Colonies as you very judiciously propose, they will soon so out number us, that all the advantages we have will not, in My Opinion, be able to preserve our language, and even our government will become precarious.[114]

By the World War I era, German organizations in the US had pulled themselves together into an influential German–American Alliance that grew accustomed to successfully using its political muscle in Washington for the benefit of the German community and its schools. When the US was at the brink of WWI, however, the aggressive approach used by the Germans and their high profile became the focal point for nationalistic anxieties. When German organizations met in Washington to influence policy just before Germany declared submarine war on Great Britain, *The New York Times* found that "[n]ever since the foundation of the Republic has any body of men assembled here who were more completely subservient to foreign influence and a foreign power and none ever proclaimed the un-American spirit more openly."[115]

The US distrust of German-Americans began to be generated by British propaganda while that country was already at war with Germany. In order to ensure broad support, the British created a moral imperative for the war by trying to "persuade the British public of the essential wickedness of the Germans."[116] As the war dragged on both "the government and the people needed to believe that their sacrifices were sanctified by moral imperatives that transcended petty economic and political considerations. Thus, more and more British were therefore willing to believe that German society itself was evil."[117]

This attitude quickly crossed the Atlantic, where German economic and political achievement were beginning to raise the hostility of the Anglo majority. This was especially so in more rural and agricultural areas where the German population was distinctive and where their economic competition with Anglos could be keen.

Seeds of nativism in the US had long been planted and sprouted whenever the nation felt particularly vulnerable,[118] so "[h]ostility toward German Americans during the war provided a new focus for the nativism that had festered in American life during the past several decades. German Americans replaced Roman Catholics and aliens as the nativist bogy for the duration of the war."[119]

It was not only nativists, however, who began to take aim at the Germans. The preservation of native languages and cultures as well as the extensive use of parochial schools was also seen as "baneful" and in opposition to the forces of social reform.[120]

The war effort hardened what began as "free-floating nationalist anxiety" into an all-encompassing campaign against "hyphenated-Americanism" generally and particularly against German-Americans. When the US actually entered the war, "hyphenated-Americans" were seen as one of the most dangerous elements – an immigrant of divided loyalty at a time when nothing less than 100% Americanism was needed to win the war. As John Higham noted the "war seemed so encompassing, so arduous, that the slightest division of purpose or lack of enthusiasm appeared an intolerable handicap to it."[121]

Then-President Teddy Roosevelt made eradicating "hyphenated Americanism" his cause and insisted on the maxim "America for Americans." He tried to make his attacks on Germans in America more palatable by saying that he was against only the "German-Americans who call themselves such" or the "professional German-Americans," not "the Americans of German origin."[122] His statement on the dangers of bilingualism is an excellent example of the linking of ethnicity, language, and patriotism that can be so effective in repressing language minorities:

> We must have but one flag. We must also have but one language. That language must be the language of the Declaration of Independence, of Washington's Farewell address, of Lincoln's Gettysburg speech and second inaugural. We cannot tolerate any attempt to oppose or supplant the language and culture that has come down to us from the builders of this Republic with the language and culture of any European country.... Whatever may have been our judgment in normal times, we are convinced that today our most dangerous foe is the foreign-language press and every similar agency, such as the German-American Alliance, which holds the alien to his former associations and through them to his former allegiance. We call upon all loyal and unadulterated Americans to man the trenches against the enemy within our gates. [123]

Anti-German sentiment increased in this war period, and actually after the war as well. There was great suspicion about the ties of the Lutheran synods to Germany and the kaiser, and the continued distrust of the use of German in the parochial schools. During the war, national hysteria reached a fever pitch with mobs raiding schools, beating Germans, including clergymen, lynching of a German immigrant and the destruction of Lutheran churches.[124] Here as elsewhere, the connection between language and ethnic identity was exploited by nativists. Several states passed laws and emergency decrees banning German speech in churches, in public meetings, even on the telephone where operators would simply disconnect calls if they heard German being spoken.[125] Proponents of Americanism, however, aimed their most strenuous efforts at the education of young children where they hoped to:

> break the German language cycle. The Americanizers particularly feared that children could not properly absorb American values and become good citizens unless they received instruction in the English language .... Moreover, many persons alleged that German-language schools tried to instill in their students a loyalty toward Germany and an admiration for autocracy.[126]

In 1919 alone, 19 states enacted laws that imposed restrictions on the teaching of foreign languages. By the end of that year, 37 states had statutes that restricted the teaching of German specifically or foreign languages generally. In some states Catholics and Lutherans were able to restrict such legislation to secular education only but this was not always successful.

The crime

Nebraska and other states passed legislation after the war was over that virtually eliminated German-language instruction in a child's early years, even in parochial schools. During the war, 151 of the synod's parochial schools in Nebraska abandoned the use of German. Still there was legislation curtailing the use of German even in church services. In 1919 Nebraska passed the Siman Act, which prohibited instruction in any foreign language in any public, private, or parochial schools, except for students who had passed the eighth grade. The penalty for each offense was a fine of between $25 and $100 dollars or imprisonment for not more than 100 days. With the passage of the Siman Act:

> ethnic communities ... realized that proponents of Americanization sought not merely to protect national security and initiate ethnic children into American ways, but to eradicate the foundations of ethnic culture. By removing foreign language instruction from the schools, the Siman Act struck at one of the principal roots of the ethnic communities.[127]

Viewing the Siman Act as a threat to the very survival of their schools, Catholics and Lutherans joined together to battle the law. Within five weeks after the bill was signed into law, the churches and synods filed a state court suit to stop its enforcement. The synods argued that the Siman Act deprived them of their liberty and property without due process of law – a substantive due process argument under the federal and state constitutions.[128]

Interestingly for bilingual education advocates today, one of the arguments made by the plaintiffs was that many of the children they taught could not understand English nor English-only instruction and that "in the parochial schools below the seventh grade the language of the parents is used in order to teach English, and that the children cannot learn English if they do not receive rudimentary education in the tongue the parents use."[129] In ruling to uphold that statute the court explicitly noted that "it ought never to be presumed that the Legislature intended to violate the Constitution," therefore it would construe the state in a manner that would save it from a constitutional infirmity.[130] Acknowledging that the state has an interest in controlling the education of its citizens "far enough to see that it is given in the language of their country, and to insure that they understand the nature of the government under which they live, and are competent to take part in it," the court also noted that "[f]urther than this, education should be left to the fullest freedom of the individual."[131]

The court then departed from the clear language of the statute and found that the intent of the law:

> is that none of the time necessarily employed in teaching the elementary branches forming the public school curriculum shall be consumed in teaching

the child a foreign language, since whatever time is devoted to such teaching in school hours must necessarily be taken away from the time which the state requires to be devoted to education carried on in the English language. Furthermore, there is nothing in the act to prevent parents, teachers or pastors from conveying religious or moral instruction in the language of the parents ... provided that such instruction is given at such time that it will not interfere with the required studies.... [I]t could not have been the intention of the Legislature to bar its parent, either in person or through the medium of tutors or teachers employed, from teaching other studies as their wisdom might dictate. [132]

The court was unpersuaded by the bilingual education arguments, however. It said that:

[i]t is common knowledge that the easiest way to learn a foreign language is to associate only with those who speak and use it. Of course, the occasional use of a few words of the language of the home in order to explain the meaning of English words would not, if good faith is used, violate the act, as seems to be feared.[133]

The court continued its flagrant disregard for the plain language of the Act finding that:

with respect to the complaint that the pastor, or the teachers in private or parochial schools, cannot give moral and religious instruction in English, it is not the medium through which such ideas are conveyed that is material; it is the lessons themselves which are essential to right conduct and good citizenship, and, as we construe it, there is no prohibition in the act to interfere with such teaching in a foreign language.[134]

The court's re-writing of the statute gave the parochial schools just about everything they could ask for but to appease the restrictionists also stressed the importance of the English language and the legitimacy of the state interests that the statute sought to serve. The parochial schools rightly understood the decision to allow them to continue to teach foreign languages during recess, and they promptly responded by extending recess periods and doing just that.

This accommodation, however, angered the language-restrictionists and they charged Robert Meyer, an instructor at the Zion Evangelical Lutheran Congregation's school, with teaching Bible stories in German to ten year old students. Meyer was convicted and charged the $25 fine. While Meyer was appealing his conviction based on the court's interpretation of the Siman Act, the legislature passed the Norval Act specifically closing the loophole created by the court.

Three years later in *Meyer v. Nebraska*,[135] Judge Letton, who wrote the earlier decision construing the Siman Act, found himself dissenting as his brethren upheld the more restrictive Norval Act. The court upheld Meyer's conviction.

Meyer had argued that instruction in religious studies in the German language was necessary for these students to be able to participate in religious services with their German-dominant parents. The schools wanted, said Meyer, to:

> keep the parents and children in a religious way in contact with each other and not diminish the influence of the parents in the home – for instance, so that the children can take part in the devotional exercises of the parents at home, attend public worship with the parents and worship with them – for that reason we wanted to have the children learn so much German that they cold be able to worship with their parents. That was the ultimate and only object we had in teaching German.[136]

Such a benign rationale, however, did not appease the court. It refused to see the religious implications of the case but said the case presented a "question of the direct and intentional teaching of the German language as a distinct subject."[137] For the court, the "salutary" purpose of the statute was clear:

> [t]he Legislature had seen the baneful effects of permitting foreigners, who had taken residence in this country, to rear and educate their children in the language of their native land. The result of that condition was found to be inimical to our own safety. To allow the children of foreigners, who had emigrated here, to be taught from early childhood the language of the country of their parents was to rear them so that they must always think in that language, and, as a consequence, naturally inculcate in them the ideas and sentiments foreign to the best interests of this country. The statute, therefore, was intended not only to require that the education of all children be conducted in the English language, but that, until they had grown into that language and until it had become a part of them, they should not in the schools be taught any other language. The obvious purpose of this statute was that the English language should be and become the mother tongue of all children reared in this state. The enactment of such a statute comes reasonably within the police power of the state.[138]

The use of foreign languages was not only unpatriotic, but something apparently to be feared – it reflected a mind and an identity unknown and perhaps unknowable: a fear born of a deep sense of vulnerability that what was spoken in a foreign language could not be benign but must be mysterious, secretive and cunning.

Since religious instruction could be carried out as easily in the English language as in German, then freedom of religion was not jeopardized. Religion will not provide a shield, reasoned the court to actions that "disturb the peace, or corrupt the public morals, or otherwise become inimical to the public welfare of the state," as apparently studying in German was.

In his dissent, Judge Letton pointed out that the court's new decision overruled its prior ruling. The state, said Letton, cannot use the police power to arbitrarily limit the kind of education a parent can give. Letton asked rhetorically:

> [h]as [the state] the right to prevent the study of music, of drawing, of handi-

work, in classes or private schools, under the guise of police power? If not, it has no power to prevent the study of French, Spanish, Italian, or any other foreign or classic language, unless such study interferes with the education in the language of our country...[139]

Letton was unpersuaded by the argument that the public welfare demanded a restriction on the teaching of foreign languages. Instead, he called the legislation what it really was: "[i]t is patent, obvious, and a matter of common knowledge that this restriction was the result of crowd psychology; that it is a product of the passions engendered by the World War, which had not had time to cool."[140]

The case was appealed to the US Supreme Court, which consolidated cases from Idaho and Ohio with Meyer's case.[141] Since the legislation in these states was similar to that in at least a dozen others, the German-language cases took on national significance.

The Supreme Court decision

In a landmark decision, the US Supreme Court found that the Nebraska statute violated the Fourteenth Amendment of the Constitution that ensures due process. It felt that the due process clause was meant for more than just the arbitrary restraint on physical liberty, but must also encompass substantive aspects so that individuals can "enjoy those privileges long recognized at common law as essential to the orderly pursuit of happiness by free men."[142]

While the court was sympathetic to the state's desire to "foster a homogenous people with American ideals," it ultimately found that the state went too far:

> [t]hat the state may do much, go very far, indeed, in order to improve the quality of its citizens, physically, mentally and morally, is clear; but the individual has certain fundamental rights which must be respected. The protection of the constitution extends to all – to those who speak other languages as well as to those born with English on the tongue. Perhaps it would be highly advantageous if all had ready understanding of our ordinary speech, but this cannot be coerced with methods which conflict withe the Constitution – a desirable end cannot be promoted by prohibited means....[143]

The Due Process Clause had mostly been used to protect individuals from arbitrary governmental actions that compromise established private rights. At a minimum, hearing and notice of a governmental action that would result in a "grievous ... deprivation" must be afforded.[144] In *Meyer*, however, the court established additional "penumbral" rights that were to be protected by the Due Process Clause: the right of the modern language teacher to be free in pursuing his profession and the right of parents to direct the education of their children. These rights were considered substantive individual rights that were to be afforded the protection of the Due Process Clause in a legal analysis that did not distinguish between the question of what specific interests are entitled to due process protection, and the inquiry into what process is actually due.[145] This came to be called, "substantive due process" because it strove to import otherwise unenumerated substantive rights into a provision that purportedly was only concerned with ensuring that an adequate process was followed. Substantive due process analysis reached its peak in the first half of the twentieth century and has since been in a period of retrenchment.[146]

Meyer's legacy

Language rights activists today cite to *Meyer* continuously for its strong words on how constitutional protections are to be afforded those not "born with English on the tongue." In a single simple phrase, the Supreme Court undermined the perception of language as tied to loyalty, citizenship and rights. In a historical moment of fear bordering on hysteria, the Supreme Court felt the pulse of the country and saw the language-restrictive legislation for what it was – free-floating fear converted into xenophobic legislation. By the time the case was decided, however, the Court itself noted that World War I was over and the US had been victorious. The feared German takeover had not come to pass, indeed victors could be generous. Had the Court decided the case ten years earlier, there is reason to believe that the Court would not have been so benevolent.

For instance, in 1944, the Supreme Court had upheld the internment of Japanese American citizens under similar historical circumstances. In *Korematsu v. US*,[147] however, the Court heard and decided the case in the middle of the war when the anti-Japanese fervor was reaching a fevered pitch. There, the Court credited the government's rationale for interning citizens as necessary for public safety with no real showing by the government that the internees were of divided loyalties, suspected of treason, willing, or even able if willing, to help the Japanese in the war. The Court in *Meyer* seemed to leave open the possibility for just such governmental deference at war time, by specifically finding that it was hearing the case at a time of peace. It might have been that even the flimsiest governmental justification would have sufficiently legitimized the anti-German legislation had the Court decided the case during war.[148]

Although the substantive due process analysis relied on by the *Meyer* Court holds little sway in today's period of cautious courts, the significance of the *dicta* in *Meyer* concerning the constitutional protection of language minorities cannot be gainsaid. Indeed, courts continue to rely on *Meyer* for this proposition.[149] Although the proper holding of *Meyer* involves the scope of parental rights, the parents whose rights were being undermined were language-minority parents trying to educate their children in their native tongue. Implicated in the deceptively short decision are issues of the status of language-minority parents and educators, the value of native language retention and foreign language learning; essentially giving language-minority parents the right to retain their native language for themselves and for future generations. Although public opinion may not agree, the Court at least found nothing inimical to the health of the nation for foreign languages to be sustained if not flourish.

Despite the educational context of the decision, *Meyer* ought not to be read as endorsing or mandating bilingual education in public schools. The instruction at issue in *Meyer* was a decidedly private, parochial school that was probably being supported by the German Lutheran community itself. The *Meyer* Court would probably not have agreed with publicly supported instruction in a non-English language for children not dominant in English; the Court's sympathy for the needs of a state to "foster homogenous" people is clear. While it wanted to give language minorities in the country the same constitutional rights as the English-dominant, it certainly was not prepared to offer more than that.

To the extent that teaching a foreign language involves speech and the imparting of ideas, *Meyer* also implicated First Amendment rights.[150] Again, the scope of the decision was not to give language minorities additional rights and privileges but to ensure that language not be used as a rationale for denying them the same rights accorded to others. This First Amendment aspect of *Meyer* will be discussed in Chapter 2. Suffice to say at this point that the use of the First Amendment to invalidate language-restrictive legislation is an emerging and tricky area of law complicated by the unique personality of language not only as a conveyor of information but as laden with expression itself.

Interestingly, the Court did not rely upon the Equal Protection Clause for its decision, perhaps because ethnic Germans were the targets as opposed to an identifiable racial group. A few years later in *Yu Cong Eng. v. Trinidad*,[151] however, the Court would use both the Due Process and the Equal Protection Clauses to strike down more language-restrictive legislation.

Yu Cong Eng v. Trinidad[152]

The language-restrictive legislation passed by the Philippine government in 1923 criminalized the keeping of accounting ledgers by businesses in languages other than English, Spanish, or a local dialect. Known colloquially as the Chinese Bookkeeping Act, the statute was defended by the government as necessary to ensure that Chinese merchants were complying with tax laws. The Chinese merchants, however, kept their ledgers in Chinese because that was the language they understood. To require them to keep ledgers in another, incomprehensible language would render their financial records meaningless to them, keep them at the mercy of locals who understood the "mandatory" languages, and might lead to the financial ruin of the Chinese businesses.

The place of the Chinese in the Filipino economy was inextricably tied to the birth of the legislation. The Supreme Court spent a considerable amount of energy reviewing the history of the Chinese in the Philippines and the nature of their economic contributions. The Chinese presence in the Philippines pre-dated that of the Spanish in the sixteenth century.[153] They were classic middlemen with a distribution system that covered the Philippine Islands and shopkeepers with small shops or "tiendas" that extended to even the smallest settlements or "barrios."[154] The Chinese were "bakers, porters, shoemakers, locksmiths, weavers, and worked in other trades. Moreover, they produced goods at low prices. The economic success of the Chinese aroused not only the usual envy and resentment but also... fears that gold was being drained away to China."[155]

It certainly could not have helped the social situation of the Chinese that they were more sojourners than settlers in the Philippines leaving families to return to in China, living separately and retaining their native languages. As the Court stated:

> not more than eight Chinese merchants [out of 12,000] in the Islands can read or write proficiently in any other language than Chinese, and ... the great majority of them could not comply with the act. The merchants' establishments are made up of young Chinese persons who come from China, begin at the beginning and are promoted from time to time to become the head of the business. The books are always kept in the Chinese language, and each Chinese establishment is completely separated from the native mode of living.[156]

The Court apparently had some level of approval for the Chinese as it balanced their insularity with an image of industrious workers making profound contributions to the Philippine economy. Indeed, an American businessman testified in the lower court to the effect that, should the Chinese be driven out of business "there would be no other system of distribution available throughout the Islands, for the reason that here are not Filipino merchants sufficiently numerous with resources and experience to provide a substitute."[157] The legislation brought protests not only from the Chinese government but from the governor of the Philippines, the Insular Committee of the House of Representatives and from chambers of commerce in the US as not only a national embarrassment but a disaster for the Chinese businesses.[158]

The Supreme Court relied on *Meyer* and other cases that fleshed out substantive due process analysis to strike down the legislation to the extent that it prohibited the merchants from keeping any books in their native language. The Court made no claims for language rights generally, insisting that:

> Of course, the Philippine government may make every reasonable requirement of its taxpayers to keep proper records of their business transactions in English or Spanish or Filipino dialect by which an adequate measure of what is due from them in meeting the cost of government can be had .... But we are clearly of opinion that it is not within the police power of the Philippine legislature, because it would be oppressive and arbitrary, to prohibit all Chinese merchants from maintaining a set of book in the Chinese language, and in the Chinese characters, and thus prevent them from keeping advised of the status of their business and directing its conduct.[159]

No doubt the extreme effect of the legislation on the Chinese and the domino effect it could have on the Philippine economy played a significant role in the Court's decision to strike down the legislation as violative of the Due Process and Equal Protection Clauses of the Philippine Autonomy Act of Congress[160]

In view of the history of the Islands and of the conditions there prevailing, we think the law to be invalid, because it deprives Chinese persons situated as they are, with their extensive and important business long established, of their liberty and property without due process of law, and denies them the equal protection of the laws.[161]

Yet the Court clearly saw that the act was "chiefly directed at the Chinese merchants.... So far as the other merchants in the Islands are concerned, its results would be negligible and would operate without especial burden on other classes of foreign residents."[162] It must have found this targeted kind of legislation distasteful as, without further comment, it cited *Holden v. Hardy*[163] for the proposition that courts must look at the intent of the legislature to discern whether its "action be a mere excuse for an unjust discrimination, or the oppression or spoilation of a particular class."[164] Had the legislation not been so targeted, its effect so complete and disastrous and its intent so embarrassing to the federal government, it's an open question as to how the Court would have decided the issue.[165]

Farrington v. Tokushige[166]

The context

Since 1819, American missionaries had been arriving in Hawaii to try and convert the deity-worshiping islanders. The missionaries bought up land, and established large sugar plantations that required the importation of Chinese and Japanese workers. Between 1885 and 1900, 70,000 Japanese contract laborers came to Hawaii.[167] From 1901 to 1907, another 11,000 Japanese laborers immigrated to the islands.[168]

On August 12, 1898, the US annexed Hawaii as a territory, and organized a territorial government in 1900. One of the first acts of the federal government was to make English the official language of the islands and to require its use in the public and private schools.[169] As the Japanese working population grew, so did the student population. Japanese students in public and private schools of Hawaii increased from 1,320 in 1900 to 19,354 in 1920; out of a total of 65,369 pupils of all races on December 31 1924, 30,487 were Japanese. Private foreign language schools in Japanese and other languages had been established in Hawaii prior to 1898. Although the schools served religious purposes as well, for the Japanese laborers who intended on returning home, the schools served simply a practical purpose – the retention of the native language amongst children who would need to re-assimilate into Japanese society.

On the heels of World War I and the mounting legitimacy of xenophobic campaigns like the "Yellow Peril," the governor of Hawaii, a US mainland appointee, introduced legislation severely controlling the operation of foreign language schools. In 1925 the "Foreign Language School Act of the Territory of Hawaii" was enacted; there were 163 foreign language schools in the territory; nine Korean, seven Chinese and the remainder in Japanese. There were 20,000 pupils enrolled in the Japanese schools; 300 teachers employed; the schools owned property aggregated to be worth $250,000.[170]

The Act defined "foreign language" as other than the English or Hawaiian languages. It brought these privately owned and operated schools under strict governmental control. It imposed an onerous regulatory schema that prescribed who could teach at the schools, the curriculum, the texts and limited enrollment to those who were at least 14 years of age or who had completed the eighth grade. In order to acquire a permit to teach in the schools, a would-be teacher needed to satisfy the department of public instruction that she was "possessed of the ideals of democracy, knowledge of American history and institutions, and knows how to read, write and speak the English language."[171]

Further, before a permit could be issued to allow the operation of the school, the applicant for the permit had to sign a pledge to abide by the terms of the act and "to the best of his ability, so direct the minds and studies of pupils in such schools as will tend to make them good and loyal American citizens, and will not permit such students to receive instructions in any way inconsistent therewith."[172] Not surprisingly, the object of the act was to "fully and effectively regulate the conducting of foreign language schools ... in order that the Americanism of the pupils may be promoted."[173] The government defended the passage of the law as an exercise of its police power.

That this kind of legislation was passed in 1925 shouldn't be surprising. The historian John Higham, called this period the "tribal twenties." He characterized the twenties as "tempestuous" and explained that:

> ...the tempestuous climate of the early twenties is not to be accounted for simply as a resumption of storms after a temporary lull. The very fact that the lull did prove temporary, that old hatreds came back to life after the war instead of being consumed by it, needs explanation. In some degree the causes lay in the objective circumstances of 1920. That year, as part of a general adjustment to peace time conditions, two factors which time and again in American history had encouraged anti-foreign outbreaks vividly reappeared. One was economic depression, the other a fresh wave of immigration.[174]

The physical location of Hawaii, separate from the rest of the nation, closer to the Japanese than to most Americans, the presence of a large, unknown native population and the superiority complex of the Americans during this time – these factors alone would have bred anti-foreigner sentiments; coupled with the economic slump and the certain vestiges of the "Yellow Peril" campaign, the resulting legislation was unfortunately typical.

The 1925 law was challenged by owners and operators of the 146 Japanese schools; the lower court issued a temporary injunction barring enforcement of the law. On appeal to the Ninth Circuit, the court cited *Pierce* and *Meyer* to find that the right of the pupils to acquire knowledge of the Japanese language and the right of others to teach them that language is "beyond question."[175] The court found the regulatory schema detailed in the act appalling, stating that "if such a system of regulations were enforced by one of our American commonwealths against an American college in which foreign languages are taught, it would shock the conscience of mankind."[176]

Noting the non-compulsory, private nature of the schools being regulated, the court was not sympathetic to the arguments of the territorial government:

> [the territory attempted to justify the act based on the] peculiar conditions prevalent on the Islands. They have a large Japanese population there, and it is said that within the next 15 years a majority of the electorate will be American citizens of Japanese extraction. It is further said that the Japanese do not readily assimilate with other races, and that they still adhere to their own ideals and customs, and are still loyal to their emperor. It is a matter of common knowledge that the Japanese do not readily assimilate with other races, and especially with the white [sic] race. This is in part a matter of choice and in part a matter of necessity, because on cannot assimilate alone. No doubt the Japanese tongue will be spoken on the islands for generations yet to come ... but we took the Islands *cum onere* and extended the Constitution of the United States there, and every American citizen has a right to invoke its protection. You cannot make good citizens by oppression, or by a denial of constitutional rights, *and we find no such conditions there as will justify a departure from the fundamental principles of constitutional law.*[177]

The court struck down the law as a violation of the Fifth Amendment's Due Process guarantee under the *Meyer* rationale.

Supreme Court decision

On appeal to the Supreme Court, the Court upheld the Ninth Circuit decision. Not surprisingly, the Court again stressed the extent of the damage the act would wreck on the plaintiffs. The Supreme Court found that enforcement of the act would "destroy most if not all" of the foreign language schools in Hawaii.[178] Relying heavily on *Meyer* again, the Court found that the Act:

> would deprive parents of fair opportunity to procure for their children instruction which they think important and we cannot say is harmful. The Japanese parent has the right to direct the education of his own child without reasonable restrictions; the Constitution protects him as well as those who speak another tongue.[179]

The Court gave a more explicit voice to its feelings about ethnic minorities, however, a feeling that was only hinted at in *Meyer* and *Yu Cong Eng*:

> [w]e of course appreciate the grave problems incident to the large alien populations of the Hawaiian islands. these should be given due weight whenever the validity of any governmental regulation of private schools is under consideration; but the limitations of the Constitution must not be transcended.[180]

While the Court found that there was "no adequate reason" as to why foreign language schools ought to be brought under such strict control,[181] the decision cannot offer much reassurance to language-minority communities.

Although another federal court struck down language restrictive legislation, the suspicion of foreign languages and consequently, of ethnic minorities, is given a yet stronger voice in *Mo Hock Ke Lok Po.*

Mo Hock Ke Lok Po v. Stainback[182]

Despite the Supreme Court's decision in *Farrington,* World War II brought back many of the anti-Japanese sentiments to Hawaii. In *Mo Hock Ke Lok Po* the trial court was asked to review language restrictive legislation within the context of an evaporating foreign-language culture. The court noted that:

> [b]efore the attack on Pearl Harbor there were large schools teaching the Chinese and Japanese languages in the afternoon, after the regular schools had adjourned. These schools ceased teaching during the war. There is testimony that all of such Japanese schools have been permanently abandoned. Their buildings were voluntarily turned over to the government or charity organizations.[183]

On May 1, 1943, the Hawaiian legislature passed an "Act regulating the Teaching of Foreign Languages to Children." The Act was tremendously broad, regulating essentially any situation where "any language other than English [is taught] as a course of study … as a regular and customary practice." The statute also prohibited the teaching of a language other than English to all children who had not passed the first four grades of public or private attendance and they must:

> pass from time to time in each succeeding grade a standard test in English composition and reading conducted by or under the direction of the department of public instruction attaining a score not lower than the normal for his grade; or (b) that he shall have passed the eighth grade in public school or its equivalent, or (c) that he shall have attained the age of 15 years.[184]

The Act was summarily challenged by Hawaiian citizens of Chinese ancestry who had children and wanted them to learn Chinese: a teacher of Chinese, a Hawaiian citizen, and three Hawaiian eleemosynary corporations chartered to teach the Chinese language. The Chinese were apparently trying to renew their after-school instruction, reflecting an undoubtedly suppressed desire to cultivate their native language.

Rather than offering a national security rationale for the Act, the government justified the statute as protecting children from the harm of learning a foreign language. The legislature had declared:

> It is hereby declared that the study and persistent use of foreign languages by children of average intelligence in their early and formative years definitely detract from their ability properly to understand and assimilate their normal

studies in the English language, which are required by law to be pursued ... and definitely retard their progress in understanding and assimilating such studies.[185]

The court did not question these findings, but instead focused on the approximately 10,000 children (out of over 22,000 Hawaiian children in school) who were of "above average" intelligence. The court said:

> [w]e do not agree with the defendants that such a denial to the parents of such a large proportion of children of the constitutional right to secure a foreign language for them is warranted to secure the elimination of the harm it seeks to avoid for those of lesser ability. It is for the brighter ones that there is the greater gain in such attainment – a gain not only in personal mental growth and satisfaction and in increased business opportunities but, now, in opportunities in service to his government's need of foreign language experts in its international intercourse.[186]

Following the path of *Meyer*, the court based its decision on the critical need to protect the relationship between parent and child, and the parents' right to direct the education of that child.[187] The court read the statute as being too broad, denying parents even the right to have a tutor for their children in their homes, even for free. Although the Act was struck down as a violation of the Fifth Amendment, again the court rationalized its decision on parental-rights grounds rather than seeking to create new rights for language minorities. Signaling a reluctance that is still felt today, this court, as the courts before it, struck down language restrictive legislation when it was clearly a product of xenophobia, its effects were apparent and drastic and there were no countervailing national security risks. How the courts treat language minorities when they seek affirmative rights is the touchstone that will reveal the scope and limits of judicial tolerance.

CONCLUSION

In this politically and judicially conservative era it is critically important for language rights activists to be at least familiar with the history of minority languages and bilingualism in this country. Unlike the myths portrayed by English-only proponents, this is a history that reflects a nation finding itself amidst linguistic heterogeneity and tolerance. True, it did not last, and the pressure to "Americanize" and abandon native languages proved too much for new populations. Still, it was never the English language that provided the weave that made the fabric of the nation strong.

Indeed, the linguistically repressive policies of the World War eras stand out as a stain in our national consciousness and against at least the principles of tolerance for which the nation was originally marked.

The development of the Fourteenth Amendment from its genesis as a protector of the privileges of citizenship for emancipated slaves, and then for the protection of minorities generally, was an important process for language minorities. Reading the Fourteenth Amendment broadly to cover substantive as well as procedural rights and to protect ethnic as well as racial minorities was absolutely essential if the Civil Rights Amendments were to have a life into the twentieth and twenty-first centuries. *Meyer* and its progeny are good examples of how the Fourteenth Amendment grew up in a time of crisis and the vital role that language minorities played in that maturation. However, for the last twenty years the courts have narrowed their interpretation of the Amendment, particularly the Equal Protection Clause, and have made it much more difficult for any minorities (but especially language minorities), to bring claims of discrimination under that law. As will be seen in the chapters still to come, court after court has questioned the applicability of the Equal Protection Clause to language minorities since a person of a language-minority background may not be a racial or ethnic minority. As the twentieth century closed, many more civil rights doors were shut for language-minority communities looking to the courts for justice.

Notes

1.   Norman Shumway, *Testimony before the US House Committee on the Judiciary English Language Constitutional Amendments: Hearing on H.J. Res. 13, H.J. Res. 33, H.J. Res. 60, and H.J. Res. 83*, 100th Congress 2nd Session, May 11, 1988 at 36–44 (1988).

2.   Guy Wright, *US English*, SAN FRANCISCO EXAMINER, March 28, 1983 (reprinted in James Crawford, LANGUAGE LOYALTIES: A SOURCE BOOK, University of Chicago Press, 1992) at 127–129.

3.   Heinz Kloss, THE AMERICAN BILINGUAL TRADITIONS (Center for Applied Linguistics and Delta Systems, McHenry, IL, 1983) at 193.

4.   *Id.* at 197.

5.   *Id.*

6.   *See supra*, note 3 at 202–206. Germans were also able to win public funds for the support of German language schools. After Germans demonstrated against a school law that would not expressly allow for the teaching of German, the legislature adopted an amendment stating:

> [t]he passage in the said law which requires that subjects of study be taught in English shall be and hereby repealed. The school board shall have the full power to decide what subjects and what language or languages shall be taught in their districts, though the subjects shall be those customary in the elementary schools.

Thereafter, the establishment of German and bilingual schools proceeded without much controversy. In Cincinnati, by 1870, over 10,000 public school students received bilingual instruction and, by 1902, there were over 17,000 students. Even in rural areas in the high schools, German language classes experienced higher enrollments than any other subject including US history.

7.   Juan Perea, *Demography and Distrust, An Essay on American Languages, Pluralism and Official English*, 77 MINN. L. REV. 269 (1992) at 312.

8.   *Id.* at 313.

9.   *Id.* at 314.

10. *See* www.ccket.com/laploza/calhist4.htm and www.ccket.com/nlaplaza/calhist3.htm.

11. *Supra,* note 3 at 232.

12. *Id.* at 235.

13. *Id.* at 236.

14. DEBATES AND PROCEEDINGS OF THE CONSTITUTIONAL CONVENTION OF THE STATE OF CALIFORNIA 1878–1879, Vol. 2 at 801–802.

15. *Id.*

16. An attempt to modify it by authorizing the legislature to permit translated documents as it deemed appropriate was unsuccessful. Opponents to the amendment argued that if the laws could be printed in Spanish, then they would need to be printed in numerous languages. Comments of Mr Schell and Mr Inman. Although the amendment ultimately lost, Delegate Blackmer was eloquent on the moral dimensions of the issue before the Convention:

    I do not believe, because we are stronger, because we outnumber them and are continually increasing the ratio, that we should entirely ignore the rights that these people ought to have under a free government. It is a simple question whether we will do right because it is a right, or whether we will do wrong because we have the power to do it. (Comments of Mr Blackmer)

17. In comparison, Louisiana became a state nine years after incorporation. California, acquired at the same time as New Mexico, would become a state two years later, Nevada in 1864, Colorado in 1876 and Utah in 1896.

18. Dennis Baron THE ENGLISH-ONLY QUESTION: AN OFFICIAL LANGUAGE FOR AMERICANS? (Yale University Press, New Haven, CT, 1990) at 96.

19. *Id.*

20. *Supra,* note 3 at 170.

21. *Id.*

22. *Id.* at 21.

23. *Id.* at 162. (Although at times the longer territorial phase was justified as the need for the area to achieve an acceptable population density, the assertion is patently false for New Mexico had 61,000 whites by 1850 and 327,000 by 1910. In comparison again, Colorado was granted statehood when it had only 40,000 whites, Minnesota had 6,000, and Nevada had 7,000.)

24. *Supra,* note 18 at 97.

25. *Id.* at 98. Naturally, the issue of patriotism was raised. The eternal question with respect to language minorities, speaking a different language as they do and therefore tied to a different culture if not a different nation, has been whether they can be loyal to their new country. The report's authors asked rhetorically:

    [c]an it be said that a native of New Mexico who renounced his allegiance to the republic of Mexico over forty years ago has less interest in the Government of the United States, less devotion to republican principles, or less fitness for full American citizenship than a subject of European kingdoms who has within a few years left his native home?

26. *Id.* at 100.

27. *Id.* at 103.

28. *Id.*

29. *Supra,* note 3 at 165.

30. *Id.* at 171.

31. *Supra,* note 18 at 85.

32. Still the opening prayers of the convention were conducted in French and English, the

convention proceedings were published in both languages, and the constitution itself was published in French and English. No other languages were accorded such weight.

33. *Supra*, note 3 at 141.

34. Kloss sums up the periods of "non-recognition" of the French language as reflected in Louisiana's ten constitutions:

> [w]e can speak of a direct campaign against the French language only during the middle period, 1864 to 1879. In the period after 1921, the French language was less the object of a direct campaign against it but rather was dropped as superfluous. During the period from 1812 to 1845 French could be bypassed, but not directly attacked ... during those years a considerable number of laws already respected the importance of French. Generally, speaking the legal as well as the actual conditions were not so drastic during the three less favorable periods as may be supposed from the wording of the constitution. For example, the 1864 constitution stated that the English language should be taught in the elementary schools. It is no accident, however, that in the constitutional convention the plenary session rejected the phrase, the "the English language only shall be taught," as was suggested by the committee for education. (*Supra*, note 3 at 143)

35. Julius W. Pratt, America's Colonial Experiment (Prentice-Hall, New York, 1951) at 184. (Hawaii, essentially run by white US businessmen, was not overseen by a "carpet bag" government.)

36. *Id.* at 187.

37. *See Downes v. Bidwell*, 182 US 244 (1901); *Balzac v. People of Porto Rico*, 258 US 298 (1922).

38. *Supra*, note 3 at 289.

39. *Supra*, note 35 at 267.

40. *Id.* at 268.

41. *Supra*, note 3 at 280.

42. *Id.* at 283.

43. Juan Jose Osuna, History of Education in Puerto Rico, 2nd edn (Editorial de la Universidad de Puerto Rico, Rio Piedras, PR, 1949) at 197.

44. *Id.* at 129.

45. *Id.* at 134.

46. *Id.*

47. For additional description of the many and differing language policies followed in Puerto Rico shortly after the US acquisition, *see supra*, note 43 at 341–397.

48. Arturo Morales, Puerto Rico: A Political and Cultural History (W.W. Norton & Co., New York, 1983) at 237.

49. *Supra*, note 43 at 201.

50. *Id.* at 357.

51. *Id.* at 362–63.

52. Susan J. Dicker, Languages in America: A Pluralist View (Multilingual Matters, Clevedon, 1996) at 180.

53. *Id.* at 180.

54. *Id.*

55. Quoted in *English First Issue Brief* (last revised, April 27, 1997).

56. *Supra*, note 52 at 181.

57. *Smothers v. Benitez*, 806 FSupp 299 (D Puerto Rico 1992).

58. *Id.* at 310.

59. *Id.*
60. According to the 1990 Census, 98.2% of all residents of Puerto Rico speak Spanish.More than half do not speak English at all. Less than a quarter have only low-level proficiency in English. US Bureau of the Census, US Department of Commerce, 1990 CENSUS OF POPULATION SOCIAL AND ECONOMIC CHARACTERISTICS, Puerto Rico 46, 1993. This information is not available for the 2000 Census as of this writing.
61. Norman Dorsen, Paul Bender, Burt Neuborne, Sylvia Law, EMERSON, HABER, AND DORM'S POLITICAL AND CIVIL RIGHTS IN THE UNITED STATES, 4th edn, Vol. II (Little Brown and Company, Boston, MA, 1979) at 5.
62. Which, incidentally, uses the language "privileges *and* immunities."
63. *Slaughterhouse Cases*, 83 US (16) Wall at 123 (1872). There have been disagreements over the interpretation of the legislative history of the Privileges or Immunities Clause. Its Framer, Representative John Bingham, and the republicans he spoke for were clear in their intentions for the Clause:

     [t]hat the scope and meaning of the limitations imposed by the 1st section, Fourteenth Amendment of the Constitution may be more fully understood, permit me to say that the privileges and immunities of citizens of the United States as contradistinguished from citizens of the state, are chiefly defined in the first eight amendments to the Constitution of the United States.... These eight articles I have shown never were limitations upon the power of the states, until made so by the Fourteenth Amendment. (Cong. Globe, 42nd Cong. 1st Sess. Opp. 150, 1871)
64. *Id.* at 79–80
65. *Infra*, note 107. Interestingly, the Privileges or Immunities Clause, after 125 years of almost virtual neglect, was used successfully, albeit within the narrow construction of J. Miller's reasoning, in a welfare rights case. In *Saenz v. Roe*, 526 US 489 (1999) recent residents to California who had been denied the same welfare benefits as more-established California residents, brought suit alleging a violation of the right to travel. The right to establish citizenship with any state and be treated the same as others was expressly recognized by J. Miller. However, the Supreme Court had not vigorously relied upon the Privileges or Immunities Clause to actually substantiate those rights. Indeed as Justice Rehnquist pointed out in his dissenting opinion, the Court had relied upon the Clause only once before in its 130-year history. *Saenz* at 511 (J. Rehnquist dissenting). It did so in *Saenz*, however. It is still too early, however, to judge how far the Privileges or Immunities Clause will be stretched; *Saenz* concerned the right to travel, a long-recognized right. It is doubtful that the clause will be used to cover the kinds of social justice and equity issues that were long litigated under the Equal Protection Clause.
66. Robert Kaczorowski, *Revolutionary Constitutionalism and the Era of the Civil War and Reconstruction*, 61 NYUL REV. 863, 922 (1986). In 1823, J. Washington explained that "privileges and immunities," used interchangeably with "inalienable rights" or "civil rights," were those necessary "to the security of the natural rights of life, liberty, and property." *Corfield v. Coryell,* 6F Cas. 546 (CCED Pa. 1823). He specified: the rights of a citizen of one state to pass through or to reside in any other state, for purposes of trade, agriculture, professional pursuits, or otherwise; to claim the benefit of the writ of habeas corpus; to institute and maintain actions of any kind in the courts of the state; to take, have and dispose of property.
67. *Id.* at 923.
68. *Supra*, note 61 at 5, quoting *Yick Wo v. Hopkins,* 118 US 356 (1886).
69. Laurence H. Tribe, AMERICAN CONSTITUTIONAL LAW (The Foundation Press Inc., Mineola, NY, 1978) at 993.

70. Juan F. Perea, *Ethnicity and the Constitution: Beyond the Black-White Binary Constitution*, 36 WM. & MARY. L. REV. 571, at n. 21.

71. *Strauder v. West Virginia*, 100 US 303 (1880).

72. 118 US 356 (1886).

73. *Id.* at 374.

74. *Id.*

75. 347 US 475 (1954).

76. *Id.* at 478.

77. AMERICAN HERITAGE DICTIONARY, 2nd College edn (Houghton Mifflin Co., Boston, MA, 1985) at 107.

78. Note that while "ancestry may overlap with national origin, ancestors may not have a single national origin." Gypsies for instance, have an ancestry but no particular national origin. *Supra*, note 70 at 575.

79. *Supra*, note 77 at 1020.

80. *Supra*, note 70.

81. *Supra*, note 77 at 1020.

82. *Matthews v. de Castro*, 429 US 181, 185 (1976).

83. *See Mississippi University for Women v. Hogan*, 458 US 718 (1982); *but see United States v. Virginia*, 518 US 515 (1996) requiring the state to proffer an "exceedingly persuasive justification" for barring admission of women to its premier military academy. *See also Craig v. Boren*, 429 US 190 (1976), which requires the state to show that the classification used serves an important governmental objective and the discriminatory means employed is substantially related to the achievement of important objectives.

84. *See Eisenstadt v. Baird*, 405 US 438 (1972).

85. For example, employment in major sector of economy, *Hampton v. Mow Sun Wong*, 426 US 88 (1976); interest in retaining drivers license, *Bell v. Burson*, 402 US 535 (1971); in obtaining higher education at an affordable tuition, *Vlandis v. Kline*, 412 US 441 (1973) (White J., concurring).

86. *Supra*, note 69 at 1090.

87. *Id.* at 1090.

88. *Graham v. Richardson*, 403 US 365 (1971); *Sugarman v. Dougall*, 413 US 634 (1973); *In Re Griffiths*, 413 US 717 91973). (According to Justice Rehnquist in *Nyquist v. Mauclet*, 432 US 1 (1977), alienage classifications were suspect because "aliens, *qua* aliens, are a 'discrete and insular' minority ... group, like blacks and orientals ... identifiable by a status over which the members are powerless" until they become eligible for citizenship (J. Rehnquist dissenting at 17).

89. *San Antonio v. Rodriguez*, 411 US 1 (1973).

90. *See Hernandez v. Texas*, 347 US 475 (1954) (Latinos); *Korematsu v. US*, 323 US 214 (1944) (Japanese ancestry).

91. Yet deliberate official racial discrimination was upheld in *Korematsu v. US, supra*, note 90, and in *Swain v. Alabama*, 380 US 202 (1965) concerning the apparent misuse of peremptory challenges by a prosecutor.

92. *See* generally *Loving v. Virginia*, 388 US 1 (1967); *Griffin v. Illinois*, 351 US 12 (1956); *Douglas v. California*, 372 US 353 (1963).

93. State constitutions, however, may make explicit provisions in some of these areas, thereby offering their citizens greater protections than the federal constitution. For instance, most states have constitutional provisions that provide for the establishment of free, public schools.

94. *US v. Carolene Products*, 304 US 144 (1938).

95. *See Carino v. University of Oklahoma, Board of Regents*, 750 F2d 815 (10th Cir 1984) (accent); *Hernandez v. Texas, supra,* note 90.

96. *Supra,* note 96 at 153 n.4 (1938).

97. *Hunter v. Erickson* 393 US 385 (1964).

98. *Id.* at 399.

99. *Korematsu, supra,* note 90, is an alarming case where explicit anti-Japanese regulations were allowed to stand.

100. 426 US 229 (1976).

101. *Akins v. Texas,* 325 US 398 (1945); *see also, Batson v. Kentucky,* 476 US 79 (1986). The same was said in a language rights case involving the selection of jurors:

> [a]nd as we make clear, a policy of striking all who speak a given language, without regard to the particular circumstances of the trial or the individual responses of the jurors, may be found to be a pretext for racial discrimination. (*Hernandez v. New York,* 500 US 352, 371–72, 1991)

> *See also, Romer v. Evans,* 517 US 620 (1996), where Amendment 2 of the Colorado Constitution was struck down because the "ultimate effect" of the amendment was to prohibit any governmental unit from adopting protective policies, statutes or regulations on behalf of gays and/or lesbians unless the state constitution was amended.

102. *Supra,* note 69 at 502.

103. 397 US 254 (1970).

104. *Morrissey v. Brewer,* 408 US 481 (1972).

105. *Mullane v. Central Hanover Bank and Trust Co.,* 339 US 306, 314 (1950).

106. *Richardson v. Wright,* 405 US 208 (1972).

107. *Meyer v. Nebraska,* 262 US 390 (1923).

108. *See supra,* note 69 at 678–79, 775, 789.

109. Thomas Sowell, MIGRATIONS AND CULTURES: A WORLD VIEW (Basic Books, New York, 1996) at 73.

110. William G. Ross, FORGING NEW FREEDOMS: 1917–1927 (University of Nebraska Press Lincoln, NE and London, England, 1994) at 37.

111. *Supra,* note 109 at 73–74.

112. *Id.* at 78.

113. John Higham, STRANGERS IN THE LAND: PATTERNS OF AMERICAN NATIVISM 1860–1925. (Atheneum, New York, 1965) at 196.

114. James Crawford, LANGUAGE LOYALTIES: A SOURCEBOOK ON THE OFFICIAL ENGLISH CONTROVERSY (University of Chicago Press, Chicago, IL, 1992) at 19.

115. *Supra,* note 113 at 197.

116. *Supra,* note 110 at 32.

117. *Id.* at 33.

118. *See generally,* Higham, *supra,* note 113.

119. *Supra,* note 110 at 38.

120. *Id.* at 38.

121. *Supra,* note 113 at 206.

122. *Id.* at 198.

123. *Supra,* note 114 at 85.

124. *Supra,* note 110 at 47.

125. James Crawford. BILINGUAL EDUCATION: HISTORY, POLITICS, THEORY AND PRACTICE, 2nd edn (Bilingual Education Services, Los Angeles, 1991) at 28.

126. *Supra,* note 110 at 47.

127. *Id.* at 96

128. *Nebraska District of Evangelical Lutheran Synod of Missouri, Ohio and Other States et al. v. McKelvie,* 104 Neb. 93, 175 NW 531 (1919).

129. *Id.*

130. *Id.* at 534.

131. *Id.*

132. *Id.*

133. *Id.*

134. *Id.*

135. 107 Neb. 657 (Neb. 1922).

136. *Id.* at 660.

137. *Id.* at 661.

138. *Id.* at 661–62.

139. *Id.* at 668.

140. *Id.* at 669.

141. *Bartels v. Ohio,* 262 US 404 (1923) consolidated with *Bohning v. Ohio* and *Pohl v. Ohio.*

142. *Supra,* note 135 at 399.

143. *Id.* at 401.

144. *Supra,* note 69 at 679.

145. *Id.* at 678–79.

146. But *see Debra P. v. Turlington,* 730 F2d 1405 (8th Cir 1984).

147. 323 US 214 (1944).

148. An additional factor that may have played a role in the Court's decisions and which may definitively differentiate *Meyer* from *Korematsu* is the nature of the governmental actor. In *Korematsu,* it was the federal government, with presumably the greatest interest and expertise in national security, that was arguing for the internments. In *Meyer* and *Bartels* it was state governments which presumably have little to no expertise in foreign relations and national security which were arguing for the legislation. The fact that the US government did not intervene on behalf of the states must have been telling for the Court.

149. *See Yniguez v. Arizonans for Official English,* 69 F3d 920 (9th Cir 1995) (*en banc*), *vacated on other grounds,* 520 US 43 (1997); *Ruiz v. Hull,* 191 Ariz. 441 (1998); *Sandoval v. Hagan,* 197 F3d 484 (11th Cir 1999), *rev'd, Alexander v. Sandoval,* 532 US. Indeed, the Supreme Court would rely on *Meyer* in deciding its landmark case on parental authority, *Pierce v. Society of Sisters,* 268 US 510 (1925).

150. *See supra,* note 69 at 789, citing *Meyer* as an example of governmental interference in speech.

151. 271 US 500 (1926).

152. *Id.*

153. *Supra,* note 109 at 206.

154. *Supra,* note 151 at 513.

155. *Supra,* note 109 at 206.

156. *Supra,* note 151 at 513.
157. *Id.*
158. *Id.* at 514.
159. *Id.* at 525.
160. The Philippine Autonomy Act of Congress of August 29, 1916 chap. 416, sec. 3, 39 Stat. at Large 546, Comp. Stat sec. 3810. to be read co-extensively with the US Constitution's Bill of Rights. *Supra,* note 151 at 524.
161. *Supra,* note 151 at 524–25.
162. *Id.* at 514.
163. 169 US 366 (1898).
164. *Id.* at 526 (citation omitted).
165. *See for example* Arnold Leibowitz, *English Literacy Legal Sanction for Discrimination* 45 NOTRE DAME LAWYER 7 at 25 (1969) arguing that the way the Supreme Court approached these early "language cases" left room for less extreme language restrictive legislation.
166. 273 US 284 (1927).
167. *Supra,* note 165 at n. 83.
168. *Id.* at n. 83
169. *Id.*
170. *Supra,* note 166 at 290–91.
171. *Farrington v. Tokusighe,* 11 F2d 710, 711 (9th Cir 1926).
172. *Id.* at 711–712.
173. *Id.* at 711.
174. *Supra,* note 113 at 266–67.
175. *Supra,* note 171 at 713.
176. *Id.* at 714.
177. *Id.* at 714 (emphasis added).
178. *Id.* at 298.
179. *Id.*
180. *Id. at* 299
181. *Id. at* 298.
182. 74 FSupp 852 (D Hawaii 1947).
183. *Id.* at 856–57. (Although the court noted that the abandoned schools were *voluntarily* transferred to the government, it isn't hard to imagine the kind of hostility that the language-minority community in Hawaii must have been under at that time, hardly making the relinquishment of their property to the government "voluntary.")
184. *Id.* at n. 2.
185. *Id.* at 856.
186. *Id.* at 857.
187. *Id.* at 854–55.

Chapter 2

Nativism and Language Restrictions: Echoes of the Past at the End of the Twentieth Century

INTRODUCTION

The eminent historian John Higham has shown us through his seminal work on nativism in the US[1] that xenophobic policies are usually adopted during times of national discomfort or lack of confidence. Little can make a country as uncomfortable as a significant rise in immigration that may challenge a nation's conception of itself. The recent rise in immigration has rivaled the highest immigration trends the US has ever experienced. The 2000 Census information reveals that there has been a 54% increase in the foreign-born population in the US since the 1980s.[2] Immigrants now comprise 11% of the US population the largest proportion since the 1930s. The infusion of new populations has been a tremendous boon for some small towns and sparsely-populated regions throughout the country that have been revitalized by immigrants.[3] Yet while some towns have been at least tolerant, if not simply welcoming, of immigrants, others have been hostile to what they perceive as a threat to their established way of life.[4]

Given that the immigration boom has been fed by arrivals from countries where English is not commonly spoken, the debate about whether steps should be taken to protect the English language have re-surfaced. It is no surprise, then, that there has also been a rise in interest in language-restrictive legislation over the past two decades.

In this chapter, I will discuss the possible reasons for and results of the recent growth in language-restrictive legislation, and review the arguments language restrictionists make to support their position. I will also review the myths upon which language restrictionists have based their movement and analyze the language specific data collected in the 2000 Census. This chapter will also discuss recent litigation challenging language-restrictive legislation. The first example is a small case from California in which the City of Pomona attempted to implement a new town ordinance that restricted the languages in which businesses could post their signs. Although the case was decided on the trial level, the court relied upon the First Amendment to find that choice of language raised First Amendment issues. The reasoning was novel, and continues to echo through the more recent cases decided by Courts of Appeals. Following the City of Pomona case, are longer discussions of the passage of English-only laws in Arizona and Alabama and the significant litigation in which those laws resulted. One of those cases, *Sandoval v. Hagan*,[5] would end up at the US Supreme Court. Finally there is a discussion of recent litigation challenging an English-only law, springing from Utah, *Anderson v. Utah*,[6] in which the court applied the reasoning of the earlier cases to uphold the state's English-only law. I conclude the chapter with a discussion of how language rights struggles have taken on a broad dimension that must be identified and used by advocates if they wish to secure language rights into the future.

MYTHS AND REALITIES OF ENGLISH-ONLY LAWS

Since 1981, 22 states have passed laws that in one fashion or another recognize the centrality of the English language to their social and civic life.[7] Sometimes they are called "Official English" laws – usually by their proponents, who wish to stress that private bilingualism and minority tongue usage is not being targeted. Other times they are labeled "English-only" laws, usually by opponents who argue that minority language usage itself is the un-stated target. Such legislation can take the form of a relatively benign attempt to do no more than acknowledge the primacy of the English in the country, or may be more pernicious and actively restrict the languages in which government can operate. Either way, the interest and debate surrounding the use of minority languages and the nature and extent of the government's support of those languages has rarely been higher.

In the early 1980s the English-only movement sprang up, and was organized under the banner of the non-profit institution, *US English*, with the late senator and semantist S.I. Hayakwa as its leader. The focus was on passing federal legislation that would make English the only language in which the government could operate. Under this rubric, the bilingual provisions of the Voting Rights Act were a primary focus. All efforts to pass a national English-only law have failed. However, the strategy has shifted to focus on the state level with much greater success.

Within the last ten years, the "language wars" have not only gone local but have also been re-defined with bilingual education as the focal point. For instance the media has often conflated the battle over bilingual education with the battle over English-only. Interestingly, opponents of bilingual education are not necessarily supporters of English-only, and the two issues can and should be analyzed separately.[8] Yet, deciding in which language to educate students is a distinctly different inquiry than whether the parents of these children should be able to vote in language they can understand. Supporters of English-only, however, can garner greater support by conflating the two issues, especially when there is such national anxiety over bilingual education in particular. The English-only proponents could argue that making English the only language of government will make bilingual education obsolete, because schools will necessarily have to immerse their students in English as quickly as possible if they are to have any chance to succeed in a mono-lingual country. *US English* has not been shy about pressing the bilingual education button. It's current chairman, Mauro Mujica, likened bilingual education advocates to "old-style southern segregationists" trying to keep language-minority children separate in bilingual education classrooms forever.[9] While *US English* has not supported a total ban on bilingual education, supporting instead what it feels is more moderate legislation that would place real time-limits on bilingual programs, its rhetoric is as hot and florid as any used by the bilingual education opponents. Mujica says his organization's goal is to "ensure that every student learns English," in contrast to the goal of the bilingual education "lobby" which he says sees each child "kept" in a bilingual education class as a source of additional revenue.[10]

Regardless of the exact nature of the laws passed, whether symbolic or actively oppressive, the US is seeing a re-emergence of nativism that makes conditions favorable for language restrictions to flourish and grow. The origins of this latest language-restrictionist movement can be traced to 1981, when late Senator S.I. Hayakawa, an immigrant and a scholar of semantics, proposed a Constitutional amendment designating English as the official language of the US. The amendment, destined to fail, would have prohibited the US or any state from making or enforcing any law that required the use of any languages other than English. In 1983 he founded the *US English*, "the nation's oldest, largest citizens' action group dedicated to preserving the unifying role of the English language in the US."[11] It reports itself as having 1.5 million members nationwide.[12]

Senator Hayakawa was not shy about sharing his rationale: the US was made into a strong country by the voluntary shedding of ethnic identity by immigrants of yesterday. With respect to today 's immigrants, he reasoned that "those who claim to speak for the Hispanic people" do not want to embrace the "melting pot" ideology but, for purely self-motivated reasons, wish to keep their "Hispanic" constituents segregated and conversing only in Spanish. Hayakawa took particular aim at the bilingual ballot provisions of the Voting Rights Act and the bilingual education funding of the federal government as "two legislative efforts [that] have released this outburst of effort on behalf of the Spanish language and Hispanic culture."[13]

Hayakawa blamed the "politically ambitious 'Hispanic Caucus,'" comprised of congressional Latino leaders, as looking "forward to a destiny for Spanish-speaking Americans separate from that of Anglo-, Italian-, Polish-, Greek-, Lebanese-, Chinese-, and Afro-Americans, and all the rest of us who rejoice in our ethnic diversity, which gives us our richness as a culture, and the English language, which keeps us in communication with each other to create a unique and vibrant culture.[14]

The charges against the "professional Hispanics" were blatantly racist and extraordinary for their unapologetic appeal to ethnic divisiveness:

> The advocates of the Spanish language and Hispanic culture are not at all unhappy about the fact that "bilingual education" ... often results in no English being taught at all. Nor does Hispanic leadership seem to be alarmed that the large populations of Mexican-Americans, Cubans and Puerto Ricans do not speak English and have no intention of learning. Hispanic spokesmen rejoice when still another concession is made to the Spanish-speaking public....It is not without significance that pressure against English language legislation does not come from any immigrant group other than Hispanics: not from the Chinese or Koreans or Filipinos or Vietnamese; nor from the immigrant Iranians, Ethiopians, Italians or Swedes. The only people who have any quarrel with the English language are the Hispanics – at least the Hispanic politicians and "bilingual teachers" and lobbying organizations. One wonders about the Hispanic rank and file?[15]

Then again: "[t]he aggressive movement on the part of Hispanics ... to reject assimilation and to seek and maintain – and give official status to – a foreign language within our borders is an unhealthy development."[16]

Hayakawa apparently made it "safe" for others to take up the banner against Latinos, professional or otherwise. Guy Wright, a columnist for the *San Francisco Examiner*, wrote in 1983 in support of *US English*:

> Even today most immigrants realize the value of knowing English and are eager to learn – witness the packed newcomer classes. The resistance comes from leaders of ethnic blocs, mostly Hispanic, who reject the melting-pot concept, resist assimilation as a betrayal of their ancestral culture, and demand government funding to maintain their ethnic institutions....This anti-assimilation movement ... comes at a time when the United States is receiving the largest wave of immigration in its history. This influx strains our facilities for assimilation and provides fertile ground for those who would like to turn language minorities into permanent power blocs.[17]

Here, at least is one almost honest rationale for supporting English-only: it will help keep ethnic minorities from becoming powerful voting blocs. The possibility of the political power of ethnic minorities must be the overriding reason for this kind of restrictionist movement since no other makes sense, especially when we think of an educated semantist like Hayakawa, who is surely conversant in the linguistic history of the US, making such historically inaccurate and patently false statements about the linguistic homogeneity of the country. Something more must be at work here.

Joseph Leibowicz, a lawyer from New Haven Connecticut and a scholar of American language policy, suggests that the push for passage of an English language amendment is "one part of an attack on despised programs and emergent Hispanic political power."[18] From this perspective, just waging the battle and putting opponents on the defensive against a "seemingly obvious, patriotic position – may constitute winning it."[19]

The battle has certainly been effectively waged since Hayakawa outlined this agenda in the early 1980s. Since 1981 there have been 17 bills introduced in Congress attempting in some way to make English the official language of the nation or to at least "express the sense of Congress" that English is the official language of the US. Most have not gone very far; it was not until 1996 that an English-only bill actually passed in the House of Representatives before it was left to die in the Senate. The rationale behind the bills, however, and the angry, frightened rhetoric used to argue for the passage are noteworthy because they have successfully permeated the thinking and language used by the public in passing state official language legislation, anti-immigrant legislation and anti-bilingual education legislation.

The primary reasons used for supporting English-only legislation on a federal level have been:

(1) the perception that Latino immigrants are not learning English as quickly as other immigrants and declaring English as the official language will encourage them to do so;

(2) bilingual ballots and bilingual education are disincentives to learning English; official English legislation would remove these "crutches";

(3) English is being threatened by a competing language (Spanish) and must be cloaked with a protective authority before Spanish replaces it;

(4) the nation is endangered by the same sort of linguistic discord and ethnic separatism that has plagued other bilingual countries; declaring English the official language would purportedly alleviate this.

Recurrent themes are also that it is "liberals" who rely on uneducated Latinos for their votes and they wish to keep them ignorant of the English language to ensure their voting blocs.[20]

The first three of these rationales really raise the same issue: the rate at which recent immigrants learn English. If current immigrants are learning English as quickly as prior immigrants, then bilingual education and bilingual ballots are not undermining that progress nor is another language going to become more prominent than English.[21] The last rationale also reflects an anxiety about the continued power of English, which should be alleviated by a discussion on the rates of English language acquisition which follows. However, language restrictionists consistently refer to Canada as a cautionary model against minority language accommodation so, after a lengthier discussion on the rate of English language acquisition, I will briefly address why Canada's language struggles are not pertinent in this country.

Rate of English language acquisition

Latinos are actually learning English faster and assimilating more quickly than previous immigrant groups did.[22] California researchers have found that persons of Mexican origin were making the same progress of integration as earlier European immigrants and as the state's recent Asian immigrants. The study also examined the transition of Spanish speakers to English and found that most of the first-generation native born are bilingual and more than 90% are proficient in English. Among the second-generation, more than half are monolingual English speakers.[23]

The most current information available from the 2000 Census, showing a rise in the number of households where languages other than English are spoken, adds some important details to this discussion. According to preliminary analyses of the 2000 Census, the number of residents who speak a language other than English at home increased by 41% during the 1990s from 38% recorded in the last census, ten years ago.[24] The number of minority language speakers who also speak English "very well" increased from 39% to 42% in the 1980s. What has alarmed some language restrictionists has been that during the 1990s speakers of languages other than English grew at seven times the rate of English-only speakers and the rate of those who described themselves as not speaking English "well" rose by 48.5% while those who did not speak English at all rose by 81.2%.[25] The fact that languages other than English are being spoken in homes or elsewhere should come as no surprise, given the immigration trends. As James Crawford, a journalist and author monitoring language issues for over a decade, commented on the Census figures, "for anyone who has been paying attention since the 1980s, there are no stunning revelations."[26] He concluded that the Census figures show only what we would expect: "over the past twenty years, the population of fluent bilinguals has been increasing at about the same rate as the population that speaks languages other than English."[27]

Indeed, although the bilingual population has clearly grown, the proportion of those who do not speak English "very well" is still small in comparison to the country's overall population. For instance, only 7.7% reported that they spoke English less than "very well." Only 1.3% reported that they did not speak English at all, and only 2.8% reported that they did not speak English "well."[28] Given the rise in ethnic diversity that the US is currently experiencing, the fact that the country is still overwhelmingly English-dominant is comment on just how durable the English language is in the US rather than a rallying point for language restrictions.

How Canada's language struggles are not our own

The recurrent references to the linguistic divisions of other countries (especially Canada) as living warnings to the US that official recognition of English is necessary misreads the true lessons of Canada. Canada's Francophone minority felt itself forced into passing restrictive French-promoting language laws because of the economic and cultural discrimination they had suffered at the hands of the Anglophone majority. While the national government promised to make Canada truly bilingual, the French-speaking minority never saw those promises realized and in response passed their own language laws protective of the French language.

Although US language minorities might feel likewise, the chances of their passing minority-language protective legislation is quite slim. The French-speaking minority of Canada is a relatively homogenous, geographically compact group with a long fairly stable history in Canada in which the group experienced the same discriminations over the course of their long histories together.[29] In contrast, US language-minority communities are very diverse, dispersed, politically heterogeneous, and comprise a mixture of recent and older immigrants who have little or no history in common and have come to the US for a variety of reasons, mostly economic and political; they have little interest in codifying the usage of the home languages.

Symbolic and restrictive laws

As in the past, the nation's anxiety over cultural and ethnic differences has led to language restrictive-legislation that has already begun to be challenged in the courts. Sometimes, English-only legislation can fairly be described as nothing more than a declaration of the historic importance of English to the state's population. For example, Arkansas' law states: "[t]he English language shall be the official language of the State of Arkansas; this section shall not prohibit the public schools from performing their duty to provide equal educational opportunities to all children."[30] These kinds of laws seem to have no real impact on the daily lives of the state's residents, and apparently were passed just with that intention. These kinds of laws might be called "benign," especially in comparison to more restrictive laws that were truly passed with the expressed purpose of changing the "official" language(s) in which the state and even its residents operate. Still these "benign" laws were passed at least partly in response to a perceived threat to the supremacy of the English language of the state, if not the nation. If nothing more, they serve as a reminder to the non-English speakers in the state (whether a small minority, or a larger group) that the state cannot be made over in to the image of the minority, that they must remain outsiders ostensibly until they are fully fluent in English. Language rights activists contend that the laws target more than just those who cannot speak English well. They argue that, because the language is so tied to ethnicity and nationality, they are really trying to exclude language minorities, regardless of their English fluency, from full participation as citizens and, as such, from the imagination of the national character.[31]

To what extent the condition is made real depends upon the scope and nature of the law. Simple declaration of "supremacy" of English in a state may not have any immediate impact on the way that a state operates its civic life. Not that such a lack of impact should be taken as an endorsement: there appears to be no reason for such laws or "resolutions," except to appease someone's insecurity over the state's status *vis-à-vis* minorities. The appeasement of such anxieties, as opposed to their rational deconstruction, may be the easiest but certainly not the wisest course. For instance, the English-only movement's widely-known agenda is to have the US adopt a Constitutional amendment making English the official language of the nation. As that effort has not been successful so far, they have concentrated their work at the state level, with much success. If two-thirds of the states adopt English-only laws, however, English-only advocates can push for a Constitutional amendment and use the popularity of the issue amongst the states as a potent argument in Washington DC. Congress would then have to buck the state-led trend if it did not want to follow that course. The states themselves, perhaps never even having thought to ratify a federal English-only law previously, would be hard pressed not to vote for a Constitutional amendment. Also, repeatedly, courts that are reviewing language-rights cases refer to whether or not a state has adopted an official language in discussing, at least in dicta, the legitimacy of the claims of language minorities for services.

For instance, in *Gutierrez v. Municipal Court*,[32] the court pointed out that, in striking down an English-only law imposed on municipal court employees, the state was not an "English-only state." One is led to wonder whether the decision might have been different if the state had adopted a "purely symbolic" English-only law. Indeed, in a voting rights case, the city of Chicago pointed out that it ought not to be made to comply with the federal requirement for bilingual ballots because Illinois recognized English as its official language.[33]

Even if the law is a "purely symbolic gesture," the meaning of that gesture is not an inclusive one but one that is open to greater restrictive interpretations by those who would like to see the law have a more widespread impact. So it is not unusual for employees to cite the prevalence of English as a justification for their own unlawful English-only law,[34] especially in a nation where a presiding judge equates a child's learning Spanish with child abuse.[35]

This kind of "language vigilantism" is created and coached into existence by "symbolic" English-only laws.[36] For, no matter what else we say about these laws, symbols have meanings and these symbolic laws were adopted for their very obvious meaning: those who do not speak English are not welcome here.

More restrictive laws have more obvious and immediate impact. Some would like to restrict the languages in which the governmental documents are produced, others would like to ensure that English is given primacy in school instruction and curriculum. One of the most restrictive laws passed by a state (Arizona) was the subject of a decade-long court battle, which is discussed below after the City of Pomona case.

City of Pomona: Restrictions on the language of business signs

A relatively early forerunner of this recently developing litigation was a lawsuit brought by the Asian community in Pomona, California.[37] In this case, the city of Pomona had passed an ordinance which required that businesses in the City that had advertising signs up with "foreign alphabetical characters" needed to devote at least one half of the signs' area to "English alphabetical characters." The businesses with such foreign "characters" were also displaying their address in "Arabic numerals."

The Asian American Business Group, a non-profit association dedicated to the preservation of the freedom of speech of Asian-Americans brought suit against the

City claiming that the ordinance violated the First Amendment's guarantees of freedom of speech and of association. They also claimed violations of the Equal Protection and Due Process Clauses of the US Constitution. The court found a freedom of speech violation because the ordinance did not so much regulate commercial speech, as regulate the *language* that the speech was written in – a substantive regulation of an "expression of national origin, culture and ethnicity..." said the court.[38] For the court "[a] person's primary language is an important part of and flows form his/her national origin ... choice of language is a form of expression as real as the textual message conveyed. It is an expression of culture."[39]

Since the ordinance regulated non-commercial speech, it impinged on a fundamental right and needed to be analyzed under strict scrutiny. In order to survive such scrutiny, the ordinance must be "narrowly tailored." This ordinance could not pass that test. The City argued that the ordinance was necessary to enable firefighters to easily identify buildings. However, the "Arabic numeral" requirement alone would address that concern since the number of a building is the best way to identify a structure. By also requiring the use of English-language words, the ordinance went too far.

So too, the law was too vague for Due Process purposes, since it referred to the need for "advertising copy" to be written in English, an undefined term. The court also struck down the law as a violation of the Equal Protection Clause. Since the law discriminated against those sign owners who use "foreign alphabetical characters" and since foreign-language usage use is "clearly an expression of national origin."[40] The court had little patience for arguments over whether the use of a foreign language was sufficient to implicate national origin: "[o]f course the ordinance does not expressly refer to national origin discrimination ... cities could avoid such heightened scrutiny by passing discriminatory laws that merely restrict those who speak foreign languages." The court plainly found this result inconsistent with civil rights laws.[41]

Pomona, however, was only a trial court decision, and its precedential value is limited. It's rationale, however, as well as that of the Supreme Court in *Meyer* decided so many years ago, continued to echo for another twenty years and as high up as the US Supreme Court when the more recent English-only cases were decided.

Yniguez v. Mofford: Arizona passes the nations' most restrictive law

Arizona passed an English-only law in 1988. Using the infamous initiative and referendum process, Robert D. Parks and his group *Arizonans for Official English* (AOE) became the principal sponsors for an initiative that would amend the Arizona Constitution to add an "official English" article. The proposed amendment, initially called Proposition 106, was both the most restrictive English-only law passed by a state and the broadest – if passed it would work to eradicate all non-English languages from every state or local government office, document and most strikingly, from the tongues of every state or local government employee.

The amendment would not only make English the official language of Arizona, it also prohibited the state "from using ... languages other than English" and required that the state and local governments "act" in English only. Importantly, the proposed law would also give any resident of the state a right to sue to enforce the law.[42]

Arizona, home to significant numbers of Latinos and Native Americans still struggling to save their native languages, became a battleground between nativism and diversity. That this kind of battle would take place in Arizona, originally part of Mexico and with a rich history of linguistic diversity and home to established Mexican-American and Native-American communities, is itself an interesting phenomenon.

Indeed, before Arizona became a state, English proficiency requirements were conspicuously kept out of enabling legislation. While conservative Senator Beveridge pushed for the denigration of the Spanish language in New Mexico, he did no such thing with Arizona, an admittedly Whiter, more Anglo territory. Governor Kibbey's rejection of an English literacy requirement for voters was remarkably sensitive and modern:

> A people does not, nor indeed, do individuals, usually change their speech voluntarily. The acquisition of a new language voluntarily is a refinement of education confined to a few individuals as a mere accomplishment. That a whole people should change their language denotes that there was a necessity more or less urgent to do so, or the acquisition if the result of years and often generations of association and intercourse with a people speaking a different language who have become predominant.[43]

Both he and his successor, Governor Richard E. Sloan, charged that law was a racial and not an educational test, aimed at "the best class of Arizona's Hispanic voter," and "unjustly discriminatory."[44] The English literacy requirement was passed over the Governor's veto. In 1912, however, the US Senate would quash the law as a discriminatory condition to allowing Arizona to become a state.[45]

The publicity pamphlet for Proposition 106 presenting both the pro and con sides for a constitutional amendment regurgitated the familiar arguments. AOE, which promoted the Proposition, argued that passage of the Proposition would encourage non-English speakers to learn English and put an end to the "ethnic separatism" and "ethnic distrust" wrought by speaking languages other than English.[46] This kind of sweeping language would be examined by the reviewing courts to help them determine the intent of the Amendment's drafters.

Those against the initiative included then-Governor Rose Mofford who argued that, because of the vagueness of the Proposition, if passed it would "cause more problems for Arizona than it would solve."[47]

In the Arizona general election held on November 8 1988, the amendment passed with 50.5% of the vote. The initiative became Article XXVIII of the Arizona Constitution.

On November 10 1988 Mary Kelly Yniguez, a bilingual state employee brought suit against the state of Arizona to have Article XXVIII declared unconstitutional under the First and Fourteenth Amendments of the US Constitution and Title VI of the Civil Rights Act of 1964.

Yniguez was joined in her suit by Jaime Gutierrez, an Arizona state senator who spoke Spanish when communicating to his constituents and continued to do so even after passage of the amendment. Both Yniguez and Gutierrez had signed loyalty oaths swearing to obey the Arizona constitution when they took on their state jobs. They filed their suit in federal district court for the district of Arizona.[48]

The trial court made a series of technical decisions regarding standing, the ability of certain individuals to sue, and the propriety of the selection of defendants. The law suit had been brought against Mofford, Catherine Eden, Yniguez's employer, and Robert Corbin, the state's Attorney General. The court ended up dismissing the suit against Eden and Corbin because they had not threatened Yniguez with enforcement of the Amendment. However, Mofford had stated publicly that, if passed, she intended to comply with the law, which ostensibly meant requiring Yniguez to comply as well. Gutierrez was dismissed as a plaintiff because none of the parties had the right to compel him to abide by the state constitution. Yniguez was allowed to remain a plaintiff even though no enforcement action had been taken against her. For, the court stated, the "danger associated with laws which limit First Amendment rights is to a large extent one of self-censorship, which is a harm that can be realized even without an actual enforcement action."[49] Further, Yniguez was allowed to stand in the shoes of others whose First Amendment rights might be impinged, even if hers weren't. This meant that Yniguez could assert the claims of those members of the public, the non-English speaking members of the public who needed Yniguez's bilingual ability and undoubtedly relied upon the multilingual nature of their state government. This is enormously important, for this kind of flexibility would allow the court to look to the real intent of the Amendment and its implications for the non-English speaking public. For now, however, the players in the lawsuit were Mary Kelly Yniguez and Rose Mofford.

Rose Mofford was not a defender of Article XXVIII; indeed, she had taken a public position against Proposition 106, lending the venerableness of her title to the Proposition's pamphlet literature. Once passed, her Attorney General, Robert Corbin, had issued an advisory opinion on the scope and meaning of Article XXVIII which had limited it severely. Corbin certainly must have had Mofford's blessing for such an interpretation. His limiting interpretation centered on a creative and, given the language of the Article, an unjustifiable, interpretation of the word "act" appearing in Section (3) (1) (a) of the Amendment. Corbin argued that the Article only required that English be used in those rare and official instances when the state acted as "sovereign," not when it acted through its employees on a daily basis to communicate with the public. Supposedly, this meant that the state employees could continue to speak in languages other than English when they needed to in order to help the state carry out its business, but the state could publish its laws, for instance, only in English. Indeed, the state would later stipulate in the lawsuit that the use of languages other than English by its employees helped the state act more effectively and efficiently.

The sweeping language of the Article however, coupled with the words of Corbin explaining his rationale for the Amendment, undermined any limiting interpretation.

It was just these factors that the trial court pointed to when it declined to save the Article by adopting Corbin's limitations. Yniguez argued that one of the deficiencies of the Amendment was that it was overly broad and therefore, a violation of the First Amendment. The court could have arguably saved the Article by adopting Corbin's narrow construction of the Amendment's reach. It declined to do so, however, finding that such a construction was no more than a "remarkable job of plastic surgery on the face of the ordinance."[50] Such linguistic gymnastics ought to be avoided by the courts, for they stand in such great contrast to the plain language of the law that the public confusion over what is or is not allowed is the unforeseen result.

The court found that the law meant what it basically said: it was "a prohibition on the use of any language other than English by all officers and employees of all political subdivisions in Arizona while performing their official duties except where specifically allowed by the law."[51] This construction, said the court is indeed one that might be stricken down for facial over breadth – that is, that it is overly broad on its very face as opposed to being applied by local authorities or interpreting agencies in an overly-broad manner.

Once the court analyzed the actual meaning of Article XXVII, it held that there was a "realistic danger and a substantial potential for the unconstitutional application of the [law];" it declared the Amendment unconstitutional.[52] The court was careful, however, to point out that its determination did not depend on Yniguez having a right to speak whatever language she wanted while she worked, "rather it depends upon the fact that the law is so over broad it would impinge other's rights to speak in a language they want."[53] For instance, Gutierrez's rights might be impinged as would state employees who wanted to "comment on matters of public concern in a language other than English."[54] In this round, the victory went to plaintiffs, but this decision would turn out to be only the first part of a long process that would see the case go up to the US Supreme Court and back down through state court channels before the new law was finally defeated in 1998, ten years after the Amendment was passed.[55]

In the meantime, the Ninth Circuit heard the appeal *en banc,* and Judge Reinhardt wrote the opinion.[56] At the outset he noted that the case presented "troubling questions" that reflected the tension between the need for a common national language and the country's tradition of tolerance. The court declared it would be guided, however, by the Supreme Court's reasoning and wisdom as reflected in *Meyer v. Nebraska,*[57] decided over twenty years ago.

Like the trial court, the Ninth Circuit noted that the Arizona law was the most restrictive state English-only law passed to date and also rejected the Attorney General's construction of the law as completely inconsistent with the spirit in which the law was passed and its plain language. Again, the court also repeated the trial court's maxim that in order to be declared over broad there must be a "realistic danger" that the provision will significantly compromise the speech rights involved.[58] The court also accepted that Yniguez was not only seeking to protect her rights but those of "innumerable employees, officials and officers in all departments and at all levels of Arizona's state and local governments."[59]

This English-only law, the court found, could not be more inclusive: it was broad enough to prohibit the Arizona state college from issuing diplomas in Latin and from a state judge saying "Mazel Tov" at the end of a wedding he performed.[60]

The most important part of the court's decision, however, centered on its response to AOE's argument that the choice of language in which a person decides to speak is not "pure" speech but an expressive decision that really relates to "conduct." The distinction between pure speech and *expressive conduct* is significant in First Amendment jurisprudence. For, while pure speech is strictly prohibited, actions that amount to conduct (like the Vietnam-era flag or draft-card burning) are not as protected, even though the actions are meant to be expressive.

The court, however, would not accept AOE's argument that language choice is akin to expressive conduct. Certainly all language must have an expressive component like putting pencil to paper or even the vibration of the vocal chords necessary to speak. Language, however, "is by definition speech, and the regulation of any language is the regulation of speech," concluded the court.[61] The court continued:

> [a] bilingual person, of course, makes an expressive choice by choosing to speak one language rather than another .... Nonetheless, this expressive effect does not reduce the choice of language to the level of "conduct" ... instead, it exemplifies the variety of ways that one's use of language conveys meaning.... Such variables – language, words, wording, tone of voice – are not expressive conduct, but are simply among the communicative elements of speech. Moreover, the choice to use a given language may often simply be based on a pragmatic desire to convey information to someone so that they may understand it. That is in fact the basis for the choice involved in the constitutional challenge we consider here.[62]

The court was clearly outraged at the contempt in which non-English languages were clearly held by the Article's sponsors. The languages of "Cervantes, Proust, Tolstoy and Lao-tze" could not be considered "scurrilous" such that regulation was appropriate. Further, it disagreed with the basic arguments propounded by the sponsors that tolerating diversity would weaken the nation. Referring to the Supreme Court's decision in *Meyer*, the court stated that "while Arizonans for Official English complains of the 'babel' of many languages, the [Supreme] Court ... responds that this 'verbal cacophony is ... not a sign of weakness but of strength.'"[63]

Undoubtedly significant to the court's reasoning was not creating affirmative language rights for minority language communities. Like the trial court, it emphasized that it was not compelling the state to provide bilingual or multilingual services, merely not to "gag" its employees. Apparently acknowledging the invidious nature of the Article's intent, the court said: "all the state must do to comply with the Constitution in this case is to refrain from terminating normal and cost-free services for reasons that are invidious, discriminatory, or at the very least, wholly insufficient."[64]

The court then turned to the right of the state as an employer to regulate the speech of its employees to see if Article XXVIII could be upheld under this rubric. Although a public employee's First Amendment rights are not as expansive as those of private persons, the very fact that someone is a public employee does not leave him/her without rights either. The key for the court on the resolution of this dynamic lay in the roles of the government as an employer:

> [t]he government's interest in achieving its goals as effectively and efficiently as possible is elevated from a relatively subordinate interest when it acts as sovereign to a significant one when it acts as employer. The government cannot restrict the speech of the public at large just in the name of efficiency. But where the government is employing someone for the very purpose of effectively achieving its goals, such restrictions may well be appropriate.[65]

Of course, in the instant case the government's interest in efficiency would be promoted by the continued use of non-English languages by its employees.

The speech that would be impinged by the law is also of incredible importance. The court said:

> [t]he employee speech banned by Article XXVIII is unquestionably of public import. It pertains to the provision of governmental services and information. Unless that speech is delivered in a form that the intended recipients can comprehend, they are likely to be deprived [of much needed data as well as substantial public and private benefits].

The speech at issue is speech that members of the public desire to hear.[66]

Further, "Article XXVIII obstructs the free flow of information and adversely affects the rights of many private persons by requiring the incomprehensible to replace the intelligible."[67] Since the bilingual employee must remain mute, under Article XXVIII's mandate, when asked a question by a member of the public in a language other than English, "[a]t such moments of awkward silence between government employees and those they serve, it will be strikingly clear to all concerned that vital speech that individuals desire both to provide and to hear has been stifled by the state."[68]

The scenario laid out by the court of language minorities asking questions in their native language and being met by mute stares or perhaps repeated answers only in English surely must have conjured images of the kind of nativist sentiment that gave rise to the *Meyer*-era legislation restricting use of the German language. Certainly, the court knew perfectly well that it was just these vulnerable members of Arizona's society at which the English-only law was aimed. For, as the court stated, it is "most often the recipient ... who initiates the dialogue in a language other than English."[69]

What governmental justifications, then, might be left to support the constitutionality of the law? AOE argued, as it did in the Proposition's publicity pamphlet, that the Article would protect democracy by encouraging "unity and political stability," and would encourage a common language and protect public confidence. Again implicitly drawing parallels to the *Meyer*-era, the court noted that in evaluating these justifications it would be guided by the Supreme Court's analysis in *Meyer and Farrington*.[70]

> Like the Supreme Court in *Meyer*, the Ninth Circuit, recognized the importance of (1) promoting democracy and national unity and (2) encouraging a common language as means of encouraging such unity .... The two primary justifications relied on by the Article proponents are closely linked. We cannot agree, however, that Article XXVIII is in anyway a fair, effective or appropriate means of promoting those interests, or that even under a more deferential analysis its severely flawed effort to advance those goals outweighs its substantial adverse effect on First Amendment rights. As we have learned time and again in our history, the state cannot achieve unity by prescribing orthodoxy.[71]

The law was especially egregious, noted the court, because its effect is not:

> uniformly spread over the population, but falls almost entirely upon Hispanics and other national origin minorities. In light of these considerations, the equal protection ramifications of Article XXVIII's restrictive impact strongly support our holding as well.[72]

In conclusion the court noted that:

> tolerance of difference – whether difference in language, religion, or culture more generally – does not exact a cost. To the contrary, the diverse and multi-cultural character of our society is widely recognized as a being among our greatest strengths. Recognizing this, we have not, except for rare repressive statutes such as those struck down in *Meyer, Bartels, Yu Cong Eng and Farrington*, tried to compel immigrants to give up their native language; instead, we have encouraged them to learn English. The Arizona restriction on language provides no encouragement, however, only compulsion; as such it is unconstitutional.[73]

That the Ninth Circuit was aware of the ethnically or racially discriminatory implications of the Arizona law is clear. That was surely at least in part why it continued to hearken back to the *Meyer*-era cases when xenophobic sentiments were high and more frankly expressed than today. Interestingly, however, the court did not base its decision in any real way, at least not legally speaking, on the racial implications of the law. It did not attempt to draw connections between language, ethnicity and race. It decided the case purely on First Amendment grounds only acknowledging the impact on minorities and noting, in passing, how often First Amendment jurisprudence is involved in protecting the rights of racial minorities.

That the court took this route is not really surprising, although a complex analysis of these issues is certainly welcome at this point in the nation's history. Certainly, language minorities are not new to the nation, and the issue of minority-language accommodation has been discussed and re-discussed repeatedly in the lower courts. The language-minority population is growing, and these issues will need to be addressed in a more comprehensive manner. The height of the English-only movement, which coincided with when *Yniguez* was filed, certainly seemed as propitious a moment as any. As noted throughout this book, however, courts will be cautious about developing new law, especially in the area of group rights, because of the national ambivalence toward the promotion of affirmative group rights. Deciding *Yniguez* as simply a First Amendment case allowed the court not to create new law especially and cast itself as stepping in the footprints of *Meyer*.

But what the court did say quite clearly was that minority language usage was a fundamental right that could not be abridged except for compelling governmental reasons. Although the court pointed out that it was not creating new affirmative rights for language minorities, its decision can be read as a template for how to determine the Constitutional strength of English-only laws under the First Amendment, and it can work to undermine English-only laws that seek to have more than a symbolic effect.

The reach of the Ninth Circuit's opinion, however, was severely limited by the US Supreme Court when it granted *certiorari* and decided to review the lower court's decision for technical reasons. In particular, the Supreme Court was concerned that Yniguez's case was moot, since she was no longer employed by the state at the time of the Ninth Circuit's decision. If a case is moot, the reviewing court should not issue a decision on the merits of the case, but should simply dismiss it. Also, the court was concerned that state courts in Arizona should have the first opportunity to review the constitutionality of their new state law. Ultimately, the Supreme Court decided to indeed vacate the Ninth Circuit opinion and have Arizona state courts review the constitutionality of Article XXVIII.[74]

The state courts did just that in *Ruiz v. Hull*.[75] In an un-reported decision, the state's trial court upheld the constitutionality of Article XXVIII. The case was, of course, appealed to the Supreme Court of Arizona. This time, however, the state court would follow the lead of the Ninth Circuit and, agreeing with that court on basic issues, it declared Article XXVIII a violation of the First Amendment.

Like the federal courts before it, the *Ruiz* court was also careful to point out that it was not creating affirmative language minority rights. So, while a bilingual public employee cannot be stopped from helping a language-minority member of the public by speaking his/her native language, the court would not compel the state to either hire bilingual employees or print its documents in languages other than English.

The court also said at the outset that "this case concerns the tension between the constitutional status of language rights and the state's power to restrict such rights."[76] The federal courts had not explicitly referred to "language rights," still a relatively new concept in the civil rights pantheon of rights-rhetoric. It is interesting to see the state court set out its recognition that the scope and nature of those rights was exactly the issue before it.

Another interesting note about the posture of the *Ruiz* case is that by this point

AOE, which had advocated in federal court for an expansive reading of Article XXVIII, now did an "about face" and joined the state in pushing for the adoption of the Attorney General's restrictive reading. Although the state court followed the federal courts' lead and rejected the Attorney General's advisory opinion on the scope of the Article as being inconsistent with its plain language, surely Richard Parks, head of AOE, had by now realized that the First Amendment was going to be a larger hurdle for his Amendment to leap than he had expected. Apparently, he reasoned that some kind of English-only law, even one as weak as that offered by the state, would be better than none.

The *Ruiz* case did indeed hold out some hope that less restrictive English-only laws might be constitutional. It was at least very careful to point out that its ruling on the unconstitutionality of Article XXVIII rested on the unusual over-breadth of the Amendment. The court referred to Florida's and Colorado's Official English laws as examples of probably constitutionally permissible symbolic laws. Florida's law states: "(a) English is the official language of the State of Florida. (b) The legislature shall have the power to enforce this section by appropriate legislation."[77] Colorado's law states: "English is the official language of the State of Colorado. This section is self-executing; however, the General Assembly may enact laws to implement this section."[78]

Wyoming's law was used by the court as an example of a more detailed law that avoided some of the constitutional questions presented by Arizona's Amendment. Wyoming's law states:

> (a) English shall be designated as the official language of Wyoming. Except as otherwise provided by law, no state agency or political subdivision of the state shall be required to provide any documents, information, literature or other written materials in any language other than English. (b) A state agency or political subdivision or its officers or employees may act in a language other than English for any of the following purposes: (i) To provide information orally to individuals in the course of delivering services to the general public.... (vii) To promote international commerce, trade or tourism.[79]

The Arizona court concluded:

> [i]f Arizona's Amendment were merely symbolic or contained some of the express exceptions of the official English provisions discussed above, it might well have passed constitutional muster. We do not express any opinion concerning the constitutionality of less restrictive English-only provisions."[80]

Also of interest in the Arizona Supreme Court's opinion was its willingness to expressly rely upon the rights of the language-minority population of Arizona to strike down the law. While the federal courts' First Amendment analysis mentioned the potential impact of the new law on the language minority population of the state, those opinions spent more time on the rights of the public employees than on the rights of the true targets of the law – the monolingual non-English-speaking language minorities themselves. On this point the *Ruiz* court was clear: "[b]y denying persons who are of limited English proficiency, or entirely lacking it, the right to participate in and have access to government, a right which is one of the 'fundamental principles of representative government in this country.'"[81]

The *Ruiz* court, however, like the federal courts before it, refused to delve into the race–ethnicity–language connections and refused to engage in an equal protection analysis of the Amendment. Instead it found that strict scrutiny applied to its review of the law because fundamental right to speech was involved.[82]

Legal challenges in Alabama

Arizona was not the only state to see significant litigation after the passage of an English-only law. Although Alabama's law was passed in 1990 litigation did not occur until 1998 when the small Latino population in the state began to feel an impact from the law.[83] Like *Yniguez*, the case would end up going all the way up to the US Supreme Court for technical reasons in which the issue of language was never even raised.

On July 13, 1990 Alabama passed Amendment 509, which states:

> English is the official language of the state of Alabama. The legislature shall enforce this amendment by appropriate legislation. The legislature and officials of the state of Alabama shall take all steps necessary to insure that the role of English as the common language of the state of Alabama is preserved and enhanced. The legislature shall make no law which diminishes or ignores the role of English as the common language of the state of Alabama.[84]

Approximately one year later, the Department of Public Safety adopted an English-only policy requiring all portions of the driver's license examination process, including the written exam, to be administered in English only. Interpreters, translation dictionaries and other interpretive aids were officially forbidden. Prior to the passage of Amendment 509 the Department, like 48 other states, had administered the written portion of its Class "D" driver's license exam in a "multitude of foreign languages" and, since 1970, had administered thousands of written exams in at least 14 languages other than English.

The Department continued to provide special accommodations for illiterate, hearing-impaired, deaf and disabled applicants. Also, the Department allowed non-English speaking drivers from other states and foreign countries to exchange a valid out-of-state license for an Alabama license without taking the written exam.

Martha Sandoval, a driver's license applicant not proficient in English brought suit under Title VI of the Civil Rights Act against the state on behalf of herself and all others similarly situated for declaratory and injunctive relief. Title VI prohibits governmental agencies from implementing policies or practices that have a discriminatory impact, even if they were not implemented or created with an intent to actually discriminate. Only race, ethnicity and national origin are specified as illegal bases for discrimination under the Act. Choice or use of a minority language is not specifically covered by Title VI. Advocates have had to argue that policies that restrict minority languages are prohibited because they have a disproportionate impact on people of a foreign national origin. As demonstrated throughout this text, many courts have been willing to treat language as a surrogate or proxy for national origin.

Defendants made procedural objections as well as substantive objections to the lawsuit. Substantively, the defendants argued that the English-only policy discriminates on the basis of language and not national origin and that "[l]anguage is not equivalent to national origin." "A showing that one of the plaintiffs speaks Spanish does not show in which country the plaintiff is from," argued the state. "Is the department discriminating against that plaintiff because she is from Spain? Mexico? Argentina? Or one of a number of other nations?"[85]

The court, however, found the state's analysis unconvincing: the essence of a Title VI disparate-impact claim is that the challenged policy only have a disparate impact on a protected group and that there be alternative, less discriminatory policies.

> English-only rules typically have a disparate impact on the basis of national origin....There is no dispute over the fact that persons who are not fluent in English are much more likely than those who are fluent to have been born in a foreign country. Whether persons who are fluent only in Spanish are native of Spain, Mexico or Argentina ... is irrelevant.[86]

And:

> [j]ust because the country of origin of those effected by the English-only policy is not readily identifiable, does not mean that a disparate impact does not exist. Conversely, the fact that individuals from a multitude of foreign nations are affected by the English-only policy shows a far-reaching discriminatory impact.[87]

After reviewing the demographic evidence submitted by the plaintiffs on the characteristics of Alabama's language minority population and the strong ties between language and national origin often found by federal courts and agencies, the court easily concluded that an English-only policy could indeed violate Title VI on the basis of national origin.

The court then reviewed in depth each of the justifications made by the state for its policy and found them all pretextual or otherwise meritless. The state argued that:

(1) the policy is required by Amendment 509;
(2) the policy is justified by highway safety concerns;
(3) the policy ensures examination integrity;
(4) it is administratively difficult to accommodate foreign language exams;
(5) the policy reflects the importance of the English language to the nation;
(6) foreign language exams are costly.

Of course given the extensive essentially trouble-free history Alabama had in providing foreign language exams and its continued aid toward the illiterate and handicapped, many of its justifications were not merely in constriction to the reality of the situation, but they were patently absurd. For instance, the court noted that "[i]t cannot be reasonably contested that having an examiner read the written examination to an illiterate English-speaking applicant takes as long, if not longer, than providing a non-English speaking applicant with a written examination in a foreign language."[88]

At the trial, former State Trooper Lt Col. Harold Hammond, Chief of the Department's Driver's License Division from 1978 to 1987 and second-in-command of the entire department from 1987 to 1991 testified that there were no significant problems administering the examination in a foreign language. In addition, "[t]here was no evidence that non-English speakers were more likely to cheat. Translations of the English examination were obtained at no cost to the department. There was no evidence that non-English speakers posed a greater safety risk or had more accidents than other motorists"[89] Also, "Col. Hammond never considered curtailing or ending foreign language examinations and in fact expanded the program whenever demand was great enough."[90] "It takes as long, if not longer, than providing a non-English speaking applicant with a written examination in a foreign language or an examiner retaining a translation dictionary during the exam."[91]

The court also disposed of the usual governmental response to demands for minority language accommodation – how to decide which languages ought to be accommodated given finite resources? The state argued that there was no reasonable way to cut off the number of languages in which the test ought to be translated. Again, since Alabama had indeed been providing foreign language exams in a finite number of languages, the state's assertion could be answered with its own experience. The court suggested that the state "provide the ... exam in the most common foreign languages spoken in the state.... As demand increases for the provision of the exam in a language in which the exam is not already available, the state could have the exam translated and made available in that language."[92]

What was interesting in this numbers issue was the plaintiffs' response. The plaintiffs argued that the law was not unreasonable and that, when only a small number of language minorities are effected, there might be no Title VI violation at all. This "slippery slope" argument – that the accommodation of one language-minority group would mean the necessary accommodation of all – is often raised by governmental defendants to try and defeat claims to accommodate any minority languages. There is a sense that when it comes to language there are no absolute rights, but only subjective determinations to be based on group size, as well as on administrative convenience and practicality. While there is a need to consider governmental concerns for efficiency and convenience, and for plaintiffs to appear reasonable and not frighten away courts with extreme positions, plaintiffs need not concede that Title VI violations in the language rights arena may be evaluated differently than other alleged acts of racial of ethnic discrimination. Title VI can indeed be violated if even one language minority is denied access to a governmental service that is available to others; *the remedy, not the actual violation,* however, may be different depending upon the numbers involved. The *Sandoval* court itself made a distinction between what could be required if many minorities were impacted (a translated exam), or if only a few were (the right to bring in a translator).

The court also handled the issue of cost, another red herring often raised by governmental defendants: "[e]ven assuming that the administration of the exam in foreign languages would entail some cost to the state, its interest in conserving its financial resources does not automatically trump all other concerns."[93] In this case, however, the court found that translated exams were available to the state for no cost, and that any additional expenses were essentially insignificant considering the state's budget for the Department of Public Safety.

On the state's rationale that its policy was justified because English is the national language, the court found that in fact the US had never declared English to be the national language and that, if it had, under the state's own rationale, Alabama would have to discontinue offering any services in languages other than English, not just written driver's licensing exams. The two examples that the defendants offered of a federal language policy that would justify the state's own English-only policy were the requirement under the citizenship laws of a certain knowledge of English, and the federal requirement that drivers holding a commercial truck driver's license be proficient in English.

The court, however, distinguished both federal requirements from Alabama's policy. Under the citizenship laws, minimal English skills could be justified since "[b]ecoming a citizen entails a long-term, if not life commitment to the United States. Accordingly, ensuring assimilation by providing for English proficiency may well be justified under that rationale."[94] Turning to the legislative history of the Citizenship Act,[95] the court quoted the legislative justifications for requiring not only minimal proficiency in English but also a knowledge of US history and its policy structure:

> [t]hrough the system of citizenship classes sponsored by the Immigration and Naturalization Service and the local school system, the alien is aided in preparing himself for citizenship, and every effort is made to give him fundamental and uniform knowledge of our political and social structure. In order that he may intelligently use this fundamental and uniform knowledge and so that he may be a complete and thoroughly integrated member of our American society, the committee feels that he should have a basic knowledge of the common language of the country and be able to read, write and speak it with reasonable facility.[96]

The federal government's interest in fostering "integrated" citizens is the justifiable rationale for its English proficiency requirement, to which even the US has made a myriad of exceptions. Alabama simply does not have the same interests that could justify its policy.

On the federal driver's license requirements, the court noted that those requirements were under scrutiny for possible Title VI violations as well. In any case, there may be legitimate reasons to require a certain measure of English fluency, since commercial truck drivers are required to fill out paperwork, and also required to operate vehicles under a plethora of federal regulations and need to interact with officials as a regular part of their work. Further:

> given the higher safety risk ostensibly posed by commercial vehicles that carry everything from school children to explosive chemicals, requiring a sufficient understanding of English to converse with the general public and to understand highway traffic signs and signals may well be justified on safety grounds.[97]

The court completed its exhaustive analysis of the case, issuing an opinion almost 100 pages long, with an extensive quote from *Meyer*. It found Justice McReynolds' words, written 75 years ago, still worth repeating. They were, in part:

> [t]hat the state may do much, go very far, indeed, in order to improve the quality of its citizens, physically, mentally, morally, is clear; but that individual has certain fundamental rights which must be respected. The protection of the Constitution extends to all, to those who speak other languages as well as to those born with English on the tongue. Perhaps it would be highly advantageous if all had ready understanding of our ordinary speech, but this cannot be coerced by methods which conflict with the Constitution – a desirable end cannot be promoted by prohibited means.[98]

The district court's decision in *Sandoval* was a forceful repudiation of all of the posturing of English-only proponents; it carefully and tirelessly went through each of the oft-repeated justifications for English-only laws, and simply subjected them to a rigorous but common sense analysis that exposed their weakness and their pretextual nature for what is essentially national origin discrimination. However, the court's decision was based on Title VI of the Civil Rights Act. The issue of whether private citizens really can sue to enforce Title VI against governmental agencies had just started to surface, and it appeared that the Supreme Court was prepared to resolve the question.

The district court's decision, was appealed to the Eleventh Circuit. The appellate court's opinion focused on three legal issues:

(1) did the Eleventh Amendment to the Constitution bar the plaintiff's suit against the state defendants;
(2) is there an implied cause of action under Title VI which actually allows private individual plaintiffs to sue under the Act;
(3) does an English-only policy discriminate on the basis of national origin.[99]

On the question of whether there is a right of action under Title VI, the court decided that there was one relying upon a close but conjectural reading of three prior Supreme Court cases. These cases and the issues of causes of action under Title VI are discussed in detail in the Appendix.

The court's decision was appealed to the Supreme Court on the technical but important question of whether private citizens can sue under the statute. In a landmark curtailment of civil rights law, the Supreme Court held that such a right did not exist. Only the federal government may sue governmental agencies for enforcement of Title VI. Private parties, found the Court, can only use an administrative process outlined in the statute to enforce Title VI. The precedential value of the lower court's opinion in *Sandoval* then is quite limited, since it relied on the viability of the Title VI claim. The court's reasoning, however, still unveils the discriminatory nature of English-only policies and the weakly-constructed bureaucratic arguments made to support them. The trial court's decision can be used by advocates as a model for puncturing the administrative allure of these arguments and holding agencies accountable for addressing the needs of linguistic minorities.

Utah's compromise: Finding a way to uphold English-only laws

In the November 2000 general election, by a margin of almost 2 to 1, Utah's voters approved "Initiative A," a new law declaring English to be the official language of the state. The law was carefully crafted; it carved out exceptions meant to address the First Amendment issues that were fatal to Arizona's laws, but was also clearly supposed to be something more meaty than a purely symbolic declaration.[100] The law stated that English is to be the sole language of the government, and included provisions on the education of children that required the state's educational policy-making body, the Board of Regents, to make "rules governing the use of foreign language in the public and higher education system that promote the following principles: non-English-speaking children and adults should become able to read, write and understand English as quickly as possible..."[101] The law contained many specific exceptions, however, including, in a bow to Arizona, that the law not be constructed to affect the ability of government employees or private individuals to exercise their First Amendment rights.[102] The ACLU (American Civil Liberties Union) of Utah brought suit challenging the law before it became effective.

The plaintiffs argued that the Act would restrict the expressive conduct of governmental officials by prohibiting them from communicating with the public in languages other than English, and also trampled on the rights of language minorities who would not be able to communicate with representatives of their government. The issue of the right of language minorities to have access to a linguistically comprehensible government is an important one, but one that most courts simply do not want to consider. The Utah court was no less circumspect, declining to address whether the language-minority public's First Amendment rights were being implicated at all. Instead, the court focused only on whether the Act would compromise the free speech rights of government officials and employees.[103]

The court found the section of the Act that simply declared English as the official language of Utah to be purely symbolic, no more potentially offensive than the declaration that the "dutch oven" is the official cooking pot of the state.[104] The court then focused on the other sections of the Act which state that the "sole language of government, except as otherwise provided in this section" shall be English; the third section required that "all official documents, transactions, proceedings, meetings ... representing the state and its political subdivisions shall be English."[105] The court's analysis then became an inquiry into the nature of an "official" document or proceeding. The court insisted that the Act meant something less than was apparent. "In order to be official," said the court, the document must minimally be in English. The court stated:

> I submit that no definition of "official" is necessary in order to achieve a comprehensible and constitutional interpretation of the act. It is irrelevant for purposes of the Act what type of government documents or acts might be labeled official. The Act simply mandates that if the document or other communication, whatever it may be, is to be eligible for "official" status, it must be in the English language unless it qualifies for exemption...[106]

The Act, reasoned the court, is not intended to regulate the speech of government employees, but is solely descriptive: "[i]t merely serves to classify government speech as either official or unofficial."[107] The court also found inoffensive the Act's prohibition on the use of state money to pay for "non-English activities."[108] Political subdivisions of the state can continue to use their own funds to pay for any translations they felt were needed. Further, there is no constitutional requirement that states be required to provide translated documents or notices.[109]

That the Act as now interpreted was "largely symbolic" was not lost on the court.[110] It was quick to note that such an interpretation was probably not in the minds of most of its supporters. However, it also found that the assimilative aim of the Act, as testified to by proponents of the initiative in court, was not frustrated by the court's interpretation.[111]

After criticizing the decision as causing more confusion,[112] the ACLU ultimately decided to abandon any appeal of the decision, saying that the new law as interpreted was simply symbolic, and could not be used as an excuse by agencies to curtail services to the state's language minority communities.[113] Important to the ACLU's decision was a move made by the state's Attorney General to designate one staff lawyer to advise state agencies on questions that might arise with respect to the implementation of the statute. The Attorney General had originally opposed the initiative and reached a settlement with the ACLU after the court's decision with the intention that "the law not be improperly read to prohibit vital communications between government and the people, and thereby to deny language minorities an equal voice in our State and in our communities."[114]

Additional English-only activity

The first half of 2002 was marked with a few interesting events that probably foretell the conflicting future of language rights. In March 2002 the Superior Court of Alaska ruled that the state's English-only initiative, which had been passed in 1998, violated the free speech rights guaranteed by the state's constitution.[115] Although the initiative was passed by 70% of the voters, it never went into effect because the lawsuit was immediately filed by Spanish, Yup'ik, and Inupiaq speakers from across the state.[116] The law, however, was very similar to the one struck down by the Arizona state courts in *Ruiz v. Hull* and the court was sympathetic to the arguments of the Alaska natives that the law was an unconstitutional infringement of their First Amendment rights. Judge Torrisi of Dillingham said that "language is the beginning, it is part of who we are. Beyond defining our ethnicity, it organizes our minds."[117] The group that sponsored the law, *Alaskans for a Common Language*, has said that it will appeal the decision.[118]

There was also another pro-language rights ruling out of Oklahoma early in the year. There, English-only advocates tried to have a petition to make English the official language of the state placed on the ballot for a vote. The proposed initiative was more restrictive even than Arizona's in that it made no exception for public safety or for conflicts with federal law.[119] The court found that the petition would:

> disenfranchise segments of Oklahoma citizens by interfering with their ability to access vital information necessary for a self-governing society and cause self-censorship by inhibiting communications with government officials. All of this is in contravention of the Oklahoma Constitution.[120]

Although the court's intervention and support of language rights is certainly welcome, it appears to have been academic; the supporters of the initiative had tried to withdraw the petition before the Supreme Court could review it and then, when the court refused to let it withdraw, abandoned the petition without filing supporting memoranda of law. Instead, it appears that they will try to have legislation passed.[121]

The most significant development to come out of the first months of 2002, however, is also the most ominous. Before leaving office, in August 2000, President Clinton issued Executive Order 13166 regarding access of language minorities to federally-funded programs.[122] The Executive Order specifically required that the major federal agencies (such as the Department of Education, the Department of Labor, and the Department of Health and Human Services) issue guidance to their respective agencies on how to comply with Title VI of the Civil Rights Act, which prohibits national origin discrimination. The Executive Order appeared to do nothing more than require compliance with a well-established, but often ignored, law. The Department of Justice (DOJ) issued a more specific mandate to the federal agencies on August 16, 2000, a few days after the Executive Order was issued.[123] The DOJ was careful to create a four-part balancing test that agencies should employ when determining what kind of accommodations agencies needed to make in order to provide adequate access to services under the law. The point of the DOJ guidance was to balance language minority needs for access to vital information and services while not overwhelming agencies (especially smaller providers) with translation and interpretation duties.

In compliance with the DOJ, the Department of Health and Human Services issued its guidance requiring that health and social service providers take "adequate steps to ensure that [LEP][124] persons receive the language assistance necessary to afford them meaningful access to their service, free of charge."[125] In the midst of this, however, the Supreme Court decided that that aspect of Title VI which prohibited policies that have a discriminatory effect on national-origin minorities could not be enforced privately, but only through administrative means.[126]

Shortly after, however, a group called *Pro-English* chaired by Robert D. Park, who had spearheaded the campaign to pass Arizona's English-only law through *Arizonans for Official English*, brought suit against then-President Bush seeking an invalidation of the Executive Order.[127] The lawsuit cuts to the very quick of the civil rights protections for language minorities as it argues that there is no legally cognizable relationship between language and national origin and the Executive Order impermissibly extends the reach of Title VI. Further, turning the loss in *Yniguez* on its head, individually-named doctor-plaintiffs argued that their own First Amendment rights are being violated by being required to speak in languages other than English. The lawsuit was filed in March 2002 and if it is not dismissed for procedural or technical grounds, it will be a frontal and possibly lethal, assault on civil rights protections for language minorities.

CONCLUSION

This chapter has focused on the re-emergence of nativist legislation and sentiment as reflected in the increased popularity of language restrictions. Proponents of language-restrictive legislation or English-only laws justify their position by pointing to the increased rate of immigration to the US, and the need for these immigrants to join the national culture by learning English as quickly as possible. There is an anxiety, unsupported by the facts, that Latinos, the bulk of recent immigrants, are not learning English as quickly as preceding immigrant communities. English-only laws, proponents argue, would remove the "crutches" fostered by bilingual or multilingual governmental services, bilingual ballots and bilingual education. Left without these aids, the immigrant communities would be forced to learn English more quickly.

Many English-only laws, however, are more symbolic than restrictive and have had no real impact on the provision of governmental services. Those that are more restrictive have been the subject of complex litigation in which three of the four laws analyzed were stricken down as violations of the First Amendment or anti-discrimination laws. In the last case, where Utah's English-only law was upheld, the Court essentially stripped it of most of its potential for harm. The lasting impact of some of theses decisions, however, is uncertain since *both Yniguez* and *Sandoval* were reversed by the Supreme Court on technical grounds. Still, *Ruiz v. Hull* stands, as does the restrictive reading given the statute in Utah.

Despite these judicial "wins," the underlying issues of whether language minorities have any rights to access their government that are impeded by the existence of English-only laws is still undecided. The *Ruiz* and Utah cases were decided based upon the rights of public employees, and the courts pointedly refused to answer the broader question on the rights of language minorities as members of the public.

The shift of the language rights struggles to the state arena, plus the recent targeting of bilingual education, mandated and funded on the state level, has made the local level the critical sphere for determining language rights. On the one hand, the new focus makes language rights a local issue, with no unifying federal principles as guidelines, promising at worst no greater consistency or clarity in this area than we have at present. Also, minorities generally tend to fare poorly in terms of civil rights enforcement on the local level, and traditionally have relied upon the federal government for protection from parochial prejudices. However, much law is already made, and all law is ultimately implemented, on a local level anyway. The federal government's approach for the last twenty years has been to increase the autonomy of the state on a variety of civil rights and educational issues.[128]

A state-by-state or regional approach to the issue of language rights may animate grass roots language rights activists who can create more nuanced and responsive local strategies for language minority protection than national policy makers could. Any advances actually achieved would also be insulated from attack as being imposed by distant and unknown federal players. Solutions can be worked out in the context of community values; everyone would know the players involved including the court or legislature, and the ultimate solutions should carry more authority on the ground where it is implemented. Many federal court decrees are never truly realized because of the hostility to the decision at the level in which it will be implemented. At a minimum, administrators of the governmental agencies being overseen by a federal court feel that the federal judiciary, reflecting national and not local interests, simply has little legitimacy. State judicial and legislative systems will not be subject to such criticism, although plainly neither entity has any special skill in running governmental agencies.

The downside to local problem-solving is also fairly clear: local institutions will be beholden to parochial interests that rarely reflect the interests of minorities. Still, state courts might rise to the challenge of adjudicating minority interests, especially when given clear violations of law. The decisions over the past two decades in the school finance cases in which state courts were called upon to decide complex issues of finance and equity in the face of federal fiat, are a good indication of just how well state courts can handle complex civil rights issues.[129] So too is the state court's decision in *Ruiz v. Hull,* where the court engaged in complex federal and state constitutional analysis with a conclusion that was heartening to language minorities.

Despite the growth of the English-only movement, we can be thankful that today's language rights struggles are not as virulent as they were in the *Meyer* era, with the imprisonment of Germans for speaking their native language and the burning of books and schools. This is not a credit to the language restrictionists, who use alarmist and xenophobic language at every turn. Rather, it seems that a combination of factors has contributed to a more temperate response by the public at large. The most important is that the nation is economically prosperous with no significant military opponents, although this sense of comfort changed dramatically on September 11, 2001, when terrorists attacked the US, killing thousands. Another important factor in restricting the popularity of nativist legislation, is that as a nation we have "constitutionally grown up." Whereas eighty years ago we may not have been so certain about what kinds of laws and actions might be constitutionally prohibited, today, through various media, we are sensitive to litigation, have been exposed to a certain amount of constitutional analysis and the scope of certain civil rights and liberties. We are also aware of our own history of xenophobia and seem loath to re-visit it. Whereas eighty years ago President Roosevelt was condemning "hyphenated Americans," President George W. Bush was quick to ask the nation not to attack "Arab-Americans" because of the attack on the World Trade Center in September 2001.[130]

Still, prior to the terrorist attacks on the US, the bilingual education wars were a potent reminder that there was still great ambivalence about the status and role of language minorities in the country. The continued efforts to make English the official language of the nation is another indicator that the nation is still not as tolerant or as mature as it ought to be given its potential; this is a country of immigrants, after all, which can look to its own history to see how much immigrants have contributed to the creation of the nation and how little they have caused in terms of destabilization or disloyalty.

Although language minorities are now greater in size and diversity than eighty years ago, they should not be lulled into a false sense of security. The nation is still restive about the role of these communities within its borders, and the increasing size of the non-White population can contribute to a sense of anxiety. Given the recent national crisis, language minorities may find themselves as scapegoats once more.

Notes

1. John Higham, STRANGERS IN THE LAND: PATTERNS OF AMERICAN NATIVISM 1860–1925 (Atheneum, New York, 1965).
2. *See* Bureau of the Census, US Dept. of Commerce, 2000 CENSUS SUPPLEMENTAL SURVEY (2001).
3. *See* Robert Strauss, *A Welcome Mat for Immigrants,* NY TIMES, January 13, 2002 at 14 NJ p.8; Dylan Loeb McClain, *With Jobs Plentiful, Immigrants Have Found it Easier to Fit In,* NY TIMES, June 27, 2001 at G1; Eric Schmitt, *To Fill The Gap: Cities Seek Wave of Immigrants,* NY TIMES, May 30, 2001 at A1.
4. *See* Elissa Goodman, *Hate Motives are Argued in Beating of Mexicans,* NY TIMES August 3, 2001 at B5; William Branigin. *Spread of Spanish Greeted by Some Unwelcome Signs.* WASH. POST, February 6, 1999 at A4. Eric Schmitt, *Pockets of Protest are Rising Against Immigration,* NY TIMES, August 9, 2001 at A12.
5. *Sandoval v. Hagan,* 7 FSupp 2d 1234, (MD Ala. 1998), *aff'd,* 197 F3d 484 (11th Cir 1999) *rev'd, Alexander v. Sandoval* 532 US 275 (2001).
6. *Anderson et al. v. Utah,* Mem. Dec. 000909680 (Dist. Ct 3rd Judicial Dist. Utah, March 5, 2001). The decision can be viewed at www.acluutah.org/EOmemodecision.html.
7. *See* www.ourworld.compuserve.com/homepages/jwcrawford. James Crawford points out that, since other states had passed laws before 1981, there are 24 states that have actually passed an English-only type of law. *See* jwcrawford/langleyg.state.html.

8. *See* BBC News, *"English-Only" Teaching Plans go to the Vote,* June 2, 1998. http://news.bbc.co.uk/h/english/education/newsid_104000/104311.stm; CNN.com *Scores Allay Concerns Over English-Only Institution In California,* September 20, 2000. http://www.cnn.com/2000/05/09/20/english.only; David Gonzalez, *Teachers Tackle English-Only,* THE ARIZONA REPUBLIC, February 21, 2001. At AZCentral.com/news/education/0221bilingual21.html.

9. Mauro E. Mujica, *Unblocking the Door to Opportunity.* At www.us-english.org/inc/news/op-eds/unblock.asp.

10. Mauro E. Mujica, *Bilingual Education Priorities.* At www.us-english.org/inc/official/horror/travell.asp.

11. At www.us-english.org.

12. *Id.*

13. S.I. Hayakawa, *The Case for Official English* (1985), reprinted in James Crawford, LANGUAGE LOYALTIES: A SOURCE BOOK ON THE OFFICIAL ENGLISH CONTROVERSY (University of Chicago Press, Chicago, IL, 1992).

14. *Id.* at 98.

15. *Id.* at 98–99.

16. *Id.* at 100.

17. *Id.* at 128.

18. Joseph Leibowicz, *The Proposed English Language Amendment: Sword or Shield?* (1985) reprinted in Crawford, *supra,* note 13, at 110.

19. *Id.* at 111.

20. *See* 131 Cong. Rec. s11143-01 (Statement of Sen. Syms) on the "need for a common tongue," and the sense that learning English is the "key to breaking the chains of the ghetto." *See* 136 Cong. Rec. H4977-04 Statement of Mr Montgomery; and that it is "Hispanic activists" not the "typical Hispanics" who want to see an officially bilingual nation. *See* 136 Cong. Rec. H4977-04 (Statement of Mr Meyers).

21. For immigrants, the most recent research has indicated that it is the less-assimilated students who are still fully bilingual that are out-performing the more assimilated or native-born minority students. The more recently immigrated are still hopeful about their chances for economic success, and put a lot of faith in the US educational system. It is only when they become more assimilated, lose their mother tongue and begin to experience for themselves or see the results of discrimination that their academic achievement begins to slide downward. *See* EDUCATION WEEK, June 7, 2000 Vol. XIX, Number 39 at 28, and sources cited therein.

22. K. McCarthy and R. Burciaga Valdez. (1986) *Current and Future Effects of Mexican Immigration in California,* cited in Sandra Guerra. *Voting Rights and the Constitution: The Disenfranchisement of non-English Speaking Citizens,* 97 YALE L. J. 1419. (1988).

23. *See also* Calvin Veltman, THE FUTURE OF THE SPANISH LANGUAGE IN THE UNITED STATES, Washington DC:Hispanic Policy Development Project (ERIC Document Production Service, No. Ed 295 485,1988).

24. *See* Bureau of the Census, US Department of Commerce, LANGUAGES SPOKEN AT HOME AND ABILITY TO SPEAK ENGLISH FOR US, REGIONS, AND STATES: 1990 (1990 CPH-L-133); 1990 Summary tape File 3 (STF 3).

25. *See Teach English* WASH POST (August 9, 2001 at A18). *See also* Gregory Boyd Bell, *Two Languages Don't Make for One Nation.* NY NEWSDAY, August 23, 2001.

26. Http://ourworld.compuserve.com/homepages/JWCRAWFORD/census02.htm.

27. *Id.*

28. *See* Bureau of the Census, US Dept. of Commerce, 2000 CENSUS. P035 AGE BY LANGUAGE

SPOKEN AT HOME BY ABILITY TO SPEAK ENGLISH FOR THE POPULATION 5 YEARS AND OVER – Universe: Population 5 years and Over Data Set: Census 2000 Supplemental Survey Tables.

29. *See* Jonathan Lemco, *Quebec's "Distinctive Character" and the Creation of Minority Rights, supra,* note 13 at 423.

30. Ark. Code Ann. §1-4-117.

31. *See supra,* note 18. *See also* Joshua Fishman, *Bias and Anti-Intellectualism: The Frenzied Fiction of "English-only,"* in Joshua A Fishman, LANGUAGE AND ETHNICITY IN MINORITY SOCIOLINGUISTIC PERSPECTIVE (Multilingual Matters Ltd, Cleveland, England,1989).

32. *Gutierrez v. Municipal Court,* 838 F2d 1031 (9th Cir 1988), *vacated as moot,* 490 US 1016 (1989).

33. *See Puerto Rican Organization for Political Action v. Kusper,* 490 F2d 575 (7th Cir 1973). *See also Sandoval v. Hagan,* 7 FSupp 2d 1234 (MD Ala 1998), *aff'd,* 197 F3d 484 (11th Cir 1999) *rev'd., Alexander v. Sandoval* 532 US 275 (2001).

34. *See generally,* Chapter 4, *infra.*

35. In June 1985 Judge Sam Keser of Amarillo Texas accused a mother of child abuse because she conversed in Spanish with her five year old and enrolled him in a bilingual education program. *See* Lynn Schnaiberg, *Bilingual Education Column,* EDUCATION WEEK ON THE WEB, September 13, 1995. At www.edweek.org/ew/vol-15/02bicol.h15.

36. Stephen Bende, *Direct Democracy and Distrust: The Relationship Between Language, Law, Rhetoric and the Language Vigilantism Experience,* 3 Harv Latino LR145 (1997).

37. *Asian American Business Group v. City of Pomona,* 716 FSupp 1328 (CD Calif. 1989).

38. *Id.* at 1330.

39. *Id.*

40. *Id.* at 1332.

41. *Id.*

42. The full text of Arizona's Article XXVIII reads:

ENGLISH AS THE OFFICIAL LANGUAGE

§ 1 English as the official language: applicability

Section 1

(1) The English language is the official language of the State of Arizona.

(2) As the official language of this State, the English language is the language of the ballot, the public schools and all government functions and actions.

(3) (a) This Article applies to:

  (i)   the legislative, the executive and judicial branches of government,

  (ii) all political subdivisions, departments, agencies, organizations and instrumentalities of this State, including local government and municipalities,

  (iii) all statutes, ordinances, rules, order, programs and policies,

  (iv) all government officials and employees during the performance of government business

  (b) As used in this Article, the phrase, "This State and all political subdivisions of the State" shall include every entity, person, action or item described in this Section, as appropriate to the circumstances.

§ 2 Requiring this state to preserve, protect and enhance English.

Section 2

  This State and all political subdivisions of this State shall take all reasonable steps to preserve and enhance the role of English language as the official language of the State of Arizona.

§ 3 Prohibiting this State from using or requiring the use of languages other than English; exceptions

Section 3

(1) Except as provided in Subsection (2):

    (a) This State and all political subdivisions of the State shall act in English and no other language.

    (b) No entity to which this Article applies shall make or enforce a law order, decree or policy to which requires the use of language other than English.

    (c) No governmental document shall be valid, effective or enforceable unless it is in the English language.

(2) This State and all political subdivisions of this State may act in a language other than English under any of the following circumstances:

    (a) to assist students who are not proficient in the English language, to the extent necessary to comply with federal law, by giving educational instruction in a language other than English to provide as rapid as possible a transition to English.

    (b) to comply with other federal laws.

    (c) to teach a student a foreign language as part of a required or voluntary educational curriculum.

    (d) to protect public health or safety.

    (e) to protect the rights of criminal defendants or victims of crime.

§ 4 Enforcement: standing

Section 4

A person who resides in or does business in this state shall have standing to bring suit to enforce this article in a court of record of the state. The legislature may enact reasonable limitations on the time and manner of bringing suit under this subsection.

43. Dennis Baron, THE ENGLISH-ONLY QUESTION: AN OFFICIAL LANGUAGE FOR AMERICANS? (Yale University Press, New Haven, CT, 1990) at 105.

44. *Id.* at 106.

45. *Id.* at 124.

46. Arizona Publicity Pamphlet at 26.

47. *Id.* at 32.

48. *Yniguez v. Mofford*, 730 Fsupp 309 (D Ariz. 1990).

49. *Id.* at 312.

50. *Id.* at 316, *citing Shuttlesworth v. City of Birmingham*, 394 US 147 (1969).

51. *Id.* at 314.

52. *Id.*

53. *Id.*

54. *Yniguez*, 730 FSupp at 314.

55. The next decision in *Yniguez* was a technical one that allowed Arizonans for Official English (AOE) to intervene and appeal the district court's decision because the state used to do so. After that decision, there was another one that allowed Yniguez to remain a plaintiff in the case in order to appeal the trial court's denial of an award of nominal damages even though she was no longer a state employee. *Yniguez II*, 975 F2d 646 (9th

Cir 1992). AOE had asked the court to declare the case moot because Yniguez was no longer an employee.

56. *Yniguez v. Arizonans for Official English,* 42 F3d 1217 (9th Cir 1995).
57. *See supra,* Chapter 1.
58. *Yniguez,* 42 F3d at 1228.
59. *Id.*
60. *Id.* at 1229.
61. *Id.* at 1230.
62. *Id.* at 1231.
63. *Id.* at 1232 (cites omitted).
64. *Id* at 1233.
65. *Id.* at 1234.
66. *Id* at 1236 (emphasis added).
67. *Id.* at 1237.
68. *Id.*
69. *Id.* at 1236.
70. *Id.* at 1239.
71. *Id.* at 1240–41 (cites omitted).
72. *Id.* at 1241.
73. *Id.*
74. *Arizonans for Official English v. Arizona,* 520 US 43 (1997).
75. *Ruiz v. Hull,* 191 Ariz. 441 (Sup. Ct Ariz. 1998).
76. *Id.* at 447.
77. *Id.* at 452.
78. *Id.*
79. *Id.*
80. *Id.* at 453.
81. *Id* at 454 (cites omitted).
82. *Id.* at 457.
83. *Sandoval v. Hagan,* 7 Fsupp 2d 1234 (MD Ala. 1998).
84. Alabama Const. Amendment 509. As in Arizona, the Alabama statute also gave residents a right to sue to enforce the provision but also went further in giving a right to sue to those who did business in the state.
85. *Supra,* note 83 at 1279.
86. *Id.*
87. *Id.* at 1280.
88. *Id.* at 1303.
89. *Id.* at 1243.
90. *Id.*
91. *Id.* at 1303.
92. *Id.* at 1301.
93. *Id.* at 1311.
94. *Id.* at 1309.
95. 8 USC §1423.
96. 1952 USCCAN 1653, 1736 at 1308.

97.   *Id*. at 1309.

98.   *Id*. at 1314, *quoting, Meyer v. Nebraska*, 262 US 390 at 401.

99.   *Sandoval v. Hagan*, 197 F3d 484 (11th Cir 1999). Generally, the Eleventh Amendment bars suit against a state by its own citizens or against another party when the state is the real party in interest. However, there are exceptions: if a state waives sovereign immunity; if Congress pursuant to a valid exercise of congressional power, abrogates a state's immunity; through a clear statement of intent to abrogate or if the suit is one for prospective relief of ongoing violations of federal law. The *Sandoval* court found that Congress clearly stated that states could not be immune from suit for violations of statutes that prohibit discrimination. Congress did this through a lawful exercise of its Spending Power – if a state accepts federal funds it thereby waives immunity from suit.

100.   *See* Utah Code Ann. §63-13-1.5.

101.   §63-13-1.5 (5)(a).

102.   *Id*.

103.   *Anderson v. Utah, supra*, note 6 at 1.

104.   *Id*. at 3.

105.   §63-13-1.5 (3).

106.   *Anderson v. Utah* at 3.

107.   *Id*.

108.   *Id*. at 4.

109.   *Id*. The court cited to *Soberal-Perez v. Heckler*, 717 F2d 36 (2nd Cir 1983) and *Frontera v. Sindell*, 533 F2d 1215 (6th Cir 1975), two cases concerning the right to linguistically appropriate documents arising in the social services context and discussed in Chapter 7, for support on this issue.

110.   *Id*. at 5.

111.   *Id*.

112.   *Court Ruling Curtails Utah's English-only Law But Leaves Confusion in its Wake, ACLU Says* (Press Release March 5, 2001) at www.aclu.org/news/2001/n030501e.html.

113.   *ACLU Withdraws Appeal of Official English Decision* (Press Release September 4, 2000). At www.acluutah.org/Sept4-01.htm.

114.   *Id*.

115.   Yereth Rosen, *Judge Strikes Down Alaska's Official-English Law*, REUTERS, March 27, 2002.

116.   Two cases were actually filed; one in Anchorage called *Alakayak, et al. v. Alaska*, and another filed in Dillingham called *Kritz v. Alaska*. The two cases were combined. *See Alaskans for a Common Language v. Kritz*, 3 P3d 906 (Alaska 2000) for a history of the challenges.

117.   *Supra*, note 115.

118.   *Id*.

119.   *See In Re Initiative Petition No. 366*, 2002 WL 491517 (Okla. 2002).

120.   *Id*. at 6.

121.   *See* John Greiner, *Court Kills English-Only Plan*, THE OKLAHOMAN, April 3, 2002.

122.   65 Fed. Reg. 50121 (August 11, 2000).

123.   65 Fed. Reg. 50123-01 (August 16, 2000).

124.   "LEP" is an acronym used by the federal government to designate schoolchildren who are entitled to English language support services because of their dominance in a language other than English. State and local governments may use the same or different acronyms to designate the same population. I have decided to eschew using acronyms

and simply refer to the same population of children as "language minorities," the term used throughout this book. Within this chapter, however, because legal requirements for certain services only follow children who are not considered by school systems to be "proficient" in English, here when I use "language minorities" it does not refer to all the many bilingual or multilingual students, but those who are not dominant in the English language.

125. 65 Fed. Reg. 52763.

126. The case, *Alexander v. Sandoval*, 121 S. Ct 1511 (2001) is discussed in the Appendix.

127. *ProEnglish, et al. v. Bush, et al.* The complaint, field in the eastern district of Virginia, can be found at http://www.proenglish.org/legal/bush/complaint.html.

128. The most recent example of the increased discretion given to states has been the move to bloc-granting federal educational aid given under Title I of the Elementary and Secondary Education Act. With block-granting the federal government would exercise little control over how states decided to spend the federal funds. Civil Rights groups have been concerned about this development since states could decide to ignore the neediest students and spend the money on pet projects or more popular student populations. *See* No Child Left Behind Act of 2001, Pub L No. 107–110, 115 Stat. 1425 (2002) at §20 USC §§6301.

129. *See San Antonio v. Rodriguez*, 411 US 980 (1973), where the Supreme Court decided that there is no federal constitutional right to a free, public education and that such a right, if it existed, was to be found in state constitutional provisions. This decision spawned decades' long state level litigation over the funding of public schools. *See Campaign for Fiscal Equity v. State*, 187 Misc. 2d 1 NY Sup. Ct (2001); *Abbott by Abbott v. Burke*, 195 NJ Super 59 (NJ Super. AD 1984) *rev'd, Abbott v. Burke*, 100 NJ 269 (1985), *aff'd Abbott by Abbott v. Burke*, 136 NJ 444 (1993), *clarified, Abbott v. Burke* 164 N 84 (1999); *Serrano v. Priest*, 20 Cal. 3d 25 (1977).

130. *See* Support for Arabs and Muslims in the US, NY TIMES at B1, September 18, 2001.

Chapter 3

Fulfilling the Promise of Citizenship: English Literacy, Naturalization, and Voting Rights

INTRODUCTION

This chapter discusses two of the most significant areas in which US citizenship and civic participation are defined: naturalization, and voting rights. Perhaps more than any other area of law, naturalization, or the laws that govern becoming a citizen, reflect a nation's idea of itself. There are many areas of law and policy that reflect a nation's values but "[c]itizenship is all about insiders and outsiders and the 'otherness' of the latter."[1] Similarly, voting is a fundamental issue in the US for, in a republican form of government, whoever has control of the ballot box would presumably control the country.

The role of English literacy has had an ignoble and prominent role in both areas. Requiring a demonstrated skill in the English language has been used as a xenophobic tool to shape the nation's immigration and naturalization policy and to restrict access to the voting booth in attempts to control the shape of the nation. This chapter begins with a discussion of the role of English literacy in both immigration and voting rights because they do overlap. Then the details of each area of law are discussed. The first section, on naturalization, discusses the federal legislation that requires a certain proficiency in English for citizenship, challenges to that requirement and the justification for abandoning this prerequisite.

The longer section on voting rights law discusses the passage of the federal Voting Rights Act, its particular provisions on language meant to ensure the enfranchisement of Puerto Ricans and the litigation that has helped to secure further bilingual assistance at the voting booth. For language minorities simple physical access to the voting booth is not sufficient; the freedom to vote requires an affirmative accommodation on the part of the government. In the context of voting rights, that means the provision of bilingual ballots and voting materials. At the end of the chapter, I examine the limits of these statutory rights and present an argument for the feasibility and wisdom of finding a constitutional basis for protecting the voting rights of language minorities.

THE ROLE OF ENGLISH IN IMMIGRATION AND VOTING RESTRICTIONS: A SHORT HISTORY OF XENOPHOBIA

Immigration and naturalization

English literacy requirements, whether to restrict immigration or access to the ballot, have an ignoble history that dates to the immigration waves of the nineteenth century and attempts by the Anglo-Saxon majorities of the north-east to keep control over their local governments.[2] Indeed, the first English literacy tests were passed by Connecticut in 1855 and Massachusetts in 1857 specifically to keep immigrants from the voting booths.[3]

Until around 1880, immigration to the US was unrestricted. By 1890, however, immigrants from the northern European countries began to be outnumbered by immigrants from Italy, Poland, and the Austro-Hungarian Empire. The assumption that immigrants, who looked and acted until that time a lot like the previous generations of immigrants, would easily assimilate into the US mainstream was questioned. Historian John Higham explains:

> [t]hroughout the [18]80s, Italian, Slavic, and Yiddish immigration increased. The peasants from these lands ... lived much closer to serfdom than did the folk of western Europe.... By western European standards, the masses of southern and eastern Europe were educationally deficient, socially backward, and bizarre in appearance.[4]

In addition, the nation was in crisis in the 1880s. It was experiencing severe economic dislocations, the rise of a labor movement and the anxiety of war: in short, a rich environment for the growth of nationalism. Connecticut's provision requiring English literacy for voting was "swept into the constitution by the rising tide of Know-Nothing agitation against the foreigner."[5]

Similarly, the backlash against the tide of Irish immigration to Massachusetts ushered in an English literacy test. Apparently, there the sense was that the poor of Ireland were illiterate generally and the issue was not over the English language specifically, although literacy in English was the requirement. The Whig party of Massachusetts saw a bleak future if the democratic Irish were allowed to continue to vote:

> [i]n those early days "the Irish went solidly to the Democrats, and for the first time in many years gave them a fighting chance in the struggle with the Whigs

... [and the] imperiling of the Whig success carried with it doubtless, the conclusion that the welfare of the state was seriously endangered.[6]

The Massachusetts and Connecticut provisions alone disenfranchised 35,000 citizens.[7]

Federal immigration policy was not as easy to change. The nation was built on immigration, and there had been a sense of confidence about the country's ability to assimilate the foreign-born that still held sway with many. For "[i]mmigration was one of the cornerstones of the nation's whole social structure, and a cosmopolitan ideal of nationality was woven deeply into America's Christian and democratic heritage. The stone could not be dislodged or the idea renounced with ease."[8]

Nonetheless, the 1890s would see the first major reversal in this attitude exemplified in federal law. Indeed, a popular movement, fueled by nativism developed in favor of restrictions on immigration.[9] One popular book of the time warned that:

> the population of the United States will, on account of the great influx of blood from Southeastern Europe, rapidly become darker in pigmentation, smaller in stature, more mercurial, more attached to music and art, more given to crimes of larceny, kidnaping, assault, murder, rape, and sex-immortality ... and the ratio of insanity in the population will rapidly increase.[10]

Knowing that the unwanted immigrants came from poor backgrounds and usually had little or no formal schooling, immigration restrictionists began to push for a literacy requirement at the end of 1880s. In 1891, Henry Cabot Lodge, a republican member of the House, took up the cause and enlisted the help of Senator Chandler to help him win support for the measure from both houses.[11] In 1894, with an economic depression in full force and with republican majorities in both houses of Congress, the restrictionists' time seemed to come. The intellectual parent of the movement, the Immigration Restriction League, advocated for the literacy test, arguing that Southern and Eastern Europe was "dumping on the United States an alarming number of illiterates, paupers, criminals, and madmen who endanger the American character and American citizenship."[12] The bill, requiring literacy in some language was introduced by Lodge in the House of Representatives near the end of 1896. The bill passed, but was neglected by the Senate until December 1896. The Senate passed it easily. But when McKinley, a republican, won the election of 1896 with immigrant support, fears of the immigrants began to subside. Cleveland vetoed the bill before he left office and there was no longer enough congressional interest to override the President.[13]

In 1906 Congress passed comprehensive naturalization legislation that sought to take responsibility for naturalization processing from the states. The state immigration bureaus had helped create a hodgepodge of immigration policy with some states, short on labor, advertising for and offering to pay the passage of immigrants.[14] The actual processing of naturalization claims became a federal task and the ability to *speak* the English language, but not read and write it, was added as the only substantive modification to the requirements of citizenship.

A report by the House Committee on Immigration and Naturalization stated that an alien who could not learn English in the five-year required residency period would be "so deficient in mental capacity ... or so careless of the opportunities afforded to him ... that he would not make a desirable citizen, and should be refused naturalization."[15]

Under the comprehensive legislation,[16] federal trial courts were given the authority to make ultimate determinations on citizenship applications. Some took it upon themselves to tighten the 1906 legislation by excluding those who did not *read* English under the theory that it would be impossible for them to be "attached" to the principles of the Constitution if they could not read it. In *In Re Katz*,[17] the court denied the citizenship application of a 42-year-old man who had resided in the US since 1913. His wife and three children resided with him in the country and he had been regularly employed to the extent that he had "amassed considerable savings and property."[18] Mr Katz would have seemed a model citizen, but for the court:

> an alien who claims to be attached to the principles of that great document [the Constitution], and yet has been unwilling to devote the time and effort necessary to enable him to read it, is not sufficiently interested in, nor attached to its principles to entitle him to the privilege of American citizenship.[19]

The push for immigration restrictions would not surface again until the end of the first decade of the twentieth century. In 1912, when the issue did re-surface with another push for a literacy test, President Taft vetoed the requirement in his last days of office. The rationale for President's Taft veto was important, for he relied on the objections of his Secretary of Commerce, Charles Nagel, in opposing the legislation. Nagel wrote the President that the justification for the literacy test was its use as a "practical measure to exclude a large portion of immigrants from certain countries."[20] Nagel argued that: "[t]he measure proposes to reach its result by indirection, and is defended purely upon the ground of practical policy, the final purpose being to reduce the quantity of cheap labor in this country."[21] He believed the test was "based on a fallacy in undertaking to apply a test which is not calculated to reach the truth and find relief from a danger which really does not exist."[22]

President Wilson similarly rejected the attempts to require literacy because "this bill ... propose[s] to turn away from tests of character and quality and impose tests which exclude and restrict."[23] He not only vetoed the bill, but used the considerable pressure of his office to compel Congress to act accordingly.[24] It was the advent of war that finally brought the passage of the literacy requirement in 1917. The two exceptions were for religious, but not political, persecution and for the immediate family members of immigrants who could meet the admission requirements.[25]

Despite the passage of the literacy test for naturalization, the taste for nativism was not quelled. Indeed, by 1920, the recently passed requirement had little effect on the flow of immigration. The literacy test had been conceived at the end of the nineteenth century when illiteracy in any language was common among the European immigrants. By 1920, when immigration began to peak again, the general literacy levels among the immigrant population had surged. According to Higham, the "[p]ostwar inrush of immigrants who could pass the test showed every sign of soon equaling the size of the indiscriminate, prewar movement. Net alien arrivals in the latter half of 1920 averaged 52,000 monthly...."[26] The post-war rise in unemployment, coupled with the nation's own feelings of disillusionment and the perception of the un-assimilability of the new immigrants, converged to support broader bans on immigration.

Soon after the armistice was signed, the immigration restrictionists took up a battle cry to limit immigration itself.[27] And the push did not come solely from politically conservative quarters. The American Federation of Labor, concerned about massive unemployment after the war, was a strong supporter of immigration restrictions.[28] Even the progressive journal The New Republic felt that "[t]he democracy of today ... cannot permit ... social ills to be aggravated by excessive immigration."[29]

Anti-Semitism also provided a unifying theme for the restrictionist movement. The "Jews were becoming a special bogey," says Higham.[30] In the same way that Latinos today are branded as "unassimilable," the Jews of the 1920s, composing a significant portion of the immigrant population, were called "abnormally twisted," "unassimilable," "filthy, un-American and often dangerous in their habits."[31] With public energy focused on restricting immigration, the nation's first major restriction on immigration was passed into law in May 1921. Under the law, European immigration would be restricted to a maximum of 350,000, with most of those coming from north-western Europe. The special status granted north-western Europeanry reflected the national sense that the flow of Jews coming from eastern Europe needed to be stopped.[32]

Limiting voting rights

Meanwhile, it was in 1892 that Mississippi, realizing how effective a weapon the literacy test had been in barring access to the voting booth in Connecticut and Massachusetts, passed its own English literacy requirement. It was quickly joined by South Carolina in 1892, Louisiana in 1898, North Carolina in 1900, Alabama in 1901, Virginia in 1902, and Georgia in 1908.[33] The southern states were not to be outdone by states in the north and west anxious over immigrant suffrage. Between 1889 and 1924, Wyoming, Maine, California, Washington, Oregon, New York, New Hampshire, Delaware and Oklahoma passed English literacy requirements at the height of the nation's anti-foreigner fervor.[34]

New York's English literacy requirement for voting became effective in 1922. There is substantial evidence that it was passed to specifically disenfranchise 1,000,000 Yiddish-speaking Jews. The provision had been proposed repeatedly since the late 1800s and had met repeated and successful democratic opposition.

The sponsor of the measure said that:

> [m]ore precious even than the forms of government are the mental qualities of our race. While those stand unimpaired, all is safe. They are exposed to a single

danger, and that is that by constantly changing our voting citizenship through the wholesale, but valuable and necessary infusion of Southern and Eastern Europeans races.... The danger has begun.... We should check it.[35]

At the 1915 constitutional convention in which it was again proposed, Louis Marshall of the American Jewish Committee testified against the amendment noting its impact on Jews: "[t]here are thousands of citizens in the state who cannot read and write English but who are good citizens for all that; educated men who know all they need to know about our institutions...."[36] The Jews kept up their connections to Yiddish, said Marshall, "through sentiment ... because enshrined in it are memories of a martyrdom patiently borne through long centuries of persecution."[37] In response, proponents of the amendment reminded the delegates of the Anglo-Saxon tradition they were destined to uphold:

> [i]t is not a question of nationality as such as it is a question of race. Search your hearts and see if the Anglo-Saxon in you does not assert itself for we are Anglo-Saxon after all.... Our only hope of making a nation out of ourselves rests on solidifying the elements that come to our shores and fitting them to walk in the paths to which our Anglo-Saxon ancestry and our Anglo-Saxon traditions point as the paths in which lies our national destiny.[38]

BECOMING A US CITIZEN AND THE NEED TO UNDERSTAND ENGLISH

The citizenship requirements

The United States Constitution, Article 1 section 8, leaves to Congress the power to "establish a uniform rule of naturalization" along with several other powers, such as the power to declare war, the power over foreign commerce, and the power to define and punish offenses against the law of nations.

In 1950, the nation was in the grip of an anti-communist hysteria, and any indicia of "foreignness" was a cause for suspicion. Patrick McCarrran, head of the Senate Judiciary Committee wrote that "American Communism is not ... a homegrown product, but is a wild weed which has been deliberately transplanted in this country by foreign agents."[39] In passing the English literacy provision, Congressmen clearly linked the inability to speak or understand English to political suspicion:

> The subcommittee has taken considerable testimony on the general problems relating to subversive activities in this country ... the subcommittee feels that it is pertinent here to restate that this testimony conclusively shows that anti-American and subversive activities are more easily carried on among non-English-speaking groups of aliens than among those who are thoroughly conversant with our language....[40]

The requirement now stands that applicants for citizenship, unless otherwise exempted for age or disability, must be able to "understand" the English language, which has been defined to include "an ability to read, write and speak words in ordinary usage in the English language."[41] The requirement is met if the applicant can read or write simple words and phrases and "no extraordinary or unreasonable condition shall be imposed upon the applicant."[42]

In addition to the English literacy requirement, applicants for citizenship must be able to demonstrate knowledge of the history and government of the US, must be in continuous legal residence in the US for five years and be of "good moral character."[43] Despite the sense that the English literacy requirement is relatively easy to meet, some data suggest that it may present a real barrier to citizenship for many.[44]

It has been suggested that the English literacy requirement essentially acts as an "official English" law for the US.[45] Although the English literacy requirement may be a real barrier to naturalization, its codification does not, I believe, rise to the level of an official English law. Not only does it stand in direct contravention to many federal pronouncements, such as the bilingual ballot provisions of the Voting Rights Act which accommodate the needs of non-English speaking citizens, but there are also many other avenues available to citizenship that do not require English literacy, and there are exemptions to the English literacy requirement itself. Additionally, federal regulations allow that, where an applicant has satisfied the literacy requirement, the civics exam can be given in the applicant's native language, if the "officer conducting the exam determines that an inaccurate or incomplete record of the [civics] examination would result if the examination on technical or complex issues were conducted in English...." [46]

Judicial reluctance to review citizenship requirements

In the only case to have challenged the English literacy requirement, the petitioner's attempt to launch a class action suit was roundly rejected by the federal district court in Brownsville, Texas, a heavily Chicano area. The decision was affirmed by the appeals court in 1974.[47] The court found that, although aliens are entitled to procedural due process in the processing of their claims for citizenship, the power of Congress to set qualifications for citizenship is virtually unlimited, and will not be reviewed by the court because it is a "non-justiciable" issue. Issues are considered "non-justiciable" when they are academic or moot. However, the courts will usually label a matter "non-justiciable" when it is really a "political question" that they believe is best handled by a coordinate branch of government. In these situations, the courts generally find, that there are essentially no "judicially manageable standards for reviewing the conduct" of which the petitioner complains – here, an English literacy requirement.[48] The courts are essentially throwing up their hands, declaring that they have no way to determine if what is being complained of ought to be unlawful. The reticence of the courts to question the qualifications for citizenship that Congress has established is unmistakable and currently an almost unscalable barrier to challenging these requisites.

The lumping of the naturalization powers given to Congress with other foreign relations powers in Article 1 section 8, has caused the courts to limit their analysis of the naturalization power. For instance, the Circuit Court above noted that the naturalization power was conferred on Congress within the same section as the war power and sovereignty over foreign commerce and then stated that "[i]t has never been supposed that there are any judicially manageable standards for reviewing the conduct of our nation's foreign relations by the other two branches of the federal government."[49]

The Supreme Court itself has been clear on this point: "over no conceivable subject is the legislative power of Congress more complete than it is over the admission of aliens."[50] Further, the:

> Supreme Court has traditionally viewed the power of Congress to regulate the entry and stay of aliens, as well as the process through which aliens become naturalized citizens, as an inherent incident of national sovereignty, committed exclusively to national, as opposed to state or local control.[51]

As befitting the international aspect of most of the powers enumerated in Article 1 section 8, the naturalization power is seen as a feature of international relations:

> it is an accepted maxim of international law, that every sovereign nation has the power, as inherent in sovereignty, and essential to self-preservation, to forbid the entrance of foreigners within its dominions, or to admit them only in such cases and upon such conditions as it may see fit to prescribe.[52]

Questioning the need for an English literacy requirement

The English literacy requirement for citizenship is unlikely to be overturned by the courts in the near future. Still, some commentators are urging a new analysis of the requirement and have strongly suggested that it ought not withstand political, if not constitutional, review. For instance, Professor Spiro argues that, with the collapse of communism and the growth of the multilingual media in the US and the existence of more pressing reasons for English literacy – namely economic ones – the English literacy requirement no longer makes sense and should be repudiated as a nativistic hold-over from the 1950s.[53]

Others argue that naturalization policies that are "rooted in xenophobia" should not be tolerated in a nation that has outlawed racial and ethnic discrimination.[54] Naturalization policies that discriminate on the basis of language serve to legitimize domestic unlawful discrimination. Further, goes the argument, those within the nation of the same national origin as those being excluded from it will most certainly feel a "badge of opprobrium" unfavored by our domestic laws.[55]

Despite the arguments of the anti-restrictionists, the legal and political outlook for challenging the English literacy requirement is not good. Not only are courts unwilling to question the role of Congress in this area, there is still a high degree of public concern over the rate of immigration which will cloud any discussion about lowering barriers to naturalization. Further, even if the courts were willing to even scrutinize Congressional use of the naturalization power, it is unlikely that the English literacy requirement would be held discriminatory. For the courts will easily accept the legitimacy of a federal policy that differentiates on the basis of language. As has been demonstrated in previous chapters, most courts willingly acknowledge the supremacy of English in the nation and the legitimacy of governmental policies that support that supremacy. They have also been unwilling to declare as unconstitutional language-based policies that do not discriminate on the basis of national origin, race, or ethnicity. Further, feelings of inferiority created in US citizens by a purportedly discriminatory naturalization process will most likely not be considered the kind of harm that courts can, or are willing to, address.

Still, advocates for immigrants generally should be willing to openly question the necessity and legitimacy of the English literacy requirement. For the most part, advocates fighting for language rights are stymied by the reliance of English-only proponents on the citizenship requirements as proof of the nation's legislative commitment to mandating English and the "common sense" necessity for such a requirement.

Yet the "common sense" reasons for the English literacy requirement do not withstand simple scrutiny. For instance, the importance of English to the national conception of itself and to community-building is already undermined by US immigration policy itself – it is possible to become a citizen by other means that do not hinge on English literacy. For example, residents of territories that become citizens by treaty or by acts of Congress or by admission of the territory to statehood. Further, federal laws such as the Voting Rights Act and the questionable legality of broad state English-only laws, discredit the argument that the nation has, through its citizenship laws, made literacy in English into a national goal to which rigid adherence is required.

More importantly, for practical purposes, the level of English necessary to pass the naturalization exam is not of a sufficiently high level to ensure that new citizens would be more comfortable or likely to use their new language than their native language. The biggest incentive to learning and using English continues to be economic, a rationale neither supported nor mitigated by naturalization laws.

Language rights proponents should not be afraid to take on the English literacy requirement when appropriate. The need for recent immigrants to learn English is quite clear but that should not distort the government's need to objectively evaluate its naturalization requirements. The two positions can stand together for the ultimate benefit of the nation – resident aliens who would make good citizens but for their inability to understand English well should be allowed to contribute to their new nation, and the economic incentives for their ultimate acquisition of high level English skills will remain in place.

BILINGUAL BALLOTS: THE TENUOUS VOTING RIGHTS OF LANGUAGE MINORITY CITIZENS

Discrimination at the booth: Federal intervention through passage of the Voting Rights Act

The right to vote as a citizen of the United States is considered a fundamental constitutional right.[56] Yet the idea that *every* citizen should have such a right is relatively novel and is still being refined. The US Constitution carefully balances the powers of the federal and state governments to regulate the qualifications of voters and the administration of elections. Historically, the power of the individual states to confer suffrage was considered paramount. The Supreme Court has said that "the privilege to vote in a state is within the jurisdiction of the state itself, to be exercised as the state may direct, and upon such terms as it may deem proper, provided, of course, no discrimination is made between individuals in violation of the federal Constitution."[57]

Some states have notoriously used their power over elections to limit access to the ballot box. Legislating land-holding requirements, racial criteria, residency requirements, poll taxes, and literacy tests have all been used to disenfranchise primarily African-Americans. It was within this tradition of wide state latitude that the Supreme Court unanimously upheld an English literacy test for voters administered by North Carolina.[58] There, Justice Douglas noted that while the Constitution speaks of the right to vote, it is a right to vote "as established by the laws and constitution of the state."[59] The Court was unanimous in finding that "[t]he ability to read and write ... has some relation to standards designed to promote intelligent use of the ballot. Literacy and illiteracy are neutral on race, creed, color, and sex."[60] Quite clearly, the Court did not consider itself confronted with a statute that had discrimination as its chief object. Yet, as described above, that was just the case. English literacy requirements were not the brain child of the South, nor were they originally created to discriminate against African-Americans, but the South did successfully adopt them for its own purposes.

After upholding the constitutionality of a strict literacy test requiring potential voters to read and write the English language, the Supreme Court did strike down literacy tests used in Mississippi[61] and Louisiana[62] that were more subjective in that they required registrants to "understand" or "interpret" state constitutional provisions. This time, the Court was aware of the discriminative impetus behind the literacy tests. The Louisiana test, found the Court, was part of a successful plan to deprive Louisiana negroes of their right to vote."[63] The piecemeal approach to voting rights seemed to call for a systemic, federal policy. In 1965 Congress answered the call by passing the Voting Rights Act. The Act prohibited the use of literacy tests and other discriminatory "tests and devices" from use in certain, mostly southern states.[64] Before passing the Act, Congress held hearings for nine days and received testimony from 67 witnesses; more than three days were spent discussing the bill on the House floor, and 26 days were spent in debate in the Senate. The House approved the bill by a vote of 328 to 74, and the Senate approved the bill by a vote of 79 to 18. Naturally, the affected states challenged the Voting Rights Act, arguing that Congress had no power to ban state literacy tests.[65]

The power of Congress to pass the Voting Rights Act was upheld in *South Carolina v. Katzenbach*[66] as an expression of the special powers given to Congress to enforce the Civil War Amendments through "appropriate legislation." The purposes of the Civil War Amendments, the Thirteenth, Fourteenth and Fifteenth Amendments, was to end "racial discrimination and to prevent direct or indirect state legislative encroachment on the rights guaranteed by the amendments."[67] In order to do this:

> the Framers gave Congress power to enforce each of the Civil War Amendments. These enforcement powers are broad.... The Thirteenth Amendment "clothed" Congress with power to pass all laws necessary and proper for abolishing all badges and incidents of slavery in the United States.... It is the power of Congress which has been enlarged.[68]

The Supreme Court found that "[t]he Voting Rights Act was designed by Congress to banish the blight of racial discrimination in voting, which has infected the electoral process in parts of our country for nearly a century."[69] It was clear to the Court that, in enacting the legislation, Congress had felt:

> itself confronted by an insidious and pervasive evil which had been perpetuated in certain parts of our country through unremitting and ingenious defiance of the Constitution ... [and that] Congress concluded that the unsuccessful remedies which it had prescribed in the past would have to be replaced by sterner and more elaborate measures in order to satisfy the clear commands of the Fifteenth Amendment.[70]

The power of Congress under the Fifteenth Amendment is one that is "complete in itself, may be exercised to its utmost extent, and acknowledges no limitations, other than are prescribed in the constitution."[71]

This broad enforcement power is an important one, and generous judicial readings of it have permitted Congress to successfully legislate away many of the barriers put up by states to disenfranchise minority voters. However, the legal analysis for what is "appropriate legislation" to enforce the Fourteenth Amendment, for instance, as distinguished from the analysis required to ascertain whether the Amendment has been violated itself, is murky at best. Further, and more broadly, the constitutional, as opposed to the statutory, protections to be offered language minorities are not at all clear. These two issues will be discussed below within the context of two companion Supreme Court cases, *Katzenbach v. Morgan*[72] and *Cardona v. Power*.[73]

Section 4(e) of the Voting Rights Act: Protecting language minorities at the booth

"The Puerto Rico exception"

The Voting Rights Act of 1965 contained §4(e), known colloquially as the "Puerto

Rico exception," a provision that ensured that no person who had successfully completed the sixth primary grade in a public school in, or a private school accredited by, the Commonwealth of Puerto Rico in which the language of instruction was other than English could be denied the right to vote because of an inability to read or write English.[74] The measure was sponsored in the Senate by Senators Jacob Javits and Robert Kennedy and in the House by Representatives Gilbert and Ryan, all of New York, for the explicit purpose of dealing with the disenfranchisement of large segments of the Puerto Rican population in New York. Throughout the congressional debate it was repeatedly acknowledged that §4(e) had particular reference to the Puerto Rican population in New York.[75] Indeed, a Puerto Rican citizen had brought a case in the New York state courts unsuccessfully challenging the English literacy requirement.[76] The Court of Appeals refused to find the literacy requirement unconstitutional under either the Fourteenth or Fifteenth Amendments or under the Treaty of Paris, the treaty under which the US was given control over the island and which promised the protection of the civil rights of Puerto Ricans. The American Jewish Congress had filed an *amicus* brief on behalf of the plaintiff.

Challenges to the bilingual provisions: New York defends its English literacy requirement

Shortly after passage of §4(e) in 1965, registered New York City voters brought an action called *Morgan v. Katzenbach*[77] challenging the constitutionality of the provision and complaining that the weight of their votes was being diluted by Puerto Ricans living in New York who were not literate in English but who were being allowed to vote under the Voting Rights Act and in contravention of state law.

The trial court upheld the New York law, relying heavily on *Lassiter* and the traditional deference given to states in the voting arena.[78] The Voting Rights Act was unusual, found the court, for Congress had never previously attempted to legislate voting requisites. It had certainly acted in this sphere in the past, for instance, prohibiting the imposition of poll taxes and granting women the right of suffrage; but those advances had been achieved through constitutional amendments that were ultimately ratified by the states before they could become effective. This law, found the court, went beyond the powers granted to Congress and was unconstitutional.

Also decided in 1965, the same year as *Morgan*, was another challenge brought to New York's election law. In *US v. County Board of Elections*,[79] the federal government applied for a temporary restraining order for the full application of the literacy requirement, and an order requiring the board of elections to register all persons who could qualify to vote under §4(e). This was a direct attack on New York's law, and this time the campaign for language rights was successful. The court unanimously upheld the Voting Rights Act, but limited its rationale to the specific situation of Puerto Ricans, citizens whose dominance in Spanish had been encouraged by the federal government. The district court detailed the historical relationship between the US and Puerto Rico and the impact of the federal acquiescence to the role of Spanish on the island. The court stated: "...we are confronted with American citizens of Puerto Rican birth or residence who have been encouraged by our government's Puerto Rican educational and foreign policy to use Spanish as the means of communication in both public and private life."[80] That Congress, through §4(e), wanted to ensure that these citizens in particular had the right to vote was a judgment "Congress ... was superbly suited to make."[81] Although the court was aware of the *Morgan* Court's different opinion on the constitutionality of §4(e), it declined to follow that court's reasoning.[82] Only the *Morgan* decision was appealed to the US Supreme Court.

The main question before the Court was to what standard of review should §4(e) be subjected. New York State argued that Congress could legislate under the Fourteenth Amendment only if it had found that the state's English literacy requirement was a violation of the Equal Protection Clause of the Fourteenth Amendment itself. For plaintiffs, the legislation could be "appropriate" only if it essentially was curing constitutional violations. Plaintiffs were confident that Congress had not conducted the kind of searching inquiry of the purpose and effect of New York's election law needed to sustain a finding of an Equal Protection Clause violation. Indeed, the plaintiffs were not foolish in their confidence: the Supreme Court had already decided in *Lassiter* that literacy tests were not *per se* unconstitutional, but that affirmative evidence of a discriminatory intent was necessary.

The federal government, however, argued that the Court's review was more limited, as befitting legislation carried out under the expanded powers of Congress under the Fourteenth Amendment and the deference due to a coordinate branch of government. According to the federal government's theory, the Court need not decide that New York's literacy requirement was unconstitutional (a stand it could not take given *Lassiter*), but only that Congress's exercise of its powers was "appropriate." Clearly, a much less exacting standard of review.

The Court agreed. The question for judicial resolution as the Court saw it was only whether §4(e) is "appropriate legislation to enforce the Equal Protection Clause."[83] Legislation would be considered appropriate if it is:

> adapted to carry out the objects the amendments have in view, whatever tends to enforce submission to the prohibitions they contain, and to secure to all persons the enjoyment of perfect equality of civil rights and the equal protection of the laws against State denial or invasion, if not prohibited, is brought within the domain of congressional power.[84]

Basically, legislation will be upheld as "appropriate" if it is "plainly adapted" to the end of enforcing the Equal Protection Clause and is not "prohibited by but is consistent with 'the letter and spirit of the constitution.'"[85] The Court would not accept the plaintiffs' argument that the courts need to determine whether state voting requirements were constitutional on a piecemeal basis – that question was essentially given to Congress to determine.

The Court found that both by its language and in its effect, §4(e) was "plainly adapted" to the enforcement of the Equal Protection Clause:

[t]he practical effect of §4(e) is to prohibit New York from denying the right to vote to large segments of its Puerto Rican community. Congress has thus prohibited the State from denying to that community the right that is "preservative of all rights".... This enhanced political power will be helpful in gaining nondiscriminatory treatment in public services for the entire Puerto Rican community.[86]

Indeed, §4(e) may be:

viewed as a measure to secure for the Puerto Rican community residing in New York nondiscriminatory treatment by government – both in the imposition of voting qualifications and the provision or administration of governmental services, such as public schools, public housing and law enforcement.[87]

New York attempted to justify its English literacy requirement with the same rationale often used by English-only advocates today to justify repealing §4(e): as a way to force immigrants to learn English. The Court, however, found that Congress could have justifiably rejected that reasoning: "Congress might have also questioned whether denial of a right deemed so precious and fundamental in our society was a necessary or appropriate means of encouraging persons to learn English...."[88]

While New York State argued that the English literacy requirement would help ensure "intelligent exercise of the franchise," Congress could have concluded that being literate in Spanish is as effective a requirement to meet that end as literacy in English would be "for those to whom Spanish-language newspapers and Spanish-language radio and television programs are available to inform them of election issues and governmental affairs."[89]

It was for Congress, however, and not the Court to balance all of these competing interests and determine whether to legislate and what kind of legislation would be "appropriate"; it was enough for the Court to find a basis upon which Congress could have found that New York's English literacy requirement constituted an invidious discrimination in violation of the Equal Protection Clause.[90]

The last area of inquiry for the Court was whether the remedy enacted by Congress was itself in violation of the Constitution. Here, the New York plaintiffs argued that, by not extending coverage to those not educated in American-flag schools, Congress was perpetuating its own invidious discrimination. This argument, however, was patently foolish. Congress can act to ameliorate social problems in small steps, it need not act to cure wrongs wholly: "[a] statute is not invalid under the Constitution because it might have gone farther than it did."[91] Further, Congress had a legitimate basis for recognizing through voting rights legislation the unique relationship between Puerto Rico and the US that does not exist between the US and non-Puerto Rican schools.[92]

Justice Harlan's dissents: Arguing for process over civil rights

The dissent in *Katzenbach* written by Justice Harlan and joined by Justice Stewart accused the majority of confusing the issue of how much power Congress was given actually under §5 of the Fourteenth Amendment to abolish the vestiges of slavery with what questions are appropriate for congressional, as opposed to judicial, determination. Justice Harlan asserted that, before Congress can actualize its powers under §5, the "condition" (here the English literacy requirement), that Congress seeks to address must be found to be an "infringement of the Constitution" by the judiciary.[93] That is, before Congress can act to fix a perceived violation of the Fourteenth Amendment, a court must actually first find that a constitutional violation has occurred. The constitutionality or unconstitutionality of the English literacy test was a question for the courts, not Congress, to decide. Taking the judicial inquiry in *South Carolina v. Katzenbach* as a guide, Justice Harlan noted that in that case, where Congress' enforcement powers under the Fifteenth Amendment were in question, the Court:

> reviewed first the "voluminous legislative history" as well as judicial precedents supporting the basic congressional finding that the clear commands of the Fifteenth Amendment has been infringed by various state subterfuges.... Given the existence of the evil, we held the remedial steps taken by the legislature under the Enforcement Clause of the Fifteenth Amendment to be a justifiable exercise of congressional initiative.[94]

No such voluminous history exists for §4(e), however, argued Harlan. Here, there was no legislative record showing that:

> Spanish-speaking citizens are fully as capable of making informed decisions in a New York election as are English-speaking citizens. Nor was there any showing whatever to support ... that §4(e) be viewed as but a remedial measure designed to cure or assure against unconstitutional discrimination of other varieties, e.g. in public schools, public housing and law enforcement ... to which Puerto Rican minorities might be subject in such communities as New York. There is simply no legislative record supporting such hypothesized discrimination of the sort we have hitherto insisted upon when congressional power is brought to bear on constitutionally reserved state concerns.[95]

The question for Harlan was whether New York's law was so "arbitrary or irrational as to offend the command of the Equal Protection Clause,"[96] a determination that must be left to the courts. If not, Harlan reasoned, Congress would be able to limit or even overrule the Court's constitutional jurisprudence through legislation.

Although the dissenters may have been correct in their technical parsing between the powers of Congress and the judiciary, they miss the broader societal goals of the Civil War Amendments which authorize the creation of the Voting Rights Act. The *South Carolina* Court pointed out that congressional action under the Fourteenth or Fifteenth Amendments was unconstitutional only when it "attacked evils not comprehended" by the Amendments.[97] The *South Carolina* Court spoke only in terms of the Fifteenth Amendment, but for our purposes the analysis is the same. Certainly ensuring that language minority citizens have access to the ballot is the kind of political good that the Amendments were intended to allow Congress to expedite. The point of the Civil War Amendments was to give Congress broad ameliorative powers in direct contrast to the wording and intentions of the original constitutional framers who had been suspicious of a federal government, and closely guarded the rights of the states. The nation had been through a civil war, had seen the limits and potential for harmful provincialism in state supremacy, and was prepared to enlist the federal government on the side of minorities to create a more legitimate republican form of government.

Further, the standard of proof required by Harlan would have been too heavy for many truly disenfranchised voters to carry. One commentator noted that "[t]o require documentation that Spanish-speaking citizens are as capable of being informed as English-speaking citizens, or that discrimination exists in public service areas that can be remedied by the vote, may unduly delay or prevent entirely any significant federal action."[98]

Cardona v. Power[99] was a companion case to *Katzenbach*, and was simply remanded to the New York Court of Appeals by the Supreme Court without a decision on the merits of the case. In this case the appellant, born and educated in Puerto Rico and living in New York since about 1948, brought a constitutional challenge to New York's election law requiring literacy in the English language – this was the flipside of *Katzenbach* – or an affirmative challenge to New York's English literacy requirement, one that had been unsuccessful when brought before the passage of the Voting Rights Act. Cardona argued that New York's requirement was a violation of the Equal Protection Clause. Since the Court had just decided in *Katzenbach* that Congress had authority to pass §4(e) of the Voting Rights Act, it declined to pass on the constitutional challenge but remanded the case to the state courts so that they could inquire into whether Cardona met the sixth grade Spanish literacy requirements of the Voting Rights Act. If she did satisfy the latter, then the Court need only enforce the Voting Rights Act and rule that Cardona was allowed to vote.

The case is noteworthy only for Justice Douglas' dissent, where he argued that the Court should not have shied away from the constitutional challenge, and ruled that New York's English literacy requirement was indeed a violation of the Equal Protection Clause. Douglas noted that the only teaching of *Lassiter* was that the state has broad powers over conduct of elections, and that it was not necessarily illegal to "condition the use of the ballot on the ability to read and write."[100]

However, Douglas sensed that there was a basis to find that invidious discrimination is present when distinctions are made between those who are literate in English and those who are literate in languages other than English. Douglas reasoned that since we are a:

> multi-racial and multi-linguistic nation, and there are groups in this country as versatile in Spanish, French, Japanese, and Chinese, for example, as others are in English. Many of them constitute communities in which there are widespread programs of public communication in one of those tongues – such as newspapers, magazines, radio and television which regularly report and comment on matters of political interest and public concern.[101]

The question for Douglas was whether "intelligent use of the ballot should not be as much presumed where one is versatile in the Spanish language as it is where English is the medium."[102]

Douglas resolved that question in favor of Cardona and the Spanish-literate:

> [t]he heavier burden [to qualify as a voter] which New York has placed on the Spanish-speaking American cannot in my view be sustained under the Equal Protection Clause of the Fourteenth Amendment.... Thus appellant has, quite apart from any federal legislation, a constitutional right to vote in New York on a parity with an English-speaking citizen – either by passing a Spanish literacy test or through a certificate showing completion of the sixth grade in a Puerto Rican school where Spanish was the classroom language. In no other way can she be placed on a constitutional parity with the English-speaking electors.[103]

Harlan and Stewart, again relying on the reasoning of *Lassiter*, dissented in *Cardona*. The strict scrutiny test for infringements on fundamental rights such as voting rights had not yet been developed by the courts, and the dissenters resisted Douglas' assertion that, when such important rights are at stake, greater scrutiny should be required. For Harlan and Stewart, the state need only show that it had a rational basis for the English literacy requirement it had adopted. This basis was clear, argued the dissenters: a well-informed person literate in Spanish would still have access to less information than an English-speaking voter. They said:

> [i]t is ... true that most candidates, certainly those campaigning on national or statewide level, make their speeches in English. New York may justifiably want its voters to be able to understand candidates directly, rather than through possibly imprecise translations or in a limited number of Spanish news media.[104]

Disturbingly, the dissenters also seemed to adopt New York's argument that requiring English literacy was an appropriate method for ensuring assimilation, and apparently that forceful assimilation can be as valuable to the state as ensuring legitimate election results:

> [i]t is noteworthy that the Federal Government requires literacy in English as a prerequisite to naturalization ... attesting to the national view of its importance as a prerequisite to full integration into the American political community.... Given the State's legitimate concern with promoting and safeguarding the intelligent use of the ballot, and given also New York's long experience with the process of integrating non-English-speaking residents into the mainstream of American life, I do not see how it can be said that this qualification for suffrage is unconstitutional.[105]

The Voting Rights Amendments: The right to cast an informed vote

Requiring bilingual voting assistance

In 1970 Congress extended the 1965 prohibition on the use of exclusionary "tests and devices" for five more years and then in 1975 it made the literary test ban indefinite and national in scope. The Voting Rights Act was amended in 1982 as well, and in 1992 the Voting Rights Language Assistance Act was passed extending the bilingual assistance mandate to 2007.[106] The 1975 Amendments, however, were particularly significant for language-minority communities. These Amendments codified requirements for bilingual assistance in any political subdivision in which a language minority group comprises more than 5% of the eligible voting population.[107]

In providing assistance to language minorities, Congress stated:

> [t]he Congress finds that voting discrimination against citizens of language minorities is pervasive and national in scope. Such minority citizens are from environments in which the dominant language is other than English. In addition they have been denied equal educational opportunities by State and local governments, resulting in severe disabilities and continuing illiteracy in the English language. The Congress further finds that, where State and local officials conduct elections only in English, language minority citizens are excluded from participating in the electoral process. In many areas of the country, this exclusion is aggravated by acts of physical, economic, and political intimidation. The Congress declares that, in order to enforce the guarantees of the Fourteenth and Fifteenth amendments to the United States Constitution, it is necessary to eliminate such discrimination by prohibiting English-only elections, and by prescribing other remedial devices.[108]

Additionally, Congress made the continued use of English-only election materials when the 5% trigger was met *"prima facie"* evidence that a political subdivision needed to be under federal supervision.[109] The 1975 Amendments also broadened coverage under the Act so as to include American Indians, Asian-Americans, Alaskan natives, and those of Spanish heritage in addition to African-Americans for whom the Voting Rights Act was originally intended.[110]

Defining the right to vote

In 1973, Puerto Ricans voters in Chicago brought a lawsuit under the Voting Rights Act and its Amendments to compel the City Board of Election Commissioners to provide them with ballot *assistance* in Spanish.[111] The district court had ordered the election commissioners to print Spanish language translations of directions for using voting machines to be pasted above English instructions on specimen ballots; posters in Spanish about assistance available to voters and cards in Spanish describing model voting machines were to be placed in polling places within eleven wards. Defendants were to make all "reasonable efforts" to appoint election judges who are bilingual in English and Spanish to fill vacancies in designated precincts and to place bilingual special judges in specified polling places.

Defendants complied with the court's order as to the previously-held November elections, but appealed those parts of the order that endured beyond November.

The court found that the combined effect of the Voting Rights Act of 1965 and the 1970 Amendments was to prohibit the "[s]tates from conditioning the right to vote of persons who attended any number of years of school in Puerto Rico on their ability to read or understand the English language."[112]

The question before the court was essentially "what is the right to vote?" The court relied on cases such as *Garza v. Smith*,[113] *US v. Louisiana*,[114] and *US v. Mississippi*,[115] where the courts found constitutional or statutory rights to cast "informed votes" as critical to actually implementing a right to vote. The *Garza* court had expanded the concept of the right to vote beyond the mechanistic pulling of a lever: the right to vote must include "the right to be informed as to which mark on the ballot, or lever on the voting machine, will effectuate the voter's political choice."[116] The *Kusper* court agreed:

> [w]e agree with the interpretation of the cases above that "the right to vote" encompasses the right to an effective vote. If a person who cannot read English is entitled to oral assistance, if a Negro is entitled to correction of erroneous instructions, so a Spanish-speaking Puerto Rican is entitled to assistance in the language he can read or understand.[117]

Since *Kusper*, the cases that have been decided have reiterated the need for extensive bilingual assistance in those municipalities covered by the Voting Rights Act. In *Torres v. Sachs*,[118] the court ordered New York City to provide its Spanish-dominant voters with bilingual written materials promulgated to voters or prospective voters in connection with the election process: bilingual ballots, bilingual election officials at the headquarters for the Board of Elections in each county and at polling places and places of registration, conspicuous signs at all polling places and places of registration indicating in Spanish that election officials are available to assist Spanish-speaking voters or registrants and that bilingual printed materials are available, and the publication of elections in all media "proportionately in a way that reflects the language characteristics of plaintiffs."[119]

The petition process

In *Gerena-Valentin v. Koch*,[120] the requirements of the Voting Rights Act were not read so broadly as to cover the petition process. Here, plaintiff, a City Council candidate, complained that New York City did not provide bilingual aid to voters or potential petition signatories, nor translate the petitions for the Board of Elections. The City did, however, provide bilingual aid to voters at the polling places for all elections. For the district court:

> [d]efendants provide the essential services for the exercise of Hispanic voters' franchises. The failure to provide bilingual petitions does not by itself deprive the Hispanic community of their right to vote, particularly where, as here the plaintiffs have not made any effort on their own to provide the bilingual aid they now request.[121]

For the court, the right to vote was what was meant to be protected by the Act and not necessarily a broader right to the petition process.

This distinction was made explicit in *Montero v. Meyer*,[122] where a citizen-initiated petition drive to make English the official language of Colorado was at issue. There, plaintiffs asserted that the Voting Rights Act required that bilingual petitions be used in certain counties in Colorado that met the threshold language-concentration requirements of the Act. The district court had found that the Act applied to initiative petitions. The appeals court, however, disagreed. The Act, reasoned the court, applies only to voting or registering to vote. To vote involves picking one candidate over another or for or against something. "Thus, applying the concept of voting to a process which provides no choice defies the commonly accepted usage of the term."[123] The initiative process that requires the signing of a petition if a voter agrees with it, but does not otherwise require the expression of a choice, is just such a process. The court found that the "signing of an initiated petition is not voting."[124]

Also important to the analysis was the fact that the Act applies to actions taken by the states themselves and not to actions taken by private citizens. Although the state does have a role to play in the initiative process it is a ministerial one only; it cannot affect the initiated measure, it only exists in this regard to make sure that the requisite signatures have been gathered correctly and prepares the petition for circulation. "Under the Colorado constitution," found the court, "one who circulates an initiative petition exercises an individual right solely for the circulator and not for the state."[125]

In 1989, the same issue arose in *Delgado v. Smith*,[126] where the petitions at issue were again to make English the official language of Florida.[127] Here, plaintiffs argued that the US Attorney General's Guidelines on implementing the language provisions of the Act that enumerated "petitions" as materials to be translated were conclusive on this issue. The court, however, disagreed by finding that, while agency interpretations of statutes are generally given much deference, here the agencies charged with implementing the Act are the affected jurisdictions themselves; that is, the states and or counties who are charged with providing multilingual assistance. The Attorney General's opinion as to what documents ought to be translated would be treated as advisory only.

Interestingly, given the recent litigation in Arizona concerning the First Amendment implications of a state-wide English-only law, discussed in Chapter 2, the *Delgado* court commented on the First Amendment implications of requiring the petition initiators to provide bilingual petitions. The initiative process is "core political speech," stated the court, and as such cannot be subjected to onerous governmental regulation:

> We are ... reluctant to construe a federal statute to mandate the imposition of a substantial burden on the right of political association, particularly where the clear language of the Act does not so require. It is hard to imagine that in passing the Act, Congress could have intended that private citizens seeking to further

their own political goals through the initiative petition process be subject to specific language requirements.[128]

Again, as in Colorado, the court found that the state had no real role in the initiative process sufficient to justify coverage by the Act: "[t]he state does not initiate the petition, does not draft the language of the petition, does not address the merits of the proposal, and does not participate in any way in the circulation of the petition or in the collection of signatures."[129]

There was, however, a dissent in *Delgado* written by Judge Anderson that relied on the need for a broad reading of the statute that would include the petition process as part of the electoral process covered by the Act. The Attorney General's opinion would have been given greater deference by the dissent. The point of the dissent was essentially that the Voting Rights Act was meant to empower language minorities so that they would stand on the same footing, as far as possible, with English-dominant voters with respect to the entire electoral process. The petition process is certainly a part of that electoral process, albeit a preliminary one. The dissent was also unpersuaded that imposing a bilingual requirement would undermine the petition-creators' First Amendment rights. The court found that:

> [c]learly the substance of the speech to be communicated is not affected by the Spanish translation of the proposal.... The bilingual requirement is a reasonable regulation to promote elector understanding, precisely like the other regulations adopted by Florida governing the form of initiative petitions.[130]

Not mentioned by the dissent but forming an ironic background to these cases is the fact that the very voters being excluded from the petition process, or who could be misled by petition circulators, are the Spanish-dominant voters who would be most affected by the English-only measure. It would seem that a statute, like the Voting Rights Act, created to protect the voting interests of language minorities should be read broadly enough to ensure that language minorities are not excluded from a petition drive that affects their interests more than anyone else's.

Investigating voter fraud

Olagues v. Russoniello,[131] decided in 1986, represents a kind of hybrid case putting voting rights within the Equal Protection Clause framework that nicely highlights the kind of issues involved with enfranchising language minorities in a way ignored by the courts in *Montero* and *Delgado*. This action was brought to challenge the US Attorney's investigation into possible voter fraud involving foreign-born voters requesting bilingual ballots. The investigation targeted recently-registered, foreign-born voters who requested bilingual ballots. The appellants, the voters, contended that the investigation was a violation of their rights under the Voting Rights Act and under the First Amendment, Equal Protection and Due Process Clauses of the Fifth and Fourteenth Amendments. In determining the appropriate level of scrutiny under the Equal Protection Clause, the court needed to determine whether the class of people targeted by the US Attorney was a suspect class. The district court had analyzed the case by defining the classification solely on the basis of language and found that the classification did not involve a suspect class. Strict scrutiny was not employed.

The *Olagues* court, however, employed a more nuanced analysis that addressed the fact that the intersection of language, ethnicity, and national origin could produce a class deserving of special protection. Since the challenged investigation targeted recently registered, foreign-born voters who requested bilingual ballots and bilingual ballots are only available in English and Chinese, the investigation, as a practical matter, targeted Spanish-speaking and Chinese-speaking immigrants.

The indicia of a "suspect class," said the court, is whether the class is "saddled with such disabilities, or subjected to such a history of purposeful unequal treatment, or relegated to such a position of political powerlessness as to command extraordinary protection from majoritarian political processes."[132] The presence of an immutable characteristic is not essential, said the court, as the Supreme Court has found aliens to be a suspect class. The discrimination faced by linguistic minorities was recognized by Congress, said the court, in the enactment of the Voting Rights Act. Even so, the court did not use this as a basis for finding that linguistic minorities, in and of themselves, were a suspect class. Instead, the court connected language to ethnicity to get to a more traditional protection on the basis of national origin: "[j]ust as persons of different ethnic groups are distinguished by surnames ... persons of different nationalities are often distinguished by a foreign language."[133] The court took the final step of finding that the instant discrimination, here against "Hispanics" and the Chinese, historic victims of discrimination, should be held to a strict level of scrutiny.

The court then strove to explain its ruling in comparison to cases such as *Soberal-Perez v. Heckler*[134] and *Garcia v. Gloor*[135] (discussed in Chapters 8 and 4), where language-discrimination claims in the social services and employment contexts were not successful. Here, the court said it was not being asked to strike down a generalized governmental preference for English:

> [t]he instant case as a practical matter, however, involves a specific classification of Spanish-speaking and Chinese-speaking immigrants. Thus, while a non-English-speaking classification is facially neutral with respect to ethnic group classification, the classification challenged here is not, because for all practical purposes it is a classification based on race and national origin. Therefore, we hold that the three characteristics, i.e. foreign-born voter, recently registered voter, and bilingual ballot voter, taken together in the instant case form a class that has the traditional indicia of a suspect classification based on race and national origin.[136]

An argument for a constitutional right to bilingual voting materials

Despite the common-sense force of Douglas' dissent in *Cardona*, a constitutional right to bilingual ballots has not yet been articulated. Applying current equal protection jurisprudence to the issue, however, would indicate that grounding such a right in the Constitution would be legitimate if not inevitable. For instance, voting is considered a fundamental right that cannot be limited without a compelling governmental purpose and, if it must be limited, then the means used must be "narrowly tailored" to address a specific concern and not run roughshod over voting rights. Once a state acts to make voting materials, including ballots, available in English, it will need to make them available in other languages absent a showing of a compelling reason. As one commentator has said: "[b]ecause the states have chosen to facilitate the right to vote for some it is incumbent on the states to facilitate that right for all."[137]

States could put various arguments, such as promoting a monolingual government, or claim the excessive cost of providing multilingual ballots and voting materials or (as New York did) distinguish between the voting-readiness of language-minority literates and English literates. None of these rationales, however, overcomes equal protection barriers. In order for English-only elections to be used as a method to promote a monolingual government, assuming that there were not already First Amendment problems with that approach,[138] the state would have to show that this method was the most "narrowly tailored" approach possible to meet those needs. Of course that could not be shown, since there is no empirical data to show that language minorities are more likely to abandon their mother tongues if they are unable to vote. Instead, the data in studies that exist show only that (1) language minority citizens are simply less likely to vote if not given multilingual assistance and (2) that, despite the existence of multilingual ballots since 1965, language minorities are acquiring English at a faster rate than previous generations.[139]

As for allegations of excessive cost, the judiciary has rarely accepted fiscal constraints as a response to equal protection challenges.[140] Even if it would in these circumstances, a study carried out by the US General Accounting Office of the costs incurred by jurisdictions providing multilingual assistance for the November 4, 1984 elections, revealed that in 83 jurisdictions the costs of election administrated did not exceed 7.6% of the total costs.[141] In any case, there may be legitimate ways for states to conserve funds if, for instance, very small language-minority groups were not concentrated together in sufficient numbers to otherwise justify the printing of multilingual ballots. In such cases, states could target the use of trained and oath-taking translators to assist these smaller groups.

Finally, New York's argument on the distinctions in the scope of the political education of potential English-dominant versus language-minority voters would not go far today when illiterate voters have been allowed to vote under the Voting Rights Act in many jurisdictions since 1965 and nationally since 1975. For many different reasons, the US political system may be disappointing to some, but no one has yet seriously blamed the existence of bad political leaders on the ability of the illiterate to vote.

CONCLUSION

Immigration, naturalization, and voting are defining issues for a country. It is in these areas that a country decides its ideology, whose interests it will protect, whom it will allow to be powerful. It is also a testing ground for inclusiveness and tolerance. US policy in the immigration area has swung from its *laissez faire* attitude of the early nineteenth century to one where immigrants are distrusted, feared, and blamed for a host of social ills. When a group is feared, efforts to contain and limit its power and effect on a country often find their way into legislation.

In this chapter we can see the impact of the trajectory towards xenophobia. The English literacy requirement in the naturalization process and in the voting arena really grew out of the nineteenth and twentieth centuries' anxieties over immigration, war, and economic woes at a time when US "confidence" in its economic and political structures and assimilative ability was low.[142]

Fortunately, civil rights struggles have been victorious in actually establishing the concept of voting rights and then extending it beyond actual physical access to the booth to the need for meaningful access. So in the voting rights area we have seen the country move from effectively blocking minority access to voting to federal legislation that not only ensures physical access to the booth, but, for language minorities, ensures access that is linguistically appropriate and therefore genuine. Clearly, more work needs to be done in voting rights: a constitutional right to bilingual ballots can be justified and would ensure that the rights of language minorities are not beholden to special political interests.

Such victories, however, are not reflected in the naturalization arena. When the federal courts finally came around to understanding the discriminatory nature of the state literacy tests for voting, they were stricken down as unconstitutional. No such fate awaits the English literacy requirement for naturalization. The distinction seems basic: restraints on voting affects citizens, all standing on the same footing, differently. As a political matter, differential treatment needs to be justified; differential treatment that can be justified only with reference to blatantly racist policies will not be tolerated.

Naturalization, however, affects those who have not yet been admitted into the body politic. Who exactly is admitted implicates a political judgement about what characteristics the country deems important enough to require of its citizenry. Courts have justified their reluctance to review congressional action in this area because it essentially involves a judgment call not about how citizens can be treated but about how those who are not yet citizens, and who can therefore be regulated in different ways, can be treated. The political nature of the area should not really be a stumbling point for courts since they often review legislative action in political areas. Voting rights, for instance, is a quintessentially political area. If courts were to allow the political nature of the questions involved in voting to act as a barrier for review, then literacy tests might still be with us. It is the nature of who is being regulated, citizens versus non-citizens, and the sense that a nation owes more protections to the citizen, that is operative. Advocates, however, need not let courts shrug off their responsibilities so easily: even naturalization policies can be and ought to be subjected to searching judicial review.

Notes

1. Peter J. Spiro, *Questioning Barriers to Naturalization*, 13 GEO. IMMIGR. L. J. 479 (1999).
2. *See* Arthur W. Bromage, *Literacy and the Electorate*, 24 THE AMERICAN POLITICAL SCIENCE REVIEW 946 (1930).
3. *Id.* at 947.
4. John Higham, STRANGERS IN THE LAND: PATTERNS OF AMERICAN NATIVISM 1860–1925 (Atheneum, New York, 1965) at 65.
5. *Id.* at 951.
6. *Supra,* note 2 at 952.
7. *Id.* at 954.
8. *Supra,* note 4, at 97.
9. *Id.* at 97–105.
10. *See* Bill Ong Hing, *Beyond the Rhetoric of Assimilation and Cultural Pluralism: Addressing the Tension of Separatism and Conflict in an Immigration-Driven Multiracial Society,* 81 CAL. L. REV. 863, 917 (1993).
11. *Supra,* note 4 at 101.
12. *Id.* at 103.
13. *Id.* at 104–105.
14. *Id.* at 367 n. 43.
15. *Supra,* note 1 at n. 53.
16. IMMIGRATION ACT OF 1907, C1134, 34 Stat. (1907).
17. *Petition of Katz,* 21 F2d 867 (ED Mich. 1927).
18. *Id.* at 867.
19. *Id.* at 871.
20. Juan F. Perea, *Demography and Distrust: An Essay on American Language, Cultural Pluralism and Official English,* 77 MINN. LAW REV. 269, 334 (1992).
21. *Id.*
22. *Id.*
23. *Id.* at 334–35.
24. *Supra,* note 4 at 193.
25. *Id.* at 203.
26. *Id.* at 308.
27. *Id.* at 304–305.
28. *Id.* at 305.
29. *Id.* at 302.
30. *Id.* at 309.
31. *Id.*
32. *Id.* at 310–311.
33. *Supra,* note 2 at 964.
34. Arnold H. Leibowitz, *English Literacy: Legal Sanction for Discrimination,* 45 NOTRE DAME LAWYER 7, n. 197 (1969).

35. *Infra*, note 78, *Katzenbach v. Morgan*, 384 US at 656 n.14.

36. *Supra*, note 34 at n.194.

37. *Id.*

38. *Id.*

39. Patrick A. McCarran, *The Internal Security Act of 1950*, 12 Univ. Pitt. L. Rev. 481 (1951).

40. Ricardo Gonzalez Cedillo, *A Constitutional Analysis of the English Literacy Requirement of the Naturalization Act* 14 St Mary's L. J. 899, 928–929 (1983).

41. 8 USC §1423(a)(1). The other qualifications for citizenship are a five year residency requirement, the passage of a civics exam, an attachment to the principles of the US Constitution, and being "disposed to the good order and happiness of the United States." There are many different avenues open to become a US citizen, not all of which require literacy in English. The most popular, called "Category 1," requires foreign nationals to first become legal permanent residents of the US through legal and continuous residence in the US. It is this category of citizenship, and its requirements for naturalization, which will be discussed in this chapter. Although the statutory requirements were not changed until 1950, as noted earlier, the courts had already been moving in the direction of tightening naturalization requirements. For instance, in *In re Swenson*, 61 FSupp 376 (D Or. 1945). The trial court denied the citizenship application of a 67-year-old man who had been in the country for 44 years. The immigration agency had recommended that he be admitted. The court, however, after examining the petitioner in open court, concluded that he would not be admitted as a citizen since he was of questionable moral character. Years previously, Mr Swenson had been charged with making moonshine, had been driving while intoxicated in about 1924 and had been convicted of "drunkenness" three times in the previous five years. Additionally, Swenson could not speak English well. The court stated:

   > [t]he ability to mumble a few common English words and banal expressions in a foreign accent, and to understand a few simple questions, or directions, does not demonstrate the capacity to speak English in connection with a requirement of attachment to the principles of the federal Constitution. (*Id.* at 376–77)

42. 8 USC §1423(a)(1).

43. *Id.* There are exemptions from the English literacy requirement for: (a) applicants over 50 years old who have been lawfully residing in the US for at least 20 years; (b) applicants over 55 years old who have been lawfully residing in the US for at least 15 years; and (c) applicants who are incapable due to mental or physical impairment to meet the literacy test.

44. *See supra*, note 1 at n. 35. A 1998 study commissioned by the Immigration and Naturalization Service found that, of 7,843 naturalization petitions filed, 34% of all denials were because of failure on the language and civics test. According to Spiro, the number may be even higher since applicants who fail the test initially can re-take the test and are considered "continued." Twenty-five percent of those continued are on account of failure on one of the tests. *See also* Ricardo Gonzalez Cedillo, *A Constitutional Analysis of the English Literacy Requirement of the Naturalization Act.* 14 St Mary's L. J. 899 (1983).

45. *See supra*, note 20; *see also supra*, note 34.

46. 8 CFR §312.2 (c)(ii).

47. *Trujillo-Hernandez v. Farrell*, 503 F2d 954 (5th Cir 1974).

48. *Id.* at 955.

49. *Id.*

50. *Fiallo v. Bell*, 9 S. Ct. 1473, 1478 (1977); *accord, The Chinese Exclusion Case*, 130 US 581 (1889).

51. Laurence H. Tribe, AMERICAN CONSTITUTIONAL LAW (The Foundation Press, Mineola, New York, 1978).
52. *Nishimura Ekin v. US*, 142 US 651, 659 (1892).
53. *See supra*, note 1 at 489–497.
54. *Supra*, note 40 at 901.
55. *Id.* at 923. *See also* Steve Roseberg, *The Protection of Aliens from Discriminatory Treatment by the National Government*, 1977 SUP. CT REV. 275, 327.
56. *See Carrington v. Rash*, 380 US 89 (1965).
57. *Pope v. Williams*, 193 US 621, 632 (1904).
58. *Lassiter v. Northampton County Board of Elections*, 360 US 45 (1959).
59. *Id.* at 50 (citation omitted).
60. *Id.* at 53–54.
61. *United States v. Mississippi*, 380 US 128 (1965).
62. *United States v. Louisiana*, 380 US 145 (1965).
63. *Id.* at 151.
64. Alabama, Georgia, Louisiana, Mississippi, South Carolina, Virginia, and certain counties in Arizona, Hawaii and North Carolina, must have federally supervised voter registration and elections for five years; these are called "§5 jurisdictions."
65. *See South Carolina v. Katzenbach*, 383 US 301 (1966).
66. *Id.*
67. *Oregon v. Mitchell*, 400 US 112, 127 (1970).
68. *Id.* at 127–128 (citations omitted).
69. *See supra*, note 65 at 308.
70. *Id.* at 309.
71. *Id.* at 327.
72. 384 US 641 (1966).
73. 384 US 672 (1966).
74. 42 USC §1973(b)(f).
75. *Supra*, note 72 at 647 n. 3.
76. *Comacho v. Doe*, 7 NY 762 (1959).
77. *See supra*, note 72.
78. *Morgan v. Katzenbach*, 247 Fsupp 196 (DDC 1965), *rev'd*, *Katzenbach v. Morgan*, 384 US 641 (1966).
79. 248 FSupp 316 (WDNY 1965).
80. *Id.* at 314.
81. *Id.* at 323.
82. *Id.*
83. *Katzenbach v. Morgan*, 384 US 641 at 650.
84. *Id.* (citation omitted).
85. *Id.*
86. *Id.* at 652 (citations omitted).
87. *Id.*
88. *Id.* at 654.
89. *Id.* at 655.
90. *Id.* at 656.

91. *Roschen v. Ward,* 279 US 337, 339 (1929).
92. *Supra,* note 83 at 658.
93. *Id.* at 666.
94. *Id.* at 667 (J. Harlan dissenting).
95. *Id.* at 669 (J. Harlan dissenting) (internal quotations and citations omitted).
96. *Id.* at 667.
97. *Supra,* note 65 at 326.
98. *Supra,* note 34 at 33.
99. 384 US 672 (1966).
100. *Id.* at 675.
101. *Id.*
102. *Id.* at 676.
103. *Id.* at 676–77.
104. *Katzenbach,* 384 US 641, 663 (the dissent in *Cardona* is reported within the *Katzenbach* opinion).
105. *Id.*
106. The 1992 Voting Rights Language Assistance Act extended the bilingual election requirements until 2007 and also specified that a political subdivision would be required to meet the bilingual requirements, not only if the 5% trigger was met but, alternatively, if the political subdivision contains an Indian reservation, and "more than 5% of the American or Alaska Native citizens of voting age within the Indian Reservation are members of a single language minority and are limited English proficient; and ... the illiteracy rate of the citizens in the language minority as a group is higher than the national illiteracy rate." 42 USC §1973 aa(b)(2)(A)(i)(III)-(ii).
107. 42 USC §1973 (b)(f). Although the 5% language minority trigger appears to be comprehensive enough, it does reflect a weakness in the legislation. For instance, only language minorities that are also racial and ethnic minorities are protected by the Act whereas diverse communities with substantial numbers of language minorities are not covered by the Act. Those groups that are covered include: Japanese, Chinese, Filipinos, Korean, Vietnamese, Asian-Indian, Spanish, American-Indian, Eskimo, Aleut, and Hawaiian. Hundreds of geographical communities are covered, but there are anomalies. For instance, San Francisco county is not required under *federal* law to provide bilingual ballots in Spanish but only in Chinese. *See The Attorney General's Language Minority Guidelines,* 28 CFR Part 55, June 15, 2000.
108. 42 USC §1973(b)(f)(c).
109. 42 USC §1973(b)(f)(3).
110. Voting Rights Act Amendments, 42 USC §1973b (1975).
111. *Puerto Rican Organization for Political Action v. Kusper,* 490 F2d 575 (7th Cir 1973).
112. *Id.* at 579.
113. 320 FSupp 131 (WD Tex. 1970).
114. 265 FSupp 703 (ED LA 1966).
115. 256 FSupp 344 (SD Miss. 1966).
116. *Supra,* note 113 at 136.
117. *Supra,* note 111 at 580. Interesting to note, however, the court's paternalistic attitude toward mother tongue retention by Puerto Ricans: "Puerto Ricans are not required, as are immigrants from foreign countries, to learn English before they have the right to vote as US citizens. *Their plight is as much a result of government policy as is the plight of*

Negroes trying to pass literacy tests in states which had subjected them to segregated, unequal school systems." Id. at 578. (emphasis added) (Note and citation omitted).

118. 381 FSupp 309 (SDNY 1974).

119. *Id.* at 313.

120. 523 Fsupp 176 (SDNY 1981).

121. *Id.* at 177.

122. 861 F2d 603 (10th Cir 1988).

123. *Id.* at 607.

124. *Id.*

125. *Id.* at 609.

126. 861 F2d 1489, (11th Cir) *rehrg. den. en banc,* 865 F2d 1274, *cert. den.,* 492 US 918 (1989).

127. *See also, Zaldivar v. City of Los Angeles,* 590 FSupp 852 (CD Cal. 1984). *Zaldivar v. City of Los Angeles,* 780 F2d 823 (9th Cir 1986) (where the district court held that the recall petition process was not part of the "electoral process" and where the Circuit Court suggested in dictum that the petition process probably was part of the electoral process).

128. *Supra,* note 126 at 1495.

129. *Id.* at 1497.

130. *Id.* at 1500 n.5 (Anderson, J. dissenting).

131. 797 F2d 1511 (9th Cir 1986).

132. *Id.* at 1520.

133. *Id.* at 1520–1521.

134. Endnote Text

135. 618 F2d 264 (5th Cir 1980).

136. *Supra,* note 131 at 1521.

137. Sandra Guerra, *Voting Rights and the Constitution: The Disenfranchisement of Non-English Speaking Citizens,* 97 YALE L. J. 1419 (1988).

138. *See* discussion of *Yniguez v. Mofford,* Chapter 2.

139. *See* R. Brischetto (ed.), BILINGUAL ELECTIONS AT WORK IN THE SOUTHWEST (MALDEF, 1982).

140. *See Shapiro v. Thompson,* 394 US 618 (1969); *Memorial Hospital v. Maricopa County,* 415 US 250 (1974); *Frontiero v. Richardson,* 411 US 677 (1973).

141. GAO Rep., *Bilingual Voting Assistance: Costs of and Use During the November 1984 General Election* (1986).

142. *See supra,* note 4, on "loss of confidence" at 158–193.

Chapter 4
Language Rights in the Workplace: Negotiating Boundaries Within Close Spaces

INTRODUCTION

The high rate of immigration to the US at the end of the twentieth century affects not only domestic and social public policies but the workforce as well. Its impact can be felt in all areas of employment law and policy, from the application of anti-discrimination statutes to relatively new discriminatory employment practices such as English-only workplace rules, to the growth of a body of law on accent discrimination.

Bilingual employees, a growing but decidedly minority population, are prized by their employers for their language abilities – they can communicate with consumers of minority communities or with international companies and can handle the English required by other aspects of their jobs, usually communicating with their employers or supervisors who speak only English. So, while in the school system being bilingual is either disparaged or ignored, in the business world, being bilingual can carry definite economic benefits.

However, monolingual speakers of other languages do not have the same language capital as their bilingual counterparts. They are usually found performing low-skilled or manual labor for little money. Yet their contributions to the economic life of the nation, while neglected or belittled, is real and tangible – they wash the dishes, work in the factories, mow the lawns, clean the offices, and do the back-breaking remains of work left by unionized construction and maintenance workers.

Whether bilingual or monolingual in languages other than English, the spaces in which language-minority workers perform their work are oftentimes fraught with

117

tension. Not only does their presence exacerbate the usual debate about the role of immigrants in the economy, but the issue of the language the workers speak, even amongst themselves, or especially amongst themselves, has been the subject of bitterness, animosity, regulation, and litigation.

This chapter will discuss Title VII of the Civil Rights Act of 1964, which prohibits private employer discrimination and its use to combat English-only workplace rules. The burdens of proof under Title VII as well as the guidelines developed by the Equal Employment Opportunities Commission (EEOC) will be detailed. The major cases in this area, especially *Garcia v. Gloor*[1] and *Garcia v. Spun Steak*[2], will be presented in detail.

The other major issues covered in this chapter are the compensation due bilingual employees when their bilingualism is used for the benefit of the employer, accent discrimination, and language rights within the labor union context. There have been significant developments in the area of language rights within the employment and labor context; some, but not all of it, has been positive. The true test of the power of language-minority worker rights will probably come, not in the legal field, with courts often belatedly reacting to what is already established policy, but in the work spaces themselves and in union meeting halls where employers, employees and labor leadership grapple with some of the most complex civil rights issues facing the nation.

ENGLISH-ONLY WORKPLACE RULES: A NEW KIND OF DISCRIMINATION FOR A NEW KIND OF WORKFORCE

The principal manifestation of the ambivalence felt toward language-minority workers has been the proliferation of English-only workplace rules enforced by employers of bilingual employees. Unlike state-wide or public English-only laws, these rules can be easily passed, explicitly, consciously, and in writing by an employer without company-wide discussion. They may just as easily be passed, however, informally and almost covertly with a supervisor simply verbally chastising employees for speaking a language other than English. Either way, a real and oppressive English-only workplace rule is in effect that may be challenged in court.

Title VII and the EEOC Guidelines: The statutory framework

Language rights in the workplace are principally governed by Title VII of the Civil Rights Act of 1964. Sections 703(a)(1) and (2) of Title VII provide that:

(a) It shall be an unlawful employment practice for an employer

(1) to fail or refuse to hire or to discharge any individual, or otherwise to discriminate against any individual with respect to his compensation, terms, conditions, or privileges of employment, because of such individual's race, color, religion, sex or national origin; or

(2) to limit, segregate, or classify his employees or applicants for employment in any way which would deprive or tend to deprive any individual of employment opportunities or otherwise adversely affect his status as an employee, because of such individual's race, color, religion, sex, or national origin.[3]

Title VII applies to private employers, state and local government employers, labor organizations and employment agencies.[4]

Cases can be brought under Title VII under two distinct theories: *disparate treatment* or *disparate impact*. Under a disparate treatment case, an employee would allege actions by the employer that would essentially amount to intentional discrimination – that she was treated differently than similarly situated employees by the employer *because of* her race, color, ethnicity or national origin or gender. Although disparate treatment cases are hard to win, success is possible.

Under a test in *McDonell Douglas Corp. v. Green,*[5] the Supreme Court attempted to set up an analytical paradigm that would allow plaintiffs to prove intentional discrimination even if they did not have direct evidence of discrimination. Under *McDonell Douglas,* a plaintiff must first establish a *prima facie* case of discrimination. If the plaintiff establishes a *prima facie* case, the burden then shifts to the defendant to articulate a legitimate non-discriminatory reason for its employment decision. The employer's justification in disparate treatment cases must be a significant one and must rise to the level of a *bona fide occupational qualification*. Then, in order to prevail, the plaintiff must demonstrate that the employer's alleged reason for the adverse employment decision is, more likely than not, a pretext for another motive which is discriminatory.[6] This last part requires that a plaintiff show two things: that the employer's rationale is false or unworthy of belief, perhaps because it simply makes no business sense or goes against the weight of the evidence. For instance, if an employer asserts that an employee was fired for poor performance but the employee's performance reviews were always satisfactory, the employer's reason appears pre-textual. The second portion of this burden, however, requires that plaintiffs also show that the *real* reason for the adverse employment action was, more likely than not, racial discrimination. This is an increased burden on the plaintiff that was articulated by the Supreme Court in 1995 in *St. Mary's Honor Ctr. v. Hicks,*[7] and requires that more than pretext alone be shown; it is a requirement of "pretext plus."

Until the Supreme Court decided the case *Price-Waterhouse v. Hopkins,*[8] the *McDonell Douglas* paradigm reigned. However, in *Price-Waterhouse* the Court came up with a new analytical framework for "mixed motive" cases. These are situations in which there were multiple reasons for the adverse employment decision, lawful and unlawful. *McDonell Douglas* addressed only the situation in which there was a single, unlawful motive for the challenged action. With *Price-Waterhouse,* the Supreme Court decided that, in order to succeed in court, a "plaintiff would have to show that the unlawful reason was the motivating factor" for the employment decision. An employer could escape liability even though discriminatory animus was proven by showing that it would have made the same decision regardless of the discrimination. There was such a public outcry over the *Price-Waterhouse* decision that Congress passed the Civil Rights Act of 1991 reversing the Supreme Court's decision. Under the 1991 Civil Rights Act a plaintiff can establish "an unlawful employment practice" by showing that "race, color, religion, sex or national origin was a motivating factor for any employment practice, even though other factors also motivated the practice."[9]

Although the evidence-shifting paradigm described above appears to change the burden of proof from one side to the other, the ultimate burden of persuading the judge or jury that the employer intentionally discriminated is always on the plaintiff.[10] The burden the plaintiff must carry in such cases is a heavy one, as she must allege specific facts that establish the existence of a *prima facie* case; failure to do so can end in the early dismissal of the case with a summary judgment for the defendant.

Fortunately, plaintiffs can also proceed under a disparate impact theory as well. Here as with Title VI disparate impact cases, the attack is made on a policy, procedure, rule or action that appears to be non-discriminatory on its face, yet has a disproportionately negative impact on a member of a protected group. "[I]mpact analysis is designed to implement Congressional concern with the 'consequences of employment practices, not simply the motivation.'"[11] For "it is well settled that Title VII is concerned not only with intentional discrimination, but also with employment practices and policies that lead to disparities in the treatment of classes of workers."[12]

In 1971, the Supreme Court articulated a disparate impact theory of employment discrimination making it much easier for employees to prevail against discriminating employers than a disparate treatment theory alone would allow.[13] The employer must justify the continued use of the practice with a business necessity. Even if the employer can establish business necessity, however, the employee can still win by showing that there was a less discriminatory alternative available to the employer that would also meet his business requirements.[14] Under either theory, the basic question that the courts must determine is whether the employer engaged in conduct that impermissibly discriminated against certain persons.

EEOC Guidelines: Creating a space for national origin discrimination

As with Title VI, an administrative agency was created to enforce the statute, here, Title VII. At first, the agency, the EEOC, had the power only to investigate complaints brought to it, but it gained the power to affirmatively litigate cases and to subpoena documents and witnesses. Unlike the Office of Civil Rights charged with enforcing Title VI, which relies on reconciliation between parties and almost never litigates cases, the EEOC does in fact bring employers to court, and wins financial judgments against them. Indeed, a plaintiff looking to act under Title VII must begin her journey to court by first filing a complaint with the EEOC.[15]

While there is still much confusion in Title VI cases as to which category – race, ethnicity or national origin – is the best fit for language rights claims, under Title VII, the EEOC has defined "national origin discrimination" to specifically include language-based discrimination. The Guidelines, however, are not law and courts need not, and as will be seen below, do not always accord them deference. Indeed, the legislative history of Title VII does not address whether language is considered a characteristic of national origin. For instance, during congressional debates, Representative Roosevelt stated: "[m]ay I just make very clear that 'national origin' means national. It means the country which you or your forbears came from.... " Representative Dent said: "[n]ational origin, of course, has nothing to do with color, religion, or the race of the individual. A man may have migrated here from Great Britain and still be a colored person."[16]

In 1980, the EEOC adopted *Guidelines on Discrimination Because of National Origin*,[17] which defines national-origin discrimination broadly as including, but not limited to, "the denial of equal employment opportunity because of an individual's or his or her ancestor's place of origin; or because an individual has the physical, cultural or linguistic characteristics of a national origin group."[18]

The EEOC's Guidelines go on to specifically address "English-only rules" or employer policies or rules, written or unwritten, that prohibit the speaking of languages other than English in the workplace. The EEOC has explained that it believes "an individual's primary language is often an essential national origin characteristic" and that a rule requiring employees to speak only English at all times in the workplace is a burdensome term and condition of employment that violates Title VII except in limited circumstances.[19] The EEOC then divided English-only rules into two categories:

(1) those that were blanket prohibitions on the speaking of languages other than English which applied to employees at all times that they were on the employer's premises and
(2) those that prohibited languages other than English only at specified times.

The first kind would be presumptively discriminatory and no employer rationale would probably be able to justify the existence of such a rule. The second could be saved by the employer's offer of a "business necessity" for the rule; the rule was necessary for the performance of the job at issue or operation of the business. An employer that enforces an English-only rule without first informing its employees about the rule and consequences for not adhering to it would not be able to justify the existence of the rule; the rule obviously could only be justified as a business necessity if the employees know about and are expected to abide by the rule.

The EEOC has stated that:

[i]n recognition of the fact that the primary language of an individual is often an essential national origin characteristic, the Commission will presume that rules requiring employees to speak only English in the workplace adversely affect an individual's employment opportunities on the basis of national origin where that individual's primary language is not English.[20]

The EEOC assumes that an English-only rule that is effective at all times while at the workplace is a "burdensome term and condition of employment that disadvantages an individual's employment opportunities," therefore the EEOC will "closely scrutinize" such a rule.[21] Such a rule will rarely if ever pass such scrutiny, for an employer would be hard pressed to find a reason why its employees must speak only English at all times, including during personal conversations or time away from work. Essentially, there will be no legitimate business reason for such overly-broad rules.

An employee can bring an action under Title VII for the existence of an English-only rule, for retaliation if the employee opposed the rule and was adversely treated by the employer because of that opposition, or may use the existence of the rule as evidence of discriminatory animus by the employer. A plaintiff may also claim that the existence of the rule contributed to a hostile work environment. To establish a *prima facie* case of harassment or hostile work environment under Title VII, an employee must prove that:

(1)   the employee belongs to a protected group;
(2)   the employee was subject to "unwelcome" harassment;
(3)   the harassment complained of was based on national origin;
(4)   the harassment affected a "term, condition, or privilege" of employment in that it was "sufficiently severe and pervasive to alter the condition of the employee's employment and create an abusive working environment"; and
(5)   the employer knew or should have known of the harassment and failed to take prompt remedial action.[22]

To establish such an environment, the plaintiff must show that the conduct alleged was so severe or pervasive that it is viewed both objectively by a reasonable person and subjectively by the employee as being abusive.[23] In making this determination a court should consider:

(1)   the frequency of the discriminatory conduct;
(2)   its severity;
(3)   whether it is physically threatening or humiliating, or a mere offensive utterance; and
(4)   whether it unreasonably interferes with an employee's work performance.

In one case, *Garcia v. Spun Steak*, which will be discussed in detail below, the court did suggest that the draconian enforcement of an English-only rule may alone be sufficient to create a hostile work environment. This is obviously a heavy burden for plaintiffs as a hostile environment implies a space "permeated with discriminatory intimidation, ridicule and insult."[24]

Applying disparate treatment theory to English-only rule cases

The EEOC has declared that an English-only rule is a term and condition of employment, the unequal application of which may constitute disparate treatment. The legality of an English-only rule may be analyzed under the disparate treatment theory if there is a claim that the rule is being applied differently to groups that are similarly situated. It should be noted that, while most English-only rule cases involve charges of national origin discrimination, Title VII also prohibits the disparate application of a rule on the basis of race. Such a disparate treatment scenario might arise where an English-only rule was applied only to Spanish-speaking workers, for instance.

Proof of disparate treatment might include comparative evidence, statistical evidence, or direct evidence of discriminatory motive. The point with evidence in disparate treatment cases is the search for indicators of improper motive. So, comparative evidence would consist of evidence that compared the complaining employee with other similarly situated employees to see if the aggrieved employee was indeed treated differently.[25] Statistical evidence may be used to establish that an English-only rule has been applied differently to similarly situated employees of a different race, sex or religion or national origin group. Direct evidence refers to the proverbial "smoking gun:" statements, for instance, by the employer's officials that indicate a bias against members of the plaintiff's ethnic or national origin group, or evidence that the employer did not take corrective action against its agent(s) who acted discriminatorily when the employer knew of or should have known of the actions. The EEOC offers the following example: "[s]tatements by the respondent that it prohibits speaking Spanish but not other languages during working hours 'because persons speaking Spanish are generally loud and disruptive' would constitute direct evidence of a discriminatory motive."[26]

Applying disparate impact theory to English-only rule cases

The EEOC has found that the disparate impact analysis applies to English-only workplace rules where:

(1)   the employer has a policy requiring English to be spoken in the workplace;
(2)   the rule is facially neutral, that is, it applies to all employees;
(3)   the rule disproportionately affects one protected group.

In *Saucedo v. Brothers Well Service, Inc.*,[27] the first federal district court case to deal with an English-only workplace rule, a disparate impact theory was used. "Brothers Well Service," the employer, was a small family-owned oil drilling company; the employees were engaged in what the court called "demanding, dangerous" work requiring "considerable teamwork."[28] John Saucedo was a Mexican-American employee of the company. He received no training for this work and in terms of company rules was simply told by the driller, John Erdelt, his immediate supervisor, that the general supervisor, "Doc," Holliday did not allow any "Mescian talk."[29] Erdelt did not tell Saucedo that the penalty for speaking Spanish was termination. Doc Holliday, through deposition, testified that he told all employees, but could not remember telling Saucedo specifically, that speaking Spanish on the job was "tantamount to quitting."[30] The court did not chose to credit Holliday's testimony and found that the only notice, such as it was, thoat Saucedo actually received about the English-only rule, was the ambiguous statement made by Erdelt.

Saucedo inadvertently violated the rule by using two words in Spanish to ask another bilingual employee where he wanted a particular metal part to be placed. The court went to some pains to detail that Saucedo was not involved in any dangerous well-drilling activity at the time and that his communication in Spanish resulted in no injuries. However, when the other Mexican-American employee argued with Holliday over the firing of Saucedo, Holliday physically attacked him. Nohavistza, the owner of Brothers, saw this and did nothing against Holliday but allowed Saucedo to be taken home and discharged. This was discrimination, found the court. Indeed, the court stated that "[a] rule that Spanish cannot be spoken on the job obviously has a disparate impact upon Mexican-American employees. Most Anglo-Americans obviously have no desire and no ability to speak foreign languages on or off the job."[31] Brothers neither attempted to justify nor negate the existence of the rule.

Bilingual and monolingual employees: Making distinctions without differences

Garcia v. Gloor: English-only before the EEOC Guidelines

The EEOC has explained that it undertook to revise its Guidelines to address English-only workplace rules, an action not taken since 1974, because of the Fifth Circuit's ruling in a case called *Garcia v. Gloor*,[32] where the court found that an employer's English-only rule did not discriminate against Mr Garcia, a bilingual employee of the company.

In *Garcia v. Gloor*, Hector Garcia, was hired by Gloor Lumber and Supply Co. as a salesman in Brownsville, Texas. Brownsville is, and was at the time of the litigation, a heavily Chicano/Latino area. In order to cater to this community, most of Gloor's employees were bilingual, although some who worked in the lumber yard spoke only Spanish. Mr Garcia testified in court that, while bilingual, Spanish was his primary language. Mr Garcia's duties included stocking his department and keeping it in order, assisting the department salespersons and selling lumber, hardware, and supplies. Gloor had a rule prohibiting employees from speaking Spanish on the job unless they were communicating with Spanish-speaking customers. The rule did not apply to the yard workers and did not apply to conversations held during work breaks. Garcia testified that he had difficulty following the English-only rule because of his preference for Spanish. On June 10, 1975 another Spanish-speaking employee asked about an item requested by a customer and Garcia replied in Spanish that the article was not available. Alton Gloor, an officer and stockholder of the company overheard the conversation, and had Garcia discharged.

The lower court found that Garcia had been fired for a number of reasons, one of which was violating the English-only rule "at every opportunity since the time of his hiring."[33] Gloor offered evidence to justify firing Garcia including reasons why the English-only rule was legitimate:

(1)   English-speaking customers objected to communications between employees that they couldn't understand;
(2)   it encouraged employees to become fluent in English;
(3)   supervisors, who did not speak Spanish would be better able to oversee the work of their subordinates.[34]

The lower court found that these were valid business reasons.

On appeal, the Fifth Circuit had to decide whether the enforcement of the English-only rule against Garcia and the other bilingual employees was a violation of Title VII. The court specifically noted that it would interpret the language of the statute itself and any developing case law and would not follow EEOC guidelines, since the agency had adopted "neither a regulation stating a standard for testing such language rules nor any general policy, presumed to be derived from the statute, prohibiting them."[35]

The court then determined that Title VII did not prohibit these rules since the protection against national origin discrimination was not the same as an action taken on the basis of language: "[n]either the statute nor common understanding equates national origin with the language that one chooses to speak."[36] Instead, the court reasoned that it was discrimination based on immutable characteristics that the statute was meant to prohibit.

> Save for religion, the discriminations on which the Act focuses its laser of prohibition are those that are either beyond the victim's power to alter ... or that impose a burden on an employee on one of the prohibited bases. No one can change his place of birth (national origin), the place of birth of his forebears (national origin), his race or fundamental sexual characteristics.[37]

For bilinguals, reasoned the court, speaking a language other than English was a choice; one that could be controlled by the employer in the same way that an employer could control the attire of his employees through a dress code. The irony of the situation that Gloor Lumber created – hiring bilingual employees, but prohibiting them from speaking to one another in Spanish, was apparently lost on the court. Indeed, the very bilingualism of the employees was what made them both more attractive to employers like Gloor Lumber and yet, under the court's reasoning, un-protected by Title VII:

> Mr Garcia was bilingual. Off the job, when he spoke one language or another, he exercised a preference. He was hired by Gloor precisely because he was bilingual, and apart from the contested rule, his preference in language was restricted to some extent by the nature of his employment. On the job, in addressing English-speaking customers, he was obliged to use English; in serving Spanish-speaking patrons, he was required to speak Spanish. The English-only rule went a step further and restricted his preference while he was on the job and not serving a customer.[38]

For monolinguals who do not speak English, language "might well be an immutable characteristic like skin color, sex or place of birth. However, the language a person who is multi-lingual elects to speak at a particular time is by definition a matter of choice."[39] The court refused to accept that Mr Garcia's use of Spanish was an "inadvertent slip" into a more familiar language, although Garcia testified that he had trouble speaking only in English. Although the court paid lip service to the possibility of finding a rule that punished such slips illegal, for the court, once a person was bilingual, such slips could not be considered inadvertent. If the court had allowed room for such inadvertent slips, then it would necessarily have realized that distinguishing between monolinguals and bilinguals in this context really made no sense: bilingualism is a continuum and the "inadvertent slip" makes this manifest and undermines any bright lines between monolinguals and bilinguals.

Manuel del Valle, a former chief administrative law judge for New York's Division of Human Rights wrote that *Gloor* "transformed an allegation of language-based national-origin discrimination into one of insubordination, that is, the refusal of an employee to obey a rule of the workplace."[40] The "modality" created by the *Gloor* court, reasoned del Valle, "sanctions discrimination against the Hispanics who have taken the first tentative steps to master English and with this proficiency achieved a modicum of employment opportunity."[41] "The bilingual," then:

> is compelled by this thinking to separate his or her linguistic behaviors into English and Spanish compartments in order to secure equal treatment from his or her employer; such separate but equal taxonomies serve only to intimidate the bilingual and stigmatize the bilingual's salient national characteristic: language.[42]

Garcia v. Spun Steak: Purposefully disregarding the EEOC

Despite the EEOC's detailed Guidelines issued after and in specific response to *Gloor*, the Ninth Circuit in *Garcia v. Spun Steak*[43] specifically declined to adopt the EEOC's presumption of unlawfulness, and instead stuck by the *Gloor* modality of distinguishing between monolingual and bilingual employees. The court declined to follow the EEOC's lead because it found that its regulations, which put the burden on the employer after the employee, only showed that the existence of English-only policy was contrary to the statute and, therefore, *ultra vires*. In *Spun Steak*, Spanish-speaking employees of a poultry and meat packaging company brought an action under Title VII for their employer's English-only workplace rule. Apparently, prior to 1990 Spanish-speaking Spun Steak employees spoke Spanish freely to their co-workers during their work hours. After receiving complaints that some workers were using their bilingual capabilities to harass and to insult other workers, Spun Steak investigated the possibility of requiring its employees to speak only English in the workplace. Spun Steak had received specific complaints about plaintiffs Garcia and Buitrago; non-Latino co-workers complained that they had made derogatory comments about them in Spanish.[44] Spun Steak employed 33 people, 24 of whom were Spanish-speaking. Virtually all of the Spanish-speaking employees, including Garcia and Buitrago, were Hispanic with varying degrees of proficiency in English; only one employee spoke no English at all.

After its investigation, Spun Steak adopted the following English-only rule in order to promote "racial harmony in the workplace":

> [I]t is hereafter the policy of this Company that only English will be spoken in connection with work. During lunch, breaks, and employees' own time, they are obviously free to speak Spanish if they wish. However, we urge all of you not to use your fluency in Spanish in a fashion which may lead other employees to suffer humiliation.[45]

In November 1990, Garcia and Buitrago received written warnings for speaking Spanish during working hours. For two months after this, they were kept from working next to each other. The employees and their union, Local 115 filed charges with the EEOC which found "[r]easonable cause to believe [Spun Steak] violated Title VII of the Civil Rights Act of 1964 ... with respect to its adoption of an English-only rule and with respect to retaliation when [Garcia, Buitrago, and Local 115] complained."[46] The trial court granted summary judgment for the employees finding that, as a matter of law, the employees had made out the *prima facie* case and that the justifications offered by Spun Steak were inadequate.

The Ninth Circuit reversed finding that, while any negative effects of the English-only rule would be suffered disproportionately by Latino workers, the crux of the issue was whether the Latino workers would suffer any significant adverse effects at all. The Latino workers argued that the rule denies them the ability to "express their cultural heritage on the job," denied them a privilege of employment enjoyed by English-speakers and created an atmosphere of inferiority, isolation, and intimidation.

The court went through each of these claims individually. It first found that, while an "individual's primary language can be an important link to his ethnic culture and identity," Title VII does not

> protect the ability of workers to express their cultural heritage at the workplace. Title VII is concerned only with disparities in the treatment of workers; it does not confer substantive benefits.... Just as a private employer is not required to allow other types of self-expression, there is nothing in Title VII which requires an employer to allow employees to express their cultural identity.[47]

The court's most controversial reasoning came next. Speaking on the job at all is a privilege that this employer has construed narrowly, said the court.

> When the privilege is defined at its narrowest (as merely the ability to speak on the job), we cannot conclude that those employees fluent in both English and Spanish are adversely impacted by the policy. Because they are able to speak English, bilingual employees can engage in conversation on the job.... The bilingual employee can readily comply with the English-only rule and still enjoy the privilege of speaking on the job.[48]

The Spanish-speaking employees argued that trying to abide by the English-only rule was a hardship for them because switching from one language to another was not fully volitional or voluntary act. The court responded:

> we fail to see the relevance of the assertion, even assuming that it can be proved. Title VII is not meant to protect against rules that merely inconvenience some employees, even if the inconvenience falls regularly on a protected class. Rather, Title VII protects against only those policies that have a significant impact. The fact that an employee may have to catch himself or herself from occasionally slipping into Spanish does not impose a burden significant enough to amount to the denial of equal opportunity.... The fact that a bilingual employee may, on occasion, unconsciously substitute a Spanish word in the place of an English one does not override our conclusion that the bilingual employee can easily comply with the rule. *In short, we conclude that a bilingual employee is not denied a privilege of employment by the English-only policy.*[49]

The court left open the possibility that Spun Steak's one employee who spoke no English could be adversely affected by the policy.

The court's decision in *Spun Steak* was a direct assault on the presumption of discrimination against English-only rules contained in the EEOC Guidelines, and the court was not shy about its feelings about those guidelines:

> [i]n holding that the enactment of an English-only while working policy does not inexorably lead to an abusive environment for those whose primary language is not English, we reach a conclusion opposite to the EEOC's long-standing position ... we are not bound by the Guidelines.... We will not defer to an "administrative construction of a statute where there are 'compelling indications that it is wrong.[50]

The Guidelines are wrong, reasoned the court, because, when Congress enacted Title VII it wanted to "strike a balance" "in preventing discrimination and preserving the independence of the employer."[51] Although Congress did not mention this, the court reasoned that balance requires that employees prove a discriminatory effect in disparate impact cases before the burden of proof shifts to the employer. The Guidelines, said the court, shift the burden to the employer before the employee has been held to the task of showing an impact. Yet, as pointed out by a dissenting judge in a later opinion in this case, the court's reasoning on this issue was so strained that, if followed to its logical endpoint, would invalidate even EEOC guidance that simply presumed that a six-foot-tall employment qualification would have a disparate impact on women.[52]

The *Spun Steak* decision marked an unfortunate moment for language rights, not only in the workplace but generally. For, while the case arose in the employment context, the decision institutionalized a misunderstanding of bilingualism and bilinguals. The court went out of its way to repudiate a federal agency's interpretation of a statute, usually accorded great deference, and to diminish, almost to the point of ridicule, the burdens that bilinguals face in adhering to an English-only policy. The reality of code switching – the inadvertent switching between languages common amongst bilinguals – was not taken seriously by the court. The court also made simplistic assumptions about language, as if the world could be divided between monolinguals who could not comply with the English-only rule, and bilinguals who could. The possibility that bilinguals have varying degrees of competence in the two languages, making it easier for some bilinguals to comply with the rule than others, was not even raised by the court.

When an application was made for a rehearing of the case, this time by the full court rather than a three-judge panel, the application for rehearing was denied.[53] However, Judge Reinhardt wrote a strong dissent attacking the panel's opinion in the original decision. Referring to that decision, Reinhardt wrote:

> [m]y colleagues have in their wisdom concluded that bilingual employees do not suffer significant adverse effects from an English-only rule because they have the 'choice' of which language to employ, and can thus "readily comply" with the rule.... This analysis demonstrates a remarkable insensitivity to the facts and history of discrimination. Whether or not the employees can readily comply with a discriminatory rule is by no means the measure of whether they suffer significant adverse consequences. Some of the most objectionable discriminatory rules are the least obtrusive in terms of one's ability to comply: being required to sit in the back of the bus, for example .... nonetheless, the majority focuses narrowly upon the ability to comply, substituting its own unenlightened conception of discriminatory impact for that adopted by the EEOC on the basis of its store of knowledge, wisdom and experience in the field of employment discrimination.[54]

Reinhardt also saw that the negative impact of being forced to comply with an English-only rule was greater than what could be quantified as a "practical" effect: "English-only rules not only symbolize a rejection of the excluded language and the culture it embodies, but also a denial of that side of an individual's personality."[55] Indeed, "[h]istory is replete with language conflicts that attest, not only to the crucial importance of language to its speakers, but also to the widespread tactic of using language as a surrogate for attacks on ethnic identity."[56]

Reinhardt also took aim at the sloppy reasoning of the original *Spun Steak* panel and called it for what it was:

> [i]t is clear that the real basis of the majority's objection to the EEOC presumption is that the majority does not agree with the Guideline on the merits. This substantive disagreement is at least rational (though the majority's view is wrong), but it should not be transformed into a wholly baseless attack on agency authority to promulgate general rules.[57]

Unfortunately, other Circuits have also followed *Spun Steak* and *Gloor* in rejecting the EEOC regulations and in making false distinctions between monolingual and bilingual employees.

Spun Steak & Gloor: Progeny and loopholes

Many courts have analyzed the intricacies involved in English-only workplace rule cases since *Spun Steak* and *Gloor* were decided. While some courts have decidedly used these cases to restrict language rights, a few lower courts found the loopholes in *Spun Steak* and *Gloor* to uphold, at least preliminarily, the rights of bilingual workers. Four cases are discussed here, two that precluded claims because of *Gloor* and *Spun Steak* and two that did not.

In *Long v. First Union Corp. of Virginia*,[58] Latino tellers were told not to speak Spanish while at the bank. The court did not follow the EEOC Guidelines, and required the plaintiffs to make out a *prima facie* case of discriminatory impact without any presumptions in their favor. The plaintiffs would have to show that the seemingly-neutral policy actually had a disproportionate impact on Latinos. Following the rationale of *Spun Steak*, however, the court found that "[t]he plaintiffs, who are all bilingual, may speak to each other while at work and are not adversely affected by the speak English-only policy."[59] Further, the employer's justification for the rule, that other employees were complaining of the use of Spanish by Latino workers and were made uncomfortable by it, was considered legitimate. Although plaintiffs argued that such a justification does not rise to the level of business necessity, the court dismissed this argument for "[s]upervisors may well have a business need to see that their unit runs smoothly and efficiently."[60]

In *Velasquez v. Goldwater Memorial Hospital*,[61] Iris Velasquez was hired as a bilingual, Spanish-speaking patient representative. During the three-month probationary period, Velasquez had several memoranda placed in her personnel file regarding her behavior or attitude, described as rude at one point. During this time she was also chastised for speaking Spanish, and was told that "you are not allowed to speak in Spanish here."[62] Velasquez was fired one week after she was told that she could not speak Spanish. Under the *St. Mary's* paradigm, Velasquez was unable to show that the hospital's proffered reasons for the termination were simply pretexts for discrimination without relying upon the existence of the language-restrictive policy. The court, then, needed to decide whether "an employer's adoption of a language policy is evidence of discriminatory animus such that plaintiff may survive summary judgment on the strength of the sole issue of fact of whether or not such a policy exists."[63]

The court decided to analyze the case under two theories – one in which an English-only policy existed, and one in which a no-speaking-Spanish policy existed. Following the reasoning in *Gloor* and *Long* the court refused to adopt the EEOC presumption of discrimination for English-only policies. Velasquez, reasoned the court, needed to show that she was terminated because of her national origin; showing that she was terminated for violating an English-only policy was insufficient since a "classification based on language does not by itself 'identity members of a suspect class' and will not support an inference of intentional national origin discrimination."[64]

The court did, however, conclude that a "no-Spanish" policy, if one existed, would be discriminatory. The court said: "if the policy prohibits employees from speaking Spanish, then language, a seemingly neutral characteristic, could be used to disguise a discriminatory motive."[65] This, however, would have required Velasquez to show that employees of other national origins were allowed to speak their non-English language, and that only Spanish was repressed. Velasquez could not show this. Under the court's reasoning then, an employer, for whatever xenophobic reasons, who represses all languages other than English is not acting in a discriminatory manner. But an employer who, for other xenophobic reasons, restricts only certain languages other than English, is discriminating. Ironically then, English language homogeneity is acceptable and apparently a sensible business rule, any departures from the English standard, however, may be proof of discrimination.

The limitations of this court's reasoning are exposed if we use a hypothetical 'monolingual' Spanish-speaking employee as a plaintiff. In such a case, the court could have been open to the possibility that the English-only rule would have fallen more heavily on Latinos than others. For the hypothetical plaintiff, an English-only rule would have amounted to a no-speech rule, which would be an unreasonable burden to place on employees, especially when the rule would have had to be borne only by Spanish-dominant employees. Yet, other employees who were Latino but bilingual, under the court's analysis would not have experienced discrimination. So alleging that the rule singled out only Latinos would have been impossible. Putting *St Mary's Honor Center* together with *Spun Steak* gives us unknown and mostly, unfair, results.

In *EEOC v. Synchro-Start Products, Inc.*,[66] the company employed approximately 200 employees, many of whom were Latino. Since at least September of 1997, the company had required its employees to speak only English during work hours. The rule was applied to employees with varying degrees of proficiency in English. The company did not explain the consequences of violating the rule to its employees before implementing it. The court began by distinguishing the case before it from the three Circuit cases, which had upheld the validity of English-only rules. First, the court was considering a motion to dismiss rather than a summary judgment motion where evidence for both sides has already been gathered. Second, the EEOC in this case had specifically alleged that the rule was applied to employees whose English language skills were imperfect or non-existent. With respect to these employees, the court found that the EEOC had a liable claim, but refused to stop there.

> [B]ut this court, writing on a clean slate in this Circuit, goes beyond that easy case to find it possible to impose liability across a broader spectrum – perhaps even as to those bilingual employees who can "readily comply with the English-only rule and still enjoy the privilege of speaking on the job.[67]

The court then analyzed the *Spun Steak* court's refusal to follow the EEOC Guidelines. *Spun Steak*, said the court, read too much into the EEOC regulations. The EEOC did not abrogate legislative intent by placing the burden of persuasion on the employer. It did, however, create a presumption of discrimination that becomes a conclusion only if the employer has no business necessity for the rule. The presumption acts as a "tie-breaker," "[a]nd in those terms the questions really becomes one of interpretation [of the statute] rather than of any effort to override legislative intent – a proper sphere for extending deference to the agency's knowledge and experience."[68]

Two lower courts in Texas also allowed challenges to English-only policies to survive based on the loopholes in *Gloor* and *Spun Steak*. In *EEOC v. University of the Incarnate Word*,[69] the magistrate judge issued a recommendation to the court that denied the university's motion for summary judgment. Sr Ann Finn, head of housekeeping, had verbally implemented an English-only workplace rule amongst the mostly Mexican housekeeping staff. The plaintiffs alleged that she called them "stupid Mexicans," and that she "physically abus[ed] the housekeeping staff, by pulling the housekeepers' ears, pulling their hair, and/or slapping their arms, hands or shoulders."[70] Sr Finn's animus toward the Spanish language was purportedly so great that she did not allow the bilingual housekeeping staff to translate her orders or directions into Spanish for the Spanish-speaking-only staff.[71] The policy was purportedly a blanket policy, applied at all times, including breaks and lunch periods.

The University asked the court to grant it summary judgment on a number of issues and relied on *Gloor* and *Spun Steak* to argue that the bilingual employees were not, as a matter of law, harmed by any English-only policy, to the extent that one existed.[72] The magistrate, however, found that *Gloor* did not apply when plaintiffs were complaining of a blanket policy applying at all times and that *Spun Steak* did not apply when the level of bilingualism or monolingualism amongst the employees affected by the policy was unclear. Both issues needed to be resolved by a jury.

Subsequent to this decision, the case was settled with the EEOC. Amongst other things, the University agreed to adopt a non-discrimination policy, abandon its English-only policy, hold supervisors accountable for violations of these policies, and pay $1,000,000 toward a settlement fund to be distributed amongst 19 eligible employees and former employees.[73]

In *EEOC v. Premier Operator Services, Inc.*,[74] the court was faced with an extreme English-only policy whereby bilingual Spanish-speaking telephone operators were prohibited from speaking in Spanish to one another at all times; the employer going so far as to plan to install a public telephone outside its building so that the Latino employees would have to go outside the building in order to make phone calls in which Spanish might be spoken.[75] Ironically, the Latino employees were prized for their Spanish-speaking ability, and the employer had ensured that they were bilingual by testing their proficiency in Spanish before hiring them.[76]

The sign used by the employer to warn of the existence of the English-only policy is a glaring example of the kind of racism for which the policy is only the most tepid example:

> Absolutely No Guns Knives or Weapons of any kind are allowed on these

Premises at any time! English is the official language of Premier Operator Services, Inc. All conversations on these premises are to be in English. Other languages may be spoken to customers who cannot speak English.[77]

The English-only policy was further memorialized in a memo that the plaintiff class members were required to sign as a condition of continued employment. Those that did not sign it were summarily discharged. Others who did sign under protest and who subsequently filed charges with the EEOC were also discharged.[78] All who were discharged were replaced with non-Latino employees.[79]

Some of the most important findings made by the court dealt with the issue of how to define a bilingual, an issue glossed over by the *Gloor* and *Spun Steak* courts. The court relied upon the testimony of a linguistics expert who talked about "code switching" – the unconscious switching between languages that is found in the speech patterns of many bilinguals.[80] Therefore, bilingual employees were being harmed by the English-only policy since they could not choose to comply with it. The court stated:

> [n]onobservance of the English-only policy was not simply a matter of individual preference for the class members. On a daily basis, the Hispanic employees of Premier were faced with the very real risk of being reprimanded or even losing their jobs if they violated the English-only rule, even if such non-compliance were to be inadvertent. There was no comparable risk posed by the policy for defendant's non-Hispanic employees.... [81]

The court ultimately found that the English-only policy resulted in the disparate treatment of the Latino employees and also had a disparate impact on Latinos. Further, the court specifically found that the EEOC Guidelines were entitled to substantial deference[82] and that the employer's conduct was so extreme and in disregard of the rights of its employees and of federal law that it awarded punitive damages. All told, Premier Operators would have to pay its Latino employees $650,000.[83]

Employer justifications: Will any rationale do?

The EEOC approach: Requiring a "compelling justification"

The Guidelines adopted by the EEOC are clear: an English-only rule is presumptively discriminatory on the basis of national origin, regardless of whether the aggrieved employees are bilingual or monolingual. In order to respond to this presumption, an employer must articulate a legitimate business justification for the rule. In its Compliance Manual, the EEOC has indicated that such a rule will be justified only if "necessary for the safe and efficient job performance or the safe and efficient operation of the business."[84]

In *Gutierrez v. Municipal Court of the Southeast Judicial District, County of Los Angeles,*[85] the court noted that the EEOC's standard of requiring "business necessity" "prevents an employer from imposing a rule that has a disparate impact on

groups protected by the national origin provision of Title VII unless there is a sufficient justification under the Civil Rights Act of 1964 for doing so."[86] The court distinguished this level of justification from an even stricter standard required if the
employer is found to have a adopted the rule for the purpose of discriminating
against a protected group: "[t]hus, even a limited English-only rule must meet the
stricter BFOQ [bona fide occupational qualification] test ... if it is the product of
discriminatory intent."[87] Business necessity alone, however, found the *Gutierrez*
court:

> must be sufficiently compelling to override the discriminatory impact created
> by the challenged rule .... In addition, the practice or rule must effectively carry
> out the business purpose it is alleged to serve, and there must be available no
> acceptable less discriminatory alternative which would accomplish the pur-
> pose as well.... As the Tenth Circuit put it: "[t]he practice must be essential, the
> purpose compelling.[88]

The EEOC's Manual offers two examples of when an English-only rule would be
permissible for safety reasons:

> Example 1(Safe and Efficient Job Performance): R—, a chemical refining plant,
> alleges that its speak-English-only policy was initiated for safety reasons since
> the chemicals used in its operations are dangerous and good communication
> between employees is necessary in the event of an emergency. The rule applies
> to all employees including clerical employees, technicians preparing and
> processing the chemicals, and laborers who load the finished product onto
> trucks for distribution. While respondent may be able to justify as a business
> necessity the applications of the speak-English-only rule to employees working
> directly with dangerous chemicals, it will not be able to justify the rule with
> regard to clerical positions, in the absence of evidence that the rule is necessary
> to the safe performance of the clerical jobs.[89]

> Example 2 (Safe and Efficient Operation of the Business): R—, the operator of an
> oil rig, has a speak-English-only policy that applies to all of its employees when
> they are on the deck of an oil rig. R— has produced evidence showing that the
> rule is necessary because its dangerous round-the-clock drilling operations on
> the deck require that all employees present on deck, whether they are directly
> involved in work operations or not, be able to communicate quickly and
> respond effectively to any emergency situation. In these circumstances, R— has
> established that the speak-English-only rule is essential to the safe and efficient
> operations of its business.[90]

One commentator, however, has noted that sweeping claims for safety even in
what might be considered dangerous occupations, should not be "rubber stamped"
by the courts:

> The reviewing court ... should consider the composition of an employer's work
> force to determine whether English-only communication enhances or interferes

with safety and efficiency. Furthermore, an English-only rule based on safety and efficiency often may be unnecessary. A rational employer hires and retains employees who are capable of understanding the safety requirements of a job and of performing their jobs satisfactorily. Where ability to speak and understand English is necessary, an employer may properly require such an ability as a prerequisite for employment.... Additionally, a rational employer will train his employees, probably in English, to handle situations that could arise on the job. In a crisis situation, it would be completely irrational for a trained and capable Spanish-speaking employee to defy his experience, training, and common sense by attempting to communicate in Spanish to people who will not understand him.[91]

In other words, the impetus behind even seemingly well-justified English-only rules can be an unnecessary suspicion of language-minority employees or a kind of racist paternalism assuming that they will not act in the same rational and intelligent manner as other employees and that a preemptive English-only rule will "keep them in line."

For the EEOC, it seems that, in order to be acceptable, an English-only rule must be necessary, not just a mere managerial convenience; the rule must effectively carry out the business purpose it is supposed to be serving. According to the EEOC, "if there is no nexus or connection between the rule and either safe and efficient job performance or the safe and efficient operation of the business as a whole, the [employer] has not shown that the rule is a business necessity."[92]

Revisiting *Gloor*, for a moment, it should be obvious that Gloor Lumber's justifications would not have withstood scrutiny under the EEOC Guidelines. Indeed, some of Gloor's justifications seem to have come right out of the mouths of southern lunch counter owners in the 1950s and 1960s justifying their refusal to serve African-Americans: the White customers wouldn't like it. Similarly, Gloor explained, the English-speaking customers, and a much larger number of employees, are made uncomfortable by conversations in languages other than English within their earshot. In *Gutierrez*[93] the court noted that "[e]xisting racial fears or prejudices and their effects cannot justify a racial classification."[94] The affidavits submitted in that case indicated that the use of Spanish "unnerved" the supervisors. The court saw this "nervousness" for what it was: "[t]he supervisors' feelings toward the use of the Spanish language may reflect a prejudice toward the use of a tongue that they do not understand, and also may indicate a bias against Hispanic-Americans."[95]

Employers may require bilingual employees to speak only in English to English-speaking consumers; not only does this seem quite rational on the employer's part but if an employee cares at all about his/her job, a matter of course. Yet, an English-only rule ought not to be necessary. Given the rule's narrowly-tailored range, it would probably pass legal scrutiny anyway *unless* it also prohibited bilingual employees from speaking to language-minority customers in the minority language that the customer preferred to conduct business.

Other defenses raised by an employer may include the need to reduce disruptions, the need for clear communication between employees, the need to improve employee's English-language skills, the need to reduce racial or ethnic tensions. None of these reasons, however, should pass legal muster. For instance, it is hard to see how prohibiting native language conversations will reduce disruptions. Factory workers speaking to one another casually on an assembly line will not be more disruptive than the workers who speak to each other in English, and the mechanical-like work will most likely be completed without interruption. Perhaps, however, the disruption rationale should be understood to include a "racial or ethnic harmony" component; that is, that racial or ethnic tensions are aroused when some employees are speaking one language to another in the presence of other employees who don't understand them. Employees who are upset by this practice, however, may already have biased feelings towards the language-minority group that results in suspicion or hostility towards their conversations. Employers may take many actions to deal with this type of tension, including sensitivity courses for its workers. An English-only rule, however, will not reduce tensions. At best it will only shift them so that the language-minority group feels insulted, and at worst (and more probable) it would actually exacerbate them, as the policy is not only illegal (and therefore can be ignored and/or challenged by the language-minority group), but also would show favoritism towards the majority language groups. As with the safety and efficiency concerns, the EEOC and the courts should look closely to see whether communications between employees is actually served by an English-only rule and whether that communication is important to the job performance.

Judicial review of employer justifications: The need for standards

The reality, however, has been quite different than the theory of business justifications. Courts have been very deferential to the rationales of employers, even if they are unsupported by substantial evidence or justify a racist and/or suspicious attitude amongst employees or customers. For instance, in *Tran v. Standard Motor Products, Inc.*[96] a Vietnamese employee claimed that his company's English-only rule created a hostile wok environment. First the court found that an English-only rule that applied only during "working hours" as opposed to one that also covered breaks and meal times, was not a blanket English-only rule and was therefore redeemable by any business justification. Then the court found that the reasons for the policy offered by Standard Motor amounted to a business necessity. Standard Motor had argued that the rule was needed to (1) ensure that all employees and supervisors could understand each other during "cell" meetings, (2) prevent injuries through effective communication, and (3) prevent non-Vietnamese employees from feeling as if they were being talked about by the Vietnamese-speaking employees.[97]

The court did not analyze these justifications at all, it did not determine whether they were truly necessary for the performance of the work, and did not consider whether there might exist less-discriminatory alternatives.

Similarly, in *Martinez v. Labelmaster, American Labelmaker Co.*,[98] the court found that, even though an employee's supervisor had "informally" imposed an English-only rule, the rule was not presumptively discriminatory because: (1) the rule was enforced only at work stations, (2) the purpose of the rule was to "promote esprit de corps in that co-workers would not understand what their non-English speaking co-workers were saying;" and (3) the employer had provided employees with notice of the rule when the employee was hired.[99]

In *Prado v. L. Luria & Son, Inc.*,[100] the employer asserted two reasons that the court found legitimate for enforcing its English-only rule: (1) to encourage store employees to speak English amongst themselves, which would facilitate the practice of approaching customers first in English; and (2) to ensure that management understands what is being said in order to evaluate all employees' work-related communications.[101] The court assumed under the reasoning of *Gloor* that an English-only rule by "[a]n employer does not violate Title VII as applied to bilingual employees so long as there's a legitimate business purpose for the rule."[102]

It seems that the *Prado, Tran,* and *Martinez* decisions reflect a growing trend to ignore the EEOC regulations and apply lower, significantly less stringent, standards to employer rationales than the "business necessity" standards.[103] None of these courts analyzed the employers' justifications or tried to determine whether less discriminatory alternatives were available. For these courts, a rule that arguably does not apply at all times (even if it may apply during all "working times") or to bilingual employees, can be justified by the most inane employer rationale and without evidence of business necessity or job-relatedness.

A rule, however, may be upheld if it is substantively related to the job to be performed. For instance, in *Jurado v. Eleven-Fifty, Corp.*,[104] a bilingual disk jockey delivered his program only in English until he was asked to add some Spanish words in the hopes of improving his ratings amongst Latino listeners. [He did so and the ratings did not improve.] Instead, an outside consultant hired by the radio station determined that the mix of Spanish and English was actually causing confusion amongst listeners as to the music that the station broadcast. The consultant made the recommendation to the station that the bilingual format be dropped, and that was ultimately relayed to Jurado, the disc jockey. Jurado refused to comply with the order to broadcast only in English, and was subsequently dismissed. Jurado brought an action under Title VII claiming disparate treatment and disparate impact of the English-only rule. The court found that the order to broadcast in English only was not the result of discriminatory animus, but merely a programming decision. This seems right; certainly the facts of the case and the limited nature of the rule, such as it was, support the employer's story that programming and not racial animus justified the existence of the rule.

The court, however, did not stop there and went on to rely upon *Gloor*, unnecessarily, to find that as a bilingual employee Jurado could easily comply with the "rule" and that there was no disparate impact because, under *Gloor*, there was no negative impact on bilingual employees. The court could have written a tighter (and more rationally reasoned) opinion if it had actually found either that there was no English-only rule in place as traditionally understood since apparently no attempt was made to curtail the use of native languages amongst employees, only on the broadcast, or that the limited English-only rule that did exist was justified by business necessity. Here, business necessity was even objectively substantiated by an outside consultant's report work for the radio station finding that the use of Spanish during Jurado's broadcast was detrimental to ratings.[105]

Labeling words: Judicial inquiry into the existence of an English-only policy

I have suggested that in *Jurado* an English-only rule might not have been in existence at all. While determining the existence of such a rule might seem simple, courts have stumbled when they have taken to analyzing whether such a rule exists. In *Rivera v. Baccarat, Inc.*,[106] a Puerto Rican employee brought a Title VII action against her employer for her termination. She alleged that Jean Luc Negre, the new president of Baccarat, had told her not to speak Spanish on the job, that he did not like her accent and that the chief financial officer of the company told her that another employee was terminated because she was "Spanish."[107] Baccarat denied the existence of an English-only rule stating: "the only rule was that, as a matter of courtesy, employees should not speak Spanish (or another foreign language) among themselves in the presence of customers or co-workers who speak only English."[108] While logically this would appear to be an English-only rule, albeit with some attempt made at limiting its scope (although a rule that does not allow other languages to be spoken in front of other co-workers can be very broad indeed), the court found that no such rule existed. Instead it seemed to differentiate between the existence of a "real" English-only rule and a "common sense rule against offending customers."[109]

Confusion also reigned in *Dimaranan v. EEOC*,[110] where the court made a distinction between an English-only "rule" and a "directive" issued by the hospital administration that no Tagalog be spoken during a specific shift. The court was clearly sympathetic to the personnel problems plaguing the night shift of an obstetrics ward where language was ultimately used as a divisive tool. The court had found that "[i]t is beyond question that certain members of the hospital's management team sought to restrict the use of Tagalog by the Filipina nurses employed in the M/B Unit (Mother/Baby Unit) on the evening shift."[111] Indeed, the court characterizes this attempt as a "restriction limited to the evening-shift of the M/B Unit, and restricted to the use of Tagalog only."[112] All of this would actually make out a case of disparate treatment, yet the court used these facts to argue for the non-existence of an English-only rule.

The *Dimaranan* case actually is a good factual situation to highlight many of the work-place issues that arise when language-minority employees use their native language in the workplace to the consternation of other employees. Here, a Filipina nurse, Adelaida Dimaranan was a good employee of the Pomona Valley Hospital and rose from the ranks to become the head nurse of the M/B Unit. Under the tutelage of a Ms Holstein, Dimaranan received RNII status, a status awarded only to those nurses who display superior clinical skills. As head of the M/B Unit, however, complaints began to surface about her authoritarian style, favoritism towards some nurses, and her use of Tagalog. Despite counseling efforts taken by the hospital, complaints about Dimaranan continued; the complaints centered on the disorganization and the divisions among the nursing staff while Dimaranan was in charge, the "dividing factor appeared to be the use of Tagalog."[113] When Holstein investigated for herself she found "general discontent"[114] among nurses on the Unit and that Tagalog was frequently spoken among the Filipina nurses. She also found that non-Tagalog-speaking nurses and even patients often felt "uncomfortable and excluded."[115] It was eventually felt that, rather than trying to address the ethnic tensions, Dimaranan fostered "the Unit's disunity by continuing to use Tagalog herself and by encouraging the other Filipina nurses to use it also."[116]

In response, Connie Tanquary, Director of the M/B Unit, asked the Unit's night staff not to speak Tagalog. When complaints about the continued use of Tagalog surfaced again, Holstein responded by prohibiting the use of Tagalog on the Unit. Despite, what the court called the "language restriction," the Filipina nurses, including Dimaranan, continued using Tagalog and "hostilities continued to further divide the Unit."[117] The hospital administration decided that it did not have sufficient evidence to warrant a demotion of Dimaranan but quickly put together a "paper trail" replete with suddenly-negative evaluations to justify her ultimate demotion and transfer.

The court saw this case as a "management problem [that] ended in this Title VII action."[118] Because of the court's sympathies with the hospital administration's attempts to resolve a difficult situation, it found that the language restriction in force did not amount to an English-only policy. The limited nature of the policy, however, directed only toward the night staff of the M/B Unit, does not change the nature of the policy – the use of Tagalog was specifically prohibited; that the nurses continued to use Tagalog reflects their strength of character, not the lack of a rule. Indeed, Dimaranan was ultimately demoted, at least in part because of her refusal to abide by the rule. The existence of a specific and announced language restriction plus the negative action taken because of a violation of the rule should have been conclusive evidence for the court to determine that a rule was indeed in effect.

The question that vexed the court, however, was what avenues of redress are open to an employer faced with ethnic tensions amongst its staff that can seemingly be traced to language. In such situations, how should the use of native languages be treated? While employers often use the desire to ease employee tensions as a justification for an English-only policy with little evidence that such tensions even exist, here those tensions were writ large. One avenue the court could have taken was to find that an English-only policy did indeed exist for the night staff of the M/B Unit but that it was justified given the tensions amongst the staff. The EEOC, however, has specifically found that English-only workplace rules do not contribute to racial harmony but instead can cause or exacerbate those that might already exist. Indeed, the restrictions on the use of Tagalog could justifiably have been interpreted as a reflection of management's favoritism toward the non-Filipina nurses.

Often, an English-only policy is a seemingly quick and simple solution to problems that require more attention and more work. For instance, biases amongst employees simply make it difficult for minorities to hold positions of authority without alienating someone; the nursing staff at the M/B Unit may only have given a voice to latent mistrust and fears of minorities, here Filipinas, already found in the hospital. What the hospital tried to address through a language policy may have required a more subtle and simultaneously more comprehensive response to cultural differences, and how they surface at the workplace, as well as the role that language plays in cultural expression and personal identification. Similarly, Filipina nurses could have received instruction on the sensitive use of native languages and respecting the justifiable feelings of language-majority employees.

Further, if the hospital felt that Dimaranan's management style was simply not up to par, irrespective of her use of Tagalog, the hospital could have transferred her, without demoting her and without ever having to issue an English-only policy. Another less-authoritarian nurse possibly would not have alienated her staff as easily as Dimaranan did, and tensions between Filipina nurses and non-Filipina nurses possibly would not have been so intense.

Courts, however, are unwilling to hold employers to truly rational and justifiable reasons for their English-only rules. They tend not to second-guess the employer and will probably not require them to offer sensitivity courses as less-discriminatory alternatives to English-only policies.

Other anti-language-minority trends

The trend against language-minority employees deepens with cases like *McNeil v. Aguilos*,[119] where an African-American hospital employee brought an action against Bellevue Hospital for racial harassment because, amongst other things, she complained about the use of Tagalog by the pediatric nurses to the Filipina supervising nurse. The use of Tagalog amongst the pediatric nurses, she argued, was meant to exclude her from the flow of information and to harass and impede her work. McNeil felt so clearly assailed that she pursued her case on a variety of fronts, even arguing anti-trust violations, contending that the hospital had "created a monopoly of Filipino nurses" and that the nurses "are attempting to establish a monopoly on information in the nursing profession in order to exclude those who do not speak Tagalog."[120] The court's only decision on the case was to let it proceed to trial and to deny the motions for summary judgment. As we saw in bilingual education, and as we are generally seeing in the affirmative-action field, the roll back in civil rights is being accompanied by negative lawsuits brought by members of majority groups, here a language-majority hospital worker, but also a racial minority.

Employers are not unaware of this roll-back. Labor and employment law journals indicate that courts are willing to uphold employer prerogatives in this area; there is a "trend toward greater judicial recognition of both employer prerogative and the rights of native English speakers and a corresponding diminished support for the claims of non-English-speaking employees."[121] One commentator advises employers:

to have business-related reasons on hand for their English-only rules just to be on safe ground.... An employer wishing to adopt an English-only rule should not be intimidated by the EEOC Guidelines regarding such rules. The courts have held, contrary to the EEOC's position, that English-only rules are not, *per se*, discriminatory.[122]

Advocates and activists certainly have their work cut out for them in this area. Many employers mimic English-only advocates' slogans on the need to retain the preeminence of English and a suspicion toward the attitudes of recent immigrants to justify English-only workplace rules. [Labor unions, which ought to be strong advocates for minority language workers, are usually suspicious themselves of these newcomers and neither their agendas nor their leadership reflect the kind of linguistic and ethnic diversity quickly becoming commonplace across the workforce.]

COMPENSATING BILINGUAL EMPLOYEES

In the English-only rule context, bilingual employees, frequently hired for their language skills, may find themselves being asked not to speak their native language because of the discomfort that foreign languages cause to others. Paradoxically, in the area of compensation, bilingual employees may find themselves working twice as much as their monolingual colleagues without additional compensation. Interestingly, one employer could indeed have two different language-based discriminatory practices: the over-working of bilingual employees because they are bilingual and English-only workplace rules prohibiting native language use that is not for the benefit of the employer.

In the area of compensation, bilingual employees will rarely be able to make out a claim for violation of Title VII for the employer's use of bilingual skills, unless the employee can show that she is doing a significantly greater amount of work without credit or compensation. An excellent case on this issue is *Perez v. FBI*,[123] which raises many complex issues surrounding the use of employees' bilingual skills by employers. Here, the employer was the FBI, which had a written policy that employees had to agree to before being hired. The policy detailed that the employee was being hired:

> based on particular skills or abilities that [he] might have in disciplines such as the law, accounting, language, science, engineering or any other special expertise, [he] may be required to use it intermittently or continuously throughout [his] employment, based upon the needs of the [FBI] and at any duty station where they are required.[124]

The FBI used this policy to require even minimally-proficient Latino employees to use their Spanish-language skills for duties (such as listening to wiretaps) that were tiresome, burdensome, difficult, were not credited for promotion decisions, and did not lead to greater expertise or training. Conversely, Anglo employees with

Spanish-language skills could refuse to take a language test to determine proficiency without which their language skills could not be used, and they were almost never required to do the thankless work that was required of Latinos. Latinos, on the other hand, were required to take the language test on pain of censure, and were forced to re-take the exam until a passing grade was achieved, and then their skills were essentially abused. The court found that:

> on the basis of Hispanic surname or other selection based on the agent's national origin, the Bureau singled out agents to take the language skills test and made assignments significantly affecting their conditions of employment in an adverse manner. The court further finds that no similar presumption attached to non-Hispanic agents.[125]

The court found that the Bureau placed "the weight of deplored assignments on Hispanic Special Agents."[126] In sum, the court found that:

> [t]hese valuable Hispanic linguists are passed over for in-service training or career development opportunities because their skills are needed more in Spanish language related assignments. As a result, Hispanic agents are not exposed to the managers who make the subjective evaluations and determinations for career advancements. Hispanic agents did not gain similar professional experience of Anglo peers, experiences which are necessary to advancement.[127]

The court in *Perez* was overwhelmed by the evidence of how badly and blatantly discriminatory treatment of Latinos was at the FBI. Not all claims for the discriminatory use of bilingual skills by Latino employees will be greeted so charitably. Certainly, in cases where public-service employees are involved, bilingual employees may be expected to use their skills on behalf of their employer without significant complaint. For instance, in *Cota v. Tucson Police Department*,[128] the Latino employees of the Tucson Police Department (TPD) complained that they were required to use their Spanish-speaking skills on the job without additional compensation, in violation of Title VII. The court found that the use of Spanish, when required, was incidental to the performance of the employees' on-the-job duties. The court found that TPD required only that its employees who speak Spanish use their skills when necessary and at the level of proficiency that they possess. There was an issue for these employees, however, who clearly felt that at times their level of Spanish proficiency was not up to that required by the translation work and that translating without that level of proficiency was difficult, burdensome even, and perhaps embarrassing. Indeed, "[s]everal witnesses testified that their assigned duties can be difficult (and at times impossible), to perform in Spanish. The increased difficulty or impossibility, they testified, is due to their inability to speak Spanish at the advanced level required to satisfactorily perform police work."[129]

While the court found that indeed the "Spanish-speakers" were sometimes required to use Spanish to assist non-Spanish-speakers in addition to their regular work, this additional work did not detrimentally affect them and, in any event, overtime compensation was available for those who needed more time to complete all their work because of providing translation assistance.[130]

The flipside to hiring employees because they are bilingual is not hiring or promoting them if they are not sufficiently fluent in English to perform the tasks required. For instance, in *Mejia v. New York Sheraton Hotel*,[131] the court found that a Dominican chambermaid was legitimately not promoted to a front office cashier's position with a hotel because, amongst other things, her English language skills were not sufficient for the position in which she would often have to communicate with the English-speaking public. The court stated:

> [t]he evidence in the case established beyond peradventure of doubt a serious past and current inability on the plaintiff's part to articulate clearly or coherently and to make herself adequately understood in the English language.... The requirement of the hotel for greater English proficiency than the plaintiff can exhibit was significantly related to successful job performance....[132]

While technically an employment case in that it relates to access to civil service employment, *Frontera v. Sindell*,[133] resounds with many of the issues usually found in the social services context with regard to questions of interpretation and translation even while it raises the significant issue of English fluency and the extent to which employers should accommodate language minorities.

In *Frontera*, a Puerto Rican migrant to Cleveland failed a civil service carpenter's exam given only in the English language. He belonged to Carpenter's Union Local having been admitted on the basis of an oral exam and a review of his work.[134] He sued the civil service commissioner under the Fourteenth Amendment for failing to give the exam, exam notices and instructions for the exam in Spanish as well as in English. Although the trial court had determined that there was evidence of a discriminatory impact in administering the exams only in English, it also held that the civil service commission had a compelling state interest in doing so.[135]

On appeal, however, the Circuit Court found that the district court was erroneous in deciding that there was any discrimination at all against Frontera on the basis of national origin.[136] Instead, the court found that only linguistic determination was at issue, even though it never used that terminology at all. It stated:

> [i]t cannot gainsaid that the common, national language of the United States is English. Our laws are printed in English and our legislatures conduct their business in English. Some states even designate English as the official language of the state.... Our national interest in English as the common language is exemplified by 8 USC §1423, which requires, in general, English language literacy as a condition to naturalization as a United States citizen.[137]

Clearly, once the court determined that there was no prohibited discrimination, then it was free to apply the lax standard of rational basis: did the civil service commission have a rational basis to administer the test only in English? Given its own strong feelings about the place of the English language in the national life, its decision on this point was made: "[in] conducting the examination in English the

Commission violated no constitutional or civil right of Frontera. In our opinion the test was job related."[138]

ACCENTS, ENGLISH FLUENCY AND "COMMUNICATION SKILLS": THE NEED FOR JUDICIAL COHERENCE AMONGST EMPLOYER BABBLE

Accent discrimination

Arguably, accent discrimination does not involve "pure" issues of language rights since discriminating against someone for having a foreign accent in the majority language is not about the protection or promotion of minority languages. However, just as language cannot be extricated from national origin, accent is a marker of minority language usage and again, labels the minority as an "other." The rulings in accent discrimination cases are a mixed bag, making it hard to predict how a court might rule on any given case. One commentator, after reviewing the case law, has noted that the plaintiff most likely to be successful will be one with a:

> slight trace of a European accent, but for the most part ... has adopted the speech patterns associated vaguely with North American television newscasters. She is qualified in every other respect for a job that requires some basic communication ability. Speech, is not, however, a major job function.[139]

Indeed, it does appear that whenever speaking, especially to the public, is even a small part of the employee's tasks, the employer's assertion that the applicant with an accent can't be understood, is credited by the court without further inquiry. It appears that for the courts, the presence of a true, as opposed to slight or bare, accent is sufficient to disqualify the applicant from work involving "communication skills." This attitude is especially offensive, since accent is the kind of immutable characteristic that the courts in the English-only cases complain that language-usage is not; while a Spanish-dominant immigrant may arguably become English-dominant they will certainly retain their accent marking them as coming from a Spanish-language background.

Courts, however, are more likely in accent cases than in English-only cases to at least assert the need to closely scrutinize employment decisions based on accent or, a sibling issue, English-language ability. Title VII contains no explicit prohibition on accent discrimination, although the EEOC prohibits discrimination based on a person's "cultural or linguistic characteristics" which has been interpreted as prohibiting accent discrimination. Again, the connections between accent and national origin, the protected categorization, must be made.

One of the leading cases in this area is *Carino v. University of Oklahoma Board of Regents*,[140] where the plaintiff, a native of the Philippines, was demoted, the court found, because of his noticeable accent. The plaintiff, Carino, was a supervisor at a dental laboratory operated by the defendant. However, his job title was reclassified a number of times without his consent or awareness until he learned that another person was actually hired to do the same work that he was supposed to be performing. As in other employment discrimination cases, in order to make out a *prima facie* case of discrimination, the plaintiff must meet a four-pronged test originally created by the Supreme Court in *McDonnell Douglas Corp. v. Green*.[141] In order to make out a *prima facie* case of discrimination, the plaintiff must prove:

(1) that the plaintiff belongs to a protected class;
(2) that he or she applied and was qualified for the position sought or held;
(3) that despite such qualifications, he or she was rejected or fired;
(4) that after his or her rejection, the position sought or terminated from either remained open and the employer continued to seek similarly qualified applicants or was filled by equally or less qualified individuals not of the protected group.

In the present case, the trial court applied the *McDonnell Douglas* test to Carino's case and found

(1) that the plaintiff belonged to a protected group since his national origin is the Republic of the Philippines;
(2) that he was qualified for the job of supervisor in the dental laboratories;
(3) that, despite his qualifications, he was reassigned from the supervisory position to a staff position in the old dental laboratory and not considered for the supervisory position in the new dental laboratory;
(4) after Carino was demoted and denied the opportunity to apply for the new supervisory position, another person, not of Carino's national origin, was hired for promotion.

It was then up to the College to articulate a non-discriminatory reason for the demotion. It appeared, however, that certain dental college faculty felt that Carino was unsuitable for continued work as a supervisor because of his accent. The court found this rationale unacceptable. Carino had been hired, stated the court, for his technical skills and a "foreign accent that does not interfere with a [plaintiff's] ability to perform duties of the position he has been denied is not a legitimate justification for adverse employment decisions."[142]

In *Fragante v. City and County of Honolulu*,[143] however, the trial and appellate courts ultimately decided that Manuel Fragante, a native of the Philippines, did not make out a case of accent discrimination. Fragante was a well-educated Filipino, and a career officer in the Philippines armed forces. His education and training were in English and after retiring from the armed forces he worked in supervisory and administrative capacities in the Philippines.[144] Fragante came to Hawaii in 1981 and he began working for the Honolulu Community Action Program in 1983. Meanwhile in 1981 he applied for a civil service job as a "Clerk Sr-8" with the Department of Finance, Motor Vehicles and Licensing Division. He took the required civil service exam and received the highest grade on the exam, placing him on the top of the civil service list and making him one of the top five candidates eligible for an interview.[145]

All apparently should have gone in Fragante's favor: he was a highly-qualified applicant, probably too qualified for the position sought. Then the interview occurred. The interview process was, the court indicated, an informal one. It lasted only 10–15 minutes, there were no written interview questions, no guidelines or criteria for its conduct and no instructions, nor were interviewers formally trained for the task. Further, the ratings sheets used to score the interviewees were "inadequate," and the ratings categories were "vague, qualitative in nature though reduced to quantitative terms, non-correlative, and not clearly job related nor well defined."[146] The interviewers noted in their ratings sheets that Fragante has a "very pronounced accent, difficult to understand," "[m]ajor drawback, difficult to understand. Would have problem working on counter and answering phone. Otherwise a good candidate," and "Heavy Filipino accent. Would be difficult to understand over telephone."[147] Ultimately, because of his accent, Fragante was not hired. Although he had 37 years of experience in management and administration, Fragante was not hired because he spoke, according to the interviewers with a "very pronounced accent."[148] The nature of Fragante's accent is itself in doubt, however. Although the trial court felt that Fragante had a "difficult manner of pronunciation," a perusal of the trial transcript in Fragante's case found "that in two days of testimony, under the stress of both direct and cross-examination, Fragante was asked to repeat his answer only twice, and once was for the repetition of a proper name."[149]

In accepting the Department's rationale for not hiring Fragante, the court appeared to be condoning employers pandering to public prejudice:

> [w]hile Plaintiff has extensive verbal communication skill in English it is understandable why the interviewers might reach their conclusion. And while there is no necessary relationship between accent and verbal communication ... listeners stop listening to Filipino accents, resulting in a breakdown of communication. Hawaii is a socially and linguistically complex community.[150]

The catering to such xenophobia by a government entity in the linguistically-rich state of Hawaii no less, ought to have been roundly condemned by the court, instead, it is credited as a legitimate business qualification. Such blatant pandering was not acceptable at the end of the civil rights era when racial discrimination was being attacked, yet disturbingly it lives today when national origin is at issue.

On appeal, the court noted the need for judicial caution in these cases because:

> accent and national origin are obviously inextricably intertwined in many cases. It would therefore be an easy refuge in this context for an employer unlawfully discriminating against someone based on national origin to state falsely that it was not the person's national origin that caused the employment or promotion problem, but the candidate's inability to measure up to the communication skills demanded by the job. We encourage a very searching look by the district courts at such a claim.[151]

Ultimately, however, the appellate court affirmed the trial court's ruling.[152] Still, advocates should take some heart in the fact that the *Fragante* court did conduct a searching inquiry into *Fragante's* qualifications for the job, and a prospective employer cannot simply deny employment or promotion opportunities on the basis of accent without subjecting themselves to a legal challenge.

English fluency

Just as the courts are unwilling to question employer discretion in accent cases, employer requirements for English fluency, often mixed with accent issues, are also apparently not disturbed. Most distressing, however, is the incredible paucity of analysis in these cases. It is impossible to tell from courts' conclusory statements and lack of a parsing through of facts how a court came to its decision besides relying almost completely on the allegations made by the employer. For instance, in *Tran v. City of Houston*,[153] a Vietnamese immigrant was employed by the City of Houston as an engineer in control of air conditioning and heating equipment. Tran upgraded his license to a Level II in October 1979. He then applied for a transfer to an inspector position, the primary responsibility of which was to ensure that all public commercial buildings complied with a city ordinance on energy conservation. The position required that the inspector explain the law to building owners, evaluate their use of light, heat, air, and water and then help the owners design an acceptable plan of conservation. Tran had all the qualifications necessary for the job and according to the City would have been hired were it not for his lack of oral English fluency; there was no question about his ability to write and read English fluently. The court agreed with the City's assessment of Tran's oral fluency finding that there were times when his English was "understood only with difficulty and sometimes not at all."[154] It is hard to swallow the court's decision, however, since Mr Tran had previously worked as an interpreter for the United States forces during the Vietnam War when apparently his oral English fluency was not an issue.

In order for language minority communities and their advocates to have greater confidence in the courts in this area and for the courts themselves to decide these accent and fluency cases with some predictability, appellate courts must demand that the trial courts undergo a serious factual investigation into the cases before them. Closely following the classic employment discrimination paradigm discussed above should help. Under *Griggs v. Duke Power*,[155] the Supreme Court required that employers show that a qualification, here English language ability, is truly related to the job to be performed and that there is no less discriminatory alternative available than a high level of English fluency.

One commentator has suggested a four-pronged analysis which can help courts apply this test. She suggests that courts inquire:

(1)   What level of communication is required for the job?
(2)   Was the candidate's speech fairly evaluated?
(3)   Is the candidate intelligible to the pool of relevant, non-prejudiced listeners, such that job performance is not unreasonably impeded?

(4)   What accommodations are reasonable given the job and limitations in intelligibility?[156]

Advocates and judges must remember that it is national origin discrimination, pure and simple, that is at stake here. In accent cases at least, the connection between national origin and accent is rock solid, even if in minority language usage cases it is harder to make; here, the characteristic at issue, accent, is immutable. Courts now need to act and analyze the facts before them as they ought to be doing in national origin cases – with strict scrutiny and with the attitude of outrage that race discrimination cases often evoke. Advocates must be strong in reminding courts of this and publicizing the pandering attitudes of employers and those courts that condone them.

LABOR UNIONS AND THE DUTY TO REPRESENT ALL EMPLOYEES FAIRLY

Title VII applies to labor unions and employment agencies just as much as it applies to employers, although there is less litigation against these labor institutions. Labor unions, for instance, cannot organize employees along racial or ethnic lines or keep minorities out of positions of power within the union. In addition to the civil rights obligation not to discriminate, labor unions also have what is called a "duty of fair representation."[157] Language minority members can legitimately raise questions as to whether their union is adequately representing them if their communication with the union leadership is stymied.

One case arising out of the Ninth Circuit, *Retana v. Apartment, Motel, Hotel and Elevator Operators Union, Local 14, AFL-CIO et al.*,[158] suggested that union failure to provide translation of the collective bargaining agreement and to furnish bilingual union representatives *may* breach the union's duty of fair representation. Retana, a hotel maid, had alleged that there was a "very substantial" number of Spanish-dominant union members and "many are recent immigrants and lack familiarity with the 'customs and practices of American labor management relations'."[159] She alleged that the union violated its duty of fair representation by failing to provide a bilingual liaison between Spanish-dominant members and the union; by failing to provide them with a copy of the collective bargaining agreement in Spanish; by failing to explain their rights and responsibilities as union members, including the right to have the union process a grievance on their behalf and the failure to seek the establishment of a bilingual supervisory system.[160] In reaching its decision, the court noted that the "duty imposed upon a union is broad and demanding. It must 'serve the interests of all members without hostility or discrimination toward any ... exercise its discretion with complete good faith and honesty and ... avoid arbitrary conduct."[161] In allowing Retana's complaint to survive a motion to dismiss, the court found that it was not:

> difficult to conceive a set of facts that might be proven under the allegations of this complaint, in which a minority group of union members were effectively

deprived of an opportunity to participate in the negotiation of a collective bargaining contract or in the enjoyment of its benefits by a language barrier which union officials exploited or took no steps to overcome.[162]

In *Zamora v. Local 11, Hotel, Employees and Restaurant Employees International Union* (AFL-CIO),[163] the court held that the union's rule not to provide translation at regular union membership meetings was a violation of the Labor-Management Reporting and Disclosure Act (LMRDA). Zamora and other union members had petitioned Local 11 officers through internal union procedures to provide a qualified translator at the meetings; Local 11's membership was 48% Spanish-dominant. The majority of the membership voted the proposal down, however, at its regularly scheduled meeting. The purpose of the LMRDA, stated the court, was to guarantee the "full and active participation by the rank and file in the affairs of the union" and thereby, reduce the likelihood of corruption amongst the union leadership. The LMRDA contains a "Bill of Rights" which guarantees that every members shall have equal rights to nominate candidates, vote in elections, attend membership meetings and participate in the deliberations and voting upon the business of the meetings "subject to reasonable rules and regulations" in the union's by-laws and constitution.

First, the court found that the union's non-translation rule did indeed conflict with the LMRDA's Bill of Rights. Simply, since Zamora and a bare minority of the membership cannot understand English, they cannot:

> fully participate in the give and take of "shop talk." Moreover, if union members cannot understand the discussion taking place at the membership meetings, they cannot be expected to make informed nomination and voting decisions.... Thus the practical effect of the union's non-translation rule is to restrict not only participation rights, but voting rights as well.[164]

Second, the court found that the rule could not be saved as a "reasonable rule or regulation." In determining whether the rule was reasonable, the court needed to balance the undemocratic effects of the rule with the union's interest in protecting its institutional integrity. The union argued that since the rule was voted on through open and democratic means, the court should not intervene. The court, however, felt that the rule was unreasonable, and could not be made better by the democratic means with which it was adopted:

> Given the percentage lingual makeup of the union, without translation services nearly one-half of the union members would be excluded from participatory discussion at the union meetings.... In fact, protection of the union as an institution is advanced by providing translation since this ensures common understanding of the discussions taking place among the attending members.... Moreover, given the makeup of Local 11, with nearly equal amount of English-speaking and non-English speaking members, a single-language requirement dependent upon majority rule could change numerous times within a given

year. Such an occurrence could only heighten racial tension within the union and weaken the organization as an institution.[165]

The concern that neither unions nor employers exploit language barriers also underlies labor union representation elections. Here, there is more case law defining under what circumstances bilingual voting notices and ballots must be provided mostly because of the important role that the National Labor Relations Board (NLRB) plays in implementing and monitoring the elections. Briefly, employees have a right under §7 of the National Labor Relations Act (NLRA) to elect whether they would like to have a labor union represent them or, if two unions are vying for representative status, who they would like to represent them. Employees must be able to exercise a fair and informed "§7 choice," clearly providing multilingual ballots for language-minority employees is a significant part of ensuring that the choices made are indeed informed.

Since the 1970s, several decisions by the NLRB and the federal courts have addressed the issue of providing multilingual ballots. The NLRB places the burden of making a timely request for multilingual election notices and ballots upon the employer and the union(s): "[a]bsent a timely request for bilingual materials, the Board will set aside an election only if the challenging party could show the lack of bilingual materials had a markedly adverse, outcome determinative impact upon the ability of employees to cast an informed vote."[166] So that in *Fibre Leather Manufacturing Corporation and International Leather Goods, Plastics & Novelty Workers Union, AFL-CIO*,[167] the Board set aside an election where both sides requested bilingual ballots because 15–20 of the 86 employees were Portuguese-dominant. The regional director of the Board failed to provide the requested bilingual ballots. The election was set aside, even though bilingual election observers were provided since the Portuguese employees, were not even aware of the purpose of these observers.[168]

Indeed, in *Kraft, Inc. Retail Food Group and Zenon N. Olow and Local 34, United Food & Commercial Workers of America, AFL-CIO*,[169] the Board ordered a new election where the multilingual ballots requested by the parties were so defective on their face that they were found to interfere with the employees' ability to exercise their election choices. The ballots were rife with translation errors and the appearance of the ballot, even to English-readers was confusing. The Regional Director had found that the translation issues affected only a small percentage of voters and therefore refused to order a new election. The Board overruled him, finding that "where the ballot is facially defective, we view evidence of actual voter confusion which would alter the election count as irrelevant."[170]

In *Norwestern Products and Amalgamated Food Processors Union, Local 190, Amalgamated Meat Cutters and Butcher Workmen of North America*[171] the Board upheld English-only ballots even though one-third of the workforce at issue was not dominant in English, since no party to the election requested the bilingual voting materials; the Regional Director of the Board, however, had been alerted to the fact that many of the employees did not speak or read English. In determining whether the election ought to be set aside, the Regional Director interviewed 18 of the 29 employees who did not understand English, and found that 10 of them had such a limited command of English that he was unable to communicate with them. These employees represented in 10 different languages. There is much in the decision to indicate that the multiplicity of languages was what in fact led to no party requesting bilingual materials. The Board noted:

> [r]elying on the complexity of conducting an election in ten languages, the Petitioner also argues that even if some employees could not communicate with the Board agent during his investigation of the objections, this does not establish that they were unable to understand the ballot.[172]

Over the objection of one member of the three-member panel that decided the case, the Board held that the use of English-only ballots could not have had an adverse impact on the election because the union had a history of conducting all of its affairs only in English. The dissenting member of the panel, however, wisely pointed out that the Board:

> can or should accede to agreements of parties to the use of English notices and ballots in these circumstances which are so clearly in derogation of those [§7] employee rights.... It is the needs of the employees in making a free and untrammeled choice of a bargaining representative that is controlling and significant, not the needs of a union ... to maintain an effective bargaining relationship.[173]

CONCLUSION

The cases challenging English-only workplace rules raise the most controversial issues discussed in this chapter. For it is in the English-only arena that the value judgments usually involved in language cases are stripped to their bare essentials. These cases rarely involve the kinds of administrative or monetary considerations that are at issue in cases involving translation or interpretation services. Instead, English-only cases involve employers trying to achieve a linguistically-homogenized work environment for little other reason than because that is the setting in which they feel most comfortable. They cloak their words in objective-sounding terminology; saying, for instance, that English-only promotes "safety" or workplace "harmony." Unfortunately, courts are willing to give these rationales, which are simply no more than polite covers for xenophobia, the cloak of legitimacy by calling them "business necessity."

The EEOC's presumption against English-only workplace rules is a sensible one – it allows for narrow rules with legitimate justifications, but also guards against those aspects of human nature that seek to restrict or eradicate fear-inspiring situations: here, foreigners and foreign languages. Judicial willingness to ignore the EEOC's Guidelines on this issue is problematic. First, it is rare but not unprecedented, for courts to question the validity of a governmental agency's interpretation of the statute it is charged with enforcing. Great deference is usually given to agency determinations, and this should be especially true when civil rights statutes are at issue and the agency interpretation does not undermine the purposes of the statute. Indeed, the EEOC's Guidelines create only a *rebuttable* presumption of discrimination, employers with legitimate justifications for their rules can easily overcome the presumption. As the court in *Synchro-Start* found, the EEOC presumption acts only as a "tie-breaker" and does not shift the ultimate burden of persuasion.

Second, a strict adherence to the Guidelines by the courts would avoid the incongruous vision of courts measuring levels of bilingualism and determining which employees can "choose" to follow English-only rules and which cannot. Courts have no expertise in this area and are really giving life to a fiction if they act as if bilingualism can be contained into particular boxes of linguistic behavior.

While courts and employers seem willing to ignore the Guidelines, at least the Guidelines have not been withdrawn by the Bush Administration, which is otherwise so politically conservative. This is a good sign and may indicate that there is still some respect for civil rights laws that address clearly discriminatory practices. An even better move would be to convert the Guidelines into regulations which would require that courts give them true deference. Proposed regulations need to be the subject of public hearings, and this vetting process could give the EEOC's position on English-only workplace rules real legitimacy.

What should be clear from the discussion in this chapter is that language rights in the employment context are in flux. The deference given to employers on English-only rules is also manifest in the areas of accent discrimination and compensation for bilingualism. Only in the labor context are courts and, here, the NLRB, more willing to mandate linguistic accommodation. This is probably because of the nature of a labor union – its principal mission is to advocate and fully represent its members. Its tools of operation, such as elections, have the flavor of fundamental rights, so courts are more willing to insist that they be held fairly. The union's duty to fairly represent members also has a hue of guardianship that the courts take seriously. In the face of explicit statutory requirements like the ones found in the labor laws, the courts have been more tolerant of language-minority claims.

What is needed is a forceful strategy that uses the recent boom in immigrant labor to push for more inclusive and fairer employment practices. Labor can lead the way in this area and has already made a promising start. The AFL-CIO recently announced its adoption of a new policy on recent immigrant workers that urged amnesty for undocumented immigrants. For decades, the US labor establishment depicted undocumented immigrants as the bane of organized workers as they were characterized as accepting lower, non-union-scale pay for work that could be done by unionized workers.[174] In a turn-around, the AFL-CIO has announced what many in the immigrant advocacy community already knew – that the immigration rules help unscrupulous employers exploit their illegally-immigrated employees.[175] Now, labor leaders say that "[t]he present system doesn't work and is used as a weapon against workers.... The only reason a lot of employers want to hire a large number of illegal aliens is so they can exploit them."[176]

The change in labor's policy was aptly summarized by one union leader as "a very dramatic change in policy that follows a very dramatic change in our world."[177]

How unions, employers and even majority-language co-workers deal with these dramatic changes in the demographics of the workforce will be especially critical to the future of the labor movement and more generally to language-minority empowerment.

Notes

1. 618 F2d 264 (5th Cir 1980), *cert. den.* 449 US 113 (1981).
2. 998 F2d 1480, 1484 (9th Cir 1993), *rehr'g den.*, 13 F3d 296 (9th Cir 1993).
3. 42 USC §2000e-2(a) (2002).
4. Title VII also applies to the federal government although different procedures are used for processing those complaints. However, the term "employer" does not include the United States, the District of Columbia, an Indian tribe, or any corporation wholly owned by the US or agency of the DC.
5. 411 US 792, 802-805 (1973).
6. *St. Mary's Honor Ctr. v. Hicks*, 509 US 502, 506 (1993).
7. *Id.*
8. 490 US 228 (1989).
9. 42 USCA §2000e-2 (m). Controversy continues to exist, however, as to how helpful the Civil Rights Act has really been. *See* Thomas H. Bernard, and George S. Crisci *"Mixed Motive" Discrimination Under The Civil Rights Act of 1991: Still a "Pyrrhic Victory" for Plaintiffs?* 51 MERCER L. REV. 673. (2000).
10. *Watson v. Fort Worth Bank & Trust*, 487 US 977 (1987).
11. *Supra,* note 2 at 1484 (citation omitted).
12. *Id.*
13. *Griggs v. Duke Power, Co.*, 401 US 424 (1971).
14. *Wards Cove Packing Co. v. Atonio,* 490 US 642 (1989). (In 1989, with an increasingly conservative judiciary, the Supreme Court lessened the burden on the employer – it would no longer have to affirmatively establish a defense of business necessity, but only that the employment practice being challenged serves the employer's legitimate employment goals, a much lighter burden. When Congress passed the Civil Rights Act of 1991, it also re-established the *Griggs* burden-shifting paradigm.)
15. A complaint must be filed with the EEOC within 180 days of the act complained of, and the EEOC must issue a "right to sue" letter before a complainant can become a plaintiff in court.
16. Lisa L. Behm *Protecting Linguistic Minorities Under Title VII: The Need for Judicial Deference to the EEOC Guidelines on Discrimination Because of National Origin* 81, MARQ. L. REV. 569 (1998) at 573.
17. 29 CFR §1606, (2002) *et seq*.
18. *Id.* (Prior to 1980, the Guidelines, which had been issued in 1970, were primarily concerned with the discriminatory use of English language tests for jobs that did not require English language skills, and the use of height and weight requirements that were not necessary for job performance and that tended to exclude certain national origin groups.) *See* EEOC Fact Sheet.
19. EEOC Compliance Manual §623.2(a) at 3833 (August 6, 1984).
20. *Id.*
21. 29 CFR §1606.7(a) (2002).

22. *Prado L. Luria & Son, Inc.*, 975 FSupp 1349, 1355 (SD Fla. 1997).
23. *Harris v. Fork Lift Systems, Inc.*, 510 US 17 (1993).
24. *Supra*, note 22 at 1356.
25. *See Flores v. Hartford Police Department*, 1981 US Dist. Lexis 11484 (D Conn. 1981).
26. *Supra*, note 19 at 3836.
27. 464 FSupp 919 (SD Tex. 1979).
28. *Id*. at 920.
29. *Id*. at 921.
30. *Id*.
31. *Id*. at 922.
32. *Supra*, note 1.
33. *Id*. at 266–267.
34. *Id*. at 267.
35. *Id*. at fn. 1.
36. *Id*. at 268.
37. *Id*. at 269.
38. *Id*.
39. *Id*. at 270.
40. Manuel del Valle, *National Origin Discrimination* at §29-22 (June, 1993). (Draft manuscript on file with author.)
41. *Id* at §29-25.
42. *Id*.
43. *Supra*, note 2.
44. The court's opinion did not reveal how these non-Spanish-speaking employees knew the content of the comments.
45. *Supra*, note 2 at 1483.
46. *Id*. at 1484.
47. *Id*. at 1487.
48. *Id*.
49. *Id*. at 1488 (emphasis added).
50. *Id*. at 1489 (citations omitted).
51. *Id*. at 1490.
52. *Garcia v. Spun Steak*, Co., 13 F3d 296 (9th Cir 1993) at 300, n. 7.
53. *Id*.
54. *Id*. at 298 (citations omitted).
55. *Id*.
56. *Id*. (notes omitted).
57. *Id*. at n.7.
58. 894 FSupp 933 (ED Va 1995), *aff'd*, unpublished op., 86 F3d 1151 (4th Cir 1996).
59. *Id*. at 941.
60. *Id*. at 942.
61. 88 FSupp 2d 257 (SDNY 2000).
62. *Id*. at 260.
63. *Id*. at 262.

64. *Id.* at 262, *quoting Soberal-Perez v. Heckler,* 717 F2d 36 (2nd Cir 1983).

65. *Id.* at 262–263.

66. 29 FSupp 2d 911 (ND Ill. 1999).

67. *Id.* at 913, *quoting Spun Steak,* 998 F2d at 1487.

68. *Id.* at 914.

69. *EEOC v. University of the Incarnate Word,*Civil No. SA-99-CA-1090-OG *Memorandum and Recommendation* (M.J. John Primomo) (WD Tex.).

70. *Id.* at 8 (*Plaintiff's Statement of Disputed Material Facts on National Origin Discrimination Claims*).

71. *Id.*

72. *Id.* at 20 (*Memorandum and Recommendation*).

73. *See Id.* (On file with author and US District Court, WD Tex.)

74. 75 FSupp 2d 550 (ND Tex. 1999), *injunction granted,* 113 FSupp 2d 1066 (ND Tex. 2000).

75. *Id.* 113 FSupp at 1069.

76. *Id.* at 1068.

77. *Id.* at 1069.

78. *Id.*

79. *Id.*

80. *Id.* at 1070.

81. *Id.*

82. *Id.* at 1074.

83. *Id.* at 1077.

84. *Supra,* note 19 at 3841.

85. 838 F2d 1031 (9th Cir 1988), *vacated as moot, Municipal Court of the Southeast Judicial District v. Gutierrez,* 490 US 1016 (1989).

86. *Id.* at 1040.

87. *Id.* at n. 9.

88. *Id.* at 1041–1042, *quoting, Williams v. Colorado Springs School District No. 11,* 641 F2d 835, 842 (10th Cir 1981).

89. *Supra,* note 19 at 3842.

90. *Id.*

91. Juan F. Perea, *English-Only Rules and the Right to Speak One's Primary Language in the Workplace,* 23 Journal of L. Reform 265, 313–314 (1990).

92. *Supra,* note 19 at 3843.

93. *Supra,* note 85.

94. *Id.* at 1043.

95. *Id.* at n. 15.

96. 10 FSupp 2d 1199 (DC Kansas 1998), *vacated,* 205 F3d 1324 (2nd Cir 2000).

97. *Id.* at 1210.

98. 1998 WL 786391 (ND Ill. 1998).

99. *Id.* at 6.

100. 975 FSupp 1349 (SD Fla. 1997).

101. *Id.* at 1354.

102. *Id.*

103. However, in *EEOC v. Premier Operator Services, Inc., supra,* note 74 at 6–7, the court did

not credit the employer's justification for a blanket English-only policy where the employer said it had implemented the policy to promote "harmony" in the workplace. The court found that there was no evidence that there had ever been "discord" in the workplace to begin with which such a policy was needed to correct. *Id.*

104. 813 F2d 1406 (9th Cir 1987).

105. *Jurado* also raises the interesting question, often raised negatively by courts, as to the connection between language and national origin. Jurado had claimed disparate treatment because he was told not to use Spanish during his broadcasts while an Anglo disk jockey was allowed to continue using Spanish in his format. While this might be probative in a simple employment discrimination claim, where a purported English-only rule is at issue, the continued unpunished use of Spanish by another disk jockey would tend to undermine, not support, the claim of employment discrimination based on national origin.

106. 10 FSupp 2d 318 (SDNY 1998).

107. *Id.* at 321.

108. *Id.*

109. *Id.* at 324.

110. 775 FSupp 338 (CD Cal. 1991), *withdrawn*, 1993 WL 326559 (CD Cal. 1993).

111. *Id.* at 342.

112. *Id.*

113. *Id.* at 341.

114. *Id.*

115. *Id.*

116. *Id.*

117. *Id.*

118. *Id.* at 340.

119. 831 FSupp 1079 (SDNY 1993).

120. *Id.* at 1086–87.

121. Susan J. Dicker, *Adaptation and Assimilation: US Business Responses to Linguistic Diversity in the Workplace*, JOURNAL OF MULTILINGUAL AND MULTICULTURAL DEVELOPMENT Vol. 19 (1998) at 295.

122. *Id.*

123. 707 FSupp 891, 899 (WD Tex. 1988).

124. *Id.* at n. 21.

125. *Id.* at 1793.

126. *Id.*

127. *Id.* at 1795.

128. 783 FSupp 458 (D Ariz. 1992).

129. *Id.* at 462.

130. *See also Morales v. Human Rights Division*, 878 FSupp 653 (SDNY 1995) (where use of Spanish language skills by *all*, not just Latino, employees, did not significantly affect job performance).

131. 459 FSupp 375 (SDNY 1978).

132. *Id.* at 377.

133. 522 F2d 1215 (6th Cir 1975).

134. *Id.* at 1216.

135. *Id.* at 1218.

136. *Id.* at 1219.

137. *Id.* at 1220 (citation omitted).

138. *Id.* (citation omitted). (Although the court said that Frontera's civil rights were not violated, no civil rights statute was before the court for analysis and it had already pointed out that it was not expressing an opinion as to Title VII or Title VI *Id.* at 1218.)

139. Mari Matsuda, *Voices of America: Accent, Anti-discrimination Law, and a Jurisprudence for the Last Reconstruction*, 100 YALE L. J. 1329, 1351 (1991).

140. 750 F2d 815 (10th Cir 1984).

141. 411 US 792, 802 (1973).

142. *Supra*, note 134 at 819. *See also Berke v. Ohio Department of Public Welfare*, 628 F2d 980 (6th Cir 1980).

143. 699 FSupp 1429 (D Hawaii 1987), *aff'd*, 888 F2d 591 (9th Cir 1989).

144. *Id.* at 1429.

145. *Id.* at 1430.

146. *Id.*

147. *Id.* at 1431.

148. *Id.*

149. *Supra*, note 134 at n. 28.

150. *Supra*, note 134 at 1431–32.

151. 150. 888 F2d 591, 596 (9th Cir 1989).

152. *See also Bell v. Home Life Insurance Co.*, 596 FSupp 1549 (MD No. Car.1984).

153. 1983 US Dist. LEXIS 18958 (SD Tex. 1983).

154. 1983 US Dist. LEXIS 18958, at 4.

155. 401 US 424 (1971).

156. *Supra*, note 132 at 1368. (Although the last prong refers to a requirement that the employer make reasonable accommodations, a principle usually found in disability law, this prong can be understood as requiring that there be no less discriminatory alternative to the course of conduct followed by the employers.)

157. This duty was first articulated by the Supreme Court in *Steele v. Louisville & Nashville R.R. Co.*, 323 US 192 (1944) as it interpreted the Railway Labor Act and then applied under the National Labor Relations Act. *See Ford Motor Co. v. Huffman,*345 US 330 (1953).

158. 453 F2d 1018 (9th Cir 1972). (Although the Court remanded the case for further proceedings and did not reach the merits of Retana's claim, the Court found that the trial court did have jurisdiction to hear the "DFR" claim.)

159. *Id.* at 1023 (citations omitted).

160. *Id.*

161. *Id.* at 1023, *citing, Vaca v. Sipes*, 386 US 171, 177 (1967).

162. *Id.* at 1024.

163. 817 F2d 566 (9th Cir 1987). (AFL-CIO is the American Federation of Labor-Congress of Industrial Organizations.)

164. *Id.* at 569.

165. *Id.* at 570–571.

166. David Gregory, *Union Leadership and Workers' Voices: Meeting the Needs of Linguistically Heterogeneous Union Members.* 58 U. CIN. L. REV. 115 (1989) at 135.

167. 167 NLRB 393 (1967).

168. *See also Marriott In-Flite Services v. National Labor Relations Board*, 417 F2d 563 (5th Cir 1969) (where the Fifth Circuit found that NLRB policy was to provide bilingual ballots when requested even absent a showing of prejudice; although the policy was not found in any statute, the court held one errant region to that standard), *see also Flo-Tronic Metal Mfg, Inc. and Steelworkers of America, AFL-CIO*, 105 LRRM 1144 (1980).

169. 118 LRRM 1242 (1985).

170. 1985 NLRB LEXIS 822, at *62–63.

171. 226 NLRB 653 (Oct. 29, 1976).

172. 1976 NLRB Lexis 202 at **4–5.

173. *Id.* at **12.

174. *See* Steven Greenhouse, *Labor Urges Amnesty for Illegal Immigrants*, NY TIMES, Feb. 17, 2000.

175. *Id.*

176. *Id.*

177. *Id.*

Chapter 5

Language Rights in Litigation: Making the Case for Greater Protections in Criminal and Civil Proceedings

INTRODUCTION

This chapter is concerned with the manner in which language rights arise in the context of judicial and quasi-judicial proceedings. Criminal and civil trials and quasi-judicial hearings like those held by the Immigration and Naturalization Service (INS) or involving parole are all covered. The issues are complex and involve a number of specific sources of flaw, some constitutional and some statutory. Given the complexity of the areas involved, the chapter is divided into three parts each with its own section for conclusions: criminal, civil and INS proceedings, jury service and finally, language rights in prison. Since the law is most developed and most complex in the criminal setting where the risks to language minorities are also greatest, the bulk of this chapter will focus on the criminal context. The criminal portion of the general section on proceedings takes us from the language issues that arise in the initial interrogation or search through the translation and interpretation practices at trials, pleas sentencing, and parole. There is a shorter section on civil litigation where the rights of language minority litigants are much less secure than in the criminal area. Finally, the section on proceedings concludes with a portion on INS hearings, which hold a middle ground between criminal and civil litigation.

The section on jury service is likewise divided, this time into two parts: one on the federal English proficiency requirements for jury service, and the second on the more complex emerging issues of the ability of full bilinguals to serve on juries when there may be presented translated testimony or evidence. The Supreme Court issued a recent decision on language rights in this area and it serves as an object lesson for language rights advocates.

The final section of this chapter concerns language rights in prison, with the most significant case in this area receiving detailed treatment. In this case, Latino prisoners were being denied linguistically appropriate prison services that were available to other inmates. Although the trial court did an admirable job of sorting through the evidence to uphold the prisoners' claims, on appeal the question simply became one of economics.

CRIMINAL, CIVIL, AND INS PROCEEDINGS

> Injustice is being done from time to time in communities thronged with aliens, through failure of the judges to insist on a supply of competent interpreters. The subject is one upon the profession are in general too callous, for no situation is more full of anguish than that of an innocent accused who cannot understand what is being testified against him.[1]

Criminal proceedings from interrogation to parole

From the moment the police begin to question a suspect through their arrest and trial to post-sentencing procedures, non-English speakers are at a frightening disadvantage when entangled within the US's criminal justice machinery. Issues of English-language proficiency as well as foreign acculturation can wreak havoc with, not only the accused's understanding of the circumstances in which he finds himself, but the ability of lawyers, jurors, and judges to accurately assess the accused's motivations, intentions, and even actions. Indeed, before any charge is filed, police officers have conversations with the accused and with potential witnesses or make subjective assessments of the accused's behavior that can either be used to build a case against an individual or absolve him of suspicion. It is at these points that a recent immigrant's English language deficiencies, unfamiliarity with US police process and possible police bias can result in the unknowing waiver of rights and even an unnecessary arrest.

Although there are constitutional and statutory protections for non-English speaking defendants, they all suffer from a substantial weakness: an almost unfettered discretion placed with trial courts leave them with the power to determine the scope of those rights with little appellate court guidance.

Defense counsel must always be securing a potent record for appeal, even while preparing a vigorous defense at trial. Counsel must be clear, prompt and adamant about the need for an interpreter at all courtroom proceedings from arraignment to sentencing, if necessary. Any evidence obtained against the client must be the subject of a hearing in which any role that the defendant's English language limitations, and/or foreign acculturation, is exposed and presented for consideration by the trial court. Finally, any sense that a court interpreter is not qualified needs to be raised and if necessary made the subject of a hearing. As detailed below, the issues raised by a language-minority defendant throughout the criminal justice process are significant because of the English-language hegemony of the system. Counsel must be aggressive in order to protect the client's rights within a structure that may see the "efficient administration of justice" as a rationale for summarily denying interpreter assistance.

Interrogations and searches

Sensitivity to the possible English language limitations of any individual, especially in cities with high immigrant populations, needs to become a routine aspect of police work. The infamous case of the killing of Amadou Diallo in the Bronx, New York by four police officers raised the country's awareness of the plight of immigrants in highly charged, police-controlled occurrences. In that case, an unarmed African immigrant was shot down by plainclothes policemen in a vestibule outside his apartment. There was speculation that Mr Diallo, who spoke only a slow and halting English, did not understand possible police commands not to move.[2] Mr Diallo did make a motion to take out his wallet, perhaps misinterpreting the police's words as an order to produce identification. He was shot down because the police said they thought he was reaching for a gun.

A police interrogation, a search and an arrest are all highly upsetting, anxiety-producing events that are made even more so for anyone who doesn't understand English or who is more comfortable speaking a language other than English. It is at these critical junctures, however, where evidence can be found, inadvertent admissions to crimes made, and simple questioning can turn into a full-blown arrest.

Interrogations

Before the police can question a suspect, the suspect's rights under *Miranda v. Arizona* ("*Miranda* warnings") need to be explained to them; this is essentially a detailing of the suspect's right not to incriminate himself by answering questions posed by the police and his right to a lawyer; if a suspect requests a lawyer, the police must stop any questioning until a lawyer is present; the suspect may then waive his right against self-incrimination with the lawyer present.[3] If a suspect waives his *Miranda* rights, he usually signs the bottom of a *Miranda* card stating that he fully and freely waives his rights and wants to proceed with questioning. If a suspect waives these rights, a police officer can question the suspect and take a written statement.

Under *Miranda*, there is a heavy burden on the government to demonstrate that the defendant "knowingly" and "intelligently" waived his privilege against self-incrimination and his right to counsel. In order to determine whether a valid waiver had been obtained a court "should consider all the circumstances surrounding the interrogation, including the defendant's age, experience, education, background and intelligence."[4] The issues for language-minority suspects are obvious: what does "knowingly and intelligently" mean for a non-English speaking newcomer? One commentator answers that, for a waiver to be knowingly and intelligently made:

means much more than the fact that the police translated the *Miranda* warnings into the defendant's language. Counsel must consider, in addition, the defendant's background understanding of the American legal system, and all the surrounding circumstances to determine the adequacy of the warnings and the sufficiency of the waiver.[5]

In *US v. Nakhoul*,[6] defendant challenged the admissibility of two sets of post-arrest statements, the first were made in a vehicle to police officers, and the second at Drug Enforcement Administration (DEA) headquarters. The Middle Eastern defendant was charged, with two others, with possession of heroin with intent to distribute.

In determining whether the statements made by the defendant could be used against him at trial, the court found that the statements made in the vehicle were admissible because the atmosphere was fairly congenial, Nakhoul initiated the conversation with police officers and Nakhoul nodded his assent to continue speaking after the *Miranda* warnings were read. The circumstances at the DEA headquarters, however, were substantially different. At the headquarters, the interrogation became aggressive, Nakhoul was placed in a small, windowless room, the *Miranda* rights had been read one and a half hours before and not repeated. The court found that under these conditions, Nakhoul's admissions were not admissible as they were procured in violation of his rights. The "subject's background should be considered when applying the totality of the circumstances test," said the court.[7]

Applying these standards to the case before it, the court reasoned that Nakhoul was a Lebanese national whose understanding of American laws, systems and constitutional rights may be limited; he probably didn't understand that *Miranda* rights given in the car were still applicable at DEA headquarters. Given the circumstances, the atmosphere was too coercive for any implied *Miranda* waiver to have been considered knowingly and intelligently made.[8] Therefore, the second set of statements were found to be inadmissible.

Similarly, in *US v. Short*,[9] the court found that *Miranda* warnings given only in English to a West German defendant were insufficient where she had been in the US for only three months, barely spoke English and was socially isolated while living on an army base. The court questioned the tactics of the police who came to question Short and the language used in the written statement that was admitted into evidence against her: "she was arrested by some of the same agents who had told her to come for an 'interview'... and she was separated from her children, and subjected to an interrogation in English, even though one of the agents spoke some German. Farmer [an agent] testified that she thought Short was 'ignorant,' 'a victim herself,' and evidenced 'judgment limitations.'" ... Additionally, Farmer testified that, at the interview, she wondered whether Short "'recognized that she was implicating herself.'"[10] The court could not give credence to the written statement the police attributed to her. Terms, like "fellatio" were used, which were clearly outside of Short's English vocabulary. The statement at best was the "agent's interpretation of her halting English."[11]

But in *Valdez v. Ward*,[12] the court found that a Spanish-dominant defendant had knowingly waived his *Miranda* rights after the appeals court reviewed the interrogation and trial transcripts. Although Valdez had referred to an interpreter to explain himself at trial occasionally the majority of the transcript revealed that he knew sufficient English to have been able to understand the nature of the *Miranda* warnings and therefore to waive these rights.[13]

Providing *Miranda* rights in the suspect's native language through the use of a previously translated and printed *Miranda* card is usually the safest course for the police. To waive *Miranda* rights, the accused would have had to sign the bottom of the card indicating his waiver. The presence of the translated card eliminates questions as to the quality of the translation, and substantially reduces doubt as to whether the accused understood his rights.[14] Although the defendant's signature at the bottom of the translated card is the most compelling evidence of a proper waiver, it is certainly not required and like much else, the adequacy of the *Miranda* translation, is left to the trial court to determine.

Once a trial court finds that *Miranda* warnings were properly translated, the burden is on the appealing defendant to show an abuse of discretion by the trial court in allowing the disputed statements to be used at trial. Appellate courts rarely, however, overrule trial courts on factual issues left to resolution by judicial discretion. The trial judge is assumed to be fundamentally fair and to have had the chance to view the evidence most fully, including the invaluable opportunity to account for the nuances that cannot be captured in a written transcript. The burden is heavy for a defendant appealing such a ruling:

> [t]o create a record on which to appeal a court's ruling that *Miranda* warnings were adequately interpreted, a defendant must introduce evidence of the questionable interpretation practices of the interpreter, the terms or legal concepts misused, or evidence demonstrating a defendant's lack of comprehension.[15]

Searches

Many of the same concepts that apply to the interrogation situation also apply to police searches. Generally, unless the suspect consents to the search, a police officer may not search someone unless there is probable cause to believe that the suspect committed a crime. Significant cultural issues can come into play here as a recent immigrant may not even be aware of the right to refuse a search by the police or even to walk away from a police officer; they may have such divergent experiences of the police in their native country that the concept of consenting to a search simply has no meaning. Further, they may become intimidated by the situation and feel they cannot refuse a search. Finally, they may indeed try to refuse the search but be misunderstood by the police. Again, the voluntariness of defendant's consent to a search must be determined by an examination of a "totality of the circumstances." "English language comprehension, cultural background and understanding of the American legal system may be relevant factors"[16]

In *US v. Gallego-Zapata*,[17] the defendant, a 22 year old native of Columbia, asked the trial court to suppress the drugs found in a bag he was carrying, which was seized from him at Logan Airport by narcotics officers. Gallego-Zapata had only seven years of schooling, had been in the US for only four months, and spoke extremely limited English. The police claimed that Gallego-Zapata had consented to the search. The government has the burden of proving that a search was consensual. The court stated that, in order to determine whether a search is indeed consensual, it must look to determine whether under all the circumstances a reasonable person would feel free to walk away from the police, or whether the police exerted physical force or authority in such a way to essentially "seize" the person.[18] The inquiry, said the court:

> is into the subjective mental state of the defendant, and relevant factors include age, education, intelligence, experience with law enforcement, race and sex compared with the race and sex of the officers, whether the defendant knew consent could be refused, whether the defendant was in custody when the consent was given, and whether the police misled the defendant about their lawful authority.[19]

In finding that the search of Gallego-Zapata was not consensual, the court took his background and the fact of his recent arrival to the US into account. The court stated that:

> [t]he evidence strongly suggests that [the defendant] merely submitted to what must have appeared to him to be a "claim of lawful authority." When the agents approached and stood close to him, he immediately placed his bag on the floor and answered their questions forthrightly and honestly. Later he told Agent Aquilar that he consented to the search because Agent Lemon had showed him his badge. It is not at all clear that when he began answering their questions he understood them to be narcotics officers rather than immigration officers. Furthermore, the agents and Gallego-Zapata were having difficulty communicating because of Gallego-Zapata's limited skills in English, and the agents resorted to a combination of short English sentences and sign language to convey to him that they wanted to search his jacket.[20]

The court in *US v. Gaviria*,[21] also suppressed drugs recovered during an illegal search of a Spanish-speaking defendant. The police contended that the search was consensual. After Gaviria engaged in a conversation, half in English and half in Spanish, with a Detective Underhill who had limited proficiency in Spanish, the detective asked Gaviria if he could search the bag; Gaviria allowed him to. The court relied on *Gallego-Zapata*, to find that there was no knowing and intelligent waiver of rights. Gaviria was a 21-year-old native of Colombia with limited formal education, and who spoke little English. Further, the court found that much of "what the detective was trying to say would make little or no sense to a person whose native language was Spanish."[22]

From arrest to interrogation and searches to actual trials, the role that language and culture will play in any criminal trial will be a highly individualized situation. Within the context of trials, issues of language and culture coalesce into a complex matrix where the trial court is almost always the ultimate arbiter of an accused's rights.

The trial of the non-English-speaking defendant

The ability of a defendant to understand the proceedings, and to communicate effectively with his lawyer, directly impacts on his right to a fair trial, because holding a trial, or any criminal proceeding, against someone who cannot understand the charges against him is a farce and results in no fair trial at all. One commentator has said that:

> [n]owhere is the need for the protection of the language rights of minority groups more pointed than in contacts with the legal process. Many non-English speakers are recent arrivals to this country; here, they face not only a new language, but a complex criminal justice system that may be just as new and strange as the language. "For a non-English-speaking in criminal cases, the inability of the individual to understand fully the nature of the charges and testimony against him may cost him his liberty or even his life."[23]

Despite the simplicity of the concept of the need for interpretation during trials, this area has grown to be quite complex. Federal and state constitutional and statutory protections as well as old-fashioned common law parallel, overlap and intersect with each other creating a complicated pastiche of rights and limits the legal bases for which are rarely well-articulated by the courts.

Consequently, there are both constitutional and statutory protections for the non-English-speaking defendant under the federal Court Interpreter's Act and the Fifth and Sixth Amendments to the US Constitution. The constitutional protections are reviewed first.

Constitutional protections

The Fifth Amendment states in pertinent part:

> *No person shall ... be deprived of life, liberty, or property, without due process of law...*

The Sixth Amendment states in pertinent part:

> *In all criminal prosecutions, the accused shall enjoy the right to ... be informed of the nature and cause of the accusation; to be confronted with the witnesses against him; to have compulsory process for obtaining witnesses in his favor; and to have the Assistance of Counsel for his defense.*

The Sixth Amendment alone contains many discrete procedural protections that need to be parsed through in order to determine the extent to the right of translation assistance for language minorities. Certainly the defendant has the right to know the charges against him and to confront the witnesses against him. There is also the right to obtain witnesses, which implies the defendant's ability to participate in the building of his own defense and of, course, the right to effective assistance of counsel.

These protections, however, are only as extensive or as limited as the resolution of a number of significant procedural issues allows. The resolution of these issues has been left to the discretion of the trial courts since at least 1907, when the Supreme Court decided *Perovich v. US*,[24] where it stated that the appointment of an interpreter "is a matter largely resting in the discretion of the trial court.... "[25] So it is the trial courts with no special training that must determine whether a defendant needs an interpreter and presumably whether the quality and extent of the translation offered is constitutionally acceptable. The judgment of the trial courts will not be overturned without the defendant meeting the high burden of showing either that the trial court abused its discretion or committed a clear error that must be overturned on appeal. This burden is rarely met. Further, the provision of interpretation services is within a context of English language hegemony reflected by many states, which affirmatively require that court proceedings be held in English and then proceed to carve out narrow exceptions.[26] The US Supreme Court has not decided whether there is a federal constitutional right to an interpreter in criminal proceedings for either a defendant or a witness that does not speak English. However, much state and lower federal court law has evolved in this area. For instance, in *Terry v. State*,[27] Alabama's appeals court stated, albeit in the context of a deaf defendant, that the:

> [Sixth Amendment] constitutional right ... would be meaningless and a vain and useless provision unless the testimony of the witnesses against him could be *understood* by the accused. Mere confrontation of the witnesses would be useless, bordering on the farcical, if the accused could not hear or *understand* their testimony.[28]

In *Marino v. Ragen*,[29] the court held that a defendant was denied due process of law when he was sentenced to life imprisonment when he did not have an attorney and the arresting officer acted as interpreter.

In *People v. Garcia*,[30] a Texas appellate court echoed these sentiments with regard to the trial of a non-English-speaking national of Mexico, who had come across the US border and committed burglary. He was tried in Texas, but the trial court denied him an interpreter without even conducting an investigation into his English-speaking ability. The appellate court found that Mexican nationals being tried in Texas had to be afforded the same rights under the Constitution as citizens of the US:

> [t]his, of necessity, means they are entitled to be confronted by the witnesses under the same conditions as apply to all others. Equal justice so requires. The constitutional right of confrontation means something more than merely bringing the accused and the witnesses face to face; it embodies and carries with it the valuable right of cross-examination of the witnesses.[31]

It was the Second Circuit, however, that decided the landmark case in 1970 that elevated the right to an interpreter to constitutional status. In *US ex rel. Negron, v. New York*,[32] a 23-year-old native of Puerto Rico with only a sixth grade education, was charged with murder. Indigent, Negron was assigned an English-only speaking lawyer. During the trial, Negron was given only brief summaries of the testimony against him by a court translator. Ironically, the translator was present only because there were Spanish-speaking witnesses testifying against Negron, and their testimony needed to be translated for the judge, jury and lawyers. The interpreter was allowed to meet briefly with Negron and his attorney during two recesses in the course of the four-day trial. The interpreter never translated the English language testimony into Spanish for Negron while the trial was in progress. Negron was convicted of murder. He appealed.

The Second Circuit found that Negron's trial violated the Sixth Amendment right of a defendant to confront the witnesses against him. The court found that without the aid of translation, Negron was essentially not present at his own trial. The court stated that it is "imperative that every criminal defendant – if the right to be present is to have meaning – possess 'sufficient present ability to consult with his lawyer with a reasonable degree of rational understanding.'"[33] Negron's incapacity to respond to specific testimony would inevitably hamper the capacity of his counsel to conduct effective cross-examination.

The court stated that:

> [n]ot only for the sake of cross-examination, however, but as a matter of simple humaneness, Negron deserved more than to sit in total incomprehension as the trial proceeded. Particularly inappropriate in this nation where many languages are spoken is a callousness to the crippling language handicap of a newcomer to its shores, whose life and freedom the state by its criminal processes chooses to put in jeopardy.[34]

The Second Circuit delineated the responsibility of the trial court when confronted with a non-English-speaking defendant:

> Negron's language disability was obvious, not just a possibility, and it was as debilitating to his ability to participate in the trial as a mental disease or defect. But it was more readily "curable" than any mental disorder. The least we can require is that a court, *put on notice of a defendant's severe language difficulty*, make unmistakably clear to him that he has a right to have a competent translator to assist him, at state expense if need be, throughout his trial.[35]

Since *Negron*, courts look to see whether fundamental fairness has been done to determine whether the constitutional standard has been met. In determining whether the defendant's trial has been fundamentally fair, the trial court has been given a lot of discretion, but not much guidance from higher courts on how to make its determinations. The emphasized portions of the *Negron* decision above indicate that one of the factors that courts consider when determining the fairness of a trial, is whether the court knew of a defendant's English language difficulties. This can be most easily proven by deciding whether the request for an interpreter has actually been made. As will be discussed further below, courts do put an onus on defendants to assert their rights clearly and in a timely manner; not every instance in which interpreters are denied will result in a reversible error.

Under the Fifth and Sixth Amendments, "[t]he trial court must balance the defendant's right to confrontation and effective assistance against the public's interest in the economical administration of criminal law, and the court's balancing is reversible only on a showing of abuse."[36] In reviewing the trial court's determinations:

> appellate courts appear to focus the inquiry on whether a defendant had been denied a fair trial or whether the proceedings were fundamentally unfair, considering the totality of the circumstances. The review is highly factual and varies from case to case. Where a trial court has failed to appoint a qualified interpreter, the burden falls on the defendant to show that his lack of comprehension of the proceedings was so complete that the trial was fundamentally unfair.[37]

The burden on the defendant on appeal is no small thing – there are as many gradations in someone's language proficiency as there are languages in existence. As discussed below, a defendant may seem proficient in English but may not be able to grasp idiomatic expressions or police procedural terminology. Under such circumstances a trial court could very well deny him an interpreter and have that ruling upheld on appeal.

Statutory protections

With *Negron* as an impetus, Congress passed the Court Interpreters Act (CIA) in 1978. Prior to the passage of the Act there were four federal statutes that addressed the need for interpreter services but none made it into a mandatory right.[38] When Congress held hearings before passing the CIA, they were told of the many convictions that had to be overturned on due process grounds because of judicial failure to appoint interpreters, despite the existence of the federal statutory protections. On the issue of the qualifications of interpreters, witnesses testified to situations in which courts relied on janitors, secretaries or clerk to translate and where judges imply took interpreters' own assertions about their ability to translate as a sufficient qualification.[39]

The CIA requires that federal trial courts use competent interpreters in "judicial proceedings" initiated by the United States. "Judicial proceedings" is defined broadly as "all proceedings whether criminal or civil, including pre-trial and grand jury proceedings."[40] When it is an indigent defendant that requires an interpreter, one is to be appointed at no expense to the defendant. Interpreters are to be made available for defendants or witnesses who are hearing-impaired or are persons:

> who speak only or primarily a language other than the English language ... so as to inhibit such party's comprehension of the proceedings or communication with counsel or the presiding judicial officer so as to inhibit such witnesses comprehension of questions and the presentation of such testimony.[41]

The CIA requires that the interpretation be provided "in the simultaneous mode for any party to a judicial proceeding ... and in the consecutive mode for witnesses." Despite this clear language, courts have held that simultaneous translation need not mean "continuous word-for-word" translation.[42] Instead, in gauging to see whether there has been compliance with the CIA, courts will look to see whether the purposes of the Act were adequately met by the translation that occurred; occasional lapses of the word-for-word standards will be allowed, especially if the defendant fails to object at the trial.[43]

The CIA, however, does not offer new protections to criminal defendants. Courts have repeatedly stated that the Act's protections are co-terminous with those already recognized under the Fifth and Sixth Amendments.[44] The *Joshi* court stated that the CIA "does not create new constitutional rights for defendants or expand existing constitutional safeguards."[45] Instead, "the purpose of the Act is to mandate the appointment of interpreters under certain conditions and to establish statutory guidance for the use of translators in order to ensure that the quality of the translation does not fall below a constitutionally permissible threshold."[46]

Who gets an interpreter?

According to one legal scholar, a study conducted on behalf of the Director of the Administrative Office of the United States Courts found that "because of the sophisticated language level used in [c]ourts, it is necessary to have a minimum of fourteen years of education to understand what goes on in a criminal trial and more than that in a civil trial."[47] Consequently, a defendant's level of English proficiency must be quite high in order to be able to truly understand the proceedings against him and to assist in his own defense; even a good knowledge of everyday conversational English will probably not be enough.

The *Negron* court felt that in the case before it, the defendant's difficulty with the English language was "obvious" and should have been addressed by the trial court. Rarely, however, are the issues in this area so clear cut. In determining whether a translator should be appointed, courts often and should consider a variety of factors, such as the length of the defendant's residence in the US, the nature of his professional or social interactions while residing in the country, his occupations, education, intelligence and citizenship status.[48] Some courts, however, will focus only on the defendant's fluency in speaking English.

In *Negron,* the court implied a defendant's burden to put the trial court "on notice" of the need for an interpreter. *Negron,* however, was decided on constitutional grounds. The CIA was passed in order to bring clarity to this confusing area, and presumably not leave the rights of defendants to be decided arbitrarily on a case-by-case basis. Yet the Act left two basic questions open for judicial resolution on a piecemeal basis:

- How is the trial court to be put on notice that an interpreter is required?
- How is the court to determine whether the party's comprehension of the proceedings or communication with counsel is inhibited by an English language problem?

On the first point, the case law is clear and the passage of the CIA did nothing to change the judicial analysis involved: defendants need to put the trial court on notice of the need for an interpreter.[49] Indeed, the lack of a defendant's objection to the absence of interpretation at trial did not go unnoticed by a reviewing court that was asked to determine whether the trial court may have abused its discretion.[50] In *Valladares* the court said: "[t]o allow a defendant to remain silent throughout the trial and then upon being found guilty, to assert a claim of inadequate translation would be an open invitation to abuse."[51] In *US v. Joshi,*[52] the court pointed out that the defendant did not object at trial to lapses in translation. The court said that it would be difficult "to find that a defendant received a fundamentally unfair trial due to an inadequate translation in the absence of contemporaneous objections to the quality of the interpretation."[53]

The defendant, however, may waive the right to an interpreter once it has been determined that the appointment of an interpreter is necessary. The waiver right is one that is personal to the defendant and may not be made by the attorney on his behalf. The court, however, need not accept the defendant's waiver if it feels that alternative interpretive services will not result in the "efficient administration of justice."[54]

In *US v. Carrion,*[55] the First Circuit affirmed the trial court's conviction of a defendant although it had conducted no inquiry into and made no factual determination concerning the defendant's need for an interpreter. The defendant's facility with the English language was unclear, but his co-defendants made motions for interpreters and the appealing defendant did not. Also, the defendant's lawyer, after questioning by the trial court, had assured the court that the defendant was able to communicate in and understand English.[56] The *Carrion* court felt that there had been an adequate process in place for the appealing defendant to avail himself of a translator if he needed one.

Once a request for an interpreter has been made by a defendant, the trial court must conduct an inquiry into the defendant's ability to speak and understand English.[57] Even if a formal request has not been made, if the defendant's ability to speak or understand English is, in the words of *Negron,* "obvious," then the trial court has a duty to suspend the trial if necessary and make a factual determination on the defendant's need for an interpreter.[58] Such an inquiry should be made outside of the presence of the jury. Frequently, however, the court's inquiry centers only on the defendant's ability to speak "social" English. Indeed, it is here, with the trial court left with wide latitude in determining the defendant's need for an interpreter, that the defendant's rights are either recognized or forsaken on the shoals of judicial efficiency or even court bias.

Such bias was clear in *US v. Mayans,*[59] where a trial court withdrew an interpreter for a defendant in the middle of trial. During trial, Pablo Mayans had relied upon an interpreter. When he began to testify in his own defense in Spanish, however, the trial judge asked him to try and testify without the interpreter. Mayans had testified only that he was born in Cuba, that he had lived in the US since 1971 and that he spoke English. The judge complained that the testimony would take twice as long with the use of an interpreter and that Mayans had lived in the US longer than he had in Cuba. Presumably the court felt that Mayans' length of stay in the US was sufficient for him to testify in English. The trial court's attitude seems to reflect a two-fold bias: one, where the court assumes it knows what a language minority knows or ought to know of the English language without any basis in research or study to justify that attitude; the other which reflects a distrust of defendants that turns even the most innocuous request by a criminal defendant into a struggle over honesty and trust. Here, the interplay between both those biases turned what could have been an uneventful narcotics trial into an act of linguistic discrimination.

The court overruled counsel's objections, and refused a side bar discussion with the attorney on the subject. Since the court kept insisting that the defendant could not use an interpreter, counsel withdrew the defendant as a witness. Counsel ultimately moved for a mistrial, which was denied. Mayans was convicted of narcotic offenses.

Mayans appealed the conviction, raising violations of both the Constitution and the CIA. Apparently the trial court never made a factual inquiry into Mayans' ability to speak English, although his counsel had explained that Mayans could not express himself in English. Instead, the trial court essentially decided to "test" Mayans' ability to speak and understand English during the trial and in front of the jury. This kind of procedure, found the appeals court, was a violation of the CIA:

> the trial court's error was in its insistence on evaluating appellant's language skills in the course of the trial itself, and in front of the jury, where the consequences of miscomprehension would have been grave indeed.... Because this clearly undermined the purpose of the interpreter statute, we conclude that the statute was violated in this case.[60]

The court also concluded that the procedure employed by the trial court was a violation of Mayans' Fifth Amendment right to testify on his own behalf: "[a]ppellant's only alternative to forfeiting his right to testify was to participate in the risky in-court experiment proposed by the trial judge."[61] The court concluded by saying that evaluations of a defendant's English language skills must be made outside the presence of a jury. A new trial was ordered.

Interestingly, however, the court did note that, while under the circumstances counsel's failure to specifically request an evaluation of Mayan's English language ability would not be held against Mayans, if it were, the court would have reviewed the trial court's actions under a more permissive "plain error" standard.[62] Such an observation undercuts the more accommodating aspects of the appellate decision. The court insisted on re-articulating the burden on defendants to not only express an inability to speak or understand English sufficiently to fairly participate in a trial (as was done here by counsel), but to make an express and specific request for a factual inquiry. Such an interpretation is not justified by the language or purposes of the CIA.

A trial court may simply hear a defendant speak English conversationally or be told by arresting officers that the defendant spoke English to them, and decide that an interpreter is not necessary.[63]

In *Gonzalez v. People of Virgin Islands*,[64] the trial court refused to appoint an interpreter even though requested by co-defendants' lawyers because of the court's belief that the defendants *should* know sufficient English. Defendants were Spanish-speaking natives of Puerto Rico living in the Virgin Islands; one had lived there for three years and the other for eight years. The request for a translator was not made at the commencement of the trial, but at the point when one of the defendants wanted to testify. In affirming the convictions, the Third Circuit found that "[i]t may well be that an accused who is unfamiliar with the language would be entitled under a constitutional provision ... to have the testimony of the People's witnesses interpreted to him in order that he may fully exercise his right of cross-examination."[65] But because of the length of their residence in the Virgin Islands and because one defendant ran a store in an English-speaking community there, the court was not convinced that defendants did not speak sufficient English to understand the proceedings.[66] Therefore, said the court, "the ignorance of English they now profess thus seems highly improbable"[67] The court's bias expressed as a suspicion on Gonzalez's motivation is clear. Three years or even eight years living in the Virgin Islands hardly seems to necessitate a fluency in the English used in legal proceedings. Indeed, most of us can well imagine that, with our freedom hanging in the balance, we would want to offer our story in the language in which we can express ourselves best.

The court was further bothered by Gonzalez's late request for an interpreter – not at the commencement of trial, but at the point when he was to testify: "[i]t has been held that an accused may waive his right to be confronted with the witnesses against him by failure to assert it in apt time."[68] The point about the late request might be well taken if it didn't seem to be used by the court to simply buttress its real reason for denying the interpreter – the court simply never believed in the defendant's need for one. Yet the suspicion seems unreasonable – for what good does it do a defendant to request, and get, an interpreter that is unnecessary? The strength of the state's case is neither diminished nor enforced because it reaches the defendant's ears through the screen of a foreign language. It certainly seems as if the trial court could have avoided an appeal if it had just provided an interpreter.

In *People v. Annett*,[69] the court actually ascribed bad motives to a defendant who had not been provided with an interpreter by a trial court despite the defendant's difficulty with the English language. The appellate court characterized his desire for an interpreter as motivated by convenience, not need:

> [t]he record in the instant case demonstrates not only that [appellant] was cognizant of what was being said to him, and what he was doing, but also that he was aware at the time his trial began that he could have an interpreter on simple request.... Further ... an interpreter was not a necessity for [appellant] but rather a mere convenience.... [70]

Indeed, this process by which an unqualified judge – usually proficient in only English – determines the interpreter needs of a non-English-speaking defendant, has been hotly contested. Some critics take aim at the deference given to trial courts by the appellate courts. For these critics, judges lack the linguistic ability to recognize both: (1) the need of a particular defendant for an interpreter, and (2) the competency of an available interpreter to meet that need.[71] Others see the very codification of judicial discretion as nativist. "The aporia of dependence on the judge's discretion points to a repressed meaning that is familiar.... Here, this theme reflects the deeply ingrained nativism of state legislatures and courts."[72]

Nevertheless, appellate courts usually uphold the trial court's decision, even if the trial court has made its determination based on the defense counsel's representations as to the defendant's need for an interpreter, or brief and/or monosyllabic colloquies between the court and the defendant. For instance, in *Vasquez v. State*,[73] the appellate court found no error in the trial court's decision not to appoint an interpreter for a defendant who answered "yes" twice to judicial questions. The court stated that "[a]lthough the State stipulated that the defendant did not *speak* English, the defendant may have *understood* English and that his right to confrontation was not infringed. In the absence of facts to show that [defendant] could not understand English, we find no error."[74] That a defendant's rights can hang on such fine distinctions, with neither trial courts nor appellate courts willing to spend more time to make truly conscientious decisions, makes a mockery of the rights first articulated in *Negron*.

A lone dissenting judge in a 1994 Ninth Circuit opinion upholding the absence of an interpreter, articulated the frustration advocates often feel when faced with judges that read defendants' rights grudgingly.[75] In this case, Miguel Angel Gonzalez wished to revoke his plea of guilty to narcotics charges because he was denied an interpreter and did not understand the nature and cause of the charges against him or the potential consequences of his guilty plea. At his arraignment, the arraigning judge entered into a short colloquy with Gonzalez:

Court:	Do you understand?
Gonzalez:	Yeah, little bit.
Court:	What is your problem, language problem?
Gonzalez:	Well, no. I don't know how to read that much. I understand. I understand.[76]

During the course of accepting Gonzalez's guilty plea, the trial court noted that his English language deficits were not a "major problem." As part of accepting a guilty plea, courts need to engage the defendant in a colloquy in which the defendant, minimally, must confess to the basic elements of the crime to which he's pleading. Apparently, during this colloquy Gonzalez did not understand the judge when he was asked complex questions; the judge then switched to asking Gonzalez simpler questions. For instance, the following colloquy occurred:

District Judge:	Would you tell me what your understanding of Count 1 of the indictment is; that is, the conspiracy charge? What do you think they are charging you with by alleging you participated in the conspiracy?

Gonzalez's lawyer:
> He is asking you on the conspiracy what does that mean [*sic*].
> What are you charged with? What did you do?

Gonzalez:　With the telephone call?

District Judge:　What did you do? Did you work with other people to buy drugs and sell them?

Gonzalez:　I used the telephone.

District Judge:　The point is, if you enter a plea of guilty now, you can't withdraw it later because you don't like [*sic*] the sentence that you get.

Gonzalez:　Yes.[77]

At the end of that colloquy the court stated: "[t]here is some language difficulty but not a major one."[78] Despite the court's statement that Gonzalez could understand what was going on, it did rely on the interpretation services of Gonzalez's wife, a co-defendant in the case against her husband.

On appeal, the Ninth Circuit refused to revoke Gonzalez's plea, finding that "Gonzalez's comprehension was not sufficiently inhibited as to require an interpreter" even if his responses were "brief and somewhat inarticulate."[79] Without further analysis, the court also found that for the same reasons the constitutional claims failed as well.

Gonzalez, however, is most noteworthy for the stinging dissent of Judge Reinhardt. He begins with a shot stating that:

> [o]nce again 'fairness and due process' take an unnecessary beating in the courts. How easy it would be to afford individuals the full rights Congress provided them. Instead, our careless and hasty treatment of criminal cases all too often makes it difficult for defendants to receive a fair trial. Here, we narrowly, grudgingly, and erroneously apply the Court Interpreters Act, a statute designed to make certain that defendants understand what is happening to them during criminal proceedings. By reviewing the factual, but not the legal basis for the district court's decision, the majority has created the misleading impression that the district court's casually, if not inadvertently, adopted approach to determining whether language difficulties inhibit a defendant's understanding constitutes an appropriate application of the Act. Nothing in the legislative history or statutory language supports the narrow application of the Act by the district court.[80]

Judge Reinhardt noted that the district court attempted to compensate for Gonzalez's inability to understand English well by speaking in simple words. Yet, "in this case the defendant could not even follow the simple questions posed by the district judge, thus clearly indicating that he would be unable to comprehend the full implications of a complex plea agreement written in English."[81]

For Judge Reinhardt, the essence of the problem with his brethren's decision was the deference it accorded to the district court treating its determination as a factual matter which can be overturned only if clearly erroneous. What was truly at issue here, argued Reinhardt, was a legal question – one that can be reviewed *de novo* by appellate courts and where trial courts are not presumed to have any particular expertise. The legal question involved the standards for evaluating a defendant's English language abilities. The statute, argued Reinhardt, does not require that defendants have a "major problem" with English before an interpreter be appointed; only that their "comprehension is impaired for purposes of the judicial proceedings." The Act, said Reinhardt, "is designed to prevent the appointment of an interpreter when one is wholly unnecessary rather than to subdivide those who cannot speak English fluently into groups with 'major' or 'minor' difficulties."[82]

Reinhardt also disagreed with the trial court's reliance on Gonzalez's wife for interpretation: she was a co-defendant and could not be relied upon to provide either accurate or impartial interpretation. The CIA was minimally intended to avoid the use of just such inappropriate use of unqualified individuals.

Once an interpreter is to be appointed, defendants should receive their own "defense" interpreter different from the "witness" interpreter. In *People v. Romero*,[83] the Spanish-speaking defendant was held to have been denied due process of law under both federal and state constitutions when one interpreter was used both to assist the defendant and to interpret the testimony of eight Spanish-speaking witnesses, with the consent of defense counsel. Such an arrangement denies the defendant a "spontaneous understanding of the testimony and the proceedings."[84] However, in *US v. Lim*,[85] the court found no violation of the Court Interpreter's Act (and impliedly no constitutional violation either) when the trial court "borrowed" an interpreter from the defense table to aid a witness on three occasions during the course of the multi-defendant trial. On two of the three occasions, the second court interpreter sat at the defense table with the defendants. On the third occasion, there was no second interpreter at the defense table. The court interpreter, aiding the witness, used a microphone, apparently allowing the defendants to hear the translation. Under the clearly erroneous standard, the Ninth Circuit upheld the trial court's determination that the defendants were not denied a fair trial.

An interesting case decided by the Sixth Circuit raised the issue of the need for an interpreter for a *witness* in a criminal proceeding. In *US v. Markarian*,[86] Markarian was convicted of narcotics charges. The government's case against him turned on the testimony of a witness named Hartounian who testified that she and Markarian were both involved in a heroin-selling conspiracy. On appeal Markarian argued that the court should have appointed an interpreter for Hartounian because she failed to understand common English words and that some of her testimony was unintelligible. No request for an interpreter was made by any party during the trial. However, at the sentencing hearing, Markarian's new lawyer challenged the reliability of Hartounian's testimony because of her English-language problems. Markarian had submitted the transcript of Hartounian's testimony to an expert who determined that Hartounian was not able to testify competently in English.

Despite Markarian's reliance on the CIA, the Sixth Circuit, following in the footsteps of prior courts, reiterated the judicial preference for reliance on the discretion of the trial court. Since the trial judge was bilingual and asserted that he paid "special attention to this question," and did not feel that an interpreter was necessary, the Sixth Circuit affirmed the decision.

Mechanics of interpretation

Unless otherwise statutorily specified, the qualifications of an interpreter to adequately interpret the proceedings fall within the area of the trial judge's discretion.[87] Court interpreters must also meet honesty standards that require, amongst other things that they represent honestly their certifications, training and pertinent experience to the court and report any personal bias that might cause them to give less-than-accurate interpretation. Finally, interpreters must meet standards of professionalism which essentially means that they are to avoid conflicts of interest, maintain confidentiality and avoid public comment. The appointment of an ineffective and incompetent interpreter may be a violation of the defendant's Sixth Amendment rights. The judge has the power to disqualify an interpreter at any point in the proceedings. "A judge should disqualify a court interpreter if the court interpreter is not qualified, is not impartial, has disclosed confidential or privileged information, or cannot effectively work with the defendant or witness for any legitimate reason."[88] However, "[m]inor errors or general disagreements standing alone are generally insufficient to disqualify an interpreter."[89]

The right to a "qualified interpreter" found in the CIA and in most state statutes is a hollow promise indeed if there are no qualified interpreters to be found in a particular language. The National Center for State Courts has already noted, however, that there is shortage of qualified court interpreters.[90] This is not surprising as, along with the increase in immigration, there has been an increase in the number of language minorities being caught in the criminal justice system. Judicial proceedings in federal courts for which a witness or defendant was assigned an interpreter increased significantly between 1980 and 1990.[91] For the same period, the use of Spanish language interpreters in federal courts increased from 23, 394 to 53,240.[92] It was the increased need for and chronic shortage of interpreters in the federal court of the Eastern District of New York that prompted one judge to order the state to pay for the translation of certain documents in criminal proceedings in order to avoid the court's dependency on interpreters.[93]

Some states have codes issued by the administrative offices of their courts that specify more clearly the qualifications of court interpreters and which can blunt the impact of having a court rely solely on its own discretion.[94] The three standards of conduct most often found in the codes govern accuracy, honesty, and professionalism. Accuracy requires the interpreter to "interpret or translate the material thoroughly and precisely, adding or omitting nothing, and stating as early as possible what has been stated in the languages of the speaker, giving consideration to variations in grammar and syntax for both languages involved."[95]

Naturally, as language is an elastic process, accurate interpretation is more complicated than a simply verbatim translation would imply. There are hand gestures, intonations, and regionalisms that can change not only the meaning of a word but an entire concept; they can change an act done unintentionally to one done with a culpable state of mind. Indeed, "the interpreter has an obligation to convey every aspect of the witness's testimony, not only words but also paralinguistic elements such as pauses, false starts, and tone of voice."[96] Again, it is left to trial courts to determine whether an interpreter is meeting this standard. Even in states where an administrative body certifies interpreters, they are only presumptively qualified and a trial court can still find their translation faulty and set it aside.

Because of the high need for accuracy, unrecorded conversations between the interpreter and a witness need to be limited. This can obviously be a difficult situation since often the interpreter is the only person who the non-English speaking witness can turn to for comfort or advice in what is surely an uncomfortable and probably foreign situation. Regardless, the persistence of long, unrecorded conversations between a witness and an interpreter may prompt a court to discharge the interpreter.

Translation of documents

The right to translated documents in a criminal proceeding was taken up by a federal district court in *US v. Mosquera*,[97] Here, the court relied on the CIA and the Due Process Clauses of the Fifth Amendment and Sixth Amendment to order the government to pay for translation of the indictment and statutes referred to in that instrument, in any plea agreement and statutes referred to therein and in any presentence report. Expenses were to be allocated amongst the US Attorneys Office, probation services, and the budget provided under the Criminal Justice Act.

The court felt that the Due Process Clause guarantee that a defendant has "real notice of the true nature of the charge against him" and the Confrontation Clause's requirement that the accused knows the nature and cause of the accusation, formed a legitimate basis for its order to translate.[98] Indeed:

> [d]ue process demands that criminal defendants be given the means to understand the charges lodged against them as soon and as fully as practicable. It is fundamental that a defendant must be told what he has been accused of in a language he or she can understand. This is the responsibility of the government, which brought the charges, not of the defendant. For a non-English-speaking defendant to stand equal with others before the court requires translation. Non-English-speaking criminal defendants currently are at a substantial disadvantage. A criminal defendant cannot aid in his own defense without meaningful access to relevant documents that he or she can understand.[99]

Further, the court found that oral translations were not sufficient:

> Just as summaries of testimony were inadequate in *US v. Negron* ... so too is an interpreter's oral description of the contents of a critical document insufficient .... While an oral interpretation can provide momentary understanding of representations contained in a document, a criminal defendant may need and want to review the document alone and with others to achieve a full understanding.[100]

Despite the appreciation for the hardships of the language-minority defendant and the attempt to provide a practical solution, the *Mosquera* court currently stands alone in ordering the translation of documents. Indeed, in *Canizales-Satizabal, v. US*,[101] the Seventh Circuit clarified that the *Mosquera* court did not find that the translation of documents was a constitutional or even a statutory necessity under the CIA, only that a trial court may in its discretion order the translation of documents if it finds it is necessary for the efficient administration of justice.

As with any waiver of rights, the trial court must be assured that the defendant fully understands what rights are being waived, and freely waives those rights. The role of an interpreter in this context is certainly crucial. Pleas entered into without an interpreter present when one is clearly necessary, may be vacated.[102] Likewise where the interpreter fails to interpret essential elements of a plea bargain.[103] As with trials, however, timely requests for an interpreter must be made, and a record that reveals that a defendant appeared to understand the proceedings will be used to uphold the plea bargain.

The first federal appeals court to review the denial of an interpreter under a plea situation upheld the denial.[104] In *US v. Perez*, Perez was arrested for purchasing the chemicals and glassware necessary for making methamphetamine. Perez had lived in the US for 19 years. Perez indicated at his first appearance before a federal magistrate that he had "some difficulty" with English. When questioned, Perez said that he understood everything "so far."[105] The magistrate did not provide an interpreter, but told Perez to stop the proceedings if he was confused. Perez appeared before a federal judge, not the magistrate, to plead guilty, at which time no interpreter was present. After pleading, however, Perez argued that his plea was involuntary since he did not understand English sufficiently to plea "freely." The appeals court determined, however, that Perez's assurances to the magistrate that he did indeed understand the proceedings "so far," did not put the trial court on notice that an interpreter was actually needed. The Fifth Circuit essentially found that a factual inquiry is not necessary absent an affirmative assertion by the defendant that an interpreter is necessary; indicating that a possible problem with English is, again, not sufficient notice.[106]

Parole and probation

Although the due process considerations at parole revocation or release hearings are more limited than at criminal trials, the hearings must be still be "fundamentally fair." If a language minority cannot understand the proceedings, then that fairness has been lost. In *Labbe v. Russi*,[107] decided in 1993, a French-speaking inmate was appointed a Spanish/English interpreter simply because that was who was most easily available, even though the inmate asked for a French interpreter and spoke and understood only a little Spanish. The Supreme Court of Westchester County found that the parole board's decision to use a Spanish-language interpreter was simply irrational, arbitrary and capricious, and its decision not to grant parole was overturned.[108] A new hearing was ordered where an interpreter of the inmate's preference was to be used.[109]

Judicial unwillingness to recognize the connection between language and national origin was played out with draconian results two years later in *Flores v. State of Texas*.[110] Here, Aristeo Flores, a Spanish-dominant man was convicted after a trial of driving while intoxicated. In determining whether to sentence Mr Flores to probation with a mandatory alcohol education program as part of the probation or to imprison him, the trial court noted the lack of any high quality alcohol rehabilitation programs for Spanish-speaking adults which could be made part of any probationary sentence. The court made a few statements worth noting:

> There are no provisions in this county to help Spanish-speaking people who are convicted of alcohol offenses.

> [T]he ... alcohol education program ... does have a Spanish class but it is worthless.

> The alcohol treatment programs are simply not available in Spanish. I've been trying ever since I've been here to ... get this county to admit what century we're in, but it has not yet happened.

> "If I out you on probation, that's absolutely meaningless" [*sic*].[111]

Mr Flores was sentenced to a year's imprisonment.

Mr Flores challenged his sentence on equal protection and due process grounds. The appellate courts, however, were unsympathetic. They found that Mr Flores was certainly treated differently because of his inability to speak English, but that was not the same as discrimination on the basis of national origin or ethnicity, "[t]o accept appellant's argument – that language equals national origin or race – assumes illogically that all Spanish-speaking persons should be treated as one group."[112] Further reasoned the court, language ability is a choice, and not the kind of immutable characteristic associated with suspect classifications:

> [a]n individual is free to choose the language he or she speaks and one only needs to look at the history of the United States to find millions of examples of individuals who came here speaking many different languages but who learned to speak at least one additional language, generally English. Clearly, language ability *does not equal* national origin or race. [113]

Since language *per se* is not a suspect classification and there is no fundamental right to probation, then under the court's analysis, the state's action must be reviewed under the lax standard of "reasonableness." The state's interest in sentencing Mr Flores is obviously a legitimate one, since there was no viable probationary sentence without a Spanish-speaking program, "incarceration was an appropriate punishment. Appellant was treated no differently than any other similarly-situated convicted drunk driver who could not speak English."[114]

The lack of Spanish-language education programs is not a violation of the Equal Protection Clause, found the court, because appellant needed to show that the absence of the programs was an act of intentional discrimination.[115]

The dissent argued vigorously for an expansive understanding of race and ethnicity under the Equal Protection Clause in which discrimination on the basis of language abilities would be unlawful. The dissent also noted that the option of having an interpreter for appellant at an English-only alcohol education program was not considered by either the trial court or the majority and was one means of accommodating Mr Flores's language needs.[116]

Civil court proceedings

Unlike in the criminal context, where a complex web of constitutional and statutory protections and restrictions are entangled, there is little law to untangle in the civil litigation context. Unfortunately, the case that has come to be considered controlling on the issue of interpretation in civil cases, *Jara v. Municipal Court for the San Antonio Judicial District of Los Angeles City*, is a negative one.[117]

Two years before *Jara* was decided, however, some hope was shed in this area by a lower California court. In *Gardiana v. Small Claims Court*,[118] an appeals court was asked to review the decision of a lower state court which had ordered the small claims courts to provide interpreters for indigent, Spanish-speaking litigants. Plaintiffs in the case on appeal were defendants in a small claims court action. Neither they nor the woman who sued them spoke or understood English, and the small claims court did not have qualified interpreters on staff who could assist the parties. The usual practice of the judges in these small claims courts was to seek the help of voluntary interpreters, usually members of the same linguistic community as the parties. The claims court action, however, was halted as the Gardianas took the issue of the interpreters on appeal. The claims court had denied the Gardianas' request for an appointed interpreter, stating that it did not believe that it had the power or authority to appoint interpreters at public expense for litigants in civil cases.

On appeal, the lower court ordered the claims court judges to provide interpreters, finding that they did have the inherent authority to order payment for them if volunteer interpreters could not be found. The defendants appealed and so did the Gardianas, who disagreed with the court's approval of volunteer interpreters.

On appeal again, the district court began by noting the peculiar and informal nature of small claims proceedings – proceedings in which lawyers are not present, the rules of evidence are suspended, and common sense ultimately rules. In these situations the litigants have no buffers between themselves and the court, and they are in charge of the presentation of their case. Given the nature of the small claims court, said the district court, the use of volunteer interpreters should be allowed.[119]

The stickier question, however, was the extent of the courts' power when no volunteers were available. Defendants unsuccessfully argued that the litigation should then proceed without an interpreter. The court disagreed, noting that if it followed that argument that:

[t]he court would then find itself in the position of having to conduct a judicial

proceeding in which no communication was possible with a litigant.... Although the small claims court functions successfully without lawyers, pleadings, legal rules of evidence, juries and formal findings, it cannot function without the use of language.[120]

The court concluded that: "[t]he duty of the court to appoint an interpreter when one is necessary compels it to appoint one free of charge when a party is indigent."[121]

Interestingly, the court did not confine itself to appointing interpreters only for defendants, but for all indigent civil litigants.

The case, however, was indeed limited to the specific context of small claims courts by the decision in *Jara*. Aurelio Fregoso Jara was a Spanish-dominant indigent man who was sued in civil court for property damages arising from a car accident. He asked the court to appoint an interpreter for him free of charge. The court denied the request. On appeal, the superior court affirmed the denial of the request. Jara appealed again to the Supreme Court of California. The court began by noting that there was no statutory basis for the appointment of an interpreter for a civil court litigant as there was for an interpreter for witnesses. Indeed, said the court, the burden on an interpreter for a party would be much greater than that for a witness. After setting that stage, the court then went on to determine whether the trial court has the inherent authority to appoint an interpreter for an indigent civil litigant. In analyzing this issue, the court likened Jara's situation to one in which courts must determine whether to appoint counsel or to pay for other services (such as transcripts or fees), for indigent civil litigants. In those cases refusals by trial courts to have the public pay for such services have been upheld. In the case of indigent prisoner defendants, the Supreme Court had pointed out that it did not have the power to require expenditure of public funds for the purpose of appointing counsel.[122] Attorneys were expected to provide those services free of charge.

In the present situation, members of a civil litigant's "family, friends or neighbors born or schooled here may provide aid. Private organizations also exist to aid immigrants."[123] Most importantly for the court, however, was the fact that counsel controls the proceedings in civil litigation. This is the essential distinction between the case before it and *Gardiana*, said the court. In reference to the distinction between small claims courts and civil courts, the court said: "[i]t is apparent that unless the non-English speaking party has an interpreter he is effectively barred from access to the small claims proceedings. By way of contrast, appellant possesses an attorney capable of fully representing him in the municipal court proceeding."[124]

Relying on the purported availability of English language assistance from the litigants' own community, the court found that "there is no need for courts to require appointment of interpreters at public expense to assist litigants." [125]

Justice Tobriner dissented because he felt that trial courts most certainly have the inherent authority to decide whether to appoint an interpreter free of charge, and that the majority's decision essentially precluded trial courts from even conducting an inquiry into the matter. Justice Tobriner took issue with the majority's "cavalier assumption" that members of Jara's community would be able or willing to step in and act as interpreters every day of a civil trial. Rather, that finding ought to be left to trial courts to make: "[w]hether in a given case the defendant has access to effective, alternative resources or whether he requires the assistance of a court-appointed interpreter at the expense of the county must lie with the sound discretion of the court."[126] If no other means are available, Tobriner argued that due process requires the court to appoint an interpreter. For Tobriner the due process right rested in the right, long judicially recognized, of indigents to be able to access the judicial process and "settle their claims of rights and duty" especially when property interests are at stake and even more so when they are defendants in a case and have been pulled into court against their wishes.[127]

Although Justice Tobriner's arguments were not able to overcome judicial concerns over municipal resources, his reasoning, which was based on the need to respect the discretion of trial courts, should have found receptive ears. More so than in criminal cases where so much more is at stake, the civil litigation context seems particularly well-suited for trial courts to hold factual hearings on the need and availability of free interpreters and to make appropriate findings. After reviewing so many cases in the criminal context where the discretion of trial court was held sacrosanct, it is peculiar to find a court tying the hands of trial courts on just this issue where property and not liberty is at stake. While distinctions between small claims and civil courts are well taken, the majority's decision amounts to nothing more than a resource-allocation debate. Once linguistic diversity issues are placed in this cost-cutting paradigm, their rights will certainly be considered too costly to secure and democracy is assuredly the poorer.

INS hearings

Taking an intermediate place between the constitutionally protected rights of criminal defendants and the "cavalier" attitude of the *Jara* court, are hearings held by the Immigration and Naturalization Service (INS). Here the risk of deportation if an applicant is not understood by INS examiners and/or an inaccurate record is created, is great. Deportation hearings have specifically been found to be civil and not criminal proceedings. However, individuals under threat of deportation are entitled to "full and fair hearings" prior to deportation. Recognizing the gravity of the deportation risk to asylum seekers, refugees and other candidates for lawful admission to the country, courts have often remanded cases to the INS where interpreters were not provided.

The leading case in this area is *Gonzales v. Zurbrick*.[128] In this case a 25-year-old Mexican woman was to be deported because of allegedly-admitted charges of prostitution. At two hearings the INS provided Gonzales with an interpreter, Alex Le Doulx, but she complained that she could not understand him. Le Doulx was a Frenchman who testified that he had learned to speak "Mexican" in Alexandria, Egypt where he occasionally met Mexicans and other who had resided in Mexico.[129] Le Doulx originally interpreted for Gonzales and the transcript of that hearing reflects her admission of the prostitution charge. The testimony of the main witnesses against Gonzales, however, was in English only and was not translated for her. After her complaint about Le Doulx, a new interpreter was assigned and Gonzales denied the prostitution charges and again complained that she had not been able to understand Le Doulx at the first hearing. At a re-opening of the hearing, the INS Board of Review determined that Le Doulx was not a competent interpreter but ordered the deportation after a review of the whole record, including the admissions Gonzales had made when Le Doulx interpreted.

On appeal, the Circuit Court needed to determine only whether Gonzales was given a "full and fair opportunity to be heard" or, whether there was such a defect in the proceedings as to lead to a denial of justice.[130] The court held that "certain basic requirements were violated" at Gonzales' hearing. It noted that:

> [t]he function of an interpreter is an important one. It affects a constitutional right, the right to a hearing is a vain thing if the alien is not understood. Deportation is fraught with serious consequences.... It is of vital concern not only to the alien but to the government as well; and if it is not unreasonable to expect that, where the services of an interpreter are needed, his capability should be unquestioned.[131]

Given these circumstances, Gonzales was to be released or a new, fair hearing held.

In dicta, the Sixth Circuit also noted that:

> [w]e think that the absence of an interpreter at the ... hearing is contrary to the aim of our law to provide fundamental fairness in administrative proceedings. Despite the essential discretionary power of Immigration officials in dealing with violations of the crewman provisions ... it would seem clearly not within the Service's discretion to conduct an official inquiry, without an interpreter, in a language the subject of the inquiry can neither understand nor speak. We therefore in this dictum express the hope that should petitioner seek permission to re-enter ... the Attorney General will consider the petition in the light of the *shocking circumstances* of the ... deportation hearing.[132]

It is certainly heartening that a Circuit Court would seek to limit the discretion of INS officials, usually given wide latitude. Indeed, in *Tejeda-Mata v. INS*,[133] the Circuit Court "reluctantly" did not order a new hearing when an immigration judge inexplicably denied petitioner's request for the simultaneous interpretation of the sole witnesses' testimony against him. An interpreter had been present at the hearing, and had interpreted for Tejeda-Mata until that point. Only because the court found that the testimony left untranslated was no more than a reiteration of admissions made by Tejeda-Mata himself, did it not order a new hearing. In language rarely found in the latest criminal cases, however, the court stated:

> the inexcusable refusal of the Immigration Judge to permit simultaneous translation of the testimony against petitioner by either the official interpreter or petitioner's counsel seems unquestionably to be an abuse of discretion.... Faced with such an abuse of discretion, this Court would, as a general rule, feel

compelled to reverse and remand this case for a new hearing."[134] Again, it was only because a new hearing would be a "futile gesture" that it was not ordered.[135]

These concerns over translation and interpretation services at INS proceedings were more fully explored in *Augustin v. Sava*.[136] There, Basseter Augustin came to the US as a refugee from Haiti to escape political persecution by paramilitary forces of the Haitian government. His attorney complained of a failure to provide Augustin with adequate translation services. The attorney ended up withdrawing from the case because the Immigration Judge denied the request for services, and insisted that the attorney herself should examine Augustin. The judge ended up examining Augustin himself. The transcript of the record, however, revealed that there were serious problems with the interpretation services during the hearing. The judge ultimately denied the request for asylum on the ground that Augustin had not established a well-founded fear of persecution. On a writ of habeas corpus of the federal district court, Judge Nickerson denied the petition for review of the judge's order of exclusion and deportation.

On appeal, the Second Circuit found that there was a flexible due process standard that minimally:

> warrants a hearing where the likelihood of persecution can be fairly evaluated. Since Congress intended this right to be equally available to all worthy claimants without regard to language skills, we think an applicant for relief under §1253 (h) [fear of political persecution] must be furnished with an accurate and complete translation of official proceedings. As a sequel to this right, translation services must be sufficient to enable the applicant to place his claim before the judge. A hearing is of no value when the alien and the judge are not understood.[137]

Because Augustin's hearing did not meet these minimal standards, Augustin was ordered to be released unless a new hearing was held.[138]

As often happens, however, the broad concerns of the *Augustin* decision were limited to its facts in another Second Circuit case, *Abdullah v. INS*.[139] The plaintiffs in *Abdullah* were undocumented individuals who petitioned the INS for "Special Agricultural Worker" (SAW) status. Their petitions were denied and they appealed over, among other reasons, the lack of interpreters during plaintiffs' interviews with INS Legalization Officers. The district court had held that the Fifth Amendment required such services.[140] The INS appealed.

The Second Circuit began its analysis by assuming, without deciding, that SAW applicants are entitled to Due Process protection in the determination of their SAW applications. As discussed previously, however, due process is a flexible concept and the circumstances determine "how much process is due." The Court decided to look at three factors previously articulated by the US Supreme Court in another context[141] in evaluating whether the process offered was sufficient. The factors are:

(1) the interests of the claimant;
(2) the risk of erroneous deprivation absent the benefit of the additional procedures sought and the probable value of such additional safeguards;
(3) the government's interest in avoiding the burdens entailed in providing the additional procedures claimed.[142]

On the first factor, the court distinguished the plaintiffs before it (those looking for a special enhanced immigrant status) from those traditionally given greater protections (those who may be deported or who are seeking asylum). Indeed, these plaintiffs are seeking a statutorily created status which the court felt was one of "extraordinary ... grace and generosity."[143] Although not part of the Supreme Court test, the court determined that a "subfactor" needed to be considered – one that allowed distinctions between those who the government seeks to punish or whose life it seeks to change and those, like plaintiffs, who "affirmatively [initiate] a proceeding seeking the benefits of a 'generous' statutory exception."[144]

The court also disagreed with the district court's findings on the burden to the government in providing interpreters. The district court had relied on INS regulations that envision the use of interpreters to find that the government had no interest in avoiding the burden of interpretation at legalization interviews. The Second Circuit countered that the voluntary prior assumption of a burden does not render the burden nonexistent. The burden to the INS in having interpreters at all legalization interviews would be substantial. So substantial apparently, that the plaintiffs "significant interests in obtaining an accurate determination of their eligibility for SAW status" was outweighed in the court's mind.[145]

Conclusion

The awareness of the need for interpreters in criminal proceedings and for the translation of documents seems to run relatively high, as well it should. Any notions of fairness and integrity in our criminal justice system would be destroyed if minimal safeguards such as interpretation were not provided. Still, as has been amply demonstrated, trial courts are given too much discretion and not enough mandates in deciding under what circumstances interpreters ought to be provided. The demands placed on judges to move cases quickly through the system, and their own cost consciousness, are additional stresses that undermine the good intentions of the CIA and begin to make the promise of *Negron* sound shallow indeed.

The half-hearted inquiries into English language skills decried by Judge Reinhardt in *Gonzalez v. US* are too often the stuff of everyday criminal court administration. That the trial courts may not be able to engage in a deeper inquiry may be a reflection of their own linguistic incompetence; that they don't see the need to, may be a reflection of pure nativism. Either way, rights are mauled, injustices certainly are allowed to go uncorrected, and our criminal justice system grows less fair with each passing day. The solution to this portion of the problem of the English-only courtroom, however, seems fairly clear: a defendant should get an interpreter upon request. There are no tactical advantages to using an unnecessary interpreter. Indeed, gaining time to answer a question that has been understood in English but must be translated can certainly backfire by the questionable impression the presence of an interpreter has on a jury and the lack of control over the adequacy of the translation. It seems beyond cavil that, especially in a criminal proceeding, one would want to ensure that the words we so carefully choose are actually heard by the jury. One commentator suggests that there ought to be a presumption that a defendant is not sufficiently proficient in English to ensure Sixth Amendment guarantees and is therefore entitled to an interpreter as a *per se* legal right:

> At the arraignment, or the earliest possible date of the criminal proceedings, courts should formally advise every defendant of the right to an interpreter.... If the defendant expresses the desire of an interpreter, one should be provided. The defendant's waiver of the right ... should be on the record and in writing.... Appointing an interpreter on demand may not overcome America's pervasive nativism, but it will protect the immigrant from the American justice system's English language hegemony.[146]

Clearly, with less than physical liberty at stake, courts are unwilling to require much accommodation of language minorities in civil proceedings. Again, however, monolithic rules about due process need not be the only route available for judicially-enforceable norms. The nature of the rights at stake and the kind of proceedings at issue can be used to achieve balance in accommodating linguistic diversity. The line of cases on INS hearings with their attempt to balance important individual interests and the government's interests in efficiency and cost containment can be a good place to start the analysis for civil proceeding purposes. Simply providing minimal protection in civil proceedings, as was done in *Touro,* is too low a standard to ensure that due process is done when real interests are at stake.

JURY SERVICE

The right to sit on a jury is, like the right to vote, a fundamental concept of citizenship. Yet, like the right to vote, there are still many barriers to serving on a jury especially for language minorities regardless of their proficiency in English. The first portion of this section will describe the federal requirement that jurors possess a certain degree of fluency in English, and the impact that requisite has on a criminal defendant's ability to be tried by his "peers." The second section will address an even more controversial and potentially dangerous matter: the ability of prosecutors in local or federal criminal trials to keep full bilinguals from jury service because of their very status as bilinguals. This prosecutorial power can undermine not only a defendant's right to be tried by a jury of his peers but a fundamental aspect of citizenship for language minorities – the right to sit on a jury.

Federal language requirements for jury service

In 1968, Congress adopted a law which requires that, in order to sit on a federal jury, individuals must, among other things, be able to "read, write, and understand the English language with a degree of proficiency sufficient to fill out satisfactorily the juror qualification form" and to be able to "speak the English language."[147]

This has led to potential jurors in federal trials being challenged on the basis of their English language abilities. In the criminal context, where jurors cannot be challenged on the basis of race, the US Supreme Court became involved when language-based challenges lead to no Latino sitting on a jury. That case, *Hernandez v. New York*,[148] was the third time[149] (and so far the last time) that the Supreme Court has deliberated over language rights. Cases that arise in the civil context concerning the statutory right to a juror who is proficient in English, are discussed first.

Challenges to the English literacy requirement itself turn up more frequently in Puerto Rico than on the mainland where it can work to disqualify many citizens from jury service.[150]

In *US v. Ramos Colon*,[151] a defendant filed a motion to dismiss an indictment and to strike the grand jury because the English-language requirements of 28 USC §1865 denied him an opportunity to be indicted and tried by a "fair cross section of the community" as required in 28 USC §1861. Interestingly, Ramos also argued that the procedures utilized in the District did not guarantee that the jurors serving were sufficiently literate in the English language anyway.

In order to select jurors, over 11,000 questionnaires were sent out in the District of Puerto Rico to names drawn from the master jury wheel. Of those, 4,262 were returned but 3,522 (amounting to 83% of the returned forms) were disqualified for "insufficient English."[152] Although the English-language requirement resulted in such a large proportion of disqualified jurors, the court found no violation of 28 USC §1861 – the guarantee of a trial by a "fair cross section of the community" was to be understood to apply only *after* the juror qualification provisions were implemented.

From a constitutional standpoint, jury selection is unlawful only if there is a systematic, intentional, and deliberate exclusion of members of a community from the juror lists. No such allegations were made or could be proved here. Disproportionality in the ultimate composition of the jury is not sufficient to show discrimination. As for the application of §1865 to Puerto Rico, the court found that it was necessary for making "the United States District Court for the District of Puerto Rico a viable part of the federal judicial system." The court stated:

> ...it can hardly be disputed ... that jurors have to understand the proceedings held before them and of which they constitute an indispensable and integral part. Furthermore, considering that this court is now a constitutional district court pursuant to Article III, Section 2 of the Constitution, the use of English in its proceedings, and the language qualification requirements of jurors which follow as the logical consequences thereof, is not merely a question of convenience or practicality but is a constitutional imperative in that English being the constitutional language of the United States and of its Institutions, the use of

said language in its proceedings ceases to be a question of adjective law but is a matter of constitutional substance.[153]

As to the issue of the competency of jurors to understand the English language proceedings, the court found that the juror qualification form, the *voir dire* conducted by the court, and the *voir dire* conducted by the attorneys were sufficient to guarantee sufficient English literacy. That defendant might have a better or more "scientific" method than that claimed by Congress is of no moment; the court would not engage in "enactment of legislation."[154]

In US *v. Benmuhar*,[155] the defendant again made an argument that §1865 resulted in a disproportionate number of Puerto Rican citizens being barred from being able to serve as federal jurors. The court agreed that such a disproportion did exist, but also found that there was a "significant state interest" in having a "branch of the national court system operate in the *national language*."[156] It discussed the importance of using the English language in the federal courts of Puerto Rico:

> Federal district courts in part are designed to provide trial alternatives for litigants, resident and nonresident, who seek the uniformity, expertise, and familiarity that they believe they may find in a national rather than a local forum. Primary use of the national language is both symbolically and functionally significant in achieving this goal. Nonresident citizens who do not speak Spanish may use the Puerto Rican federal district court without unusual requirements. The Attorney General of the United States may appear personally or by representative without being limited by considerations of fluency in Spanish. Other judges may sit by designation as needed without regard to their ability in Spanish. Possible translation distortions in indictments and complaints based on statutes written in English are avoided, as they are again during appellate review.[157]

A party in either a civil or criminal federal case who has lost after trial and believes that the English proficiency requirement was not met has the ability to challenge the verdict reached by the jury. For instance, in *Johnson International Company v. Jackson National Life Insurance Co.*,[158] the insurance company that lost a breach of contract trial moved for a new trial because it felt, among other things, that one of the jurors, a Japanese-American woman, did not meet the juror qualification requirements because she could not understand English sufficiently and used a dictionary to help her interpret the court's jury instructions during deliberations. The juror, Taiko Saragosa, had orally introduced herself during *voir dire*, as had the other jurors. Although the court characterized her speech as "stilted," it was also "responsive" and quite proficient. Mrs Saragosa was a native of Japan who came to the US in 1966, and was made a citizen in 1972 or 1973. Because of concerns over her use of a dictionary, the court questioned her in chambers after the trial. Among the words Mrs Saragosa needed to look up in the dictionary were "negligence" and "myocardial infarction." She told the court, however, that she understood the jury instructions and listened closely to the directions given by the court.

The court disagreed with Jackson-Life's claim that Mrs Saragosa was not competent to serve as a juror, and found instead that:

> [i]t is true that she has some difficulty expressing herself in the English language. It is also true that from time to time Mrs Saragosa used a translation book when she wanted "to make sure." However, it is equally true that Mrs Saragosa, an otherwise diligent juror, has used the English language as an important component of her everyday life in this country for about a quarter of a century. [159]

The court concluded that "[t]he fact that a juror is more expressive in one language than another does not mean the juror is incompetent."[160]

Indeed, Mrs Saragosa had been able to participate in the jury deliberation process during which time she changed her mind about her original decisions; importantly, no juror had complained that Mrs Saragosa would not participate in deliberations. The court also concluded that Mrs Saragosa's use of the English/Japanese dictionary was not prejudicial to Jackson-Life because it did not give her more than any other lay person's understanding of the term looked up, and the term was not at issue anyway.[161]

Punishing the bilingual juror: When knowing two languages is too much knowledge

While there may be legitimate reasons to require a certain degree of English literacy amongst potential jurors, proficiency in a *second* language ought not to be punished. However, as discussed in *Hernandez v. New York*,[162] below, courts have allowed prosecutors to seriously challenge jurors based only on their bilingualism without running afoul of the Equal Protection Clause.

The use of peremptory challenges to remove potential jurors from a jury has long been a concern of civil rights advocates.[163] Unlike challenges "for cause," counsel need not provide a reason for removing jurors with peremptory challenges; they can base their decision on whatever intuitive or whimsical reason they may hold about the suitability of a potential juror.

In *Batson v. Kentucky*,[164] the court took an important step forward in recognizing that the use of peremptory challenges can be used in a discriminatory way by prosecutors, and provided some limitations on their use. In *Batson*, the prosecutor had used his peremptory challenges to remove all four African-Americans from the *venire* panel. Batson, the African-American defendant, was tried and convicted by an all-white jury. The Supreme Court found that race-based challenges to potential jurors can violate the Equal Protection Clause, and required prosecutors to explain the basis of their challenges once the defendant has shown that the challenges could have been racially motivated.

In order to make out a *prima facie* case, the defendant must show that he or she is a member of a cognizable racial group, and that the State used its peremptory challenges to strike other members of the defendant's racial group from the *venire*. Since the Equal Protection Clause is involved, the defendant is essentially trying to make out a *prima facie* case of *intentional discrimination* by showing "that the totality of the relevant facts gives use to an inference of discriminatory purpose." [165]

The burden then shifts to the prosecutor, who must give a "reasonably specific" explanation of "legitimate reasons" for using his challenges.[166] The explanation must also be related to the case at trial and must be race-neutral.[167] Prosecutors cannot merely affirm their good faith in their use of peremptory challenges nor can they assert that members of a particular racial or ethnic group are simply unqualified to serve as jurors in the case.[168]

Once the prosecutor has explained the basis for his challenges, the trial court must determine if the prosecutor's explanations are indeed worthy of belief. This determination would require the trial court to ascertain whether the prosecutor is actually telling the truth by scrutinizing his demeanor and attitude and/or by finding that the questions and answers elicited during *voir dire* support or undermine the prosecutor's rationale. If the prosecutor's rationale is not accepted by the court, then the peremptory challenges are considered unconstitutional, and cannot be allowed to stand. Since it is the trial court that is making factual determinations as to the trustworthiness of a prosecutor, its judgment is given great deference by appellate courts.[169]

The *Baston* decision was important for its official recognition of a long-acknowledged reality – the not-so-hidden use of peremptory challenges to exclude jurors on the basis of race. However, the standards it set up for parties to actually establish discrimination are so subjective and difficult to apply that it has had little real impact on the jury selection process.[170] Indeed, one district court in a decision analyzed below predicted that "discriminatory practices are unlikely to diminish; rather, the ingenuity of counsel to explain their actions is likely to expand."[171] That court argued for the complete abandonment of peremptory challenges as the only real cure for discriminatory jury selection processes.

Certainly the *Batson* standards will be of limited use to language minorities who, because of judicial unwillingness to equate language with national origin or ethnicity, can rarely make out intentional discrimination. This difficulty was exemplified in the Supreme Court's decision in *Hernandez v. New York*,[172] a criminal jury selection case, which also reflects the Supreme Court's formulation of modern equal protection analysis in the language rights context. It is an unfortunate example of a conservative, inflexible court misunderstanding the nature of bilingualism and the subtleties of racial and ethnic issues at the end of the twentieth century.

The prosecutor in *Hernandez*, peremptorily challenged jurors who spoke Spanish because he felt they would not accept a translator's version of what his key witnesses said. The defendant and the victims were Latinos. The prosecutor had challenged the Spanish-speaking jurors even though, after some hesitancy, they said that they could accept the translator's version, of what was said. The prosecutor, nevertheless felt "from the hesitancy of their answers and their lack of eye contact that they would not be able to do it."[173] The prosecutor had challenged the only prospective jurors with definite Hispanic surnames, and the case was tried without Latino jurors.

Petitioner, the defendant in the trial, argued that since Spanish-language ability bears such a close relation to ethnicity, the challenge to jurors on the basis of their ability to speak Spanish is not race neutral and is, therefore, a discriminatory reason.

The narrow parameters of the modern courts' equal protection analysis are illustrated in this case where the justifiable claims of the petitioner were wrecked on the shoals of the Supreme Court's conservative and rigid review of his equal protection claims. The Court found that, since equal protection requires intentional or purposeful discrimination, the fact that language and ethnicity are closely related is not sufficient to make out an equal protection claim. Although the Court discussed the need to give a negative disproportionate impact on minorities "appropriate weight," the Court stated that, "even if we knew that a high percentage of bilingual jurors would hesitate in answering questions like these and, as a consequence, would be excluded under the prosecutor's criterion, that fact alone would not cause the criterion to fail the race-neutrality test."[174] Instead, the Court said that the impact issue could be used by the trial court in evaluating the sincerity of the prosecutor's rationale; impact could be used to determine pretext. The trial court here chose to believe the prosecutor, which the Supreme Court felt it could reasonably have done. Since the presence or absence of discriminatory intent is a finding of fact, within the special province of trial courts, the Supreme Court wouldn't overturn that finding.

The petitioner, then, lost his claim under the Equal Protection Clause because of the narrow interpretation of "race" used by the Court. The Court itself seemed conscious of this:

> [i]n holding that a race-neutral reason for a peremptory challenge means a reason other than race, we do not resolve the more difficult question of the breadth with which the concept of race should be defined for equal protection purposes. We would face a quite different case if the prosecutor had justified his peremptory challenges with the explanation that he did not want Spanish-speaking jurors. It may well be, for certain ethnic groups and in some communities, that proficiency in a particular language, like skin color, should be treated as a surrogate for race under an equal protection analysis.[175]

Despite the Court's protestations, the prosecutor *did* essentially challenge the jurors because of their ability to speak or at least understand Spanish, even though the challenge was framed in the technical language of the jurors' ability or willingness to accept a translator's version of testimony. The issue arose only with Spanish-speaking jurors; the prosecutor did not question the other potential juror about their willingness or ability to accept the translator's version. Instead, the prosecutor struck all of the Latino-surnamed jurors, even though the jurors had voiced their willingness to accept the translator's words. The unspoken question was whether a bilingual juror *could* accept a translator's version if they are hearing something different from the witness. Striking bilingual jurors because of a perceived inability to follow the translator, despite good-faith assertions that they would try to, amounts to an automatic exclusion of bilingual jurors. Unlike other jurors, whose good-faith responses are accepted by judge, prosecutor, and defense, bilingual jurors are treated with suspicion and are left unable to say or apparently do anything that would qualify them for service in certain cases. The Court was apparently aware of this possibility when it stated that:

> [o]ur decision today does not imply that exclusion of bilinguals from jury service is wise, or even that it is constitutional in all cases. It is a harsh paradox that one may become proficient enough in English to participate in trial ... only to encounter disqualification because he knows a second language as well. As the court observed in a somewhat related context: "Mere knowledge of [a foreign] language cannot reasonably be regarded as harmful. Heretofore it has been commonly looked upon as helpful and desirable," *Meyer v. Nebraska*.... [176]

However, the Court did not offer guidance on how this harsh result could be avoided given the facts of the case before it.

Justice Kaye, Chief Judge of the New York Court of Appeals, which upheld Hernandez's conviction before the case went to the Supreme Court, dissented from the state court's majority decision. Her analysis gives us an alternative to the Supreme Court's analysis. Justice Kaye found it crucial that the prosecutor's race "neutral" explanation was one that results in a disparate negative impact on a single ethnic group: "[t]he statistics before us indicate that, in Kings County, virtually all Latinos speak Spanish at home."[177] Simply excluding Spanish-speaking jurors because a Spanish-speaking witness will be called, said Justice Kaye, allows the prosecution to do "by indirection what can no longer be done directly."[178]

Justice Kaye then gave disparate impact a place in the analysis: "[a]n explanation by a prosecutor that may appear facially neutral but nonetheless has a disparate impact on members of defendant's radial or ethnic group is 'inherently suspect.'"[179] Therefore, more than simple speculation on the part of the prosecutor must form the basis of the challenge; "[t]o conclude otherwise can too easily permit discriminatory practices to continue."[180] As for the case before her, Justice Kaye found that there was not sufficient evidence to support the prosecutor's explanation. "Despite this court's repeated reference to the two jurors' initial expressed uncertainty or hesitancy, the fact remains that both individuals satisfied the court that they would accept the official court translation, and that they would be fair and impartial jurors."[181]

Justice Kaye's solution to the issue was simple: bilingual jurors should not be stricken wholesale from juries where interpreters may be used; instead, the trial court give an instruction to the Spanish-speaking jurors to follow the official court interpreter; should they perceive an error in the interpretation, they should bring that to the attention of the court and the court only, not to other jurors.[182]

The decision in *Hernandez* found the Supreme Court between two historically different periods of time reflecting the worst of both of them. First, there was the traditional suspicion of bilinguals found in *Stainback* and *Yick Wo* when linguistic minorities were a small, very identifiable group. The process of second language acquisition was a relatively unstudied one, and the connections between language and patriotism colored public perception of bilinguals.

The Supreme Court seems to be equally perplexed by bilinguals, unwilling to state the question with which it is secretly grappling – can bilinguals ignore the direct testimony of a witness and listen only to a translator? Asking the very question, of course, would indicate that the Court was looking at bilinguals as an "other," an unknowable, exotic importation, the inner mind of whom no one can really know. So the Court doesn't ask this question, but does betray its approval of this kind of thinking, as exemplified by the prosecutor. The best example of this is the Court's inclusion, in a footnote to its decision, of a portion of a transcript of another trial presenting a troublesome bilingual juror. There, a bilingual juror sat on a trial with a translator but then questioned the translator's abilities and appeared to insult her.[183] The Court included the quotation as an illustration of "the sort of problems that may arise where a juror fails to accept the official translation of foreign-language testimony."[184] The inclusion of the quotation, however, also legitimizes the prosecutor's suspicion of the bilingual jurors even in the face of their good-faith responses: even close questioning of a bilingual juror will not address their problematic aspects – a perhaps uncontrollable urge to follow the direct testimony. Although couched in the language of the late twentieth century, the Court's decision reflected the early-century attitude of bilingualism as suspicious and bilinguals as problematic.

Although its attitude was decidedly old-fashioned, the Court was caught in an assuredly modern situation: the record growth of Spanish-speaking immigrants and the challenge to the traditionally Black–White understanding of racial issues that their presence poses. Bilinguals are no longer exotics or highly marginalized. In a city like New York, Spanish-speaking bilinguals capable and willing to serve on juries are quite common. Indeed, Justice Kaye's proposed measures for the accommodation, even the positive use of bilingual jurors to ensure accurate interpretation, reflect the reality of living and working in a multilingual city. The Supreme Court, however, refused to address the pressing presence of bilinguals, and did not attempt to recreate racial and ethnic definitions in a way that would take their situation seriously. Instead, bilinguals otherwise capable of serving on a jury were marginalized by the Court itself and denied one of the fundamental aspects of citizenship – jury service.

A federal trial court in *Pemberthy v. Beyer*,[185] in order to protect language minorities, attempted to leap through the analytical spaces it felt were left open in *Hernandez*. However, it was ultimately overruled on appeal.

In *Pemberthy*, two Latino defendants convicted of drug-related charges challenged the prosecutor's use of peremptory challenges to exclude all Latino jurors from their jury. The case was tried before *Batson* was decided, so the prosecutor did not initially need to offer a race-neutral explanation for his challenges. At the trial, the accuracy of the police officer's translation of certain recorded conversations held in Spanish was a factual issue. There was no "official" translation accepted by the trial court, and the jurors needed to determine whether what was said in the tapes, as translated, amounted to drug dealing. The prosecutor asked the trial court to question those jurors who indicated that they were bilingual in Spanish and English as to their level of Spanish proficiency and their ability to accept the prosecutor's translation of the tapes. Five jurors indicated that they were bilingual; two of these were not Latino. All five were stricken by the prosecutor using peremptory challenges. Two Latino jurors were questioned closely on their proficiency in Spanish and their willingness to follow the interpretation of the tapes. Both answered that they were highly fluent in Spanish, but that they would also be able to accept the translation as offered if directed to do so by the court.

After *Batson* was decided, the trial court held a hearing in which the prosecutor was asked to offer his explanations for the challenges. The prosecutor testified that he struck all bilingual jurors because he did not believe, regardless of their assertions, that they would be able to ignore their own interpretation of the tapes and rely only on the prosecutor's translation. The prosecutor went on: "I didn't want one or two people on the jury who might know Spanish who might disagree with the interpretation as counsel would put forth to have sort of like a more important place on a jury."[186]

The Appellate Division, which held the *Batson* hearing, made specific findings of fact. The federal district court's responsibility was to apply *Batson* to this language rights case. The court easily found that the defendant had made out a *prima facie* case of discrimination under *Batson* – he was a member of a protected ethnic group, and the prosecutor systematically struck members of that ethnic group from the jury. It was then up to the prosecutor to proffer a race-neutral explanation for the striking. This is where the analysis became particularly complex since it required the court to decide whether a language-based strike is the same as a strike based on ethnicity or race.

The court began by defining the term "race" broadly. The court relied on the broad definition of race, as defined by Webster's Dictionary, as "[a]ny group of people who have the same activities, habits, ideas, etc.... "[187] Under this definition, reasoned the court, language may well be a characteristic of race. The court relied heavily on the *dicta* in *Hernandez* where the Supreme Court stated:

> [i]n holding that a race-neutral reason for a peremptory challenge means a reason other than race, we do not resolve the more difficult question of the breadth with which the concept of race should be defined for equal protection purposes. We would face a quite different case if the prosecutor had justified his peremptory challenges with the explanation that he did not want Spanish-speaking jurors.[188]

The Court in *Hernandez* was *not* presented with the *exact* issue before it, reasoned the district court– a situation where the potential bilingual jurors did not equivocate in their assurances to the court. For the district court, the situation it was faced with was the very one that *Hernandez* meant to prohibit. In concluding that language "bears such a close relationship to a juror's identity as a Latino that it is a surrogate for race and/or ethnicity," the court found that "the one characteristic that links and, in essence *defines* this community/ "race" and exposes it to irrational discrimination is their status as native Spanish speakers."[189] Under this analysis, the prosecutor's rationale for striking the bilingual jurors was no more than a race-based reason.

The court recognized the difficult situation that it was grappling with when it defined "race" broadly enough to include language, but also needed to stay within an intentional discrimination framework. It took pains to distinguish its own analysis from a disparate impact one:

> the foregoing analysis is *not* a "disparate impact" analysis. Disparate impact analysis would assign a proffered explanation race-based status based on the effect or result that all jurors of a certain race were excluded.... Although the facts ... may appear to resemble a disparate impact dynamic, a more precise description of what occurred is that the prosecutor applied a trial related reason, which reason is the very definition of the racial group. In other words, the basis for the strikes – Spanish-speaking ability – is the defining characteristic of Latinos. Such a reason can only be understood as race-based. Indeed, this is the scenario which *Hernandez* identified as race-based.[190]

The proffered reasons cannot be trial-related, said the court, because it is race-based; a race-based rationale can never be justified by linking it to the trial. Further, the prosecutor, by not believing the assurances given by the jurors, "made generalized, group-based assumptions about the capacity, behavior, and trustworthiness of Spanish speakers, without any individualized basis for concern."[191] In a footnote, the court went further and noted that, even if the prosecutor had a legitimate concern that the bilingual jurors would hold a special status amongst the jurors, "the inextricable linkage between Spanish-speaking ability and Latino ethnicity necessitates the conclusion that the State must tolerate this risk."[192]

Finally, under the third step of *Batson*, the court needed to determine whether the petitioner carried his burden of proving purposeful discrimination.[193] The court found that the prosecutor did so even if the state's rationale was considered race-neutral. The court determined that the linkage between race and language would mean that the prosecutor could foresee that his strikes based on language would result in a jury without Latinos. Also, although the prosecutor *said* that he struck the jurors because of his concern over their willingness to follow the state's interpretation of the tapes, he actually struck *all* bilingual jurors, regardless of how they responded on this point during *voir dire*. The rationale the prosecutor offered for his actions only supports a finding of intentional conduct: "[t]he prosecutor states that no native speaker could ever set aside their knowledge of the language and restrict themselves to the evidence as presented.... Thus, unless the inability to accept to follow instructions is considered an inherent quality of Spanish-speaking people, the prosecutor's concern is unfounded."[194]

Although under *Batson* the court was required to make findings of intentional discrimination, it clearly found the task unpleasant:

[t]he [*Batson*] procedure places the trial judge in the awkward position of determining the credibility of the explanations proffered by counsel. It will require the trial court, as the court does here, frequently to make findings which impugn the integrity of honorable and dedicated prosecutors.... [195]

The case was appealed to the Third Circuit where the issue of language and race was treated very differently. The Third Circuit court first addressed the issue of whether the prosecutor's real reason for peremptorily challenging the bilingual jurors was a reflection of his prejudice against Latinos, rather than a concern over translation disputes. Here, the Third Circuit disagreed with the district court over whether the state court Appellate Division had made factual findings on this issue that needed to be accorded deference. The district court had found that it had not. The Third Circuit thought that it was "clear" that the Appellate Division had made a factual finding that the prosecutor had stricken the jurors based on their ability to speak Spanish. The Third Circuit credited the Appellate Division's determination finding that it was supported by the record – most notably by the prosecutor's decision to strike all bilingual jurors, even though two of the five bilinguals were not Latino. On the issue of whether the prosecutor improperly questioned the trustworthiness of Spanish-speakers, the court said "we do not think that it is strongly indicative of bias for a trial lawyer to suspect that some people, if placed in this situation, would find it difficult, at a conscious or subconscious level, to follow the translation."[196]

The remaining question was whether the prosecutor violated the Equal Protection Clause by using peremptory challenges to strike all the bilingual jurors. The Third Circuit took its guidance, not from the plurality opinion in *Hernandez*, but from the opinion of Justice O'Connor in which Justice Scalia joined. Justice O'Connor was careful not to endorse a disparate impact standard for *Batson* purposes:

> [n]o matter how closely tied or significantly correlated to race the explanation for a peremptory strike may be, the strike does not implicate the Equal Protection Clause unless it is based on race. That is the distinction between disproportionate effect, which is not sufficient to constitute an equal protection violation, and intentional discrimination which is.[197]

Here, reasoned the Circuit Court, the lack of alliance between language and ethnicity or race is blatant, since two of the stricken jurors were not even Latino. Such strikes do not present problems under the Equal Protection Clause. "[N]o simple equation," said the court, "can be drawn between ethnicity and language. Sociologists recognize language as only one of the many components of ethnicity."[198] The district court's view that, for Latinos, ethnic identity is based on language, "seem[ed] exaggerated" to the Third Circuit.[199]

The sociological link between race and language was of no interest to the court. *Batson*, it reasoned, applied only to those classifications that are subject to strict scrutiny. "Classifications based on the ability to speak or understand a foreign language do not meet the requirements for either 'strict' or 'heightened' scrutiny."[200] The ability to speak a foreign language may indeed be relevant in some situations to the achievement of a legitimate state interest, but is not immutable and "the history of discrimination against individuals who speak a foreign language in addition to English is not comparable to the history of discrimination based on factors such as race or national origin."[201] Challenges based on language ability rather than ethnicity are subject only to rational basis review, found the court.

Applying *Batson*, then, trial courts must essentially determine the "subjective intent" of the prosecutor. The court attempted to give trial courts some guidance on how to make this kind of determination by listing factors for the courts to consider: They were:

(1) any extrinsic evidence of motivation;
(2) whether the prosecutors's strikes correlate better with language ability or with race;
(3) how strong the prosecutor's reasons are to fear that translation issues will be a problem.[202]

While the court stated that it "would be utterly unacceptable if Latinos were commonly excluded from juries based on pretextual concerns about translations," it ultimately found that "peremptory challenges that are sincerely based on translation concerns are not prohibited."[203] Although the *Pemberthy* petitioners applied to the US Supreme Court for review of the Third Circuit's decision, the Court denied *certiorari*, declining to hear the case.

In *US v. Munoz*,[204] the Fifth Circuit also relied upon *Hernandez* to decide, in a brief opinion, that striking a Latino juror because he understood Spanish was not discriminatory. The defendant was again Latino and a translation of a tape-recorded conversation held in Spanish was going to be used at the trial. A non-Latino Spanish-speaking juror was also struck. The opinion did not reveal what kind of assurances the stricken jurors had given the trial court about their willingness to follow judicial instruction on the veracity of the translation. When asked to enunciate his reasons for striking the jurors, the prosecutor said: " ...I anticipate there is going to be Spanish in the tapes. I didn't want any arguments in the jury as to their possible translation of the tapes versus what is provided in the transcript to English speakers."[205]

Without an in-depth discussion, the Fifth Circuit accepted this rationale as race-neutral for *Batson* purposes, since it was based on language ability rather than on ethnicity or race. [206]

A somewhat different issue was raised in *US v. Canoy*.[207] A convicted defendant, Marius Canoy, challenged his conviction under *Batson v. Kentucky* because the prosecutor had used peremptory strikes to exclude the only Asian individual on the *venire*. Canoy was born in and had spent most of his life in the Philippines. Canoy made out a *prima facie* case of discrimination – he was a member of a protected racial group, and the only *venire* person who shared his ethnic background was stricken by the prosecution. The prosecutor, however, argued that he struck the juror, Daniel

Ma, from acting as an alternate juror because Ma had been educated outside the US, and entirely in a foreign language. The prosecutor was purportedly concerned "with whether English was Ma's first language," even though Ma had "not exhibited any difficulty speaking or understanding English when questioned by the court."[208] The trial court accepted the prosecutor's rationale as being race-neutral.

Although the appellate court noted that the explanation offered by the prosecution – formal education in a language other than English – would likely fall most heavily on ethnic minorities, it found that the potential for such disproportionality was not sufficient evidence of purposeful discrimination under equal protection analysis. Rather, reviewing courts must rely on the factual judgments made by trial courts, which must assess whether "the government is legitimately concerned about language skills or is instead utilizing that concern as a shield for prohibited discrimination."[209] Although both the trial court and the appellate court made much of the fact that the prosecutor had not sought to excuse Ma for service until he was available to serve as an alternate, given the state of the law as articulated in *Hernandez*, there is little doubt that Canoy would not have won his *Batson* challenge in any case.

Conclusion

The treatment of language under *Hernandez* through the *Batson* framework has proved to be a poisonous concoction for language minorities. It clearly shows the limits of modern equal protection analysis, an analysis that does not allow for the real impact on minorities of governmental decisions such as peremptory challenges to be considered, because such considerations might muddy the "pure" waters of intent analysis. If language is not considered an indicator of national origin or ethnicity, then what is "race" for the *Hernandez* Court? The district court's opinion in *Pemberthy* made a good-faith attempt to grapple with this issue, and did as good a job as any court could do when it decided that characteristics that are used to mark and subject groups to discrimination are aspects of race.

The other courts, however, would not recognize this reasoning, but seemed to require some sort of fake perfect correlation between the characteristics at issue and the group to be protected. There are, however, no such characteristics; every physical, or as the courts would call them, "immutable," feature that can be thought of will not apply without exception to every member of each racial group. These courts seem to think, for instance, that dark skin coloring will mark every African-American and, therefore, that color is an aspect of race. But one need only actually look at the many-hued, and intermarried, generations of African-Americans living in the US to know that there is no one "color" associated with being African-American. Conversely, non-African-Americans may enjoy darker skin tones than some African-Americans. Further, with skin bleaches, hair dyes and hair straighteners widely available, skin color and hair texture may be more mutable than ability to speak or understand a foreign language, or more mutable than a thick accent. In short, the correlation between any aspect of race and the protected group is a matter of degree or, in legal terms, a matter of disparate impact. The courts, however, treat "disparate impact" as dirty words or a noxious substance from which the Equal Protection Clause must be protected. Even the *Pemberthy* district court went to some lengths to try and convince the appellate court that its rationale was not imbued with the deadly disparate-impact analysis. Such assurances, however, did it no good. Just as the district court ruled the *Batson* court's reliance on the revelation of subjective intent as invitations to prosecutors to become more inventive, so too must the civil rights community bemoan the fact that modern equal protection analysis has forced well-intending courts to weave complex opinions in order to advance the mission of the Equal Protection Clause.

The Third Circuit's opinion clearly articulated its vision of the Equal Protection Clause when it flatly refused to grant language abilities anything more than a rational-basis review. Its analysis on this point was quite weak, relying only upon a presumed distinction between what it termed "sociological" connections between language and ethnicity and presumably the more demanding, legally required connections between language and race. It did not address these issues or explain why the sociological evidence was insufficient to convince it that heightened, if not strict, scrutiny was unjustified. More damning is the fact that sociological evidence is the only kind of evidence the courts can rely on in determining what characteristics ought to be considered when decisions on the scope of race are made. The *Hernandez, Pemberthy* and *Munoz* courts seem to realize that they were in difficult waters. They were involved in nothing less than determining the scope of traditional civil rights laws in a country that demographically, economically, and politically no longer reflects the nation that forged those laws, yet those protections are still required. The issue at stake is whether the civil rights laws will be allowed to evolve with the nation and continue to protect the traditional African-American "minority" even as it unfolds to safeguard the newly emerging ones.

The *Hernandez* Court hinted at the complexity of the issues involved in defining race at the end of the twentieth century, but was apparently nervous of doing anything more than raising the issue. The *Pemberthy* district court did take up the challenge and did an admirable job of coming up with a realistic, workable response. Unfortunately, its reasoning and holding was roundly rejected on appeal. While the *Munoz* court was wrong, at least its opinion was not as harmful as the Third Circuit's opinion – long and detailed and putting language squarely on the bottom rung of the traditional civil rights pantheon. It is a decision we are bound to see again and again in citations by other courts on even unrelated language rights issues.

Hopefully, other Circuits will be persuaded by the *Pemberthy* district court opinion, and forge a new understanding of equal protection – one that will be serviceable to a nation on the edge of significant demographic changes.

LANGUAGE MINORITIES IN PRISON: THE EXTENT AND LIMITS OF THE EIGHTH AMENDMENT

Introduction

It seems aphoristic to say that how a country handles its criminals reflects its moral state. Certainly, few are as universally despised as those who are convicted of crimes, and few give rise to the temptation that they be given no rights, to lock them away from sight as well as memory. The Original Framers of the Constitution, through the Eighth Amendment, placed restrictions on the treatment of criminals by state and federal governments.

The Eighth Amendment, however, protects all citizens, not just the accused or the imprisoned, from unreasonable actions of the state against the physical body. The protection from severe bodily harm, and the concomitant respect for bodily integrity, are the backbones of this constitutional provision. The Amendment has been implicated in claims against the state for actions of the police in dealing with members of communities, in state requirements for vaccinations and fluoridated water, and in blood testing of suspected alcohol-related car accidents.[210]

This section will discuss the uses of the Eighth Amendment, prohibiting cruel and unusual punishment, in language rights litigation. The Eighth Amendment will be considered here only in the context in which it was raised by language minorities: that is, as prisoners. The most significant litigation in this area, *Franklin v. District of Columbia*,[211] where Spanish-dominant prisoners complained of lack of linguistically-appropriate prison services, will be discussed in detail

Latinos and corrections: Living in a linguistic prison

The cruel and unusual punishment provision of the Eighth Amendment uses fairly straightforward words to limit the discretion of the government in how it treats its citizens, especially those accused or convicted of crimes:

> *Excessive bail shall not be required, nor excessive fines imposed, nor cruel and unusual punishments inflicted.*

The prohibition against cruel and unusual punishment is necessarily defined in subjective terms. It is left up to individual communities to determine what is "cruel and unusual," there being a perverse sense, even with punishment, that familiarity dulls outrage and what might be unusual and cruel in one community may be the norm in another.

A violation of the Eighth Amendment may be found if there is a deliberate indifference to medical and mental health needs of prisoners. Governments will be found liable for violating the Eighth Amendment if they knew or should have known that inmates face a substantial risk of harm and yet disregard that risk by failing to take reasonable measures to abate it.[212]

In *Franklin*, a class of Spanish-dominant Latino prisoners who were, or would be, incarcerated in DC correctional institutions brought action, seeking injunctive and declaratory relief for violations of the First, Fifth, and Eighth Amendments and Title VI of the Civil Rights Act for the prison's failure to provide them appropriate medical, mental, educational, vocational, and religious services as well as the failure to provide interpreters and translated documents at hearings.

There had been a documented need for greater services available to the Latino community of the District of Columbia generally as a result of civil disturbances in the Mount Pleasant area. The Department of Corrections (DCDC) organized a Task Force to address the services to the Latino population within the correctional institutions. The Task Force recognized that "limited English speaking inmates are not afforded the opportunity to participate because of the language barrier and the lack of sensitivity to their needs by the system."[213] Specifically, the Task Force found that:

> [limited English Proficient] inmates could not seek appropriate mental health services, medical services; could not participate in educational and vocational programs; their ability to have their spiritual needs was impaired and their ability to participate duly in institutional and community-based programs were all impaired by the lack of bilingual staff whether psychiatric, medical or otherwise. [214]

Just 2%, or approximately 188, of DCDC prisoners were Latinos.[215] The court noted the lack of English-language proficiency amongst the Latino prisoners: approximately 80 Latino inmates "do not speak English sufficient to function effectively on a daily basis."[216] A psychologist employed by DCDC since 1983 stated that in 13 years at DCDC, she had seen only two Hispanics who could fully function in English and do "C" grade work in English-language courses. She explained that only about half of the Hispanic inmates could even communicate in English regarding basic functions and needs; the other half were essentially non-functional in English. She added that "virtually none of the Hispanic inmates in DCDC [correctional institutions] could understand English language subtleties such as the expression 'I feel blue.'"[217]

In order for an inmate to be considered for parole, the following programs, unavailable in Spanish needed to be completed: substance abuse, Alcoholics Anonymous, life skills, mental health, and psychological or psychiatric counseling. As of the date of the trial, four years after the Taskforce reported to DCDC on the "desperate need" of these programs for Latino prisoners, only 40% of the Spanish-dominant inmates had access to the programs.[218] The DCDC began a more intense "flurry of activity" addressing these needs only on the eve of trial.

With respect to access to medical and mental health care, the court found that "LEP [Limited English Proficiency] inmates have difficulty accessing the medical and mental health care system. Moreover, if and when they are able to do so, the treatment that they receive is inadequate and, at times, unsafe."[219] "Hispanic prisoners are denied necessary medical treatment because there is no program in place to insure that they can communicate with their medical providers, which limits their ability to gain access to medical services throughout the period of incarceration."[220] Further, confidentiality of Spanish-speaking patients is routinely violated, as fellow prisoners and correctional officers are used to translate sensitive, disease-specific information. Further, "[f]or medical care to be adequate, a doctor and a patient must be able to understand each other."[221] The failure to communicate makes it almost impossible for a doctor to be able to adequately diagnose and treat the patient and for the patient to understand the treatment plan, the medication being prescribed, and possible side effects.[222] The court found that "[w]ithin the Department of Corrections, poor communication has led to inadequate treatment for LEP Hispanic inmates, deficiencies of which correctional officials knew or should have known."[223]

The court pointed out the "marked insensitivity" of the DCDC medical staff to the need for interpreters. Many of the contemptuous attitudes reflected by the courts in the criminal trials of language minorities discussed above are found here again, except exemplified by the prison officials. For example, the Chief Medical Officer at one facility told the expert that Latino inmates could "understand enough" English if, for example, they could understand "positivo" after undergoing a test for HIV.[224] Another Chief Medical Officer of another facility in regard to a specific Latino inmate said that he "can speak English whenever he wants."[225] The court found that "[t]he medical staff's relaxed attitude translates to the denial of effective medical care for LEP Hispanic inmates in the DCDC system."[226] For example, the prisoners' expert testified that "a significant majority of the medical staff seemed to attribute an ability to function minimally in English as equivalent to being able to effectively communicate in a medical setting."[227]

Similar problems existed with access to mental health services. The prisoners' expert testified that provision of psychological and psychiatric services to Hispanic prisoners in the DCDC institutions was "grossly inadequate and dangerous."[228] The court made interesting findings in this regard: "[d]ue to the significance of linguistic and cultural nuances in psychiatric diagnoses, the translation of mental health encounters, even through a qualified interpreter, is inadequate."[229] Further:

> the evidence at trial established that few, if any, LEP Hispanic inmates in DCDC correctional institutions engage in meaningful verbal encounters with psychologists or psychiatrists in the DCDC mental health care system. Medication has been prescribed without a full understanding of the nature of the underlying problems, and inmates do not understand the treatment plan or the potential side effects of the medication prescribed.[230]

On the issue of translation assistance at prison hearings, the court found that the provision of interpreters at these hearings was "haphazard at best."[231] "The failure to use disinterested, trained interpreters creates additional problems, since neither the LEP Hispanic inmate nor the board have any way of knowing whether the interpretation is accurate or has been colored by the view of the 'interested' untrained interpreter."[232]

Furthermore, there was no procedure in place to advise parole boards of the need for an interpreter.[233] On the process followed at hearings, one Lieutenant had been known to tell inmates: "I know you speak English, so we're going ahead." Another hearing officer commented that "if I can't understand him [i.e. the inmate], I'll get a translator." "This ignores the real issue," said the court, "whether the *inmate* is able to understand the hearings."[234] (emphasis added). The court concluded that:

> ...the evidence at trial clearly established that the actual practice within DCDC correctional institutions often subjects LEP Hispanic inmates to Kafkaesque hearings – hearings where adjudications are made and their futures are affected by officials speaking a language that they seldom understand regarding allegations that are too infrequently explained to them in words that they understand.[235]

The court found that the plaintiffs had proved a violation of the Eighth Amendment by:

> demonstrat[ing] overwhelmingly ... that the defendant has been deliberately indifferent to the medical and mental health care needs of the plaintiff class. The plaintiffs have repeatedly shown that, for years.... Hispanic prisoners have not been provided adequate health care treatment and that the defendant had repeated notice of these problems. The plaintiffs have also demonstrated that the defendant's actual (not its written) policies and practices were the moving force denying Hispanic prisoners adequate medical treatment and placing them at substantial risk of serious harm.[236]

Indeed, the court remained un-moved by DCDC's last-minute attempts to address some of these needs. It stated: "[w]here the record clearly establishes deliberate indifference or other constitutional violations, the defendant cannot hide behind a paper shield of departmental orders or program statements that are seldom, if ever, followed."[237]

Further, found the court, "[t]o satisfy the Constitution," "a medical facility must be adequately staffed.... Nor can access to medical treatment be substantially delayed in a systematic manner due to inadequate staffing."[238]

The *Franklin* prisoners also won on their claim of DCDC's failure to provide interpreters at hearings as a violation of due process. The court stated that:

> [i]f Due Process means anything at all, it provides constitutional protection of the right to participate meaningfully in critical proceedings. For Due Process to be satisfied in the prison setting, an inmate must be provided notice of charges, must have the right to call witnesses and present evidence on his or her behalf, and the inmate must be provided with written findings. For this procedural regime to be meaningful, it should be obvious that the prisoner must be able to understand the proceedings and participate on his or her own behalf. Non-English speaking prisoners who are not provided with qualified interpreters at any of the critical stages of the discipline proceedings or during parole proceedings are denied due process of law.... [239]

However, the prisoners had also argued that the lack of educational and vocational programs for Spanish prisoners violated Title VI, the Equal Protection and

Due Process Clauses of the Fifth Amendment. The court found no violation of the Due Process Clause because there is no fundamental right to these services that must be protected by the existence of some sort of process.

The equal protection claim failed as well because the prisoners had argued that services were not available to them, not because they were *Hispanic*, an ethnic group protected by the Constitution, but because they were Spanish-dominant. Naturally this argument required the court to accept the nexus between language and national origin. The court would not do so. It said:

> [o]f course, a denial of equal protection and a violation of Title VI would result were prison programs offered based upon an inmate's race or ethnic origin. That, however, is not this case. All programs are available to all inmates. To the extent that *LEP Hispanics* are unable to participate in meaningful sense in English-language programs, those *LEP Hispanic* inmates are differently situated for equal protection purposes.[240]

The Title VI claim failed for the same reasons:

> The LEP Hispanic inmates are not being barred from participation in prison programs because of their race, color or national origin. While the programs are open to all inmates, limited English proficient inmates' participation is limited only by their English fluency. Simply put, LEP inmates are differently situated than inmates who are fluent in English. While it may be penologically sound and even highly desirable for the defendant to offer identical programs to every language group confined within the walls of its prisons, neither Title VI nor the Constitution require it to do so. The defendant simply cannot discriminate for an illegal reason and here, the plaintiffs have not shown that it has.[241]

These are very interesting findings, for the court had gone into considerable detail to show that "LEP Hispanic" inmates were indeed being denied access to programs – the programs were not available to all, and they were not available to the "LEP" sub-population of Latinos because of their language. Although the court had been able to appreciate in a very nuanced way the importance that language plays in being able to communicate sensitive and medical information to physicians, it refused to legally recognize what it knew in reality – that the national origin of Latinos was absolutely connected to language. Almost ten years after *Hernandez* was decided, raising the possibility of linkages between ethnicity and language, this federal district court, confronted with rampant discrimination based on language, did not even refer to *Hernandez*. Most likely, arguments based on *Hernandez* were made to the court; and the court was aware of the statistics that correlated Latino identity (especially Central American identity) with Spanish-dominance. Indeed, the court was aware of the background to the DCDC Taskforce's work on services to Latino prisoners – the civil unrest in the Mount Pleasant area over the Latino community's unmet needs. The Taskforce's work on Latino issues unequivocally included the need for *linguistically* appropriate services: greater responsiveness to Latinos went hand in hand with greater responsiveness to English language barriers. However, the court did away with the discrimination claims in four sentences. The only hint of a rationale lies in the one sentence where the court noted the "desirability" of programs for prisoners in every language for every "language group confined within the walls of its prisons."[242] The court, however, clearly found this "desirability" to be too much to mandate and followed the lead of those conservative courts who continually find that economic costs outweigh the rights of linguistic minorities.

In any case, the district court issued a sixteen-page injunction requiring the DCDC to make substantial changes in the way it operated its jails on behalf of Spanish-dominant prisoners.

The inroads made by the prisoners at the trial level were short-lived. On appeal, the DC Circuit Court of Appeals found that due process was not violated by a lack of interpreters at prison hearings, that the Eighth Amendment was not violated by a lack of interpreters at medical consultations, and that prisoners did not have the constitutional right to have medical personnel serve as interpreters.[243]

The Circuit Court essentially disagreed with the trial court's interpretation of the facts before it, particularly the extent and nature of the problems with the DCDC and its efforts to address the needs of the Latino population within the jails. The Circuit Court emphasized the small number of Spanish-dominant inmates at DCDC, thereby questioning the legitimacy of the trial court's mandate of systemic reform. Underlying the Circuit Court's thinking was the troubling question: does vindicating the rights of a small population legitimize mandating extensive and, therefore, expensive, reforms? Certainly, without saying as much, it answered that question negatively.

For the Circuit Court there was on the one hand the small population (150 prisoners) claiming harm and, on the other, the efforts it felt DCDC had in good faith made to accommodate the prisoners. In contrast to the findings made by the trial court and to which it showed no deference, the Circuit Court emphasized the "27 different non-medical programs to assist Spanish-speaking inmates."[244] DCDC required the Spanish-dominant prisoners to take ESL classes for six hours per day, five days per week. and shielded the program from budget cuts. The Circuit Court found the number of bilingual staff impressive, while the trial court had found that number "meager" and "inadequate." The Circuit Court also credited DCDC with the "flurry of activity" which the trial court had seen as a cynical governmental attempt at avoiding liability.

On the due process claim, the Circuit Court noted that due process within the prison setting was a limited concept, since clearly liberty was already severely curtailed. Within this context, for an interest in liberty to exist, a prisoner must be subjected to a "'restraint that imposes atypical and significant hardship' as compared with the ordinary incidents of prison life."[245] Many of the types of hearings at which the district court had directed that DCDC provide interpreters were not of the kind to implicate due process, claimed the Circuit Court. Disciplinary proceedings, housing, and classification hearings are not of a kind to constitute a "dramatic departure from the basic conditions of the prison sentences originally imposed."[246]

On the Eighth Amendment claims concerning medical care, the Circuit Court did not see the "deliberate indifference" of prison officials, but instead saw only an "imperfect enforcement" of well-intentioned policy.[247] The district court had required that DCDC either hire bilingual health care providers or else use bilingual members of the health care staff for translating at medical consultations. The trial court had justified this portion of the injunction by finding that prisoners had a limited constitutional right to medical confidentiality, a limited right to privacy that could not be usurped without some penologically valid justification. Such a right to privacy, however, simply does not exist for prisoners, disagreed the Circuit Court. Having one prisoner translate for another even sensitive medical information is no more than "one of the ordinary incidents of prison life."[248]

Had the trial court sustained the Title VI and equal protection claims, its injunction on this point would have had a firmer footing, and would have made more factual sense. For, while prisoners may indeed have little right to privacy, the real issue was the fact that the Spanish-dominant prisoners had to rely on fellow inmates for translating sensitive medical information, while the other prisoners did not. This issue could have been legitimately addressed through the hiring of more bilingual medical personnel.

The Circuit Court's true concerns, however, were ultimately revealed:

> [s]uppose plaintiffs prevailed, suppose members of their class had a due process right to be treated by prison medical personnel who speak their native tongue. Such a constitutional right could hardly be reserved only for Spanish-speaking prisoners. Prisoners who spoke or understood only Arabic, or only Mandarin or Italian or any other of the world's languages would presumably have the same constitutional right when they sought medical treatment. Implementing such a system would inevitably entail considerable disruption and expense, and might well prove to be impossible given the difficulty the District has experienced in recruiting medical staff.[249]

Economics reared its socially conservative head again.[250]

Many of the same issues concerning lack of Spanish-speaking medical staff were raised in *Leon v. Johnson*,[251] where a Spanish-dominant prisoner who had AIDS did not receive his medicine for weeks because of a lack of interpreter services at the Orleans Correctional Facility. Hector Leon, the plaintiff, was transferred to Orleans from Attica and, although he spoke only a limited amount of English, he was given an orientation manual written only in English; the manual contained instructions on how prisoners are supposed to obtain their medication. With the help of counsel, Leon was eventually able to figure out the proper process for getting his medication, but still had to rely on other prisoners in order to speak about private medical matters with prison medical staff.

Leon sued the state under the Eighth Amendment for inadequate medical care for the weeks in which he was unable to obtain his medication as well as for the lack of Spanish-speaking medical staff. Leon argued that his diagnosis of AIDS required him to be on a medical treatment regimen that was severely interrupted by his not having been informed of the medication procedure in a manner intelligible to him.[252] The court, however, did not agree that the lack of medication for even several weeks, without a showing of real harm, amounted to the kind of "physical injury" required under the Eighth Amendment. The court also found that there was no deliberate indifference to Leon's needs; at most negligence on the part of some officials was shown – not sufficient to sustain a constitutional violation. Further, found the court, Leon, who had received 2000 hours of English-language instruction at Attica, was sufficiently well-versed in English to at least ask someone for help in obtaining his medication.[253]

Leon also pressed a claim for violation of privacy because of the enforced use of other inmates to translate sensitive medical information for him. He alleged that he was "subjected to ridicule and humiliation" because of this.[254] However, it appeared that Leon only once used an inmate to translate his medical records, and it was an inmate chosen by Leon himself. On this issue, the court relied squarely on the decision in *Franklin*, where the Circuit Court had found that "Spanish-speaking prisoners with limited proficiency in English do not have a privacy right ... to force the District to hire bilingual medical personnel so that the prisoners may communicate their medical information only to such employees."[255] Since Leon used an inmate only once, and had previously voluntarily made his AIDS diagnosis known to certain prison officials, there was no "forced" use of inmates for translation that would amount to a violation of privacy.[256]

One case[257] that arose in the context of services for deaf prisoners ought to be mentioned, since it raises many of the same issues advanced by language minority inmates – the lack of appropriate services tailored to the needs of the deaf inmate community make it impossible for them to have the same access to educational, vocational, and rehabilitative services as other inmates.[258] Since these are not race-related claims, however, they are brought under the Rehabilitation Act and the Americans with Disabilities Act, which require governmental agencies to take affirmative steps to enable the deaf and disabled to have equal access to services. Here, the court found that the state's failure to provide interpreters or other assistive devices during medical treatment violated the Eighth Amendment because much medical treatment will depend upon the communication between prisoner and medical professional. The consistent lack of interpretive services results in a "systemic pattern of inadequacy of treatment ... which is causing class members unwarranted suffering."[259] The court also found that relying upon inmates and other correctional personnel who are not medical staff for interpreter services was a constitutional violation of the right to privacy unless the person being used was bound to maintain confidentiality.[260]

Conclusion

Franklin and *Leon* exemplify the judicial suspicion toward language rights generally as progenitors of expensive, affirmative action programs and, I think, an overall distaste for criminals and prisoners. It would seem that prisoners, so much more limited in their avenues for self-help, should be treated with more generosity. Yet, instead, the 188 prisoners in the DCDC are seen in strictly economic terms and not just as 188 people but as multipliers – the Circuit Court seems almost afraid of a kind of over-run of language-minority prisoners, all demanding non-essential (even esoteric) services in local dialects. Such a parade of horribles had been flashed before – in the social services context, by English-only supporters, and as will be seen later, in the consumer protection area. Yet we have seen that such a scenario has very little reality to it and that courts imbued with equitable powers have the flexibility to create remedies for constitutional violations that can be just and reasonable. In the end it isn't clear just what the *Franklin* Circuit Court is trying to address: the potential number of language-minority prisoners demanding services, or the equitable powers of lower courts to fashion remedies.

Notes

1.   5 John W. Wigmore, Evidence, §1393 (Chadbourn rev. 1974) at 176.
2.   Robert D. McFadden, *Four Officers Indicted for Murder in Killing of Diallo, Lawyer Says,* NY Times, March 26, 1999 at A1.
3.   *Miranda v. Arizona,* 384 US 434, 444 (1966).
4.   *US v. Nakhoul,* 596 FSupp 1398, 1401 (D Mass. 1984), *aff'd sub. nom., United States v. El-Debeib,* 802 F2d 442 (1st Cir 1986).
5.   Richard W. Cole and Laura Maslow-Armand, *The Role of Counsel and The Courts in Addressing Foreign language and Cultural Barriers at Different Stages of a Criminal Proceeding,* 19 W New Eng. L. Rev. 193, 201 (1997).
6.   *See Nakhoul supra*, note 4.
7.   *Id* at 1402.
8.   *Id.*
9.   790 F2d 464 (6th Cir 1986).
10. *Id.* at 469.
11. *Id.*
12. 217 F3d 1222 (10th Cir 2000).
13. *See also Davis v. US,* 512 US 452 (1994), where the Supreme Court held that only clear unequivocal requests for an attorney are sufficient to require police officers to stop questioning. An ambiguous remark like "maybe I should talk to a lawyer" is not sufficient. The Court noted, but was apparently unconcerned about, the impact such a requirement could have on a non-English speaking defendant:

     [w]e recognize that requiring a clear assertion of the right to counsel might disadvantage some suspects who – because of fear, intimidation, lack of linguistic skills or a variety of other reasons – will not clearly articulate their right to counsel although they actually want to have a lawyer present. But the primary protection afforded suspects to subject custodial interrogation is the *Miranda* warning themselves. (*Id.* at 460)

14. *See US v. Toscano-Padilla,* No 92-30247, 1993 US App. LEXIS 15411 (9th Cir 1993). *But see State v. Santiago,* 542 NW 2d 466 (Wis. Ct App. 1995), where the police officer who

translated the *Miranda* warnings testified that he gave a "street language" version of what the pre-printed *Miranda* card said, and was unable to repeat that translation in court, the trial court had no basis for determining the adequacy of the translation, and the conviction was overturned.)

15. *Supra,* note 5 at 204.
16. *Id.* at 205.
17. 630 FSupp 665 (D Mass. 1986).
18. *Id.* at 668.
19. *Id.*
20. *Id.* at 675.
21. 775 FSupp 495 (DRI 1991).
22. *Id.* at 500.
23. Leslie V. Dery, *Disinterring the "Good" and "Bad Immigrant": A Deconstruction of the State Court Interpreter Laws for Non-English speaking Criminal Defendants,* 45 Kansas L. Rev. 837, 852 (1997).
24. 205 US 86 (1907).
25. *Id.* at 91.
26. *See for example* MICH. Comp. Laws Ann. § 600.1427 (West 1996); Mo. Rev. Stat. §476.050 (1986); Utah Code Ann. §78-7-22 (1996); Vt. Stat. Ann. tit. 4 § 731 (1988); Wis. Stat. Ann. §757.18 (WEST 1981).
27. 105 So. 386 (Ct App. Ala.1925).
28. *Id.* at 387 (emphasis added).
29. 332 US 561 (1947).
30. 210 SW 2d 2d 574 (Tex. Crim. App. 1948).
31. *Supra,* note 21 at 580.
32. 434 F2d 386 (2nd Cir 1970).
33. *Id.* at 389 (citations omitted).
34. *Id.* at 390.
35. *Id.* at 390–391 (emphasis added).
36. *Valladares v. US,* 871 F2d 1564, 1566 (11 Cir 1989); *see also US v. Martinez,* 616 F2d 185, 188 (5th Cir 1980).
37. *Supra,* note 5 at 197(emphasis added).
38. The four statutes were: Rule 28(b) of the Federal Rules of Criminal procedure, the Criminal Justice Act of 1964, Rule 43 (f) of the Federal Rules of Civil Procedure and Rule 604 of the Federal Rules of Evidence.
39. Mollie M. Pawlosky, *When Justice is Lost in the "Translation": Gonzalez v. United States, An "Interpretation" of the Court Interpreters Act of 1978* 45 De Paul L. Rev. 435, 443 (1996).
40. 28 USC §1826. (The efficiency of the CIA is limited because it applies only to situations where the US has instituted proceedings against a party. State statutes, however, provide substantial additional protections for defendants being tried in state courts. For instance, Arkansas, California, Delaware, Florida, Idaho, Indiana, Illinois, Iowa, Kansas, Kentucky, Maryland, Massachusetts, Michigan, Minnesota, Nebraska, New Mexico, North Dakota, Oregon, Texas, Utah, Washington, Wisconsin, and the District of Columbia all have created statutory rights to an interpreter for a non-English-speaking defendant. Many other jurisdictions simply authorize the appointment of an interpreter for the non-English speaking defendant.)
41. 28 USC §1827.

42. *See US v. Joshi*, 896 F2d 1303.

43. *See also Valladares v. US, supra*, note 36.

44. Joshi, *supra*, note 42; *US v. Tapia*, 631 F2d 1207, 1209–1210 (5th Cir 1986).

45. *Supra*, note 42 at 1303.

46. *Supra*, note 42 at 1309.

47. Bill Piatt, Only English? Law and Language Policy in the United States, (University of New Mexico Press, 1990) at 84.

48. *Supra*, note 5 at 193; *see also Coronel-Quintana*, 752 F2d 1284, 1291 (8th Cir 1985), *cert. den.*, 106 S. Ct 66 (1985); *Valladares, supra*, note 36 at 1566.

49. *See Valladares, supra*, note 36, where the court held that §1827 does not place on the trial court a mandatory duty to inquire as to the need for an interpreter when a defendant has difficulty with English); *see also US v. Tapia, supra*, note 44.

50. *See US v. Desist*, 384 F2d 889 (2nd Cir 1967), and *Valladares, supra*, note 36.

51. *Valladares, supra*, note 36.

52. 896 F2d 1303 (1st Cir 1990), *cert. den.*, 498 US 986 (1991).

53. Joshi, *supra*, note 42 at 1310, *citing Valladares, supra*, note 36; *US v. Lim*, 794 F2d 469, 471 (9th Cir 1986); *Tapia, supra*, note 44 at 1207; *US v. Martinez*, 616 F2d 185, 187-88 (5th Cir 1980), *cert. den.* 450 US 994 (1981); *US v. Bennett*, 848 F2d 1134, 1141 (11th Cir 1988).

54. 28 USC §1827; *see also US v. Petrosian*, 126 F3d 1232 (9th Cir 1997).

55. 488 F2d 12 (1st Cir 1973*)*, *cert. den.*, 94 Sup. Ct 1613 (1974).

56. *Id.* at 15.

57. *Id.*

58. Some state courts, however, have affirmative waiver provisions for the defendant: the failure to timely request an interpreter is seen as a waiver. No burden is placed on the trial court to inquire further.

59. 17 F3d 11745 (9th Cir 1999).

60. *Id.* at 1180.

61. *Id.* at 1181.

62. *Id.* at n. 4 at 1180.

63. In *State v. Topete*, 380 NW2d 635 (Neb. 1986) (the court used information that the defendant spoke English in the jail to deny him an interpreter).

64. 109 F2d 215 (3rd Cir 1940).

65. *Id.* at 217.

66. *Id.*

67. *Id.*

68. *Id.*

69. 59 Cal. Rptr 888 (Cal. Ct App. 1967), *cert. den.*, 390 US 1029 (1968).

70. *Id.* at 890.

71. *Supra*, note 23 at 847.

72. *Id.* at 860.

73. 819 SW 2d 932, 937–38 (Tex. Ct App. 1991).

74. *Id.* (emphasis added).

75. *Gonzalez v. US*, 33 F3d 1047 (9th Cir 1994).

76. *Id.* at 1053.

77. *Id.*

78. *Id.* at 1050.

79. *Id.* at 1051.

80. *Id.* at 1052.

81. *Id.* at 1053.

82. *Id.*

83. 200 Cal. Rptr 404, 406 (Cal. Ct. App. 1984).

84. *Id.* at 406; *see also In re Dung T* 206 Cal. Rptr 772, 776–78 (Cal. Ct App. 1984) (right of defendant to own interpreter is available under the California Constitution.)

85. 794 F2d 469 (9th Cir 1986).

86. 967 F2d 1098 (6th Cir 1992).

87. *See* Franklyn P. Salimbene, *Court Interpreters: Standard of Practice and Standards for Training*, 6 Cornell J. L. & Pub. Pol'y 645, 657 (1997). Under the CIA the Director of the Administrative Office of the United States Courts certifies court interpreters based on results of criterion-referenced performance exams. 1827(b)(1). An otherwise qualified interpreter may be used only if a certified interpreter is not reasonably available. The Director is to keep a list of certified interpreters.

    The test used for certification is quite difficult, with written and oral portions. The written test has both English and Spanish sections, each of which tests the candidate's reading comprehension, language usage, proficiency at sentence completion, and knowledge of antonyms and synonyms. The level of English tested is at the fourteenth grade.

    After passage of the written portion, candidates must pass an oral portion which is conducted in a simulated courtroom and which is judged by a panel comprising an active court interpreter, a specialist in the Spanish language, and an international conference interpreter. Even after passage of the oral portion, additional training in simultaneous and consecutive interpretation and sight translation is required.

88. Charles M Grabau; Llewellyn Joseph Gibons. *Protecting the Rights of Linguistic Minorities: Challenges to Court Interpretation.* 30 New Eng. L. Rev. 227, 275 (Winter 1996).

89. *Id.*

90. *Id.*

91. *Supra*, note 86, at 647.

92. *Id.*

93. *See US v. Mosquera*, 816 FSupp 168 (SDNY 1993), *aff'd*, 48 F3d 1214 (2nd Cir 1994).

94. Court rules exist in California, Minnesota, New Jersey, and Oregon. *See* William E. Hewitt, *Court Interpretation: Model Guide for Policy and Practice in the State Courts* (Williamsburg: NCSC 1995); also contains a model code of professional conduct for court interpreters.

95. *Supra*, note 86 at 649–650.

96. *Id.* at 651.

97. *Supra*, note 92.

98. *Supra*, note 92 at 173.

99. *Id.* at 175.

100. *Id.*

101. 73 F3d 364 (7th Cir 1995).

102. *See Parra v. Page*, 430 P2d 834 (Okla. Crim. App. 1967).

103. *Chacon v. Wood*, 36 F3d 1459 (9th Cir 1994).

104. *US v. Perez*, 918 F2d 488 (5th Cir1990).

105. *Id.* at 489.

106. *See also US v. Japa*, 994 F2d 899 (1st Cir 1993).

107. 601 NYS2d 643 (Sup. Ct New York County 1993).

108. *Labbe* v. Russi, 601 NYS2d 648 (1993).

109. *See also Solari v. Vincent*, 77 Misc. 2d 54, 353 NYS2d 639 (Sup. Ct Duchess Cty 1974). *But see Haderxhanji v. NYS Parole Board*, 97 AD2d 368, 467 NYS2d 381 (AD 1st Dept 1983); *Torres v. Hammock*, 105 Misc 2d 1073, 430 NYS2d 775 (Washington Cty 1980); *Rivera v. Jeffes*, 402 A2d 316 (Commonwealth Ct of PA 1979), where the courts applied similar standards to those used in criminal trials: if inmate's English-language skills seemed sufficient from the record, a lack of an interpreter was not grounds for overturning a parole board's findings.

110. 904 SW 2d 129 (Tex. Cr. App. 1995).

111. *Id.* at 132.

112. *Id.* at 130.

113. *Id.* (emphasis in original).

114. *Id.* at 131.

115. *Id.*

116. *Id.* at 138.

117. 145 Cal. Rptr 847 (Sup. Ct Cal. 1978).

118. 130 Cal. Rptr 675 (Ct App. 1st District Cal. 1976).

119. *Id.* at 681.

120. *Id.*

121. *Id.*

122. *See Payne v. Superior Court*, 17 Cal. Rptr 405 (1976).

123. *Supra*, note 115 at 184.

124. *Id.* at 185.

125. *Id.*

126. *Id.* at188.

127. *Id.* at 189.

128. 45 F2d 934 (6th Cir 1930).

129. *Id.* at 936.

130. *Id.*

131. *Id.*

132. *Id.* (citations omitted, emphasis added).

133. 626 F2d 721 (9th Cir 1980).

134. *Id.* at 726.

135. *Id.* at 727; *see also Leung v. INS*, 531 F2d 166 at168 (3rd Cir 1976), where court noted that the INS Review Board "should make allowance for language difficulties when they potentially prejudice an alien's case."

136. 735 F2d 32 (2nd Cir 1984).

137. *Id.* at 37.

138. *But see Kaoru Yamataya v. Fisher*, 189 US 86 (1903), where the Supreme Court was not moved by an immigrant's insistence that she had been denied an opportunity to be heard because of a lack of interpretation services at an immigration hearing.

139. 184 F3d 158 (2nd Cir 1999).

140. *Abdullah v. INS*, 921 FSupp 1080 (SDNY 1996).

141. *See Mathews v. Eldridge*, 424 US 319 (1976).

142. *Supra*, note 139 at 164.
143. *Id.* at 165 (quoting with approval from the legislative history of the Immigration Reform and Control Act).
144. *Id.* at 165.
145. *Id.* at 166.
146. *Supra*, note 23 at 893–95.
147. 28 USC §1865(b)(2)(3) (The provision is part of more comprehensive legislation intended to systematize the selection of jurors and eliminate subjective and potentially discriminatory qualifications imposed by local courts.) *See also* P.L. 90-274 (Jury Selection and Service Act of 1968 House Report No. 90-1076, 1968.)
148. 500 US 352 (1991). The state court case where this litigation began before being appealed to the Supreme Court is *New York v. Hernandez*, 75 NY 2d 350, 361.
149. The first *Meyer v. Nebraska*, 262 US 390 (1923), was arguably not over language right per se, but about parental rights. The case, however, has precedential value and its *dicta* is cited by almost every higher court that has addressed language rights issues. The second instance of Supreme Court review on a language issues was in *Lau v. Nichols* concerning bilingual education and is discussed in Chapter 6.
150. *See US v. Aponte-Suarez*, 905 F2d 483 (1st Cir 1990), *cert. den.*, 111 S. Ct 531, 498 US 990; *US v. Hayes*, 479 FSupp 901 (DC PR1979), *aff'd in part, rev'd in part on other grounds*, 653 F 2d (1st Cir 1981).
151. 415 FSupp 459 (D PR1976).
152. *Id.* at 462.
153. *Id.* at 465 (cites and notes omitted).
154. *Id.* at 466.
155. 678 F2d 14 (1st Cir 1981).
156. *Id.* at 19 (emphasis added).
157. *Id.* at 20. (Still, the court at least said that it was open to the possibility of having the state interest met by less-discriminatory alternatives if the defendant had provided any; he did not.)
158. 812 FSupp 966 (D Neb. 1993).
159. *Id.* at 979.
160. *Id.*
161. *See also US v. Tormes-Ortiz*, 977 F2d 677 (1st Cir 1992), *cert. den.*, 113 SCt 1588 (1992), in which defendant's counsel objected to the possibility that jury deliberations were being held in Spanish, only after a conviction was returned. The court castigated counsel for not reporting what he thought was misconduct immediately, but deciding to gamble on the outcome instead.
162. *Supra*, note 148.
163. *See Strauder v. West Virginia*, 100 US 303 (1880) (the Supreme Court recognized that statues that prohibited African-Americans from serving as jurors violated the Equal Protection Clause).
164. 476 US 79 (1986).
165. *Id.* at 98.
166. *Texas v. Dept. of Community Affairs v. Burdine*, 450 US 248, 258 (1981)(citations omitted).
167. *Id.*
168. *Id.*
169. *Batson* has since been extended to civil trials, to cover gender-based and ethnic, as well

as racial groups, and to peremptory challenges made by criminal defendants as well. Also, the party opposing the challenges need not share the same race, ethnicity or gender as that of the excluded juror. *See Edmonson v. Leesville Concrete Co.*, 500 US 614 (1991); *Powers v. Ohio*, 499 US 400 (1991); *Georgia v. McCollum*, 505 US 42 (1992); *JEB v. Alabama ex. rel. T.B.*, 511 US 127 (1994).

170. *See* Michael J. Raphael, and Edward J. Ungrarsky, *Excuses, Excuses: Neutral Explanations Under Batson v. Kentucky,* 27 U. MICH. J. L. REFORM 229 (1993).

171. *Pemberthy v. Beyer,* 800 FSupp 144 (D NJ 1992), *rev'd*, 19 F3d 857 (3rd Cir 1994), *cert. den.*, 513 US 969 (1994).

172. *Supra,* note 148.

173. 75 NY 2d 350 at note 1

174. *Supra,* note 148 at 362.

175. *Id.* at 354.

176. *Id.* at 371.

177. *Id.* at 361.

178. *Id.* at 362.

179. *Id.*

180. *Id.*

181. *Id.* at 363.

182. *Id.* at 364.

183. *Id.* at n.3.

184. *Id.*

185. 800 FSupp 144 (DNJ 1992).

186. *Id.* at 153.

187. *Id.* at n. 15.

188. 500 US 371.

189. *Supra,* note 185 at 160 (emphasis in original).

190. *Id.* at 161 (citations omitted).

191. *Id.* at 162.

192. *Id.* at note 25.

193. 476 US 98 (1986).

194. *Supra,* note 185 at 165.

195. *Id.* at 167.

196. *Pemberthy v. Beyer,* 19 F3d 857 (3rd Cir 1994).

197. *Supra,* note 185 at 375.

198. *Supra,* note 196 at 869–870.

199. *Id.* at 870.

200. *Id.*

201. *Id* at 871.

202. *Id.* at 872.

203. *Id.* at 873.

204. 15 F3d 395 (5th Cir 1994).

205. *Id.* at 398.

206. *Id.* at 399.

207. 38 F3d 893 (7th Cir 1994).

208. *Id.* at 898.

209. *Id.* at 900.

210. *See Jacobson v. Massachusetts*, 197 US 11 (1905); *Dowell v. City of Tulsa*, 273 P2d 859 (Okl 1954), *cert. den.*, 348 US 912 (1955); *Schmerber v. California*, 384 US 757 (1966).

211. 960 FSupp394 (DC Dist 1997), *overruled*, 163 F3d 625 (DC Cir 1999), *rehr'g den.* 168 F3d 1360.

212. *See Ramos v. Lamm*, 639 F2d 559, 575 (10th Cir 1980), *cert. den.*, 450 US 1041 (1981), where the Circuit Court stated: "[d]eliberate indifference to serious medical needs is shown when prison officials have prevented an inmate from receiving recommended treatment or when an inmate is denied access to medical personnel capable of evaluating the need for treatment.)"

213. *Supra*, note 211, 960 FSupp at 401–402.

214. *Id.* at 402.

215. *Id.* at 401. Strangely, the court found it meaningful that the majority of the prisoners were from Central America because "[u]nlike Hispanics from Puerto Rico, Hispanics from Central America typically have little or no exposure to English or the way of life in the US " *Id.* The court was apparently unaware of the prevalence of the Spanish language in Puerto Rico.

216. *Id.*

217. *Id.* at n.14.

218. *Id.* at 403.

221. *Id.* at 406.

222. *Id.* at 407.

223. *Id.* at 409.

222. *Id.*

223. *Id.* at 410.

224. *Id.*

225. *Id.*

226. *Id.*

227. *Id.*

228. *Id.* at 411.

229. *Id.* at 413.

230. *Id.* at 414, 429. (The court credited the testimony of the prisoners' expert who spoke of why the use of *unqualified* interpreters at medical care encounters seriously threatens an inmate's health. Errors in translation can have deleterious effects on the communication between patient and clinician, making it distorted and obscured. A diagnosis and treatment intervention provided on the basis of misinformation can have serious consequences for the patient. For example, the seriousness of a patient's suicide intent can be minimized or, worse, missed, because the clinician was not able to follow subtleties in language and cues to gear the interview.)

231. *Id.* at 418. (The hearings concerned discipline, parole, housing, and adjustment of status. At adjustment board hearings alleged disciplinary violations are adjudicated; findings of hearing are a permanent part of a prisoner's record and can have a negative impact on parole considerations amongst other things.)

232. *Id.*

233. *Id.* at 420.

234. *Id.* (emphasis added).

235. *Id.* (Also, at the parole hearings, DCDC did not provide Spanish versions of documents used. *Id.* at 419.)

236. *Id.* at 428.

237. *Id.* at 406.

238. *Id.* at 429. On this same issue, the Seventh Circuit found an Eighth Amendment violation when the prisoner's doctors could not communicate well in English with English-dominant prisoners. *Wellman v. Faulkner,* 715 F2d 269 (7th Cir 1983). (The court stated that "an impenetrable language barrier between doctor and patient can readily lead to misdiagnoses and therefore unnecessary pain and suffering. This type of language problem, which is uncorrected over a long period of time and of which there is no prospect of alleviation, can contribute to unconstitutional deficiencies in medical care.")

239. *Supra,* note 211, 960 FSupp at 432.

240. *Id.* (emphasis added).

241. *Id.*

242. *Id.*

243. *Franklin v. District of Columbia,* 163 F3d 625 (DC Cir 1999).

244. *Id.* at 636.

245. *Id.* at 631 (citations omitted).

246. *Id.* at 634 (Regarding at what level of custody – maximum, close, medium, minimum or community – a prisoner shall be held.)

247. *Id.* at 636.

248. *Id.* at 638.

249. *Id.*

250. An application for re-hearing *en banc* was made and denied. *Franklin v. District of Columbia,* 168 F3d 1360 (DC Cir 1999). The dissenters to that denial argued that the panel of Circuit judges who decided the appeal did not credit the trial court's findings of fact as they should have, and yet did not rule that these findings were clearly erroneous and therefore invalid as a matter of law. The district court had made numerous and significant findings on how the written policies of the DCDC were "honored in the breach" and that the last-minute actions taken by the DCDC were mere "window dressing." *Id* at 1361. Further, on the Due Process claim, the dissenters felt that there may indeed have been hearings in which significant liberty interest would be at stake – disciplinary hearings, for instance, where "good time credits" could be risked – so a true analysis of the kind of process followed would have been appropriate. *Id.* For further findings in this area, a remand to the district court would have been the right course, rather than the wholesale disregard of that court's findings.

251. 2000 WL 674698 (WDNY 2000).

252. *Id.* 2000 WL at 3.

253. *Id.* at 4.

254. *Id.* at 5.

255. *Leon* at 6, *quoting Franklin, supra,* note 243.

256. *Id.* at 7–8.

257. Clarkson v. Coughlin, 898 FSupp 1019 (SDNY 1995).

258. *Id.* at 1032–33.

259. *Id.* at 1048.

260. *Id.*

Chapter 6

Bilingual Education: Learning and Politics in the Classroom

INTRODUCTION

The education of language-minority children is one of the most controversial and significant issues raised by the new immigration. Although immigrant students raise a host of complex issues especially for school systems that have not gone through any structural reformations in response to these students' arrival, these issues have not been systematically analyzed.[1] Instead, the education of language-minority children is centered around the debate on the efficacy and desirability of bilingual education.

Bilingual education in its richest sense is about helping all language minorities be fully bilingual and bicultural, "shared by two equal languages"[2] in the belief that a diversity that begins from within is the only kind that can inspire the kind of societal revolution of the soul necessary for respecting the greater diversity of all people.

This chapter reviews the political, legal, and research history of bilingual education, beginning with an explanation of its intents and purposes, the ambivalence with which it has been treated in the US since the federal government became involved in its legislative birth, and the impact that ambivalence has had on bilingual programs throughout the nation. All cases involving bilingual education from its roots in the school desegregation cases of the 1960s and 1970s to the present struggle for the very survival of bilingual education are related here. At the end is a section on recommendations for advocates and activists wishing to continue to fight for bilingual education, despite the severity of the struggle.

What is clear throughout is that the legislative, judicial, and public response to bilingual education is a weathervane by which the national sentiment toward language minorities and new immigrants can be gauged. For bilingual education, unlike any other language right is "purely" about using public funds to nurture the native, non-English, language. This is a frightening concept for many, even if the use of the native language is justified as limited and in the ultimate service of learning the English language. The flagrant use of native languages in public classrooms is still considered to be somehow subversive.

THE POLITICAL NATURE OF BILINGUAL EDUCATION

Bilingual education is not, and cannot be, the only tool used to achieve the whole-sale reform in the treatment of language minorities. Its place in the struggle for that reform can neither be denigrated nor abandoned. Bilingual education is, perhaps, the defining issue for determining the extent and scope of what "empowerment" will mean for language-minority communities. To advocate for bilingual education is to argue for the value of heterogeneity and the intrinsic worth of diversity for their own sakes while realizing that such an attitude, if properly reflected in national policy, will be a fertile ground from which respect for and amongst language-minority communities can grow.

Unfortunately, within the already emotionally charged arena of language rights, bilingual education stands at its heated center. It is where subtle issues of nationalism must be worked out; where the process of defining a national identity collides with other complex issues such as the role of public education in our country, the process of language acquisition, and the mythology of easy assimilation. Bilingual education is also one of the most difficult language issues to defend. It is easier to support bilingual ballots, rooted as they are in the notion of making the democratic process available to all regardless of English language ability; even many political or social conservatives would not lightly repeal legislation requiring bilingual ballots. It is also more popular to oppose English-only rules, either within the work-place or in public – advocacy that speaks to the public's deep-seated pride in the guarantees of the First Amendment can provide a basis for success.

In contrast, the term "bilingual education," is greeted by the general public with either blank stares or with deep suspicion. It appears to be an affirmative-action type of program that by its very terms is teaching children to be bilingual and suggests that fluency in English is at best on a par with other languages and at worst is being subjugated to other "native" (and therefore, suspicious) foreign languages. The result has been an incredibly emotional argument between sides that start out at such different ideological positions that consensus has not yet been possible.

One of the reasons for so much heat and so little light is that, on a fundamental level, bilingual education places at the forefront the need to understand and explain the attitude toward the ambassadors of bilingual education: bilinguals themselves. Bilinguals are potent reminders of the place and the people that gave birth to the US and, for some, a threat of what it might become. As a nation of immigrants, US history is rooted in the sweat, labor and ill-treatment of thousands of "foreigners" who neither looked nor sounded like assimilated Americans. They have been paid poorly, housed poorly and often educationally neglected. It would seem as if they ought to feel little allegiance to this nation. Yet, they have not been the backers of any revolution. Instead, from these well-springs, the US has been able to build a country and a citizenry. Still, which American can look on the faces of these recent immi-grants and not see their own ethnic selves; their parents or grandparents? Banishing these immigrants, these bilinguals, to the periphery of our minds, denying them and with that denying ourselves and our needs too, the nation has tried to rid itself of its old, ethnic, self. A self that is perpetually a stranger, not quite fitting in, yet belonging nowhere else. Banishing bilingual education is necessary if the country is to hold on to the myth of it itself as needing no old ethnicities – as self-promoting, self-actualizing, and self-reliant.

Given the array of factors involved, it is clear that bilingual education is not so much an educational issue in the US as a political one. Indeed, bilingual education cannot be understood, supported or condemned without reference to the status of bilinguals and bilingualism in the nation. Parents, advocates, and bilingual educa-tion teachers need to be aware of its political nature and use that awareness to direct the shape and flow of their strategies for reform of bilingual education in the US.

One grave error that no advocate should commit, however, is to assume that bilingual education is either a panacea for the miserable education afforded most language-minority children in the US or that minority languages can be retained only through the use of bilingual education in public schools. Instead, bilingual education advocacy should be seen as an integral and important part, but only a part, of a struggle for language-minority recognition and civic empowerment. The current political and legal dimensions of bilingual education, however, are terribly far removed from those goals.

What is bilingual education?

Bilingual education is not merely a disinterested exercise in the application of theory and research to real life situations. It is also an exercise in social policy and ideology.[3]

At its very simplest, bilingual education can be defined as a method to teach school age children a foreign language while they learn other subjects in their native language as well. In the US, the goal, of course, is to teach language-minority chil-dren English. As with the other areas of language rights, however, to truly under-stand bilingual education in the US, its political and social dimensions must be explored as well.

Professor Colin Baker points out that:

[a]t the outset, a distinction needs making between education that uses and promotes two languages and education for language-minority children. This is a difference between a "classroom where formal instruction is to foster bilin-gualism and a classroom where bilingual children are present but bilingualism is not fostered in the curriculum."[4]

Multiple approaches to teaching a second language can be and often are labeled "bilingual education" even when the native language of the student is rarely used, if at all. The political and social bases of different programs can be revealed by trying to determine the goals of the program. Some of the various goals, whether or not expressed, for programs labeled as providing a "bilingual education" are:

(1)   to assimilate individuals or groups into the mainstream of the majority society;
(2)   to unify a multilingual society;
(3)   to enable people to communicate with the outside world;
(4)   to provide marketable language skills;
(5)   to preserve ethnic and linguistic identity;
(6)   to reconcile and mediate between different linguistic and political communities;
(7)   to spread the use of a colonizing language;
(8)   to strengthen elite groups and preserve their position in society;
(9)   to give equal status in law to language of unequal status in daily life;
(10) To deepen understanding of language and culture.[5]

Understanding the specific goals of a bilingual education program is critical for evaluating the effectiveness of the program, in revealing the society's attitude toward language minorities and helping to judge the arguments of those who criticize bilingual education for not meeting its goals.

Bilingual education programs can be seen on a continuum with *maintenance* or *developmental* programs, with the richest use of the native language at one end of the spectrum, and *"structured immersion"* classes (barely "bilingual") at the other end. Developmental or maintenance programs treat the native language of the students as an asset – the first block for building toward full bilingualism. The expectation is that it will take the students between four and seven years to become fully bilingual in two languages, and the goal is not simply oral, but academic fluency. There are few of these programs in the US; they require strong program leadership, talented well-trained teachers, sufficient resources, smaller class sizes, rich bilingual texts, and a well-prepared and implemented curriculum. They are usually funded by special federal money that often will not be guaranteed beyond one or two pilot years. The currently popular "dual language" programs, in which language-minority and language-majority students are taught in the same classrooms with the goal of full bilingualism for both groups, is one type of developmental program. These kinds of enrichment programs aim to "extend the individual and group use of minority languages leading to cultural pluralism ... and to the social autonomy of an ethnic group."[6]

The major differences between developmental and transitional programs go beyond curriculum to philosophy, teacher training, and parental involvement. The linguist Rolf Kjolseth describes these two oppositional models of bilingual education. The Pluralistic Model is the ideal model. It is characterized by an:

> educational program ... created through the collaboration of parents and school; it is a political and social issues around which the entire community is mobilized. Research into the varieties of the minority and majority languages spoken in the community is undertaken to determine which varieties will be

used as media of instruction, the choice of instructional materials and the types of teacher training to be instituted. The program lasts a minimum of nine years. School personnel are of local, ethnic origin; their background and education ensure that they are appropriate bilingual and bicultural role models for their students. The student body is composed of both majority and minority-language members.... The content of instruction includes the cultures of both language groups and stimulates community language planning efforts. Parents are involved in the program through extracurricular activities, demonstration classes, and a bilingual adult education program that replicates the design of their children's program.[7]

Much more common, however, is what Kjolseth terms the "Assimilation Model":

This bilingual program is created by the educational system; the community is invited to become involved but has no decision-making power. Teachers are either majority-language members or minority-language members living outside the community. They are trained to teach the standard variety of the minority language and its "high" culture.... The student body is exclusively minority-language. The program, which usually lasts three years, may begin by using the standard variety of the minority language alone or in combination with the majority-language standard as the medium of instruction, but in a short time the minority language is phased out in favor of the majority language. The content of the curriculum emphasizes the culture and values of the majority language.[8]

On the other hand, the most prevalent form of bilingual education in the US is transitional bilingual education, which is usually time-limited and does not attempt to retain the native language.[9] Rather, there is an expectation that the native language will be lost and replaced by the a majority language. Content area courses are still taught through the native language to the extent required by the child's English language skills. The goal, of course, is that students end the bilingual program in one to three years receiving all of their content courses in English, and then transfer into the mainstream. Approximately 76% of the language-minority students in the US are enrolled in classes that offer only instruction in English as a Second language (ESL), which teaches students English but offers no native language component.[10] Some 40% receive transitional bilingual education services and 37% receive instruction aimed at maintaining or enhancing the native language.[11] It is important for advocates to realize that *the large majority of language-minority children are not in any kind of bilingual education class at all.*[12] Critics of bilingual education often use the continued under-achievement of language-minority children (especially Latinos) as proof of the failure of bilingual education programs. Given the small numbers enrolled nationally, however, that argument has little bite. Rather, it may indicate just the opposite: greater and more extensive interventions are needed, bilingual education being just one of them, to raise academic performance.

As noted above, in the US, most language-minority children are not enrolled in bilingual education programs, but either in ESL-only classes or in no real "program" at all but receive extra help from teacher aides or other students.[13] Some of these interventions are called "structured immersion." As its name implies, this seeks the wholesale immersion of these children into English-only classrooms, but attempts to help the child survive by providing some words or "cues" in the native language so that the child can hopefully glean some sense from the instruction. ESL classes may or may not be a part of this approach, which is currently most popular among opponents of bilingual education because of its emphasis on the rapid acquisition of English.[14]

In the US bilingual education has been cast as a remedial program for poor language-minority children who speak native languages other than English and who, therefore, must become fluent in English as quickly as possible. Their native languages are not valued and the retention of the minority language is not one of the goals of most bilingual education programs. Indeed, "bilingual education" is not used as a term to describe the goal of fluency in two languages, but as a method to reach another goal – fluency in English at the expense of retention of the mother tongue.

In evaluating programs, Skutnabb-Kangas describes the common US bilingual programs as asssimilationist; they are bilingual programs "the goal of which is monolingualism for minority children."[15] The underlying assumption of these types of programs is that the children need not be taught bilingually once they have learned enough of the majority language to be able to follow instruction in monolingual English classes. These children are often transferred to mainstream English-only classrooms once they have achieved a certain surface oral fluency that masks the lack of a deeper understanding of the language that would enable them to successfully academically compete with their majority-language classmates. "The result is often that they fail miserably at school, regardless of superficial oral fluency.... All the transitional bilingual programmes belong to this type."[16] Administrators of these programs may pay lip service to the importance of retaining the mother tongue, but "the real attitude is often evident when we look at the degree and kind of effort made to ensure equality between the languages."[17]

In the US, English is designated as the language of instruction with specific exceptions for the provision of ESL and bilingual education classes when needed in order to ensure that students become proficient in English. Bilingual education teachers are often the least experienced, are frequently language minorities themselves and sometimes have trouble meeting minimum state certification requirements, and are most vulnerable to job cuts because they are uncertified and young. Further, language-minority students are often segregated in the schools with the nation's worst academic performances and the fewest material resources.

Skutnabb-Kangas concludes: "if such a comparison reveals several respects in which the languages have not been made equal ... that shows that the real goal probably is closer to monolingualism than bilingualism, regardless of all the pious phrases."[18]

The theory of bilingual education

Although the decision to use an enrichment bilingual education program rather than a transitional or a structured-immersion approach is usually a political one,[19] there is a strong theoretical basis for bilingual education that is nevertheless attacked by opponents. Bilingual education is partly based on a theory called the "developmental interdependence hypothesis," developed mostly by the linguist Jim Cummins. "This hypothesis suggest that a child's second-language competence is partly dependent on the level of competence already achieved in the first language. That is, the more developed the first language is, the easier it will be to develop the second language."[20]

In 1991, at the behest of the Bush Administration, J. David Ramirez, on behalf of the US Department of Education, conducted a longitudinal study of structured English immersion, early-exit and late-exit transitional bilingual education programs for language-minority children.[21] The research was conducted to answer the question: which of the three alternative instructional programs helped Spanish-speaking "limited English proficient" (LEP)[22] students "catch up" to their English-dominant peers? The study followed 2,000 elementary children for four years. Conducted as it was at the request of a politically conservative administration, many were surprised when Ramirez concluded that the late exit bilingual education programs were the most beneficial kind of programs in the long run.[23] Ramirez noted that:

> [i]t appears that students who were provided with a substantial and consistent primary language development program learned mathematics, English language reading skills as fast or faster than the norming population.... It's their growth in these academic skills; atypical of discouraged youth, it provides support for the efficiency of providing language development in facilitating the acquisition of English language skills.[24]

On the other hand, Ramirez concluded that providing these students almost exclusive instruction in English does not help them catch up. Instead, by the sixth grade, these students may fall further behind than their English-dominant peers.[25] Contrary to national policy, the data also documented that learning a second language would take at least six years.[26] Like Rolf Kjolseth's model program, the teachers in the late-exit programs were more likely to have a background similar to that of their students, were more likely to be sufficiently proficient in Spanish to be teaching Spanish-dominant students, and tended to have more advanced training than the teachers in the other programs.[27]

The study also found, however, that after four years in their respective programs, language-minority children in the English-immersion and early-exit bilingual programs were of comparable skill in math, language arts, and reading when tested in English.[28] The study has significant implications for English -language instruction for language-minority children; if we truly want academic achievement for language-minority schoolchildren, the nation will heavily invest in long-term, high-quality natural language instruction.

More recently, Drs Virginia Collier and Wayne Thomas of George Mason University conducted a major research study of five large urban and suburban school districts across the US collecting the records of over 700,000 language-minority students from 1982–1990.[29] They focused on the length of time needed for these students to be academically successful in a second language, and the student, program, and instructional factors that influenced their academic achievement. They too found that long-term developmental types of bilingual education programs were by far the most successful.[30]

The children in well implemented one-way and two-way bilingual classes outperformed their counterparts being schooled in well-implemented monolingual classrooms, as they reached upper grades of elementary school. Even more important, they sustain the gain they have made throughout the remainder of their schooling "long after the program does not continue beyond the elementary school years."[31] In contrast, students who were schooled in English tend to show dramatic gain in English development in the early grades but then " lose ground relative to native speakers of English so they reach the upper grades of school."[32]

Collier and Wayne concluded that it takes "typically bilingually-schooled students" who are achieving in grade levels in their native language from four to seven years to reach the average English achievement of an English-proficient student.[33] Immigrants with two to five years of achievement on grade-level home country schooling in the native language take from five to seven years to reach the 50th NCE in English when schooled only in English.[34] The typical English immigrant schooled all in English in US will need between seven to ten years or more to reach the 50th NCE, and " the majority of these students do not ever make it to the 50th NCE, unless they receive support for L1 academic and cognitive development at home."[35]

The characteristics of the programs that were most successful were:

- an integrated school environment with English speakers and language minorities learning each other's languages;
- a perception among staff, students and parents that the program was a kind of "gifted and talented" programs with high expectations for all students;
- equal status of the two languages, which created self-confidence amongst the language-minority children;
- healthy parental involvement;
- instructional approaches that emphasized: whole language, natural acquisition through all content areas;
- cooperative thinking, interactive and discovery learning, cognitive complexity of all lessons. [36]

The birth and near demise of the Bilingual Education Act

Bilingual education had a promising beginning in this nation, as detailed in Chapter 1 which dealt with the role of bilingualism during the country's formative years. However, these periods of publicly-supported bilingual education were relatively brief, and did not reflect a national policy of minority-language promotion. Instead, they reflect at least two well-established US characteristics: (1) the preference for local control and decision-making especially in the area of education, and (2) a preference for practical and useful solutions with a minimum of dogma or ideology attached. The states that had large and well-organized language-minority populations were under pressure to meet these communities' demands, and often simple practicality, such as the need to communicate with constituents, and the availability or non-availability of English-dominant teachers, led to the public support of bilingual or even minority-language only schools.

Publicly-supported bilingual education did not continue for more than a few decades. It was not until the Civil Rights Era, when the nation's attention became riveted by the educational issues of poor minority students and of language-minority children, that bilingual education became a focus.

Interest in bilingual education was not serendipitous; the educational plight of many Latino schoolchildren was increasingly visible during the early and mid 1960s. The drop-out rate for Latinos, Chicanos and Puerto Ricans was often the highest amongst all ethnic groups.[37] Chicanos had endured segregated and second-rate schooling in many southwestern states; both Puerto Ricans and Chicanos had seen their native languages ridiculed and suppressed either through the outright punishment of children for speaking Spanish or by legislation changing the national language of Puerto Rico to English.[38] The educational fall-out of these policies were not surprising: Latino students left schools in droves, alienated, uneducated, and isolated in their own countries.[39]

In a precursor to the Civil Rights Era, a case brought in 1947 by students of "Mexican descent" highlights the educational history with which Latino students in the US were struggling. The suit was brought against the Westminster School District of Orange County, California, for segregating the Mexican students in separate schools for children of Mexican or "Latin descent."[40] The students complained that they were being deprived of their rights under the Equal Protection and Due Process Clauses of the Fourteenth Amendment. The school district argued that segregation had been upheld in the past, and that the linguistic differences of the Mexican-American children justified the segregation in this instance. It should be noted that this case arose before *Brown v. Board of Education* was decided and therefore, before the intrinsic evil of involuntary segregation was accepted. The court ended up finding for the students by enforcing California's ignominious law on segregation: California law only allowed the segregation of Indians and children of "Chinese, Japanese or Mongolian parentage."[41] The school district, by segregating Mexican children through administrative decree, was in violation of its own discrimination law.

Even though official segregation of Mexican-Americans was not upheld by the courts, such segregation continued throughout the southwest and was nominally justified by school districts on the basis of English language skills. Professor Joan Moore summarized the situation in the southwest:

[i]n the past the physically segregated school was a natural reflection of the prevailing belief in Mexican racial inferiority. No southwestern state upheld legally the segregation of Mexican American children, yet the practice was widespread. Separate schools were built and maintained, in theory, simply because of residential segregation or to benefit the Mexican child. He had a "language handicap" and needed to be "Americanized" before mixing with Anglo children. His presence in an integrated school would hinder the progress of white American children.... [42]

Latino educators and leaders argued that bilingual education programs that reflected the value of native languages and consequently the value of the Latino students themselves could be a remedy for their educational plight. Puerto Ricans in cities like New York were experimenting with bilingual classes and were beginning to see successes. In 1966, the National Education Association (NEA) issued a pamphlet, *The Invisible Minority, Pero No Vencibles,* which focused on the disastrous education received by most Mexican-American children in Tucson's schools. The document became the impetus for a conference held in Tucson that involved influential congressmen. Along with poor facilities and uncertified teachers, the NEA had highlighted the scandal of "sink-or-swim" instruction rampant in many Tucson schools. [43]

In 1968, Congress passed landmark legislation authorizing school districts to offer bilingual education programs for what it defined as "limited English proficient" ("LEP") students. The name of the legislation was the Bilingual Education Act (BEA), and it was Title VII of the Elementary and Secondary Education Act (ESEA) that focused money and the nation's attention on the educational issues facing children of poverty. The ESEA was passed in 1965 as part of President Johnson's Great Society program. It was, and still is, a massive federal grant-in-aid program for schools with the mission to equalize educational opportunities between poor and more affluent students and to eradicate racial discrimination. ESEA was expanded to include the BEA three years later as a specific nod to the special needs of language minorities. The BEA did not require that districts offer bilingual education programs, but it did reserve a pot of money for districts to create instructional materials, and encouraged parental involvement and authorized resources to support teacher development and staff training to address educational issues of "LEP" students."

Passage of the ESEA and Title VII were infused with a sense of helping poor students overcome their "deprivations." Early research on the development of infant minds had found that infants interacted with the world to a much greater extent than previously thought; they actually tried to comprehend, that is, find patterns and stability in the information they were receiving. Interacting with infants and providing intellectual and visual stimulation were considered critical to the infant's cognitive development. Infants that did not receive this kind of stimulation were considered "deprived."[44] The idea of social or cognitive deprivation found a footing in the politics of culture, perhaps because of the increasing consciousness about the social and educational plight suffered by most of the nation's minorities. In any case, the concept of "cultural deprivation" grew with its implicit condemnation of the "culture" of Latinos and blacks. For, it was the divergent and, therefore, deprived culture of these children that was leading them to educational failure. Change the culture, the theory went, and thereby change the outcome. This approach has the convenience of "blaming the victim" and not requiring systems (such as schools) to change dramatically. If the culture that the children are coming from is "deprived," then it is their home life, not the "enriching" schools, that has to be changed. This attitude was carried over into federal programs like the Bilingual Education Act with its emphasis on "remedying" language-minority children.

The BEA was passed under the sponsorship primarily of Senator Ralph Yarborough of Texas. The legislation, reflecting its era, included a poverty criterion for the enrollment of students and defined its goal as the speedy acquisition of English. The children who were enrolled in the bilingual programs were not only to be "poor" but also "educationally disadvantaged because of their inability to speak English."[45] The hearings were well-attended by Latino parents and community leaders who saw passage of the BEA as a first step in breaking the cycle of Latino educational failure and unemployment. They asked the federal government to endorse a pedagogy that would maintain their native language as well as reduce the cultural and linguistic gap between the students and their schools.

Those who testified, however, pushed for various goals. Some parents wanted the government to foster bilingualism for all students, regardless of their home language; others wanted bilingualism fostered only for their own children, still others wanted only the most effective method for learning English quickly.[46] School administrators testified of their concerns about implementation of programs and costs. Some educational experts who testified were concerned about the evidence on the effectiveness of bilingual education programs, and others saw Latino educational failure as requiring large-scale compensatory programs with bilingual education being a feature of that effort. In trying to define the goals of the BEA more specifically, Senator Yarborough made his intentions less than clear: "[i]t is not the purpose of this bill to create pockets of different languages throughout the country ... not to stamp out the mother tongue, and not to make their mother tongue the dominant language, but just to try and make those children fully literate in English."[47]

The Act that was finally passed was not a "mandate" for bilingual education as many language-minority communities had hoped. Instead, Congress adopted a "research orientation" and a capacity-building focus that the federal government felt only minimally intruded on the educational discretion of local school districts.[48] While the Act's genesis was concern over the educational failure of Spanish-dominant students, the Act's coverage was extended to all "children who came from environments where the dominant language is other than English."[49]

The ambiguity over the Act's goals, and the pressure of more conservative groups during the appropriations process, kept funding minimal. Congress did not appropriate any funds under the Act for 1968 at all, even though $15 million had been authorized.[50] Between 1969 and 1973 annual funding never exceeded $35 million, even though up to $135 million was available. "Given the government's own estimate that over 3 million NEP [non-English proficient] and LEP children needed special assistance, the amounts allocated between 1968 and 1973 never exceeded about $10 per child in the target population and probably averaged about $5 to $6 per child."[51] The Latino community's initial euphoria over the passage of the BEA, which had been misconstrued as a mandate for bilingual education, must have been quickly dampened.

Yet the needs of language-minority children were finally being made visible on a national platform: for a forgotten population, any victory can seem sweet. Further, the effects of the BEA were not inconsequential, despite its limited funding.

In 1971 Massachusetts became the first state to pass a bilingual education law mandating that bilingual education be used by school districts that received state funds if they had enough children with the same native language and in one or two contiguous grades that could be used to form self-contained bilingual classes. The Massachusetts legislature noted:

> The General Court finds that there are large numbers of children in the Commonwealth who come from environments where the primary language is other than English. Experience has shown that public school classes in which instruction is given only in English are inadequate for the education of children whose native tongue is another language. The General Court believes that a *compensatory* program of transitional bilingual education can meet the needs of these children and facilitate their integration into the regular school curriculum.[52]

In 2002, 30 states had statutes expressly allowing native-language instruction.:

> Of these, nine require it under certain circumstances; twenty-one provide some form of financial aid to bilingual programs and most set standards for certifying bilingual or ESL teachers. Although laws in seven states still prohibit instruction in languages other than English, these bans are no longer enforced.[53]

By 1973, when the BEA was up for re-authorization, bilingual education had many supporters. The House Committee on Education and Labor noted in its report on the Act that "[t]here is evidence that the use of the child's mother tongue as a medium of instruction concurrent with an effort to strengthen his command of English acts to prevent retardation in academic skill and performance."[54] It went on to note that the "lack of bilingual education programs undoubtedly has a lot to do with the disproportionate drop-out rate among children with limited English speaking ability."[55] This attitude was reflected in the new and unprecedented requirement that schools receiving funding needed to use the student's native language "to the extent necessary to allow a child to progress effectively through the educational system." In addition, the poverty criterion was abandoned and funding for programs was growing. Title VII's budget was $45 million and supported 211 school projects in 26 languages.[56] Funding, however, was still not keeping up with need: at $45 million only 6% of eligible children were being served in programs.[57]

Even with the Act up for re-authorization, however, the issue of its goals remained murky: Latino leaders and advocates pressed for the development and maintenance of native languages along with the acquisition of English language skills. While the Act did not adopt these goals, it did not explicitly reject them either. A perception grew that the federal government was "coddling" immigrant children by trying to take necessarily sharp edges off the immigrant experience; that "soft" issues like "self-esteem and "comfort" were replacing the "crucible" of the melting pot at the expense of national cohesion.[58] Importantly, Albert Shanker, then-president of the American Federation of Teachers, which represented thousands of teachers, did not express support for bilingual education. Instead, in a 1974 editorial he wrote:

> [t]he American taxpayer, while recognizing the existence of cultural diversity, still wants the schools to be the basis of an American melting pot. While the need for the child to feel comfortable and be able to communicate is clear, it is also clear that what these children need is intensive instruction in English so that they may as soon as possible function with other children in regular school programs.[59]

Bilingual education was caught between competing interests and goals on a national level, and a lack of information on a local level. While Congress prepared itself for the re-authorization of Title VII, parents, students, and teachers in schools were not cognizant of the complex educational issues facing Puerto Rican and immigrant children; they did not know about the competing goals of bilingual education or the basis for its methodology; in short, although federal leaders, advocates and the professionals were ready for at least a transitional model of bilingual education, the nation was not.

The AIR Report: An early stab at bilingual education

Something of a backlash against bilingual education began in 1977 with the release of the first large-scale, comparative evaluation of bilingual education in the US.[60] The report was conducted by the American Institutes for Research (AIR) and commissioned by the Office of Planning, Budget and Evaluation. AIR made four important findings:

(1) on English tests, students in bilingual education programs obtained slightly lower scores than comparable students in regular programs;
(2) on math tests, students in bilingual education programs performed somewhat or better than comparable students in regular programs;
(3) there was no significant difference in the attitudes toward school children in bilingual education programs and regular programs;

(4)   the ability of students in bilingual education programs to read Spanish did not improve significantly.[61]

The sense of the AIR report was that there was no documentary evidence for the overall effectiveness of bilingual education programs as compared to providing no program or assistance at all.[62] Further, the AIR researchers felt that bilingual education was being implemented in schools in ways that undermined the congressional intent that the programs be transitional in nature. AIR reported that 86% of the bilingual education program directors said that Spanish-speaking children were retained in the programs even after they had learned enough English to join mainstream classes. Many critics, like Noel Epstein, education editor of the Washington Post, used the AIR report findings to condemn bilingual education as "affirmative ethnicity."[63] Like affirmative action, bilingual education was seen as government's "misguided attempt to compensate for past discrimination."[64] In a point that would continue to be made for decades and is still made today, bilingual education was seen as institutionalizing a private function – the inculcation of ethnic pride and maintenance of "home" languages.

The "ethnic" separatist *feel* of bilingual education was also attacked as contrary to established constitutional principles of desegregated schools. In order for bilingual education programs to be possible, there must be a "cluster" or sufficient number of students of the same native language and in or around the same grades to be able to create a bilingual education program and justify the hiring of a bilingual teacher. These students need to be kept together in order to maintain their programs. Yet in the 1970s in the US there were many education desegregation cases that called for the racial and sometimes ethnic mixing of students – a concept that at least at first blush appears to be contrary to the interests of bilingual education. In the beginning it was indeed seen that way and many Black–White desegregation cases were complicated by the presence of a small but vocal language-minority community that wanted no part of the desegregation efforts.[65] Instead, they wanted to stay together to support their bilingual programs. This was seen, however, as "clannish" and enhanced the sense of an ethnic enclave with values and interests that were different than those of the rest of the nation.

Congress grappled with these divisive issues in the 1978 amendments to the BEA. The native language of the students in programs could be used only to "the extent necessary" to further the goal of English acquisition; Title VII programs were to be transitional only not developmental or used to maintain native languages; in identifying eligibility for programs, student's oral, written and reading comprehension in English were to be assessed.[66] Addressing the segregatory aspects of bilingual education, the Act was amended to include a mandate that elective classes, like art, music and gym, must not be segregated. Lastly, 40% of a bilingual education program's seats could go to majority-language children to assist language-minority children in their acquisition of English.[67] Presumably, the language-minority children had nothing of value to offer the English-dominant children.

By 1980, the Office of Planning, Budget and Evaluation had issued a series of studies that effectively undermined the theoretical basis for the federal government's support of transitional bilingual education programs.[68] In 1981, a report was issued that laid the blame of language-minority academic failure on poverty as much as on a "linguistic mismatch" between the students and their schools.[69] The report stressed the need for local discretion in resolving the educational issues facing these students, and recommended that the government allow for other instructional practices than just bilingual education.[70]

Throughout the continuing history of the BEA and its periodic re-authorizations, the main weaknesses have been its ambivalent purpose – the undecided question of whether or not to make it explicitly assimilationist, the Act's limited funding opportunities, and the need for intensive teacher training. The passage of the BEA brought the issue of bilingual education and the education of language-minority children to the forefront of national consciousness. However, the sensitive issues it raises are still unresolved: issues such as whether language minorities, especially those who recently immigrated to the US, ought to be treated like African-Americans, as in need of special programs to compensate for past discrimination; whether the education of language minorities is an issue to be decided on the local level or whether the federal government should be involved; what are the goals of education for language-minority students and are they different for language majority students, and should they be? The legislation ought not to be confused with traditional civil rights legislation, which explicitly seeks to fix perceived injustices, and to do so through forceful mandates and if necessary, authorized court action such as the Fair Housing Act. The BEA is essentially a federal bureaucratic tool that provides some additional funding for language-minority programs. Most districts, however, rely on their own state and local dollars to provide services and must comply with more explicit state laws, where they exist.

The most important tool for language-minority communities in their struggle for special educational programs are two traditional civil rights laws – Title VI of the Civil Rights Act of 1964 and §1703(f) of the Equal Educational Opportunities Act.

Bilingual education and school desegregation: A tension surfaces

The law of bilingual education, as opposed to its political and pedagogical life, really began as a feature of desegregation cases in the early 1970s. Desegregation case law itself began with Brown v. Board of Education,.[71] *Brown* was *the* case that set the stage for how minority students' claims for educational justice were to be shaped and analyzed. In *Brown* the Supreme Court set aside the "separate but equal" doctrine of *Plessy v. Ferguson*,[72] and unanimously held that segregated schools could never be equal, that state-imposed segregation was a negative stamp set upon Black children's "hearts and minds," the effects on which might never be undone. The plaintiffs, African-American schoolchildren who were forced to go to segregated schools that were also inferior to all-White ones, complained that such treatment was a violation of the Equal Protection Clause. The case became the touchstone for shaping claims for "equal educational opportunities." The main feature of *Brown* – that the state take no purposeful action to skew educational opportunities available to minority students – would be fleshed out, analyzed, discussed, and limited in many cases to come.

Although *Brown* appears to be a case for the assimilation of African-American children into the American mainstream, some have argued that *Brown* does not proscribe the maintenance of diversity; the Court did not define an integrated society as one in which the distinct African-American cultural heritage was to be suppressed.[73] Rather, it was the forced nature of the segregation that was problematic; similarly, "forced assimilation" of a disparaged ethnic or racial group may also amount to a constitutional wrong if such treatment results in the continued negative labeling of the group.[74]

Under the blueprint of *Brown*, in order to make out a claim of unlawful segregation, plaintiffs must show that there is a state-sponsored system of segregation by race or ethnicity. Plaintiffs would also present evidence of a negative effect of that segregation on minority students. Once unlawful segregation was found, the courts' remedial powers were broad. Courts could order the re-alignment of school district lines, the re-assignment of students amongst schools, the busing of students, enhanced compensatory programs for minority students, the building of new schools, the creation of magnet schools, and so on – all toward the end of eliminating the vestiges of the discrimination "root and branch."[75] Within this broad scope, the provision of bilingual education classes as compensatory programs for language-minority students was a natural outgrowth.

The case of *Guey Heung Lee v. Johnson*[76] begins to address the issue of the protection of bilingual education programs against desegregation efforts. This case deals with the rights of Chinese-American students living in San Francisco to retain their programs already in existence in the face of a federal court order to desegregate schools. The courts would need to handle these complex issues quite sensitively for the ideals and aspirations of one minority group (here African-Americans) which had been given an imprimatur of national policy in *Brown* were in competition with the relatively novel claims of a recently-arrived minority community expressing a different ideal (here Chinese-American communities wishing to maintain segregated bilingual education classes).

The district court that heard the case and ordered the desegregation of all races, not just Black and White, did not exhibit the kind of finesse and sensitivity required. The court said only that "[t]hose who oppose desegregation, however, well intentioned, would deprive children of the most meaningful opportunities to know members of different races."[77] The court's order noted that "[b]ilingual classes are not proscribed. They may be provided in any manner which does not create, maintain or foster segregation."[78] The Chinese community appealed to try and halt the implementation of the desegregation plan. Sitting as a Circuit Court Judge, Justice Douglas explained why he would not delay implementation of the plan:

> *Brown v. Board of Education* was not written for Blacks alone. It rests on the Equal
> Protection Clause of the Fourteenth Amendment, one of the first beneficiaries

of which were the Chinese people of San Francisco.... The themes of our school desegregation cases extends to all racial minorities treated invidiously by a State or any of its agencies.[79]

Although the Chinese students were certainly segregated, it is unclear whether they had actually brought a complaint against the state.

The case of *US v. Texas*[80] provides a nice example of a "classic" desegregation case that addressed language-minority issues. The Texas Education Agency, the state department charged with operating the public schools, had been found to be maintaining a segregated system of education through the creation and support of nine all-Black schools. Apparently, one school district had a majority of Mexican-American students. For this group, the court ordered a plan to help the students in "adjusting to those parts of their new school environment which present a cultural or linguistic shock."[81] The court envisioned a "joint learning and adjustment process" that would involve the participation of both Anglo and Chicano students. The court seemed to be mandating a dual language, native-language maintenance program that seems almost "revolutionary" in these conservative times. The court explained that the district needed to implement language programs

> that introduce and develop language skills in a secondary language (English for many Mexican-American students, Spanish for Anglo students) while at the same time reinforcing and developing language skills in the primary language, so that neither English nor Spanish is presented as a more valued language.... [82]

In creating this comprehensive program, the court relied upon the testimony of plaintiffs' expert, Dr Jose Cardenas, an educator and researcher. Cardenas argued that the Mexican-American children were failing in the Texas schools because of their cultural incompatibility with the majority, Anglo culture of the school system. Dr Cardenas testified that the Mexican-American students exhibit numerous characteristics which have a causal connection with their general inability to benefit from an educational program designed primarily to meet the needs of so-called Anglo-Americans. These characteristics include cultural incompatibilities and:

> English language deficiencies – two traits which immediately and effectively identify those students sharing them as members of a definite group whose performance norm habitually will fall below that of Anglo-American students who do not exhibit these traits. It would appear that it is largely these ethnically linked traits-albeit combined with other factors such as poverty, malnutrition and the effects of past educational deprivation – which accounts for the identifiability of Mexican-American students as a group which have, as a consequence, elicited from many school boards throughout Texas, and indeed, throughout the southwestern United States, the different and often discriminatory treatment shown in the record in this case.[83]

Even though Cardenas' definition of Mexican-American school children as quoted by the court is laden with unfashionable deficit-based language, it gave rise, at least on paper, to an enriched educational program that is rarely seen. By placing the emphasis on the school system's Anglo-oriented curriculum rather than on language alone, Cardenas touched on an issue that we are still studying – how do we re-make schools to reflect the educational needs of the current student population?

Cardenas had developed a "Theory of Incompatibilities" that was published in 1969 and laid the blame of pervasive minority-student failure at the doors of schools; there exists a fatal incompatibility "between the characteristics of minority children and the characteristics of a typical instructional program."[84] Cardenas identified over forty "incompatibilities" between minority students and their educational systems, which he grouped into five areas – poverty, culture, language, mobility, and societal perceptions. These incompatibilities are interdependent, so the existence of only one feature will probably not lead to student failure and, likewise, the reform effort that focuses on only one element will not succeed in addressing failure. Cardenas is emphatic in stating, despite the ambiguous language quoted by the court, that "past failures of minority children are the result of inadequate school programs, and *not* the fault of the child and his background.[85] Although we may not speak in terms of "cultural incompatibilities" today, and instead speak of "educational reform," it is edifying to see that there is a theory that embraces the realities of cultural and linguistic diversity and puts the burden on schools to respond positively.[86]

While the *Texas* case was a victory for plaintiffs, another case was moving up toward the Supreme Court that would undermine educational litigation for years to come. In 1973, in *San Antonio Independent School District v. Rodriguez,*[87] the Supreme Court had found that there was no fundamental right to an education guaranteed by the Constitution. Poor minority students had brought suit against the state of Texas for its inadequate funding of their schools in comparison to the wealthy, White school districts. The students argued that, because the funding was so inadequate, the education they were able to receive was dismal and not comparable with that offered in the wealthy districts. These students, found the Court, would need to look to their state constitution for a right to an education; the Court was simply unwilling to become involved in what it saw as ultimately a local issue.

The impact of *Rodriguez* has been drastic. Lawyers have had to file lawsuits state by state in order to have educational adequacy issues determined on a piecemeal basis on this fundamentally critical issue; the nation has become a patchwork of lawsuits, funding formulas and judicial decisions that take years if not decades to have implemented by recalcitrant state legislatures.[88] The implication of *Rodriguez* for bilingual education is obvious – if there is no constitutional right to an education under the Fourteenth Amendment, there is clearly no constitutional right to a *bilingual* education. Indeed, in the *Keyes v. School District No. 1,*[89] another desegregation case, the appellate court overruled a district court that had imposed the Cardenas Plan as a cure for Fourteenth Amendment violations. The appellate court relied on *Rodriguez* to state that:

local control permits citizen participation in the formulation of school policy and encourages innovation to meet particular needs. Educational policy, moreover, is an area in which the courts' lack of specialized knowledge and experience counsels against premature interference with the informed judgments made at state and local levels.[90]

The Circuit Court was clearly overwhelmed by the comprehensiveness of the Cardenas proposals:

[t]hese proposals, it must be emphasized, touch virtually every aspect of curriculum planning, methodology and philosophy presently the responsibility of local school authorities. [Plaintiffs propose], for example, the inclusion of specific courses in the curriculum, adoption and publication of specific educational principles, provision of early childhood education ... and adult education of minorities and provision of adequate clothing for poor minority school children.[91]

The court felt that the school system must be prepared only to help move students from their native language to English so that they can benefit from the education offered. Going far beyond that minimum, the imposition of the Cardenas Plan improperly stepped on the toes of local school officials, whose expertise and discretion needed to be acknowledged.

THE RISE OF TITLE VI AND BILINGUAL EDUCATION AS A CIVIL RIGHT

Although the Fourteenth Amendment became a poor tool for pursuing the goals of cultural pluralism in education, other statutory avenues opened up. In 1964, Congress passed the Civil Rights Act. Title VI was passed by President Johnson as the federal government's promise to African-Americans that it was prepared to "get tough" on civil rights violators. In uncompromising language, the statute made it unlawful for any entity that received federal funding to discriminate against someone on the basis of "race, color, or national origin." The scope of the statute was broad, for almost every public entity receives federal funds.[92] However, the statute has a special application for language-minority children because its prohibition on national origin discrimination was read by the Supreme Court in *Lau v. Nichols*, discussed below, as also prohibiting linguistic discrimination.

Serna v. Portales[93] was apparently the first case to raise the issue of bilingual education outside of the desegregation context, and relied upon Title VI for its claims. Plaintiffs, "Spanish surnamed children" claimed violations of both the Equal Protection Clause and Title VI in that the district failed to provide the "learning opportunities which [satisfied] both their educational and social needs."[94] Although Title VI was raised, the court applied an equal protection analysis to the case. Plaintiffs claimed that the education offered at the Lindsey School, which had a minority of "Spanish-surnamed" (presumably Mexican-American) children was tailored to middle class, English-speaking children, "without regard for the educational needs of the child from an environment where Spanish is the predominant language spoken."[95] The court found that the "IQ" scores of the Spanish-surnamed children were below those of Anglo children. The court found that these scores were indicative of something amiss, and coupled that concern with the testimony of plaintiffs' experts on the negative effects "upon Spanish-surnamed children when they are placed in a school atmosphere which does not adequately reflect the educational needs of this minority" to find a violation of the Equal Protection Clause.[96]

The efforts already made by the school district to alleviate the "problems" raised by these children were simply inadequate said the court:

> [u]nder the circumstances, it is incumbent upon the school district to reassess and enlarge its program directed to the specialized needs of the Spanish-surnamed students at Lindsey and also to establish and operate in adequate manner programs at the other elementary schools where no bilingual-bicultural program now exists.[97]

Six months ago, after the trial court decided *Serna,* and undoubtedly while the appeals papers were being filed to the Tenth Circuit, the Ninth Circuit decided the landmark case, *Lau v. Nichols.*[98]

Lau v. Nichols: Bilingual education litigation comes into its own

The actual case, *Lau v. Nichols,* began as part of a San Francisco desegregation case filed by African-Americans. By the time it was decided by the US Supreme Court, however, it would be considered the *"Brown v. Board of Education* decision" for national-origin minority students.[99] The case, however, was actually the "last resort" for a Chinese-American community that had been fighting for the adequate education of its children for years. According to Ling-Chi Wang, a community leader at the time and parent organizer, Chinese-American parents had been petitioning the San Francisco school board for bilingual education for three years prior to resorting to litigation. Despite demonstrations, research, the development of community alternatives and the packing of school board meetings, all to demand bilingual education, the board refused to act.[100] In the words of Ling-Chi Wang:

> [m]ore and more Chinese American children were dropping out of school and forming street gangs that engaged in the violent activities for which Chinatown became well known. This was a time of mounting anger and frustration with a bureaucracy mired in inertia and indifference.[101]

When the school district did act, it was with a token – one hour per day of ESL instruction. The school district was caught in a desegregation lawsuit in which the immigrant communities were not interested and the school board for its part, was not interested in dealing with the Chinese community.[102]

In 1970, the following facts were stipulated by both plaintiffs and defendants:

(1)   2,856 Chinese dominant students in the district needed special services;
(2)   1,790 received no special help at all;
(3)   only 433 of those who did receive help did so on a full-time basis.

The language-minority community at issue was approximately 2,500 recently-immigrated Chinese-dominant families. Prior to the lawsuit, approximately half of the Chinese-American schoolchildren who needed English language support services were receiving them. While they were allowed to enroll in school, many simply sat uncomprehendingly in classes conducted only in English. They received neither translation assistance nor classes in English to help them eventually understand the instruction.

The parents brought a case under the Equal Protection Clause of the Fourteenth Amendment of the Constitution, and the still-novel statute, Title VI of the Civil Rights Act of 1964.

When the case came to the appeals court, the court was singularly unsympathetic and/or simply disingenuous as to the students' claims for relief. The students argued that the San Francisco Unified School District violated Title VI, the Fifth, Ninth and Fourteenth Amendments to the US Constitution, and Article 55 of the California Constitution. The students claimed that the school district's failure to provide English language educational services for approximately half of the Chinese-dominant schoolchildren in the district was a violation of their right to an equal educational opportunity. The Ninth Circuit judges characterized the students' claims as being for "bilingual compensatory education in the English language" for all non-English-speaking Chinese students.[103] However, the exact nature of the relief requested appears to have been a source of confusion itself.

The district court had denied the schoolchildren's relief, finding that, since the school district had provided all children the *same* educational opportunity, it could not have been engaged in illegal discrimination. The Ninth Circuit summarized: "[the school district] had no duty to rectify [the students'] special deficiencies, as long as they provided these students with access to the same educational system made available to all other students."[104] This meant that, for the court, the special needs of students did not create an additional obligation on the school district.

The Ninth Circuit characterized appellants' argument as an "extreme" extension of *Brown*.[105] According to the court, appellants wanted schools to undertake the affirmative duty of providing special assistance to students where educational "disabilities," whatever the origin, undermined their ability to "take as great an advantage of classes as other students."[106] "According to appellants, *Brown* requires schools to provide 'equal' opportunities to all and equality is to be measured not only by what the school offers the child, but by the potential which the child brings to the school."[107] The court stated:

> [e]very student brings to the starting line of his educational career different advantages and disadvantages caused in part by social, economic and cultural background, created and continued completely apart from any contribution by the school system.[108]

The reliance on the *Brown* rhetoric of "equal educational opportunity," as expansive and generous as that language sounds, backfired in this case. For, while *Brown* required equal opportunities, its analysis also required an impermissible state action that *led* to the abrogation of opportunity. For the court, a state's failure to make things right in the world was not what the Equal Protection Clause was born to fix, as understood in *Brown*.

More may have been at work in this court, however, than simply a close reading of the *Brown* requirements. Over and over, the court made derogatory comparisons or used negative language to refer to the Plaintiffs.[109] Finally, the court made two statements that reveal a deep adherence to the national assimilation mythology.

Taken together or separately, the statements are extraordinary reflections of deep bias. The first statement arose in the context of rejecting a comparison made by plaintiffs. Plaintiffs argued that the state has an obligation to help these students, just as the state has an obligation to provide free counsel and waiver of fees to indigent convicts in a criminal case. Although the indigency is not the fault of the state, argued the plaintiffs, the state under the Constitution is required to help the defendant gain access to a system in which he is compelled to interact. The court responded by stating that, while the ability of a convict to pay a fine or lawyer has no relationship to the purposes for which the criminal justice system exists, here, apparently, the neglect of the English-language needs of these students does play a role in the educational process. The court asserted that English is the language of the nation and of California:

> [t]he state's use of English s the language of instruction in its schools intimately and properly related to the educational and socializing purpose for which public schools were established.[110]

Without saying as much, the court endorsed a sink-or-swim approach to language-minority education.

In the second statement, the court went on to say that the blame for the status of these language-minority children:

> lies within the children themselves. The classification claimed invidious is not the result of laws enacted by the state presently or historically, but the results of deficiencies created by the appellants themselves in failing to learning the English language. For this the Constitution offers no relief....[111]

These words give a moral underpinning to the school district's callous disregard for the education of these students; what the first statement assured defendants was the right pedagogical decision, the second statement blesses with moral certitude.

The students fared only a little better in the rhetoric of the dissenters. Although the dissenting judges eloquently argued that there was no educational opportunity for a child who doesn't understand English to be to be compelled to go to an English-only classroom, the judges were careful to paint the plaintiffs' claims as benignly or as "English-centric" as possible:

Plaintiffs do not seek to be taught in Chinese, in whole or in part. They seek only to learn English. They claim ... that they cannot learn English effectively unless it is taught to them by persons who have a facility in the only language they understand; i.e. Chinese. It seems abundantly clear that as soon as the plaintiffs have achieved enough proficiency in English to understand their teachers and classmates somewhat in the course of instruction, they will expect no further Chinese to be uttered in their classes. They do not seek instruction in the Chinese language or to be taught anything in Chinese except how to speak English.[112]

Despite the apparent good, but confused, intentions of the dissenters, plaintiffs' counsel had in other fora, at least, unequivocally stated that the students' struggle was one for bilingual education.[113]

Although the district court and the appellate court both analyzed *Lau* within an equal protection context and found that the Constitution was not violated, when the case went before the Supreme Court, the Constitution took second-seat to the still-novel Title VI.[114]

The Supreme Court side-stepped the constitutional issues and put together an analysis that could assuage the concerns of lower courts. The Court noted that under California law, all students must attend school. Relying upon the heavy hand of the state's involvement in public education, the Court felt that the state must then ensure that the student it compels to attend, must actually be receiving a comprehensible education. This seems to give at least a nod to *Brown* and the requirement of state action. But the Court went on to rely on the regulations of the Department of Health, Education and Welfare (HEW)[115] and its requirement that under Title VI school districts must take steps to rectify the English-language deficiencies of language-minority children. The Court stated:

[i]t seems obvious that the Chinese-speaking minority receive fewer benefits than the English-speaking majority from respondent's school system which deprives then a meaningful opportunity to participate in the educational program – all earmarks of the discrimination banned by the regulation.[116]

The Court went on to find that:

[i]mposition of a requirement that, before a child can effectively participate in the educational program, he must already have acquired those basic skills is to make a mockery of public education. We know that those who do not understand English are certain to find their classroom experiences wholly incomprehensible and in no way meaningful.[117]

The Supreme Court's decision not to rely on the Constitution for relief was the safe course. Courts are loath to interpret the Constitution when they can decide a case on statutory grounds. That alone might explain the Court's decision. Yet, with the lower courts relying on the Equal Protection Clause, certainly the constitutional implications or even the lack of implications for plaintiffs' claims, could have been discussed.

The Court, however, chose the safe route and for the parents certainly the most limited one. Language-minority children who are not proficient in English have not really been the subject of historical discrimination in the way that African-Americans were. While the segregation of African-Americans was based on race, and had no educational justification, some could feel that the segregation of language-minorities could be justified on pedagogical grounds – the intensive teaching of English or the acclimation of a foreign group. Giving these children constitutional rights akin to African-Americans under *Brown* may have felt like giving them more than their due. Further, a constitutional duty to address English language deficiencies could not be so easily limited on the basis of practicality – again the courts have voiced their concerns about the number of children involved, and the need not to burden a school district with heavy obligations on behalf of a few children. Justice Blackmun was emphatic when, while concurring with the majority, he felt a need to state that had the number of children affected been smaller, the Court may not have decided the case the same way:

> [a]gainst the possibility that the Court's judgment may be interpreted too broadly, I stress the fact that the children with whom we are concerned here number about 1,800. This is a very substantial group that is being deprived of any meaningful schooling ... I merely wish to make plain that when, in another case, we are concerned with a very few youngsters, or with just a single child who speaks only German or Polish or Spanish or any language other than English, I would not regard today's decision ... as conclusive upon the issue whether the statute and guidelines require the funded school district to provide special instruction.[118]

This was prescient. For in *Otero v. Mesa County Valley School District*,[119] discussed below, the trial court balked at the possible financial implications of finding an equal protection violation: "...if there were an Equal Protection right to bilingual/bicultural education, the needs of a single student would give rise to that right, and our nation's schools would bankrupt themselves in meeting equal protection claims to bilingual education in every conceivable language and dialect."[120]

The Supreme Court might also have been sensitive about appearing to undermine its recent, controversial decision in *Rodriguez*. Just one year before, the Court had found that there was no federal constitutional right to an education. Although *Brown* stands for the proposition that what is available to one must be made available to all on equal terms, affirmatively mandating certain pedagogical practices as constitutionally required would run counter to *Rodriguez*'s holding. Indeed, in *Otero*, decided after *Lau*, the analysis of *Rodriguez* was used to deny the plaintiffs' constitutional claims for a "Cardenas-model" of education:

> [t]he plaintiffs ... in the present case argue for a right to differential treatment of minority children in the educational process. As the [Supreme] Court stated in *Rodriguez*: "[E]very reform that benefits some more than others may be criticized for what it fails to accomplish. But the thrust of the [state's educational]

system is affirmative and reformatory, and therefore, should be scrutinized under judicial principles sensitive to the nature to the state's efforts.[121]

Despite the victory in the Supreme Court, back in San Francisco the Chinese community needed to stay organized, focused, and intransigent in order to make the court order real. Against the wishes of the school board, the community formed a citizen's task force to develop a plan to implement the *Lau* decision. With the help of the Center for Applied Linguistics in Washington, the community was able to develop a 700-page *Master Plan for Bilingual Education*,[122] which called for a maintenance bilingual-bicultural program of instruction. The Chinese community was able to rally support for the report and its recommendations through the use of its multilingual, multiracial task force. According to Ling-Chi Wang, "[u]sing the Supreme Court decision as a rallying point, they formed a broad coalition for the first time and focused on their issues.... After several months of intensive lobbying, the board finally and reluctantly approved the master plan."[123] Ultimately, the community was able to use its newfound power to elect a school board sympathetic to bilingual education.

Although *Lau* did not endorse bilingual education, many lower courts understood the Court's decision to be a mandate for bilingual education: the only way for a school district to "cure" language minorities would be by creating and implementing bilingual education programs. After *Lau*, school districts around the country settled lawsuits with parents' groups seeking bilingual education. Most importantly, however, the federal government's Office for Civil Rights (OCR) for the HEW developed what came to be known as "*Lau Guidelines*" in order to determine whether school districts were in compliance with Title VI.[124] The Guidelines detailed the proper identification and assessment of language-minority schoolchildren and programs that would meet the school districts' legal obligations, as understood under *Lau*. As such, the *Guidelines* promoted transitional bilingual-education programs. For instance, students who are monolingual speakers of languages other than English, or who primarily speak a language other than English, and who are in elementary school are to receive bilingual instruction; ESL-only was not considered an educationally or legally viable option.[125] Hundreds of school districts across the nation were brought into compliance with the *Guidelines* in settlements with the HEW, at pain of losing federal funds.

The effects of the Court's decision not to rely on the Constitution were felt directly after *Lau* despite the generous interpretation given the case by the HEW. In *Otero v. Mesa County Valley School District*,[126] the Court was very clear on the limits of *Lau*'s holding and denied plaintiff schoolchildren relief, at least partly because there "is no constitutional right to bilingual/bicultural education."[127]

The plaintiffs in *Otero* had also relied upon the "Cardenas Plan" to argue that Spanish-surnamed" students were being deprived of an equal educational opportunity under the Fourteenth Amendment. Unlike in *Texas*, however, the Mexican-American population in the Mesa County Valley School District was quite small, comprising only 8.2% of the district's population. This population was itself spread throughout the district and again throughout the elementary, junior, and high schools.[128] The elementary schools had the highest concentration, but the total "minority" population did not exceed much more than 16% at 2 of the 19 schools in the district.[129] Complicating matters further, many of the Mexican-American children were not Spanish-dominant. Although the students were almost invariably poorer than Anglo students and did not perform as well in school, the genesis of the problem apparently did not lie in their levels of English proficiency, for less than 3% of all Mexican-American elementary children spoke or understood Spanish.[130] The court was "unconvinced that any adherent problems encountered by Mexican-American students in District 5 [were] attributable to cultural deficiencies or language problems."[131]

The court rejected plaintiffs' attempt to have the "Cardenas Plan" mandated by the court. The numbers of the students involved, the good-faith efforts of the school district to identify and assess students who needed additional services, and the support for local control by school experts were factors that the plaintiffs could not surmount:

> [p]laintiffs want to restructure the curriculum of Mesa Valley School District No 5, and they want to tailor it to accommodate plaintiffs' concept of the alleged needs of an astonishingly small number of students, what plaintiffs really want is to substitute their judgment for the thoughtful, independent judgment of the elected school board....[132]

Perhaps most frightening for the precedential value of *Lau*, however, was a footnote in *Keyes v. School District No.1*.[133] *Keyes* was a complicated school desegregation case with a bilingual education claim woven in through the fabric of the litigation. The court cited to *San Antonio v. Rodriguez*[134] for the lack of a Fourteenth Amendment claim to any kind of systematic and comprehensive educational programming for language-minority children. It accurately pointed out that the *Lau* Court never reached the constitutional question. However, as reflected in the language of the footnote, neither did the court believe that *Lau* required bilingual education despite the HEW Guidelines. The court said:

> [w]e note that in the 1973–74 school year, Denver school authorities identified 344 students in the system with language difficulties arising from their Spanish-speaking backgrounds. School authorities determined that 251 of the students needed special help in acquiring language skills necessary to perform satisfactorily in school. A number of programs were directed to the needs of those students. On the basis of the facts and after reviewing the record, we were unable to find any support for a violation of §601 [of the Civil Rights Act of 1964].[135]

The fact that the court failed to analyze the programs offered to see if they met the *Lau* Guidelines, but was satisfied only that a "number of programs" were being offered, is compelling. Perhaps the court realized that the language of *Lau* could not carry all the weight with which the HEW Guidelines had burdened it.

The demise of Title VI and the rise of the EEOA

In 1974, the same year that *Lau* was decided, Congress passed the Equal Educational Opportunity Act of 1974 (EEOA).[136] Interestingly, the implications of the EEOA for bilingual education would prove to outlast the original focus of the bill and the major educational issue on the nation's mind at the time: school desegregation.

The EEOA was originally prepared by the Nixon Administration as a means of reducing judicial use of busing as a remedy in school desegregation cases.[137] Section 1703 (f), however, stated that:

> [n]o state shall deny equal educational opportunity to an individual on account of his or her race, color, sex, or national origin, by (f) the failure by an educational agency to take appropriate action to overcome language barriers that impede equal participation by its students in its instructional programs.[138]

In 1972 the President had explained that the EEOA " would further establish an educational bill of rights for Mexican-Americans, Puerto Ricans and Indians and others who start their education under language handicaps to make certain that they, too, will have equal opportunity."[139] HEW Secretary Elliot Richardson expressed the intent of the legislation in testimony before the House Committee on Education and Labor. He explained:

> [i]t would be a legal right to receive bilingual education as set forth in the beginning of §[1703(f)] ... this is basically declaratory of the position we have taken in the enforcement of Title VI of the Civil Rights Act of 1964 through a memorandum issued in 1970 [HEW Guidelines]. This would be the first time that Congress ever declared that there is a right to receive bilingual education. It would mean, therefore, that in the future the refusal to provide it would be a violation of law.[140]

The legislative history of §1703(f), then, is clear that it was a right to bilingual education that was being developed, and within that context the assumption that *Lau* was an endorsement of bilingual education is undeniable. Indeed, it has been said that the EEOA was really a codification of the *Lau Guidelines*.[141] Despite legislative history, however, and in the absence of an express Supreme Court decision, the legal basis for a right to bilingual education is no longer recognized, as the vitality of *Lau* began to wane within ten years of its writing.

The legal viability of *Lau* was undermined in *Regents of the University of California v. Bakke*[142] by questioning whether a violation of Title VI included an intent requirement. *Lau*, by endorsing the HEW Guidelines, had undoubtedly found that it did not.[143] With the passage of the EEOA and the questioned vitality of *Lau*, plaintiffs began bringing claims for bilingual education under both Title VI and EEOA. *Rios v. Reed*[144] is an example of the lines that began to be obscured between Title VI and the EEOA, and also provided a picture of how bilingual education programs were typically implemented before litigation was brought.

The plaintiffs, who were Puerto Ricans, brought the action on behalf of their children, who attended the Patchogue-Medford School District. The district had 11,000 students of whom approximately 800 were Latinos, approximately 186 of them in the bilingual program. In 1978 the district's bilingual program had six full-time bilingual teachers, one part-time bilingual teacher, and six bilingual aids.[145] One bilingual teacher reported to a supervisor who did not speak Spanish and had no training in or understanding of the methodology of teaching English as a second language or in bilingual education. Further, the school principals who evaluated the performance of the bilingual teachers were also unfamiliar with bilingual education and also did not speak or understand Spanish. Only two of the bilingual-education program teachers actually had any formal training for bilingual teaching. The other teachers were qualified to teach Spanish, apparently as a foreign language.[146]

Prior to 1975, identification of children with English language deficiencies was informal – either through observations made by school personnel or by a child or parent's admission of English-language difficulties. In 1975, the ability to *speak* English was formally measured, but there was no assessment of children's ability to read or write in English or Spanish. There were no established procedures for referring students to bilingual instructors. Often casual conversations amongst teachers at lunch revealed the possible need for bilingual instruction.[147] Instruction for "English language deficient students," as they were labeled by the court, was in the English language. Some instruction was offered to kindergarten students and first graders in Spanish; but in each successive grade these students received less instruction in Spanish, and few continued in the programs in the middle schools until they were in the high school.[148] No textbooks in Spanish were available. Language minorities received an average of 40–50 minutes a day in subject-matter instruction in Spanish, and the remainder of the school day in English.[149] The program did not have a systematic instructional plan for subject matter to be taught in Spanish. Nor did it offer Spanish cultural instruction.[150] Finally, no standards were developed to determine when students had reached the required level of proficiency in English to enable them to exit the programs: "[a]t times bilingual teachers made the determination; at times students [were] dismissed from the program against the advice of the bilingual teacher."[151]

The court stated that:

> [t]he purpose of the statutes, i.e. Title VI ... the Equal Educational Opportunity Act of 1974, and the Civil Rights Act of 1871, as they relate to bilingual education is to assure the language-deficient child that he or she will be afforded the same opportunity to learn as that offered his or her English-speaking counterpart. Taken together, the statutes, and the legislative history ... mandate teaching such children subject matter in their native tongue (when required) by competent teachers. Though not expressly provided by statute, the legislative history suggests that the program must also be bi-cultural as a psychological support to the subject matter instruction.[152]

Applying this standard to the school districts program, the court found that the district had failed to live up to its obligations:

[t]he statutory obligations upon the school district require it to take affirmative action for language-deficient students by establishing an ESL and bilingual program and to keep them in such program until they have attained sufficient proficiency in English to be instructed along with English-speaking students of comparable intelligence.[153]

Further:

a denial of educational opportunities to a child in the first years of schooling is not justified by demonstrating that the educational program employed will teach the child English sooner than programs comprised of more extensive Spanish instruction. While the District's goal of teaching Hispanic children the English language is certainly proper, it cannot be allowed to compromise a student's right to meaningful education before proficiency in English is obtained.[154]

Although the court glosses over many difficult pedagogical issues concerning the assessment and placement of language minorities, its support for bilingual education and its refusal to adopt an English-centric view of education for language-minority children, is refreshing. The seeds for the undoing of bilingual education, planted as early as the 1968 passage of the BEA, however, began to bear fruit only three short years after *Rios* was decided.

Castaneda v. Pickard: The federal mandate for bilingual education erodes

In *Castaneda v. Pickard*,[155] the Fifth Circuit established a three-part test for determining whether a district was in violation of §1703(f). The court simply ignored the assumption that *Lau* contained a mandate for bilingual education and presented its own analysis that, through quiet acquiescence by potential plaintiffs and the explicit adoption by OCR has become the law of the nation in this area.[156]

Castaneda was decided in 1981. By that time the AIR report discussed above had dealt bilingual education advocates a serious blow. Further, the endorsement of the use of native language instruction by the federal government could no longer be assured. In the 1978 amendments to the BEA, the native language was to be used only to the extent necessary to allow a child to achieve proficiency in the English language.

Meanwhile, the *Lau* Guidelines, which had been only informally adopted, were being attacked by school districts that felt that OCR was being heavy-handed. By 1980, OCR had used its Guidelines and its threat of withholding federal funds to negotiate 359 "*Lau* Plans" that enabled many language-minority children to receive special English-language instruction for the first time. In doing so, however, OCR was in a delicate position, because it had never gone through the final rule-making process in establishing its Guidelines. It would need to go through the process of proposing regulations, soliciting public comment, and issuing final rules before they could have the force of law. President Carter's administration prepared regulations even more restrictive than the *Guidelines*, mandating the creation of bilingual programs in schools where at least 25 "LEP" children of the same language group were enrolled in two consecutive elementary grades.[157] The Education Department received a record-making 4,600 public comments on the proposal, most of them negative. The public confusion between Title VI and the BEA that was contained in Title VII was also fed when representatives of the Department of Education's Title VII staff defended the *Lau* Guidelines, issued by the HEW, in hearings being held across the nation. "The effect was to strengthen "the popular misconception that the new regulation and the Title VII program [were] one and the same.... The opposition made the most of it and was able to weaken both the grant-giving and enforcement aspects of bilingual education."[158]

In1980, bilingual education received another setback from the OCR itself when it grudgingly approved an "ESL-only" approach to the education of language-minority children in Fairfax, Virginia. Since 1976, Fairfax County had been resisting OCR pressure to establish a bilingual program. With language-minority students representing more than 50 language groups, administrators argued that intensive ESL was the only practical approach. After OCR relented, the *Washington Post* "hailed the 'Fairfax model' as a triumph for local control over a hard-line government policy." ESL, a necessary component of bilingual education, was now popularized as a promising "alternative method."[159]

With Ronald Reagan's landslide victory in 1981, any hope of converting the *Lau* Guidelines into regulations were dashed. Reagan had come into office with the promise to "get government off our backs" and his Secretary of Education echoed the sentiment, characterizing the mandating of native language instruction as "an intrusion on state and local responsibility.... We will protect the rights of children who do not speak English well, but we will do so by permitting school districts to use anyway that has proven to be successful."[160]

The *Castaneda* court captured the mood of the country perfectly. The court relied on the EEOA §1703(f) in determining whether the Raymondsville Independent School District had met its obligation under the law. It questioned the continued vitality of *Lau*, given the decision in *Bakke*. The court ruled that, in passing the EEOA, Congress had thrown its support to *Lau*, "affirming that educational neglect violated the civil rights of language-minority children, whether or not they had been victims of deliberate discrimination."[161] Good-faith efforts by districts are not enough, said the court. It came up with a three-pronged test to define what "appropriate action" meant under §1703(f). The program for language-minority students:

(1) must be based on a sound educational theory;
(2) must be implemented effectively with sufficient resources and personnel;
(3) after a trial period, the program must be effective – students must be learning English.[162]

Although the *Castaneda* court applied its three-pronged test, seriously citing the RISD for not training its teachers appropriately, the truth is that almost any program can be supported by an educational theory, and some "approaches" may need so few funds that adequate funding is not an issue. Yet the test would allow some number of years to pass by before it could be determined whether a violation of law occurred. If the children were learning English, then apparently the program would be found to be effective. Yet, if half the language-minority population had dropped out and only those that remained actually learned English, would the program still be considered successful? As anti-bilingual education laws spring up throughout the nation, the extent and limits of the *Castaneda* test will themselves be tested.

THE 1990S: BILINGUAL EDUCATION FIGHTS FOR SURVIVAL

The 1990s brought the most vehement attacks on immigrants and bilingual education since the 1940s. This time, however, the nation's only war seemed to be with itself. In the 1940s, the US could point to specific ethnic populations (the German, the Japanese, even Italians) as "the other," those whose loyalty to the nation could be questioned as the nation fought a war against the native countries of these "ethnics." The 1990s, however, were more complicated. The nation's economy was booming, unemployment was at a record low, the Cold War was over, and democracy and capitalism seemed to be the declared victors. Many in the nation, however, did not have a sense of the economic well-being and security that ought to have followed. Instead, many in the middle class found themselves laid-off as companies retrenched or moved or outsourced to other countries, or else workers simply found themselves without the new technological skills needed to compete. Full-time workers found themselves holding down two or three part-time jobs in order to make ends meet. Home-grown companies like Chrysler merged with European companies, and cut back their US workforce. Others, like Kodak in New York, could no longer offer the cradle-to-grave security that an entire community had come to rely upon.[163]

The flow of immigration, however, was not decreasing. Instead, the late 1980s and the early 1990s saw an increase in immigration rivaling the nation's largest influx of immigrants in the early 1900s.[164] The most visible faces of these immigrants were the brown ones of Mexicans in California and the Midwest and of Dominicans and Central Americans in the East. Anti-immigrant organizations called for stricter immigration controls and better-guarded borders to stop the flow of undocumented immigrants from Mexico.[165] Congress responded strongly with legislation aiming to reduce immigration by making the US as inhospitable as possible. The legislation that was ultimately passed virtually eliminated social services for those who were not US residents.[166]

Meanwhile, California took the offensive against immigrants through the liberal use of its initiative and referendum process. In 1994, California voters passed Proposition 187, called the "Save Our State" initiative. It would deny undocumented immigrants access to public schools, hospitals, and social services. Thankfully, implementation of the most harmful parts of the bill were overturned through court action.[167] But the acrimony and divisiveness that the referendum process promoted has had a lasting effect on the state, especially in areas where older White residents live side-by-side with new, younger immigrants. The social compact whereby residents act in the best interests of, and for the future benefit of, the larger community was shattered. The older White residents simply could not envision the immigrants as safeguarding the future of their city and the immigrants saw themselves as outsiders in a city in which they were the growing majority.[168]

The birth and life of Proposition 227

If the passage of Proposition 187 wasn't bad enough, the other shoe dropped in 1997 when "English for the Children," Proposition 227, was introduced. Proposition 227 attempted to eliminate bilingual education from California. It stated in part that:

> ...all children in California public schools shall be taught English by being taught in English. In particular, this shall require that all children be placed in English language classrooms. Children who are English learners shall be educated through sheltered English immersion during a temporary transition period not normally intended to exceed one year. Local schools shall be permitted to place in the same classroom English learners of different ages but whose degree of English proficiency is similar. Local schools shall be encouraged to mix together in the same classroom English learners from different native-language groups but with the same degree of English fluency. Once English learners have acquired a good working knowledge of English, they shall be transferred to English language mainstream classrooms.[169]

Parental waivers to allow their children to be enrolled in bilingual education classes were theoretically possible, but practically almost impossible. They were allowed only under narrow circumstances in which the parent had to overcome a presumption that bilingual education would not be the most appropriate educational setting.[170]

The roots of Proposition 227, now called "English for the Children," lay in the boycott of the Ninth Street Elementary School in Los Angeles by Latino parents who said that they no longer wanted their children to be involved in the bilingual education program. Approximately 100 parents kept their children at home for four days in February 1996. Although only four parents had actually availed themselves of the school's opt-out provisions, the parents argued that individually they were overwhelmed by the school system, and afraid to ask for English-only instruction. They complained that they faced attacks from other Latinos, and that their pride in their language and culture would be questioned. Mayor Richard Riordan threw his support behind the parents saying that bilingual education "is about an experiment that has failed our children."[171]

The boycott was spearheaded by Alice Callaghan, an activist Episcopal priest who ran *Las Familias del Pueblo*, a neighborhood community center serving Latinos. The boycott, dubbed as a backlash against bilingual education from those it was designed to serve, caught the imagination of the media across the nation. Rarely have Latino parents, seen as its primary beneficiaries, criticized bilingual education. Just as rarely do recently-immigrated Latinos engage in orchestrated and highly public actions of civil disobedience.

The disappointment of the parents in the bilingual education program, and their anger, however, were palpable, at least in the press accounts. They complained that their children were learning neither English nor Spanish well, that the programs were themselves racist and segregatory, and that they were being run by people who made money from keeping the children in the programs. Alice Callaghan charged that the children in the bilingual education program were "[a]t no place in the day ... learning to read and write in English."[172]

The following quotations from the parents, which appeared in the papers, capture the essence of their feelings and also the depth of the issues with which bilingual education advocates must grapple:

> At school, it should be English. We are in foreign lands now. And in foreign lands you speak the foreign language. We don't want him to speak macerated English like we do.[173]

> For me, bilingual education doesn't work. I think sometimes it's racist to keep the kids apart, not give them the same opportunity to learn in English that everyone else has.[174]

> ... the truth is, I'm in a better position to teach my kids Spanish and they're [teachers] in a better position to teach them in English.[175]

> [The programs] have had much negative effect. They have to speak, read and write English to have success in this country. In the bilingual program they don't learn either language well.[176]

> We want our children to be taught in English ... that's why we came to the United States ... If not, better to keep her in my country. There she can learn Spanish.[177]

On the other side, the school and its staff ended up sounding defensive. They argued that only a few parents had chosen to opt out, that the concerns with bilingual education had never been raised at prior parent meetings, and that the parents were being manipulated by Callaghan. Certainly, something about the parents's remarks sounds platitudinous, and one can easily envision a scenario of manipulation. Imagine, for instance that a despairing parent complains to Callaghan or one of her staff at the center about her son's dismal grades. Callaghan questions her about her son's education and learns that he's in bilingual education. Callaghan makes a few generalized statements about the need to learn English and how in bilingual education students are kept apart from the "White kids" and are taught nothing. The Los Angeles' School District's incentive pay of $5,000 annually to bilingual education teachers provides the perfect "motive" for the existence of bilingual education at all: bilingual education teachers want to "keep" kids in the program so that they get the extra money. "It's all about money," said Alice Callaghan, and she certainly shared those feeling with the parents.[178] It's not difficult to imagine that parents, undoubtedly impressed by Callaghan's school savvy and her work in the Latino community, would be convinced that bilingual education was the reason for their child's academic problems. Everything else, bad schools or bad programs or simply the complexities and time required to learn a second language, are all more complex and require more time-consuming work to resolve than withdrawing a child from a program.

Manipulation or not, however, unless bilingual education teachers and advocates are as prepared to defend bilingual education as the opponents are to destroy it, then the battle is lost before it is begun. Minimally, what the parents' words reveal is that they are alienated from their children's school and teachers. Parents who are afraid to opt out of bilingual education are not parents who feel at home in the schools; they are not confident of their ability to defend themselves, but unfortunately are certain of their inevitable need to do so.

Ron Unz, the Silicon Valley software businessman who fathered Proposition 227, credited the Ninth Street School boycott for the inspiration for his initiative.[179] Most certainly to deflect charges of racism and/or ignorance of education issues, he took Georgia Matta Tuchman, a Latina and former school teacher, as his co-chair. Together they took a virulently anti-bilingual education position to a statewide, and even a national, level and made the parents of the Ninth Street School into placards for their initiative. With the perception that Latino parents supported English-only instruction and charges that bilingual education was actually discriminatory, the initiative gained widespread and diverse support.[180] In the end, Proposition 227 received only about 30% of the Latino vote, but it was passed with overwhelming White support and with a cumulative total vote of over 60%.

While Ron Unz was spending over $700,000 himself to finance his war on bilingual education,[181] the Orange Unified School District began voluntarily moving away from bilingual education programs. In 1997 the school district asked the California Department of Education for a waiver from the state's bilingual education law to implement a new program for language minorities. Through operation of law and without explicit approval, the waiver was granted for one year. The proposed program would move away from bilingual education and toward a predominantly English curriculum with supplemental assistance for the students with little English proficiency. The additional assistance would take the form of tutorials, summer school and a pre-kindergarten program. All students would receive "English Language Development" instruction as well. The theory for the program was that "language proficiency is best obtained by lingual immersion."[182]

Parents of language-minority children in the Orange County Schools brought suit alleging that the new program would violate Title VI and the EEOA. Although a temporary restraining order was granted in state court, the case was removed to federal court where the restraining order was ultimately dissolved. The federal court, in deciding whether to extend the temporary restraining order into a preliminary injunction, reviewed the *Castaneda* factors to find that the parents could not show that the proposed program would not meet those standards. The court relied heavily on the state's experts, especially anti-bilingual education researcher, Christine Rossell. Dr Rossell was so adamant in her opposition to bilingual education that she even took on the federal government when she testified that language-minority children who are not given any special programs at all do no worse than students who are placed in bilingual programs.[183] Thankfully, the court would not follow Rossell down that path and explicitly re-affirmed that the EEOA "clearly contemplates appropriate *affirmative action.*"[184]

Orange County's alternative program was allowed to continue at least until Proposition 227 became law in 1998.

Challenging Unz in California

No sooner did the proposition become a law, than lawyers from Multicultural Education Training and Advocacy, Inc. (META) in San Francisco, and the Mexican American Legal Defense and Educational Fund based in Los Angeles, filed a lawsuit to enjoin the State from implementing the law.[185] Since Proposition 227 had only just been passed, and had not yet been implemented by any school district, the lawyers had to make the difficult claim that the law was illegal on its face, which meant that it could not be implemented in any way except unlawfully. The lawyers relied on the Supremacy Clause of the Constitution, the Equal Protection Clause, Title VI of the Civil Rights Act, and §1703(f) of the EEOA.

The federal district court, however, refused to declare Proposition 227 irredeemably unlawful. It found that the EEOA under *Castaneda* actually allowed for the possibility of innovation, even retrograde innovation, and would not foreclose schools and districts from trying out the various kinds of interventions that the bill would allow, even if it essentially foreclosed them from choosing bilingual education.[186] The fact that schools would need to emphasize learning English over all other subjects even to the possible detriment of students overall academic achievement, was not unlawful.[187]

In *McLaughlin v. State Board of Education,*[188] another attack was made on Proposition 227. This time school districts argued that under existing California education law they could seek a waiver from the State Board of Education from any other provision of the state's education law including the new anti-bilingual education law, so they applied to the Board for waivers from all provisions of Proposition 227. The now-codified Proposition was silent on how its provisions would interact with the existing state waiver law. The Board of Education denied the requests for waivers on the ground that the law allowed parents only to waive their right to an English-only education for their children, and then only in particular circumstances.

The lower court sided with the districts on the theory that, since the waiver provisions were in place when the *Unz* initiative was adopted by the public, then it could be assumed that it was passed with the knowledge that the waiver law was controlling.[189] The appeals court reversed, however. It felt that the initiative process was a unique one and members of the public could not be held to the same standards of statutory knowledge as legislators. Instead, the initiative and referenda materials distributed to the public used the parental, as opposed to an administrative waiver as a central argument for the approval of the initiative.

The court concluded that the words of the new law were simply too emphatic and inflexible to allow any other interpretation, but that it was intended to amend the waiver provisions of the Education Law.[190] Invoking the principle of "drafter's oversight" or "neglect," the court stated that:

> [the new law] inflexibly declares that absent a parental waiver, the interests of LEP children are always best served by English-only instruction. It is only when a parent decides that English-only instruction is not appropriate for his or her child that an individual waiver need be sought.[191]

The court left open the possibility that school districts might be able to seek exemptions from specific portions of the law, since that question had not been presented to it for decision.[192]

However, the court did not look behind the initiative process, in which supposedly the public is the "drafter," to the reality of initiative politics, at least as it was employed by Unz, where politically-savvy and well-funded individuals actually drafted the language of the initiative and then proceeded to "sell" it to the public. Certainly while the public at large cannot reasonably be held to the same standards of statutory knowledge as legislators, when initiative drafters essentially act as legislators, more is required from the court than a perfunctory and simplistic analysis that discharges them of any real responsibility to do their work well and to present their initiative honestly.

In *Doe v. Los Angeles United School District*,[193] parents waited one month after Proposition 227 was adopted to challenge Los Angeles' implementation of the law, asserting that the district's inadequate teacher training, lack of prepared curricula and instructional materials, and delay in developing transition criteria and waiver procedures, were evidence of its inability to meet the *Casteneda* standards. The court did not grant an application for a temporary restraining order, but did certify a class of all future and current "LEP" students in the Los Angeles school district. That case is currently in settlement negotiations.

Finally, teachers themselves brought suit claiming that Proposition 227's provisions allowing teachers to be sued for violating the law were a violation of their First Amendment rights.[194] The teachers had argued that the vague and broad language of Proposition 227, which required English-language instruction frightened them into not speaking in languages other than English in a variety of non-instructional settings and, therefore, "chilled" their exercise of their free speech rights.

The court, however, was not sympathetic. It found that the state can "dictate to teachers that they teach in English," and the Proposition covered only instructional or curriculum matters, over which teachers have no free speech rights.[195] Although there may be some slight disagreement as to which language speech may be conducted in within the classroom, it is clear that it is instructional speech, and not speech outside the classroom, that is being regulated.[196] Further, the court clarified the new law so that there could be no question over what the Proposition actually accomplished. The court said that the words used in the Proposition, that instruction be "overwhelmingly" in English, meant that "only a very small amount of speech in the students' native language is permitted."[197]

The California courts' decisions clearly represent significant victories for the opponents of bilingual education in California.[198] The opponents have effectively blended a mixture of potent ingredients to create a kind of noxious potion that can be used to destroy many civil rights, not just bilingual education. There is a folksy reliance on "commonsense" and the opinion of the "common" man or woman and a concomitant distrust of "experts," "researchers," "administrators," and even those teachers whose educational judgment does not reflect this common understanding. The soothing message is that parents and the public generally know enough about education and about learning English, through a mixture of their own experience and that of their grandparents, to make their educational judgments at least as trustworthy as that of traditional educators. Public fears and mistrust of recent immigrants and the kind of backlash that those fears have generated are made palatable, first by enlisting the support of token language minorities such as Gloria Matta Tuchman, and then disparaging the experts and advocates as not representative of the true immigrants. According to this scenario, the poor, untutored, immigrant has been led astray by left-wing elitist advocates who are really trying to hold on to their own special-interest, job-promoting programs, and needs to be led back to the model of the imagined model immigrant of the past. The supposition is that there is certainly no one better to do that than the US public, with its own legitimate experiences of immigration and English language learning.

Arizona

Unz's strategy was also successful in Arizona, where a copycat proposition, Proposition 203, was voted in by more than 63% of the state's population.[199] Proposition 203 is even more restrictive than Proposition 227 in that waivers into bilingual education are almost impossible to obtain.[200] The state was targeted by Ron Unz and his supporters as the next place to continue his "experiment" of English immersion.[201] In an indication that it may be getting easier and easier to defeat bilingual education in the initiative process, Ron Unz, who also financially supported the Arizona proposition, spent only $172,000 in the state for signature-gathering purposes.[202]

There appears to be little chance of an immediate slow-down by opponents of bilingual education. According to a national education newspaper, "[t]he Center for Equal Opportunity is financing efforts to put an anti-bilingual measure on the 2002 Colorado ballot. Another strategy under consideration is to run initiatives in a bloc of smaller states that permit such ballot measures..."[203]

Prior to the passage of Proposition 203, a less politically-charged case, yet one that represents the brutal reality with which poor school districts must struggle in trying to educate their poor and language-minority students, arose in Arizona.[204] In that case language-minority children and their parents in the Nogales Unified

School District (NUSD) brought an action against the state for violating Title VI of the Civil Rights Act and §1703(f) of the EEOA for failing to adequately educate them in English and failing to enable them to master the standard academic curriculum.

The NUSD was a poor school district with an overwhelmingly Mexican-American population. The school district had a high proportion of "at-risk" students, those who were entitled to free or reduced lunch as an indicator of poverty, and all of its schools were eligible to receive funds under Title I of the ESEA for their high proportion of poor students. Although the NUSD received a base allocation from the state to educate its students, and a small amount more for educating its language-minority children, the state money simply did not go far enough, and the district was unable to raise enough money in taxes to make up the short falls. In the court's words, the NUSD was always in a situation of "robbing Peter to pay Paul."[205]

The NUSD had adopted a "*Lau*" program to educate its language-minority students; a mixture of ESL and transitional bilingual education programs. The program's goal was to have the students graduate from high school fully proficient in both English and Spanish. The reality, however, was quite different. The NUSD simply did not have enough resources to attract and more importantly, keep, trained ESL and bilingual education teachers in sufficient numbers to educate its large numbers of language-minority children.[206] In order to deal with this problem, the district essentially implemented a triage program; as soon as language-minority children reached oral proficiency in English, they were put in all English class-rooms.[207] To adequately implement the transitional bilingual education program at the elementary level, NUSD needs at least 60 more teachers with either bilingual or ESL endorsements.[208] In the middle school, the focus for the *Lau* program was the 100 newcomer students, although there were approximately 700 language-minority children.[209] The other students were mainstreamed because they presumably had attained oral proficiency in English. To properly implement the ESL program in middle schools, NUSD needed approximately 160 more "LEP-endorsed" teachers.[210] It was the same story in the high school.[211]

Except for the state's base-level funding for NUSD, the court found that:

> the State does not provide any assistance regarding implementation or opera-
> tion of NUSD's "Lau" program; it provides no money, training programs or
> materials or technical assistance. Instead, it would tell other districts to look to
> NUSD for its own language endorsed teachers.[212]

The court found that the "State's minimum base level for funding the '*Lau*' programs was arbitrary and capricious, and bore no relation to the actual funding needed to ensure that language minorities in NUSD were achieving mastery of 'essential skills.'"[213] Therefore, the court held that the state was "violating the EEOA because the state's arbitrary and capricious "*Lau*" appropriation was not reasonably calculated to effectively implement the "*Lau*" educational theory which it approved and NUSD adopted."[214] Defendants were also found in violation of EEOA for not following through with practices, resources and personnel to transform its educational theory into practice.[215]

The court, however, did not rule in favor of the students on the Title VI claims. The correlation that existed in NUSD between at "at risk" students and language minorities "destroy[ed] any race-based inferences that might otherwise be drawn. Based on the evidence presented at trial, the students at NUSD might very well fail the tests because they are low-income 'at-risk' students."[216] "At-risk" students are not protected from discriminatory treatment. For advocates trying to bring Title VI claims in this area, the court's decision on this claim at least serves as a reminder of the need for detailed and precise data analysis that might or might not be possible to gather. Otherwise *Flores* is a good case that highlights the significant but un-exotic struggles that poor school districts must face, and which often undermine the ability of schools to properly implement meaningful bilingual programs. Of course the case was couched in terms of giving children an opportunity to learn English, rather than as one that sought developmental bilingual education services; but, with parents and advocates at the grassroots-level struggling for a better education, this litigation could have been the beginning of better things in Nogales. Unfortunately, it is unclear what the impact of the passage of Proposition 203 will have on the instructional program at NUSD; it may be that the efforts of the parents over so many years will be washed away with the results of one day's elections.

One indicator of the state of education for language-minority children since the passage of Proposition 203 is reflected in the lawsuit *Morales v. Tucson Unified School District*[217] In this case, the Morales family sued the Tucson school district for denying the family's request for a waiver under the law which would have allowed seven-year-old Jasmine Morales to remain in a bilingual education program. Under the law, parental requests for waivers are granted only if the student has such special needs that the required structured English-immersion classes would not be appropriate. Jasmine had been making good progress in the bilingual program, both in her English skills and in her academic content. After the shift in program, however, she was allegedly traumatized by the change, and began losing her academic and English-language skills.[218] The lawsuit claimed that the program being offered by Tucson as required by Proposition 203 was in violation of the EEOA because it was not an appropriate program, and that it also was in violation of the Due Process Clause because it did not require parental notification or provide for an appeal of any decision. The case is pending in the federal court in Arizona.

Probably without nearly as much success, bilingual education is also under attack in New York City.

New York

Often mentioned in the California press concerning the Ninth Street School boycott was a lawsuit brought by Latino parents of the Bushwick Parents Organization (BPO) from Brooklyn, New York in 1996. The lawsuit charged that the New York State Commissioner of Education violated the law by allowing students to stay in bilingual education classes for more than three years. New York City's bilingual education programs are governed by two sets of laws, state and federal. Under state law, children are allowed to remain in bilingual education or ESL classes for three years. After that time, the school district must assess the students "individually" to determine whether they need to receive "English language support services" for more than three years.[219] The assessment is actually done annually, regardless of whether the student is in the program for one year or four years.

The federal law is embodied in the "ASPIRA Consent Decree," which was the product of litigation brought by Puerto Rican parents and children in 1974 to address the intolerable educational underachievement of Puerto Rican students in the New York City schools.[220] The litigation ended in the Consent Decree, which mandated a transitional bilingual education program for Spanish surnamed children who were found to be more proficient in Spanish than in English. Still, parents could opt their children out of these programs and enroll them in ESL-only classes. The ASPIRA Consent Decree, named after the Puerto Rican advocacy organization that was the lead plaintiff, became a model for school districts across the country and is still in existence today although it is under attack by a conservative mayoralty and press.

The BPO court papers claimed that "tens of thousands of immigrant children in New York City have been permitted to languish for up to six years in bilingual classes, learning neither English nor other subjects particularly well."[221] Bilingual classrooms were called "prisons" from which Latino children had to escape. Again, the effort was spearheaded by a White clerical activist, Sister Kathy Maire. Sister Maire was a leader of the BPO, and connected the parents with the Public Education Association (PEA). The PEA was then under the stewardship of Ray Domanico who has been with the Manhattan Institute, an ultra-conservative think tank. PEA connected the group with a conservative lawyer at the large law firm, Paul, Weiss, Rifkind, Wharton and Garrison. Yet in informal conversations and flyers, the BPO had expressed support for bilingual education but disappointment with how the programs were being administered, specifically in the Bushwick district.[222]

The lawsuit that was brought had little legal merit and did not reflect any support for bilingual education. The BPO argued that, under state law, the Commissioner of Education had to *personally* verify whether students still needed bilingual education before they could be allowed to continue in the program beyond three years. Although the BPO sued the Commissioner, the Puerto Rican Legal Defense and Education Fund (PRLDEF) acting on behalf of ASPIRA intervened for the organization as a defendant to protect its interest in the integrity of the Consent Decree. In court papers PRLDEF argued that *individualized* assessment as specified under the law, not personalized assessment, was required and was being provided through individually-administered standardized tests. The case was indeed quickly dismissed, but not before local and national media trained their attention on the poverty-stricken community of Bushwick, New York. Unfortunately, very little that was positive came of the lawsuit – a group of activist Latino parents who continued to pledge their theoretical support for bilingual education was lost to the cause of bilingual education, the community was torn apart by the lawsuit, the justifiable complaints about the quality of the schooling in Bushwick generally went unaddressed, and national conservative think tanks used the lawsuit for their own purposes.

Unlike the Ninth Street boycott, however, the BPO lawsuit did not give rise to an Unz-type of initiative, nor did it stimulate anti-bilingual education attitudes across the state. Still, the specter of Latino parents calling bilingual education a "prison" from which children had to escape is sobering. Moreover, the vision of progressive organizations such as PRLDEF and ASPIRA standing on the same side as a state defendant speaks volumes about how the bilingual education struggle has changed. For critics, BPO is nothing less than a forlorn example of a grassroots parent-centered organization taking on the established bilingual education bureaucracy and its apologists. Its loss made it look that much more like the David to our Goliath. As the lawyer for PRLDEF involved in the litigation, the reality is more complicated and more anguished. Unlike the opponents, advocates have no short and pithy slogans that can explain language acquisition, or that can mobilize parents against bad programs and to fight for better ones, or that can counteract the weight of equating English with patriotism and material success. When language restrictionists turn the attention of Latino parents toward fighting bilingual education only rather than fighting for a good education for all, they must take responsibility for dissipating the energies of parents that could be used to struggle for a real reform of urban education.

The struggle for bilingual education in New York continues. The New York City Mayor, Rudolph Guiliani, publicly stated his belief that the city's bilingual education programs were not working and needed to be strictly time-limited.[223] He appointed a mayoral Taskforce, headed by his former Deputy Major Randy Mastro, to study the provision of services to language minorities in the City and make recommendations for change. While the Taskforce was doing its work, Board of Education Member, Irving Hamer, who headed a Board subcommittee on "ELLs" (language-minority children), issued its own report and data on the academic achievement of language-minority children and their rates of English-language acquisition.[224] In an apparent surprise to many, the majority of students in transitional bilingual education programs were learning English within three years, and there was only an 11% difference in the percentage of bilingual-education participants reaching the three-year mark when compared to those students taking ESL-only.[225] The study did not control for socio-economic status, so that difference may be explicable on grounds other than pedagogical ones. It would appear that bilingual education in New York City was working, in as much as English acquisition is the goal, against the odds.

Still, the Taskforce was adamant about its desire to make radical changes to the services provided to language minorities in New York City. Even before issuing a written report, Mr Mastro used local tabloids to push for what he termed an "English immersion" option; he would like parents not only to be able to choose between bilingual education and traditional ESL-only, but also to have the choice of an accelerated approach to learning English.[226] Mr Mastro went so far as to hold a public hearing on his "proposal" before actually committing it to writing, and he invited Ron Unz to testify.

The New York City schools Chancellor, Harold O. Levy, issued his own proposals for "reforming" bilingual education in the City which were presented as recommendations to the City's Board of Education.[227] He adopted a Mastro/Giuliani-created alternative to traditional ESL called "accelerated English." He went one step further, however, and proposed that students should not be assigned to any program as soon as possible (as the city had been doing under the ASPIRA Consent Decree for years) but should wait until after the parents had indicated their programmatic choice for their children.[228] The parents would be able to choose between traditional bilingual education, traditional ESL-only, dual-language programs, and the new accelerated English-acquisition programs. This would change the way bilingual education programs are implemented from an opt-out framework (where students would be initially assigned to bilingual education classes and parents would have the opportunity, to be exercised at any time, to take their child out of programs) into an opt-in model. Chancellor Levy also proposed that parents be able to unilaterally remove their children from an English-language support service, (whether it be transitional bilingual education or ESL-only or accelerated English, for instance) if they wanted to after three years of service in a program regardless of the child's English proficiency.[229]

Such a complete reliance on the judgment of parents is unprecedented. In no other matter are parents given such authority over curriculum or pedagogy. By pinning his reform effort on to parental choice, the Chancellor effectively threw his support to those who, like Ron Unz, question the educational legitimacy of bilingual education and bilingual teachers, and exalt the "common sense" of parents at the possible expense of the education of their children. Cleverly, he also exonerated the school system from actually having to implement any deep change to programs that might be costly by putting the onus on parents to simply take their children out of programs if they were unhappy. Not surprisingly, the Chancellor's budget proposal for implementing his recommendations contained little new money for really reforming bilingual education and ESL-only programs, such as reducing class size.

Interestingly, there was nothing in the Hamer report or the underlying data that indicated that parental choice, or lack of choice, was an issue that needed to be addressed or that any of the issues that did indeed need to be addressed could be effectively tackled through greater parental choice. Still, on February 27, 2001 the Board of Education formally adopted the Chancellor's recommendations, and set the stage for a potential legal battle with the plaintiffs in ASPIRA.

Although an "Unz-like" initiative is ultimately unlikely in New York City, the terms of the debate have changed dramatically since the ASPIRA Consent Decree was signed by a federal court judge in 1974. Native language instruction is no longer stressed for its own sake, and bilingual education teachers are treated as part of the problem rather than as part of a solution. The race to learn English, with the opponents and the proponents of bilingual education taking sides, is the only factor that is considered valuable. In the meantime, the drop-out rate for immigrant student language-minority students continues to climb. According to the most recent statistics issued by the New York City Board of Education, 30.6% of the language minorities in the Class of 2000 dropped out compared to just over 19% for the entire Class, and 30.3% actually graduated, making it more likely that a student who was not proficient in the English language would drop out than graduate.[230] For those who were defined as recent immigrants upon entry into the Class of 2000, 28.1% dropped out compared to 19.0% for non-immigrant students.[231]

New Mexico

The conservative think tank, Center for Equal Opportunity, which has targeted affirmative action and bilingual education for eradication, campaigned for language-minority parents to act as plaintiffs in an ill-fated attempt to bring down bilingual education in Albuquerque, New Mexico. A flyer put out by the organization promised parents of children in the City's bilingual education programs that "[y]our child stands to receive $10,000 for damages and discrimination."[232]

Not surprisingly, in 1998, Latino parents brought a lawsuit against the Albuquerque Public School District (APS) for violations of Title VI of the Civil Rights Act, the Equal Educational Opportunities Act and the Fourteenth Amendment. Some of the parents complained that their children were being mis-identified as "LEP" and placed in bilingual education classes and thereby "denied the equal educational opportunities afforded to other similarly situated Anglo or English-speaking students within APS" because of their national origin.[233] They also complained that they were never informed that they had a right to opt out of the bilingual-education programs. Other parents complained that, although their children did indeed require English-language support services, they were not given an opportunity to enroll in ESL-only classes, but only in bilingual education classes and that they were therefore denied an opportunity to learn English.[234]

The complaint alleged that:

> APS's actions of forcing non-LEP students into bilingual programs; placing students in a bilingual program that is deficient in instruction and course offerings; placing both LEP and non-LEP students in a bilingual program that is not equivalent in the quality of instruction given in mainstream courses; failing to provide English-as-a-Second-Language (ESL) instruction,

among other things violated Title VI.[235] Further, the district's failure to provide other kinds of instructional programs (presumably more English-centric ones), was also a violation of law.[236] In a real twist of civil rights history, the parents even complained that New Mexico's bilingual education law was discriminatory because it demanded that Latino students be treated differently than other students by requiring that bilingual programs "provide for the educational needs of linguistically and culturally different students," and "emphasize the history and cultures associated with the students' mother tongue."[237] By targeting instruction in the history and culture of language-minority groups, these language restrictionists revealed the heart of their agenda, which goes beyond restricting just language and goes to the repression of minority identities.

The plaintiffs requested amongst other things that the court enter an order "requiring Defendant to cease from offering native language academic instruction."[238]

Other Latino parents intervened in the lawsuit represented by META, Inc., demanding the continuation and improvement of the bilingual program in the Albuquerque schools.

The court ultimately dismissed all of the plaintiffs' claims against the state's bilingual education law, finding that, for equal protection purposes, the law created no illegal classifications nor did it distribute resources in a way that was based on classifications. For instance, the classes on history and culture of language minorities were to be attended by all students. Indeed, found the court:

> on its face this statute does not divide the students but unites them: it specifically provides that bilingual educational programs in the state must accommodate everyone, children who speak 'minority' languages, Native American children, and all others who wish to participate in the program.[239]

The plaintiffs also charged that the school district implemented the bilingual education law unlawfully by using a "'capture and keep' method to increase the number of LEP students and thereby increase the funding it receive under the [bilingual education law]."[240] Yet the court found that the school district followed appropriate standards for testing and placing students in bilingual education classes. Although the results of English-proficiency tests would predictably result in "some grouping based on national origin, the uncontradicted evidence demonstrates that the purpose of the classification is to provide for the specialized needs of these students, not to discriminate."[241]

For many of the same reasons that the constitutional claims failed, the plaintiffs' Title VI disparate impact claim also failed: only students who need services were receiving them, and there was no apparent harm to them in getting those services.[242]

In a separate opinion, the court also disposed of the alleged violations of §1703(f) of the EEOA. On this issue, the court went through the analysis of §1703(f) claims as outlined in *Castaneda*, but found that it could not yet determine whether the Albuquerque schools' program was indeed properly teaching children English in its bilingual programs, because the school district had not yet set up a proper data analysis system.[243] However, in accordance with an agreement entered into with OCR, the school district was in the process of doing so. In any case, as to individually named students, there had been no showing by the plaintiffs that those students had not made adequate progress.[244]

RECOMMENDATIONS

The education of language-minority children is at a critical point. Bilingual education, previously supported as a minimal gesture toward helping these students learn a new language and become acclimated to a new world, has fallen into disrepute. Yet there is information that newly-immigrated students who retain their native languages and cultures are more likely to see higher academic achievement than those who quickly attempt to assimilate.[245]

At the same time, as of fall 1999, only nine states did not yet have a system of assessment that operates on the belief that the curriculum and testing of students should and can be standardized.[246] Although the federal government appropriated more funds to education from 1992 to 2000, there is still an unbridgeable "minority achievement gap" and a sense that US students generally do not compete well on international norms.[247] The most creative solutions being presented are those that rely upon public disinvestment from education: voucher programs, charter schools and the operation of schools by private companies. New York City, one of the most influential school systems in the nation because it is the largest, has already opened up several charter schools and in 2000 it hired a private company to operate five of its worst-performing schools.[248] According to New York City Board of Education member Terri Thomson, the private company may be able to teach the Board of Education what really works best in education.[249]

The implications of all these endeavors for language-minority children, let alone for all children, is unclear. History, however, has taught us much about how language minorities generally and their students in particular have been treated by large school systems – they are generally neglected and forgotten unless and until they fight for their deserved recognition and a place in the school system.

In order to stop this cycle of neglect, struggle, and then limited compromise, we need to help language-minority communities to become empowered and, therefore, visible to policymakers from the beginning, at the policy-creation stage. Commitment to bilingual education is, I believe, still one of the most significant and *transgressive*, and therefore, empowering, ideas available to language minorities, because it begins with the demand that language-minority communities be met on their own terms, as valuable co-equals with the English monolingual majority. It is not the only place in which educational reform for language minorities must take place, but it is a potent starting point, because it demands respect and, once respect is obtained, educational reform for language minorities can proceed apace.

In 1996, Colin Baker wrote that only one thing was certain about the future of bilingual education – that nothing is certain.[250] The methodology has been applauded, supported, mandated, ridiculed, vilified and left without legal protection. Like other civil rights, bilingual education certainly pushed against the individualistic grain inherent in the shape of US law. These civil rights were defined at a distinct moment in US history when a self-critical awareness prompted the middle classes to try to make the "American dream" real for the poor and dis-empowered. That generosity of spirit, however, was still restrained in that it was limited to sharing a portion of the bounty of the nation with those considered the long-suffering and deserving poor with the understanding that they would soon no longer need that kind of support. Yet it was still a unique moment in US history, and does not appear to be an era that will repeat itself in the near future.

Although the challenges to the civil rights activists and advocates are greater, no challenge comes without the opportunity for self-reflection, creativity and, if we are strong, a renewed commitment to those invisible many who, while often quiet, are neither speechless nor powerless. For those who are willing to struggle on, a reinvigorated, multi-tiered advocacy strategy must be pursued that should weave together the following elements.

Development of grassroots parental activist leadership

Opponents of bilingual education have painted a portrait of bilingual education advocates as self-interested elites who think they "know better" than immigrant parents about educating their children, often to the detriment of the child and against the best instincts of parents. If the activism for bilingual education rests only on the shoulders of professionals, it will not succeed.

Professionals can impart knowledge on the historical struggle of language minorities in the US, the connections with other minority groups, the place of language in our individual and national personalities, the political nature of education and the place of bilingual education within the vision of a quality education.

The work of professionals here needs to retain that flavor of humility and self-effacement that comes with truly loving and respecting language-minority communities, understanding that our role is not to act as the ultimate leader. We need to share the learning we have gained through struggle, legitimize the communities' struggle, empower them to move on to take over their own empowerment, and hopefully leave behind a thoughtful, wise coalition of parents and students who can act in the best interests of their children and communities.

Development of committed bilingual education teachers

Poorly designed programs, implemented either by hostile, uninterested teachers and districts, or by well-meaning but untrained staff, has had a negative impact on the ability of many to wholeheartedly support bilingual education. Bilingual education teachers must themselves become deeply aware of the political nature of their work; indeed, of the politics that brought about the political nature of their very own existence. For the most part, bilingual education teachers would not exist, indeed the license requirements would not have been developed, were it not for the struggle and loud advocacy of concerned language-minority communities.

Great faith in the ability of language-minority teachers to help educate language-minority students in a caring, legitimizing and supportive environment was one of the hallmarks of the struggle for bilingual education. A career that is born in this way cannot be seen simply as a job with good benefits. Bilingual education teachers must learn of the historical struggles that led to bilingual education, must keep abreast of the current political climate, and must use their access to parents to educate and organize communities. Most importantly, perhaps, they must be excellent at what they do. Litigation and advocacy will never alone eliminate the biases of the public toward bilingual education and bilingual educators, and there is indeed a double standard with regard to bilingual education – as there is for every minority-serving program.

Bilingual educators must informally or through their own organizations monitor and evaluate their own programs using high criteria, they must develop their own professional development practices, and share and disseminate best-practice information. They must mentor each other and move vigorously to expose and either improve or disband failing bilingual programs. In short, bilingual educators were not created by the education bureaucracy, and neither they nor our children are best served by that bureaucracy. Bilingual educators cannot now rely upon that bureaucratic system to do what is best for them, for their programs or for language-minority children. Bilingual educators must fill in the gaps themselves; they must be excellent, self-monitoring, self-helping and self-criticizing. This is the minimal role of professional bilingual educator associations.

Contextualize bilingual education within a struggle for educational reform

As discussed previously within the context of empowering education in language minorities as outlined by Jim Cummins, the struggle for bilingual education must be understood within the context of a good education for all. Good bilingual education programs are found in schools with strong leadership imbued with a clear vision for educational excellence. It is my own feeling that schools should express an unabashed commitment to language-minority schoolchildren and to bilingualism for all as an ultimate goal. When language-minority schoolchildren are moved to the center of reform in this way, their needs will not only *not* be forgotten, but will form the basis for substantive school reform that will be equitable for all. Schools must live the sentiments expressed by the playwright Ariel Dorfman – allowing two languages to live in one body is to begin to "embody differences" that can lead to authentic tolerance and the "salvation" of our species. Putting bilingual education within this context should also help in spreading the appeal of bilingual education to other mainstream educational organizations that do not have the struggle for bilingual education on their agendas.

Develop support for bilingual education among various language-minority groups

Since the inception of bilingual education, the general public has viewed it as a special educational program for Latino children only. Indeed, the recent attacks on bilingual education have focused in the program's popularity amongst Latinos in order to divide the support of the language-minority communities for the programs and to emphasize its "special interest" nature. Latinos certainly are more likely to be enrolled in bilingual programs than other language groups are. However, this probably has more to do with the fact that bilingual education programs need a minimum number of students enrolled in order to be sustainable, and Latinos are the largest single ethnic group, speaking the same native language, in the nation. Opponents of bilingual education seem to want to use the relatively higher enrollment of Latinos as an indication that they are more interested in retaining their native languages than other groups are . There has been no study, however, to indicate that other language-minority groups are not interested in retaining their native languages. Indeed, states with large and diverse language groups offer bilingual programs in as many languages as the demographics of the area will accommodate. New York City alone offers bilingual programs in Haitian-Creole, Korean, Russian, and Chinese in addition to Spanish.[251]

Still, national leadership on this issue has been Latino-dominated, and it is certainly the time, if it has not already been so, for leadership in this area to reflect the diversity of the language-minority communities in the nation, and other language groups have to make advocacy for bilingual education a visible priority for their organizations. If the base of support for bilingual programs is to widen, which seems critical, then Latinos and other language groups must highlight and nurture cross-cultural support for these programs. New York City has had experience with unified efforts in support of bilingual education, but these mostly occur at times of crisis.

On the other hand, Latinos have established organizations for which bilingual education is or was a top agenda item. Unfortunately, many of these organizations have either been overwhelmed by their own needs, lulled into a false sense of security by the provision of federal and state laws on bilingual education, or have been cowed by the vociferous criticism of bilingual education. These organizations need to reinvigorate their bilingual education strategies by reaching down to the grassroots level, as well as across to other language groups. To date, that outreach has either not been done or has been done half-heartedly. Collaboration – sharing of strategies, joint events, sessions on cross-cultural understanding – needs to be developed by grassroots organizations on the local level. Latino bilingual education teachers can be especially helpful as they reach out to their colleagues in ESL or other bilingual programs to share information on building successful programs. Recognizing the political nature of bilingual education, they can strategize with each other, their parents, and their students on building cross-cultural support for bilingual education in their own communities.

Build coalitions with mainstream, non-ethnic education groups

In order for bilingual education to be taken seriously as part of an educational reform strategy, it must become part of the agendas of other, non-ethnic, mainstream educational organizations. Just as the educational bureaucracies must be taught how to *see* language minorities as part of the educational landscape, so too do established educational organizations and funds that may have more political leverage than smaller, less powerful ethnic organizations. Building coalitions with these kinds of groups is critically important for language minorities, and they may meet with as much resistance as if they were trying to change the minds of a long-term education bureaucrat. For many established organizations already have their agendas set, many have bought into the misperceptions of bilingual education, or may see it as "too ethnic" an issue that might undermine their work in other areas such as finance, assessment, or teacher development. It is up to language-minority communities to begin to speak to these other organizations, and not just to each other any longer, to educate them on how the needs of language-minority students have a role in their work and to continue to keep pressuring them until language minorities and bilingual education are concepts they can recognize easily and begin to support.

Involve lawyers to the extent necessary to assist communities in realizing educational and empowering efforts

Lawyers can help language-minority communities in building organizations and coalitions to advance the goals of bilingual education, and education generally, that is empowering. For instance, the recent move towards "standards" and high-stakes testing has opened up new avenues for litigation. However, the lawyers cannot and should not dominate the strategic thinking of a community seeking empowerment. Lawyering within the context of promoting social change must take place within a context of community support, mobilization, and leadership. This is undoubtedly more complicated and time-consuming than a lawyer-dominated process. However, the ultimate goal, community empowerment, can only be approached from this angle if it is to be obtained at all.

CONCLUSION

Bilingual education has come a down a long and tortured path. In many ways this should not be surprising. This simply is a nation that cherishes its immigrants only to the extent that they assimilate quickly; entrenched ethnic or linguistic ties seem to cause a kind of national anxiety where the very foundations of the country are feared to be jeopardized. In the area of social and educational rights, the nation values primarily its tradition of individualism and local control of schools. The school desegregation efforts were similarly ill-fated because that struggle also sought to take control of education, a simultaneously and intensely personal and political act, from local communities in order to re-make the national landscape into one in which minorities are equally reflected.[252]

From its compromised legislative beginnings to today where programs are being threatened around the country, bilingual education has fallen probably more quickly and more steeply than any other civil right. The stakes for the opponents seem high – with immigration being the nation's defining characteristic and new immigrants coming in at record numbers, the very face and fate of the nation appears to be at issue. The strategy against bilingual education has a desperate quality to it; from its ethnic divisiveness to its vilification of advocates, language rights activists and simple bilingual education teachers, the nation has not seen this kind of vitriol since the World War eras. Yet, the rhetoric has purportedly not been aimed at the language-minority parents and children themselves, but at the teachers and advocates in a stunning and perhaps unprecedented use of table turning: those who have advocated for and struggled for the empowerment of language minorities are called racist and our motives, suspicious. If it were not for the potent place that immigration has in the national consciousness, such hubris would not be as successful as it has been. It is because of the national myth about the painless assimilation of previous generations of immigrants without governmental assistance, and the insistence by bilingual education opponents that neither the nation nor the world has changed so much as to make today's immigration experience any harder, that language-minority communities can be convinced into abandoning bilingual education. When this is mixed with the time-tested equation of language with nation and patriotism, then the support of the general public is ensured.

Unfortunately, for advocates there simply is no easy way to combat this propaganda. The truth about our nation's history, about racism and about economics and even about urban education, or about language acquisition, cannot be reduced to simple statements or to a few elements on an initiative ballot. The work that must be done, as reflected I think in the recommendations above, is hard, complex, time-consuming and neither exotic nor terribly newsworthy. However, it may be the most worthwhile work that a language-rights activist can do if it is real empowerment that is sought.

Notes

1. These issues involve parental and community involvement in education, teacher training, and even school organization and structure.
2. Ariel Dorfman, HEADING SOUTH, LOOKING NORTH: A BILINGUAL JOURNEY (Penguin Putnam, 1999) at 42.
3. Colin Baker, FOUNDATIONS OF BILINGUAL EDUCATION AND BILINGUALISM, 2nd edn, (Multilingual Matters, Clevedon, 1996) at 203.
4. *Id* at 172.
5. *Id*. at 173–174.
6. *Id* at 173.
7. Susan J. Dicker, LANGUAGE IN AMERICA: A PLURALIST VIEW (Multilingual Matters, Clevedon, 1996) at 137.
8. *Id*. at 138.
9. US General Accounting Office, PUBLIC EDUCATION: MEETING THE NEEDS OF STUDENTS WITH LIMITED ENGLISH PROFICIENCY (Washington DC, 2001) at 18–20.
10. *Id*. at 18.

11. *Id.*

12. *Id. See also* US General Accounting Office, DESCRIPTIVE STUDY OF SERVICES TO LIMITED ENGLISH PROFICIENT STUDENTS, Vol. 1 (Washington DC, 1993) at 26.

13. *See Id.*

14. Diane Ravitch, a vociferous opponent of bilingual education and a fellow at the conservative think tank, Brookings Institution, has specifically supported structured immersion over bilingual education. *See* Diane Ravitch, *First Teach Them English*, NY TIMES, September 5, 1997.

15. Tove Skutnabb-Kangas, BILINGUALISM OR NOT: THE EDUCATION OF MINORITIES (Multilingual Matters, Clevedon, 1987) at 131.

16. *Id.*

17. *Id.*

18. *Id.* at 132.

19. The decision may also be influenced by funds; structured immersion approaches may be cheaper to operate. Yet, how a school district opts to spend its money is at least partly informed by the values and goals it has for its students.

20. *Supra*, note 3, at 151.

21. David Ramirez, *Final Report: Longitudinal Study of Structured English Immersion Strategy Early-Exit & Late-Exit Transitional Bilingual Education Progress for Language Minority Children Executive Summary* (USDOE Washington, DC) BILINGUAL RESEARCH JOURNAL 10:12 1992.

22. Limited English Proficient. *See supra*, Chapter 2, note 124.

23. *Supra*, note 21 at 38–39.

24. *Id.*

25. *Id.* at 38.

26. *Id.* at 45.

27. *Id.* at 19.

28. *Id.* at 23.

29. Wayne P. Thomas and Virginia Collier, SCHOOL EFFECTIVENESS FOR LANGUAGE MINORITY STUDENTS (NCBE George Washington University, Washington DC, 1997).

30. *Id.* at 9.

31. *Id.* at 15.

32. *Id.* at 35–36.

33. *Id.* at 36.

34. *Id.*

35. *Id.* at 36.

36. *Id.* at 15–16.

37. *See* Alfredo Lopez, THE PUERTO RICAN PAPERS: NOTES ON THE RE-EMERGENCE OF A NATION at 113–123. Bobbs-Merill Co., 1973. *See also* US Commission on Civil Rights, PUERTO RICANS IN THE CONTINENTAL UNITED STATES: AN UNCERTAIN FUTURE (1976) at 92.

38. *See* Jose A. Cardenas, MULTICULTURAL EDUCATION: A GENERATION OF ADVOCACY (Intercultural Development Research Association, 1995) at 10–16.

39. *See* Sandra Del Valle, *Bilingual Education for Puerto Ricans in New York City*, HARV. EDUC. REV. (1998) at 196; See also Isaura Santiago Santiago, *Aspira v. The Board of Education Revisited*, AMERICAN J. OF EDUC. (1986) at 151–56.

40. *Westminster School District of Orange County v. Mendez*, 161 F2d 774 (9th Cir 1947).

41. *Id* at 780.

42. Joan Moore, MEXICAN-AMERICANS at 78–79 (Prentice-Hall, New York, 1970).

43. James Crawford, BILINGUAL EDUCATION: HISTORY, THEORY, POLITICS AND PRACTICE, 2nd edn (Bilingual Educational Services, 1995) at 33.

44. Jerome Bruner, THE CULTURE OF EDUCATION (Harvard University Press, Cambridge, MA, 1996) at 71–72.

45. *Supra*, note 43 at 32.

46. Rachel F. Moran, *The Politics of Discretion: Federal Intervention in Bilingual Education* 76 Cal. L. REV. 1249 (1988) at 1265.

47. *Id.*

48. *Id.* at 1264.

49. Bilingual Education Act of 1968 §702, 81 Stat at 816.

50. *Supra*, note 46 at 1264.

51. *Id.* at 1265.

52. Act of Nov 4, 1971 Mass. Acts 943 (uncodified preface; emphasis added).

53. *Supra*, note 43 at 33.

54. HR 805, 93rd Cong., 2nd Sess. 66.

55. *Id.* at 767.

56. *Supra*, note 43 at 37.

57. *Id.*

58. For instance, in 1989, US Secretary of Education William Bennett in reference to the Bilingual Education Act decided that "a sense of cultural pride can not come at the price of proficiency in English, our common tongue," quoted in, Rachel Moran, *Of Democracy, Devaluation and Bilingual Education*, 226 CREIGHTON L. REV. 255 at n. 93.

59. *Supra*, note 43 at 39.

60. *Supra*, note 46 at 1286.

61. *Id.* at 1285.

62. *Id.* at 1288.

63. Noel Epstein, LANGUAGE, ETHNICITY AND THE SCHOOLS POLICY ALTERATIONS FOR BILINGUAL-BICULTURAL EDUCATION (Washington DC's Institute for Educational Leadership, 1977).

64. *Supra*, note 43 at 39.

65. *See generally* Tony Baez, Ricardo Fernandez, Ricardo A. Navarro, Roger L. Rice, *Litigation Strategies for Educational Equity: Bilingual Education and Research* ISSUES IN EDUCATION, VOL. 3 (AMERICAN EDUCATIONAL RESEARCH ASSOCIATION, WASHINGTON DC, 1995).

66. *Supra*, note 43 at 41.

67. *Id.*

68. *Supra*, note 60 at 1299.

69. *Id.*

70. *Id.*

71. 347 US 483 (1954).

72. 163 US 537 (1896).

73. *See* Kevin M. Fong, *Cultural Pluralism*, 13 HARV. L. R-C. L. L. REV. 133, 143 (1978).

74. *See Id.* generally.

75. *Green v. Kent County Board of Education*, 391 US 430 (1968).

76. 404 US 1215.

77. *Johnson v. San Francisco Unified School District*, 339 FSupp 1315, 1320 (ND Cal. 1971).

78. *Id.* at 1322.

79. *See supra,* note 76 at 1216–17.

80. 342 FSupp 24 (ED Texas 1971).

81. *Id.* at 28.

82. *Id.* at 30.

83. *Id.* at 26.

84. *Supra,* note 38 at 22.

85. *Id.* at 29 (emphasis in original).

86. *See also Cisneros v. Corpus Christi Ind Sch Dist,* 467 F2d 142 (5th Cir 1972), where a large Mexican-American population was involved in a school desegregation case, but where language and culture were not mentioned as part of claims or in remedy; and *US v. Texas Education Agency,* 532 F2d 380 (5th Cir 1976).

87. 411 US 1 (1973).

88. *See Campaign for Fiscal Equity v. State,* 187 Misc 2d 1 NY Sup. Ct (2001); *Abbott by Abbott v. Burke,* 195 NJ Super 59 (NJ Super AD 1984) *rev'd, Abbott v. Burke,* 100 NJ 269 (1985), *aff'd Abbott by Abbott v. Burke,* 136 NJ 444 (1993), *clarified, Abbott v. Burke* 164 NJ 84 (1999); *Serrano v. Priest,* 20 Cal. 3d 25 (1977).

89. *Keyes v. School Dist. No. 1, Denver Colorado,* 521 F2d 465 (10th Cir 1975).

90. *Id.* at 482, *citing Rodriguez, supra,* note 87 at 42.

91. *Id.* at 481.

92. The scope of Title VI is discussed in detail in the Appendix.

93. 351 FSupp 1279 (D New Mexico 1972), *aff'd,* 499 F2d 1147 (10th Cir 1974)

94. *Id.* 351 FSupp at 1280.

95. *Id.* at 1281.

96. *Id.* at 1282.

97. *Id.*

98. 483 F2d 791 (9th Cir 1973).

99. ARC Associates, Revisiting the Lau Decision: Thirty Years After: A National Commemorative Symposium (ARC Associates, 1996) at 19.

100. *Id. at 13.*

101. *Id.*

102. *Id.* at 14

103. *Supra,* note 98 at 792.

104. *Id.* at 793.

105. *Id.* at 794.

106. *Id.*

107. *Id.*

108. *Id.* at 797.

109. *Id.* at 799 (where plaintiffs' claims for relief were compared to requests for "welfare").

110. *Id.*at 798.

111. *Id.*at 799.

112. *Id.* at 802.

113. *See* Edward Steinman. *The Supreme Court Says We Must – Now What? Problems and Issues in Bilingual Education Selected Papers From the 1979 Denver Conference.* (The Lau Taskforce Remedies Comprehensive Bilingual Education Programs Planning, October 1980).

114. *Lau v. Nichols*, 414 US 563 (1974).
115. HEW would later be divided into three separate departments, including the Department of Education. The Office for Civil Rights for the Education Department is the agency that presently enforces school districts' compliance with Title VI of the Civil Rights Act.
116. *Supra*, note 114 at 568.
117. *Id.* at 566.
118. *Supra*, note 114 at 572.
119. 408 FSupp 162 (D Colo.1975).
120. *Id.* at 169.
121. *Id.*
122. *Supra*, note 19 at 15.
123. *Id.*
124. *See* Office for Civil Rights, *Task Force Findings Specifying Remedies Available for Eliminating Past Educational Practices Ruled Unlawful Under Lau v. Nichols* 1975, reprinted in Keith A. Baker and Adrian A. de Kanter (eds), Bilingual Education (Lexington Books, Lexington, MA, 1983) at 213.
125. *Id.*
126. 628 F2d 1271 (10th Cir1980).
127. *Id.* at 170.
128. *Id.* at 165.
129. *Id.*
130. *Id.* at 165.
131. *Id.* at 166.
132. *Id.* at 164.
133. *See supra*, note 89.
134. *Supra*, note 87.
135. *Supra*, note 89 at n.22.
136. The Act was passed as an amendment from the floor of the House to the Education Amendments of 1974. Although the bill has no legislative history, there is a history attached to the identical bill introduced in 1972, which had failed to receive Senate approval.
137. Jonathan D. Haft, *Assuring Equal Educational Opportunity for Language Minority Students: Bilingual Education and the Equal Educational Opportunity Act of 1974.* 18 Colum. J. L. & Soc. Probs. 209, 233 (1983).
138. 42 USC §1703(f).
139. *Supra*, note 138 at 237, *citing*, *Educational Opportunity and Busing: The President's Address to the Nation Outlining his Proposals*, 8 Weekly Comp. Pres. Doc. 590, 591 (March 16, 1972).
140. *Supra*, note 138 at 238, *citing* Equal Educational Opportunities Act: Hearings on HR 13915 Before the House Commission on *Education and Labor*, 92nd Cong. Sess. 140–41 (1972) (testimony of Elliot Richardson).
141. *See supra*, note 138 at 261.
142. 438 US 265 (1978).
143. As discussed in the Appendix, this question was partly put to rest in *Guardians Association v. Civil Service Commission of the City of NY*, 463 US 582 (1983), where the plurality of the Supreme Court found that if the *regulations* of Title VI are cited by a

plaintiff in addition to the statute, then an *effects* test could be applied – essentially, this standard required only that the policy, practice or regulation being challenged by plaintiffs have a disproportionately negative *effect* on a particular ethnic group. Once such a negative effect is established, the burden of proof shifts to the defendant to show that there is a legitimate business or educational necessity for the practice. Plaintiffs can still win, however, if they can demonstrate the existence of an alternative practice that would reach the same goal but would not have a negative impact. As further discussed in the Appendix, however, the usefulness of Title VI has been limited by a recent Supreme Court decision finding that there is no private right of action under Title VI.

144. 480 FSupp 14 (EDNY 1978).

145. *Id.* at 18.

146. *Id.*

147. *Id* at 19.

148. *Id.*

149. *Id.*

150. *Id.*

151. *Id* at 20.

152. *Id.* at 22.

153. *Id.* at 23.

154. *Id.*

155. 648 F2d 989 (5th Cir 1981).

156. *See* OCR Guidelines, *supra,* note 124.

157. *Supra,* note 43 at 42.

158. *Id.*

159. *Id.*

160. *Id.*

161. *Supra,* note 124.

162. *Id.* at 1010.

163. Jayson Blair, *Lucent Layoffs are New Hires to other Technology Firms,* NY Times, March 18, 2001; Kenneth N. Gilpin, *Kodak Cuts its Profit Forecast for Third Time This Autumn,* NY Times, Dec. 13, 2000 at 610; Bloomberg News, *Kodak Hurt by Stemp Plans to Lay off Employees,* September 20, 2001 at C2.

164. Michael Fix and Jeffrey S Passel,. *Immigration and Immigrants: Setting the Record Straight* (1994) (Urban Institute Washington DC) at 19–21. Eric Schmidts, *New Census Shows Hispanics are Even with Blacks in US,* NY Times March 8, 2001 at A1.

165. *See* Dan Stein, *Making Immigration Great Again,* Speech at Commonwealth Club, July 28, 1997.At www.fairus.org/html/09012707.htm Dan Stein, *Current Problems in Interior Enforcement of the Nations Immigration Laws,* Testimony on July 1, 1999. At www.fairus.org/htm/08317906.htm. *See also,* the website for FAIR, The Federation for American Immigration Reform, generally, at Fairus.org, and the website of the American Immigration Control Foundation. At www.aicfoundation.com.

166. The Immigrant Responsibility Act of 1997, 147 Cong. Rec. H. 4395 (1996).

167. *League of United Latin American Citizens v. Wilson,* 997 FSupp 1244 (1997), holding Proposition 187 unconstitutional because it is pre-empted by the federal government's sole authority to regulate immigration.

168. *See* Fear and Learning at Hoover Elementary, video (on file with author.)

169. West's Ann. Cal. Educ. Code §305.

170. The waivers are possible for "(a) children who already know English ... ; or (b) Older children: the child is age 10 years or older, and it is the informed belief of the school principal and educational staff tat an alternate course of educational study would be better suited to the child's rapid acquisition of basic English language skills; or (c) Children with special needs: the child has already been placed for a period of not less than thirty days during that school year in an English language classroom and it is subsequently the informed belief of the school principal and educational staff that the child has such physical, emotional, psychological or educational need that an alternate course of educational study would be better suited to the child's overall educational development." 227 WEST'S ANN. CAL. EDUC. CODE § 311(a)–(c).

171. Jim Newton and Doug Smith, *Riordan Backs Move to End Bilingual Classes*, LOS ANGELES TIMES, front page. April 10, 1998.

172. CHRISTIAN SCIENCE MONITOR, May 23, 1999.

173. ORANGE COUNTY REGISTER, April 11, 1996.

174. *Id.*

175. *Id.*

176. THE WASHINGTON TIMES, February 18, 1996.

177. LOS ANGELES TIMES, February 13, 1996.

178. *See* THE WASHINGTON TIMES, February 18, 1997 (where Alice Callaghan is quoted as saying "this is very much about money").

179. *See* website for *English for the Children*, at onenation.org.

180. Amy Pyle, *Bilingual Schooling is Failing Parents Say*, LOS ANGELES TIMES, Jan. 16, 1996.

181. *See Proposition 227: English Language in Public Schools. Initiative Statute.* At www.ss.ca.gov/prd/bmprimary98_2/prop227-2.htm.

182. *Quiroz v. State Board of Education*, 1997 WL 661163 at 5 (ED Cal. 1997).

183. *Id.* at fn.5.

184. *Id.* at fn.5 (emphasis added).

185. *Valeria G. v. Wilson*, 12 FSupp 2d 1007(ND Cal. 1998).

186. *Id.* at 1019.

187. *Id.*

188. 75 Cal. App. 4th 196, 89 Cal. Rptr 2d 295 (First Dist. 1999).

189. *Id.* 89 Cal. Rptr 2d at 304.

190. *Id* at 310.

191. *Id.* at 312–13.

192. *Id.* at n. 23.

193. 48 FSupp 2d 1233 (CD Calif. 1999).

194. *California Teachers Association v. Davis*, 64 FSupp 2d 945 (CD Calif. 1999).

195. *Id.* at 954.

196. *Id.* at 956.

197. *Id.*

198. Another case stemming out of California arose in the context of the use of English-language standardized tests for the assessment of language minorities. The San Francisco Unified School district refused to administer the test to language minorities who had been enrolled in school less than thirty months. The school district filed suit against the state for requiring it to give the exam to all students enrolled in the schools for more than twelve months, alleging violations of Title VI. *California Department of Education v. San Francisco*

Unified School District, 1998 WL 241603 (ND Cal. 1998). The case, however, was settled before any decision on the merits of the suit was made by a court.

199. James Crawford, *Bilingual Education: Strike Two*. RETHINKING SCHOOLS, Vol. 15. No.2, Winter 2000/2001.

200. ARIZ. REV. STAT. Article 31 English Language Education for Children in Public Schools §15-753.

201. In a speech at the Harvard Club in New York City on December 6, 2000, Ron Unz referred to the education being offered to language-minority children in California under his initiative as an "experiment" on more than a million schoolchildren.

202. *See* Mary Ann. Zehr, *Arizona Curtails Bilingual Education*, EDUCATION WEEK, November 15, 2000.

203. *See Id.* While this book was in production, initiatives were indeed introduced in Colorado and Massachusetts; the initiative failed in Colorado, but passed in Massachusetts.

204. *See Flores v. Arizona*, 172 FSupp 2d 1225 (D Ariz. 2000).

205. *Id.* at 1235.

206. *Id.*

207. *Id.* at 1232.

208. *Id.*

209. *Id.*

210. *Id.*

211. *Id.* at 1233–1234.

212. *Id.* at 1235.

213. *Id.* at 1239.

214. *Id.*

215. *Id.*

216. *Id* at 1240.

217. *Morales v. Tucson Unified School District* (D Ariz. 2001).

218. *Id. Complaint for Injunctive and Declaratory Relief* at ¶¶ 35–36.

219. Although the state law limits the amount of time children can spend in bilingual or ESL-only classes, tellingly, the lawsuit focused only on violations of law for children in bilingual classes.

220. *See* Isaura Santiago-Santiago, *supra*, note 39 at 196; Sandra Del Valle, *supra*, note 39 at 156.

221. *Bushwick Parents Organization v. Mills*, 5185-95 (Sup. C. Albany County), ARTICLE 78 PETITION.

222. *See* Letter from Maria Perez "for Bushwick Parents Organization" to Congresswoman Velasquez dated September 26,1995 (on file with author).

223. Lynette Holloway, *Mayor Urges Changes to Bilingual Education*, NY TIMES Dec. 19, 2000 at B3.

224. New York City Board of Education, ELL SUBCOMMITTEE RESEARCH STUDIES: PROGRESS REPORT (2000).

225. *Id* at 3.

226. Andy M Mastro, *How New York Can Fix Bilingual Education*, DAILY NEWS, September 24, 2000.

227. New York City Board of Education, CHANCELLOR'S REPORT ON THE EDUCATION OF ENGLISH LANGUAGE LEARNERS (2000).

228. *Id.* at 14.

229. *Id* at 16.

230. New York City Board of Education. THE CLASS OF 2000: FOUR YEAR LONGITUDINAL REPORT AND 1999-00 EVENT DROPOUT RATES (2001), Figure 5 at 17.

231. *Id.* Figure 6 at 18.

232. *See* Flyer at http://.ourworld.compuserve.com/homepages/jwcrawford/10k.htm

233. *Carbajal et al. v. Albuquerque Public School District*, 98 Civ. 279 (D New Mexico). Complaint at ¶30.

234. *Id.* at ¶¶ 75–79.

235. *Id.* at ¶128.

236. *Id.* at ¶129.

237. *Id.* at ¶138.

238. *Id.* at 29.

239. *Carbajal v. Albuquerque Public School District* 98 Civ. 279. Memorandum Opinion and Order at 24 (New Mexico 1999).

240. *Id.* at 26–27.

241. *Id.* at 29.

242. *Id.* at 32.

243. *Carbajal v. Albuquerque Public School District*, 98 Civ 279. Findings of Fact and Conclusion of Law at 20 (D New Mexico 1999).

244. *Id.*

245. *See* Richard Rothstein, *Achievers and Delinquents Via Melting Pot Recipe*, NY TIMES, April 24, 2002. *See also* Ruben G. Rumbaut, *The Crucible Within: Ethic Identity, Self-Esteem, and Segmented Assimilation Among Children of Immigrants*, in THE NEW SECOND GENERATION, Alejandro Portes (ed.) (Russell Sage Foundation, New York, 1996) at 119–170.

246. *See Quality Counts 2000*, EDUCATION WEEK, January 13, 2000.

247. *More Money for Schools*, EDUCATION WEEK, January 17, 2001; Debra Viadero, *Lags in Minority Achievement Defy Traditional Explanations*, March 22, 2000; NEWS SUMMARY EDUCATION WEEK, *US Lags in International Test*, NY TIMES Dec. 5, 2001.

248. Edward Wyatt, *City Plans to Let Company Run Some Schools, in a First*, NY TIMES, Dec. 21, 2000 at A1.

249. *Id.* While this book was in production, the city's plan to privatize certain schools was stopped by a local court.

250. *Supra*, note 2 at 171.

251. New York City Board of Education. ELL SUBCOMMITTEEE RESEARCH STUDIES: PROGRESS REPORT (2001) Figure 11.

252. For an excellent overview of the school desegregation struggles, *see* J. Harvie Wilkinson III. FROM BROWN TO BAKKE. THE SUPREME COURT AND SCHOOL INTEGRATION: 1954–1978. (Oxford University Press, 1979).

Chapter 7

Native American Education: The US Implements an English-Only Policy

INTRODUCTION

The link between the status of groups in society and the way their language and culture are treated was carved out with painful precision in the history of Anglo treatment of the North American Indians. We need not conjecture about the possible implications of culturally and linguistically repressive policies; their tragic results are etched in our nation's soul: the loss and near extinction of hundreds of native languages and consequently native cultures, the educational neglect of generations of Native American children, and the erosion of literacy, self-sufficiency and community, with a concomitant rise in unemployment, alcoholism, teenage suicide, and alienation.

It has become axiomatic to declare that the US presently has no official language, and never has had one. This sweeping generalization, however, does not honor the experiences of Native Americans who were subjected to strict, unapologetic and expressly English-only and identity-repressive policies; these policies rose to the level of mandate and reflected the deep suspicion if not hatred with which Native Americans were regarded. Native Americans have the disheartening distinction of being the first victims of US xenophobic language and educational policies: policies that reflected the deep contempt with which Native American culture, language, customs, indeed entire way of life, were held.

Although the history of the treatment of Native Americans by White settlers goes beyond language policies to extend to cultural repression and forcible relocation, as we have seen, language, culture, the status of minority groups, and the identity of individuals and communities are all inter-related. In essence, how the Native Americans were regarded generally and the social and economic context of their treatment led inexorably to a reactionary and repressive approach to their language. This chapter will focus on the establishment of an English-only policy within Native American communities by the federal government in the area of education, arguably the most significant force in repressing or nurturing native languages for future generations.

US EDUCATION OF NATIVE AMERICANS: EXPERIMENTS IN LANGUAGE REPRESSION

Current results of past regressive policies

Language-minority groups today have much to learn from the treatment of Native Americans, for, unfortunately, the attitudes and rationales that were used to justify Native American repression will seem alarmingly familiar to those engaged in defense of language-minority rights today. Also, the solutions suggested to the mis-education of Native Americans, including maintenance of native languages and community or tribal control of education, are also as relevant today for language-minority communities as they were for Native Americans a hundred years ago. Being able to look back to the experiences of Native Americans means that advocates don't have to rely on conjecture, as sensible as it may be, to discuss the origins and results of policies aimed at crushing minority identities; our own nation can serve as a living example of regressive linguistic policies and the high price they exact on minorities.

In 1969, Congress issued a report on the failed Indian educational policies of the federal and state governments. It found one main theme that imbued the educational philosophy regarding Indians and virtually guaranteed its failure: a policy of coercive assimilation. The roots of this policy were (1) "a continuous desire to exploit, and expropriate Indian land and physical resources; (2) a self-righteous intolerance of tribal communities and cultural differences."[1] The results of this philosophy are clear: Native American children today are more than twice as likely as White children to drop out of school, have the lowest educational attainment of any ethnic group, and are experiencing the highest unemployment rate of any ethnic group.[2] For the Cherokee, after 60 years of state responsibility for Cherokee education, one commentator writing in 1974 noted that:

> 40 % of all adult Cherokees were functionally illiterate, the median number of school years completed was less than six years, and the level of education was below the average of the state as a whole and for the rural Whites living near the Cherokees. The Cherokee drop-out rate in public schools was as high as 75 %. An appalling 90 % of the Cherokee families in one Oklahoma county were on welfare, and in another county, 90 % of all Choctaws were living below the poverty line.[3]

The blame, some argue, lies squarely on the shoulders of an Anglo school system that neither respects nor tolerates Native American languages, cultures or philosophy. The educational mission of Anglo education for the Indians was a destruction of these languages deemed "primitive and barbarous"; the elimination of native cultures were seen as an impediment to colonization and in any case inferior and unworthy of either emulation or preservation. For the Indians, argues one commentator, Ray Folsom, it was not segregation, but forced integration that was problematic:

> [b]y coercing Indian children to accept the dominant culture and discard the Indian values, the integration of Indian children into White public schools has been a form of racial discrimination. This form of discrimination, the integrating of the Indian culture, has caused the same sense of inferiority, the same lack of motivation for educational achievement, and the same resultant social problems which the *Brown* [*v. Board of Education*] court found compelling.[4]

Folsom has noted that:

> because the white teacher had never really been accepted as representing in any way the parent's philosophy or the child's conscience, neurotic tension caused by the culture conflict of the classroom often leads to delinquency, suicide, and alcoholism. The demands of the dominant society for cultural assimilation are met by hostility, withdrawal, and feelings of rejection by the Sioux student.[5]

Mission education

The Anglo school system established for the Native Americans was marked from its inception by a lack of respect or even bare tolerance for Native American languages and cultures.

The tragic educational and economic state of Native Americans today can be traced to the "civilizing" efforts of Anglos since at least the sixteenth century, when the Spanish and French began staking out new territories in North America and sought to establish their European languages and religions among the native populations. In 1617, King James I of England called for the education of the Indians, which included the teaching of English. Protestant clergymen responded to the King's call and, with the King's approval, sought the conversion of the Indians to Christianity as well as undertaking their secular education. The goals of the educational policies, however, were suspect from the start: "the objective from the outset seems to have been to coerce the Indian to accommodate the White man. Thus, the educational practices of the colonial powers were often rigidly pragmatic and less frequently adaptable to Indian ways."[6] Indeed, the Anglos came to the Indians with preconceived ideas about their own superiority and an assumption that the Indians would willingly abandon their culture and mores.

The relationship between the English language and religious indoctrination is an interesting one, and is significant to the development of English-only policies. The missionaries' work was enmeshed with the education of Native Americans. They established schools in which the teaching of English, Euro-American civilization and the depreciation of tribal languages and cultures were the main objects.[7] The missionaries who came from England to North America attached great importance to reading the Bible. While some missionaries translated the Bible into Indian languages, many more:

> preferred to teach the Indians English rather than utilizing Indian languages, which they viewed as barbarous and inadequate mediums for conveying Christian doctrines and as incompatible with efforts to foster the civilization of the Indians. Indeed, by referring to the Indians themselves as "barbarous" and "barbarians" ... the English and other Europeans in effect branded the Indians as inferior on the basis of their language.[8]

Yet, despite the preference of the missionaries for instruction in English, many mission schools ended up being bilingual and even multilingual because of the Indians' attachment to their language.

Traditional Native American education as practiced by the tribes could not be more different than traditional European education being introduced by the Anglos. Although educational practices varied by tribe, several characteristics cut across the varied educational methods employed. For instance, in native education individualism was subordinate to the interests of tribal groups; children learned by application and imitation rather than by memorization, and value was placed on sharing and cooperation rather on than competition.[9] Education was achieved through "legend, precept, example, and sanctions."[10] Religion, community involvement, respect for elders, and the use of positive and negative reinforcement were used.[11] Indeed, tribal customs on the rearing of children were held to be divinely instituted, and were scrupulously adhered to and carried from one generation to another.[12] For the Cherokee, strong discipline of their children was unthinkable. They were motivated by the belief that "reason will guide their children, when they become used to it, and before that time they cannot commit fault. To chastise them would be to debase the mind, and blunt the sense of honor, by the habit of a slavish motive to action."[13] Native American education was meant to provide the child with "the essential qualities needed to exist within the tribal social structure. The home provided a forum in which to practice his newly learned skills; relatives provided discipline, morals, manners, and generosity. Religion was the center of all Indian educational undertakings."[14]

In contrast, the Indians saw the European philosophy of education as an attempt to bind "its students to the possessions it helps them attain; students become slaves to the very goods they seek. The more the educated person accumulates, the more real freedom is lost as he falls in the trap of materialism."[15] In addition to representing different world views, the Indians were troubled that the education that the Anglos offered simply was not practical for them, a theme that would recur throughout the Anglo attempts at education. One Indian speaking in 1744 on behalf of six Native American nations in 1744 stated:

> [s]everal of our Young People were formerly brought up in the colleges of the

Northern Provinces; they were instructed in all your Sciences, but, when they came back to us, they were bad Runners, ignorant of every means of living in the woods, unable to bear either Cold or Hunger; knew neither to build a Cain, take a deer, or kill an enemy, spoke our language imperfectly, were therefore neither fit for Hunters, Warriors, nor Counselors; they were totally good for nothing.[16]

The Native American, Big Soldier, summed up the Indian perspective on Anglo education and life beautifully: "[y]ou whites possess the power of subduing almost every animal to your use. You are surrounded by slaves. Everything about you is in chains, and you are slaves yourselves. I fear if I should exchange my pursuits for yours, I too should become a slave."[17]

The Indians' philosophies of life were reflected in their language. As with all languages, the creation and development of Native languages was infused by the world view and daily life of the Native Americans who spoke them. "[s]cholars have been able to link the uniqueness of the forms of expression in any given Indian languages with the particular interests, needs, situational demands, and cultural priorities of the tribes(s) using that language in daily conversation..."[18] There are few language systems as distinct from one another as the European language system is from the Native American language system. "Many Indian languages place little emphasis on time or verb tense; others make little differentiation between nouns and verbs or separate linguistic units; still others build into a single word thoughts that in English can be expressed only in an entire sentence."[19] Further:

> where Indian language expression is concerned, the reference contrasts quite markedly with the reference perspective allowed by the language of the surrounding society.... For members of many Indian communities, the power of the Indian language to give highly specific culture-based reference perspectives is important, especially if much of the day's conversation must be carried out in English. Under such circumstances, Indian language fluency reminds the speaker that no single language has a monopoly over truth, logic, or precision of expression; for any reference given in English ... there is always another way to say it, and another reference perspective which can be brought to the discussion.[20]

Today, there are around 200 Indian languages, at the time of the Anglo encroachment there were more than 1,500. Although the languages can generally be grouped into several categories, the richness and diversity of Indian language helps explain the attachment Indians felt for their native languages even in the face of Anglo coercion to change – with so many languages, the extent of tribal and community identification with languages was bound to be strong. Indeed, "[m]uch of the distinctiveness which characterizes a particular Indian language has come to highlight its speaker's culturally salient, socially significant reality."[21] Not surprisingly, for the Indians, learning a new language really meant learning and being absorbed into a new culture. "[F]rom a psychological point of view, there are as many different worlds upon the Earth as there are languages. Each language is an instrument which guides people in observing, in reacting, in expressing themselves in a special way."[22]

This tribe–language connection certainly played a role in Anglo's decision to repeatedly attempt to restrict the use of Indian languages:

> ...Indian languages appear to have given the tribal membership a readily available means through which they could invest in the continuing vitality of the tribal life style and its cultural and social significance.... The languages were, and remain, important parts of the tribes' cultural inventory. And as English became a more visible part of the daily life of Indian peoples, even greater importance came to be placed on the maintenance of the ancestral language tradition within many communities.[23]

Colonial education of Indians

From 1778 to 1871 the new US government entered into almost 400 treaties with various Indian nations.[24] In 1794, the first treaty between whites and native groups was signed that contained a provision for the education of the Indians.[25] Initially, treaties were created that contained educational provisions, but these provisions were rarely fulfilled by the Anglo government. In 1885, the Superintendent of Indian Education noted that the federal government had failed to give effect to most of these provisions. Indeed, $4 million would have been needed to fulfill the obligations of just eight treaties; yet from 1778 to 1876 more than 400 treaties had been signed and ratified. The Secretary of the Interior argued that:

> this money is now due. A large part of the money so agreed to be paid was in consideration of land ceded to the Government by the Indians, It is not a gratuity, but a debt due the Indians, incurred by the Government on its own motion and not at the request of the Indians.[26]

Indians could do very little to enforce treaty provisions, for most of the treaties relied on the honor of the President to give them effect. Indeed, the Supreme Court would characterize the relationship between Native American tribes and the US government as that of a ward and its guardian.[27] Although it was called a "trust" relationship, the Court would later hold that the US could unilaterally abrogate its treaties with the tribes, vitiating any legitimate concept of the word "trust."[28] In any case, the US was impatient with the Indians and although it formed "Peace Commissions" to enter into treaties and establish reservations for the Indians, any dissent would trigger a military solution for the "suppression of Indian hostilities."[29]

It was not until the "Civilization Act" was passed in 1819 that Congress allocated some money to actually fulfill treaty obligations for education. The initial $10,000 allocation was for the purpose of "introducing the habits and arts of civilization" to American Indians: the Indians "should be taken under our guardianship, and our opinion not theirs, ought to prevail in measures intended for their civilization and happiness."[30] Funds under the Civilization Act were administered by the federal government, but the operation of the "mission schools" was left to the religious organizations. "The main objective of both the government and the missionaries was to encourage the Indians to become settled, practicing farmers and to discard their native traditions."[31] In short, "to make the whole tribe English in their language, civilized in their habits and Christian in their religion."[32] The US's assumption of the education of Native Americans was aimed even perhaps more strenuously to the elimination of native cultures and languages than was the education under the independent missionaries. The new US government realized that the Native Americans, with their deep respect for the land and their mobile lifestyle, would be an impediment to the colonization of North America. They used education and land reclamation policies as coercive tools to not only "assimilate" American Indians to the Anglo lifestyle but to forcefully destroy American Indian culture. The Anglos rationalized that the more the Indians' cultural mores resembled the Europeans, the less likely they would be to oppose expansionism. "Indeed in the eighteenth century the main thrust of education seemed to be to destroy the Indian so as to save the person within."[33] The disrespect with which Indians were held meant that even Christianized Indians were not accepted into White society.

> Christianized Indians, or those American Indians who were educated in the colonial schools, were relegated to the frontier to serve as a buffer between the settlers and the tribes beyond the frontier. Laws in the colony prevented Indians from holding any office, testifying in court, or hunting on patented lands. In an effort to restrict the privileges that came with being White, any child born of Indian blood was termed a mulatto and considered a second-class citizen. Conversion to Christianity did not alter his or her status.[34]

In the colonial era, the efforts at Anglo education for Indians were generally unsuccessful attempts at acculturation. The point of US educational policy at this time was to do with words what was to be avoided by gun – to "kill the Indian and save the man."[35]

Mission education, like the colonial era that preceded it, was a general failure. According to one historian, the failure was due to three somewhat overlapping causes:

(1) the "Indian mission" was to "remake the Indian religiously, linguistically and culturally";
(2) "opposition to his mission by thousands of Indians consecrated to their own religion, proud of their own culture and desirous of perpetuating it";
(3) the role of unscrupulous white traders in Indian society, which generated suspicions amongst the Indians of all Whites.[36]

The result of these efforts was a "small number of poorly attended mission schools, a suspicious and disillusioned Indian population, and a few hundred alumni who for the most part were considered outcasts by Whites and Indians alike."[37]

Tribally controlled education: A light amidst educational failure

Amidst this landscape of educational failure, there was a bright spot. The so-called Five Civilized Tribes (the Cherokee, Creek, Choctaw, Chickasaw, and Seminole Nations) were allowed to control their own education from approximately 1830 to 1898. This coincided with the initiation of removal policies that would see the forcible removal of 60,000 Indians from their native homelands to the western, underdeveloped part of the nation. Probably the Indians realized that, in order to survive, they would need to adopt the mores of the Anglos.[38] Following passage of the Indian Removal Act in 1830, tribal management of Indian schools was allowed amongst these five tribes, who saw value in educating their members in Anglo ways; although financed by the federal government, there was little federal administration or implementation of the schools. Finally, Indians began to see educational policies that actually worked: the Choctaw and the Cherokee established the most comprehensive school system, with a network of more than 200 schools and academies.[39] While the Indians controlled their own schools, they placed a premium on education, often allotting their "removal money" for the establishment of schools. The tribal schools were a mix of neighborhood schools, boarding schools and male and female academies or seminaries operated under contract by religious groups. The Five Civilized Tribes were eager to use native teachers, and created special licensure exemptions for them. The course of study typically included vocational or industrial arts, as well as an academic program and recreation. While the study of English was included, the use of native languages was common in the schools. The goals of education for these tribes was to prepare their students for "meaningful citizenship in the tribe."[40] The students were expected to serve their tribes as governors, senators, representatives or Supreme Court judges.

After the Civil War, as Oklahoma moved toward statehood, tribal life fell into a process of dissolution, spurred by the building of railroads through Indian territory, the wholesale movement of Whites into the Territory, and the refusal of the federal government to help the tribes keep some control of their land. Through statutes that ended the communal ownership of land and the federal takeover of tribal schools, the tribes' control over their land, the education of their youth and, therefore, their future were endangered. One of the first acts of the federal government once it assumed complete control of the schools was to open them up to the enrollment of White children who, in the developing state, had no system of education to turn to that was as well organized as was the tribes' network. The implications for the Indians of this new forced integration were reflected in the rationale offered for the integration: "[t]he Indian must lose his identity by absorption, and such absorption will be rapid and positive; and he must soon cease to be recognized as a separate and distinct race."[41]

The educational losses that resulted from this change in control were swift and tangible:

> ...the documented results of the loss of tribal control over the education of their youth was nothing short of phenomenal: among the Cherokee a 90% literacy

rate became a 40% illiteracy rate within several decades of federal and state control. The primary cause for such educational atrophy ... was the "almost complete alienation of the Cherokee community from the White-controlled public school systems.[42]

The Cherokees regarded the schools as "White man's" schools and saw the teaching of English as coercive. "Cherokees finally have become totally alienated from the school system .... The tribe has surrendered to the school bureaucracy, but tribal opinion is unchanged."[43]

Removing the tribal environment: Off-reservation boarding schools

Almost inconceivably, things got even worse. In 1879 the nature of American Indian education was drastically changed. Whereas previously educational efforts were primarily carried out by missionaries who tried to Christianize the Indians as part of the Anglo effort to "civilize," in 1879 Army Captain Richard Pratt used his military background to develop a military style school for the Native American children, the Carlisle School. "An integral part of his educational theory required taking the children away from their families, tribes, and environments."[44] The rationale was that the sooner, or the younger, that Indian children were taken away from their families and submerged in White culture, the more likely they would be to "successfully" assimilate into the dominant society, in much the way immigrants were doing. In this way, reasoned the Board of Indian Commissioners, the Indians would become self-sufficient and in 20 years time, the federal government would be able to withdraw support. Captain Pratt outlined his philosophy:

> I defy you to find any Indian in them when they are grown. I believe if we took one of these Indians – a little papoose from his mother's back, always looking backward – into our families, face it the other way and keep it under our care and training until grown, it would then be Anglo-Saxon in spirit and American in all his qualities.[45]

The Carlisle Indian School was the first of these Indian boarding schools to open in the reservation-remote Carlisle Barracks, Pennsylvania and became the nation's center for Indian education. Starting in 1879 with the placement, or "outing," of 16 Indian children in White homes, by 1890 Pratt had placed 662 students in these homes. The academic instruction at these schools emphasized English-language skills, industrial and vocational training in European farming and household chores. The Carlisle School prohibited students from speaking their native languages and from participating in traditional Indian cultural activities.[46] In an 1897 annual report, Pratt boasted of his schools:

> [o]ur statistics show that we had 68 different tribes and different languages in our school membership. I venture the assertion that in no other institution in existence are there so many different nationalities and languages as are

gathered here, with the object of molding all into one people speaking one tongue, and with aims and purposes in unison.[47]

Since Indian languages were viewed as barbarous, the retention of their own language as they learned English was not ever considered; instruction in Indian languages was seen as a hindrance to the ultimate civilization process. Consequently, Indian students were punished for speaking their native languages; even corporal punishment was considered appropriate. Indian school teacher Minnie Jenkins recalls that she:

> once had 35 Mohave kindergartners lie "like little sardines" across tables, and then spanked them for speaking Mohave; other punishments included forcing students to stand still in the school's public hall or to march around the schoolyard while other children were playing, and washing a student's mouth out with soap. Even the misunderstanding of English might lead to punishment.[48]

Inevitably, many students were ashamed of their native language as they assimilated their school lessons, which stressed the superiority of English: "[o]ne Sioux student at Carlisle Indian School wrote to the school superintendent in 1887 to report 'with much sorrow' that she had spoken one Sioux word without thinking ... and that she had been so upset that she could not eat her dinner and wept at the dining table."[49]

The devastating psychological effects of the English-only rules on the students, putting aside social and educational tragedies for the moment, were acute. Charles A. Eastman, who attended the Santee Indian School, wrote of his experiences: "[f]or a whole week we youthful warriors were held up and harassed with words of three letters. Like raspberry bushes in the path, they tore, bled and sweated us – those little words rat, cat and so forth – until not a semblance of our native dignity and self-respect was left."[50]

Because of the distance from the children's homes to the schools, many children did not make it home during the summer months but were placed in Anglo homes. The result was that these children spent up to eight years away from their families, returning afterward as strangers to their families homes, languages, and cultures. Yet return they did, for Pratt never achieved his goal of completely submerging the Indian into White society; students who left the Carlisle School did return to their reservations.

At first, attendance at the boarding schools was voluntary, as missionaries convinced Indian families that the Christianizing of their children depended on it. Later, in 1891 as part of the Indian Appropriation Act, Congress passed mandatory education requirements for Indians and since the boarding schools were the only schools available, these were the ones attended. The Carlisle School was just one school that was implementing the federal government's English-only policy. In 1805 the Bureau of Indian Affairs issued regulations that made English-only the policy for all Indian schools:

[a]ll instruction must be in English except in so far as the native language of the pupils shall be necessary medium for conveying the knowledge of English, and the conversation of communication and between the pupils and with the teacher must be, as far as practicable, in English.[51]

All schools run by the federal government, as well as those operated by religious groups under contract with the government, were expected to comply with the regulation. The "course of study" prepared by the Commissioner of Indian Affairs stressed that learning English was to be the main area of study for the first-year students and "by the end of four years of instruction, students were expected to be able to speak English "fluently and correctly."[52]

The boarding schools were poorly administered, often dirty, often located in remote areas, relied upon the manual labor of its students for their operation, taught only rudimentary skills in reading and math, often lacked appropriate educational materials, gave their students poor diets, had an abundance of unqualified personnel, and were often so unsanitary that they became breeding grounds for diseases such as tuberculosis. Because of the competition for students and the Indians' unwillingness to send their children so far away from them, essentially giving their children up to the government, the Indian service resorted to "kid-catching" especially on the reservations of the Navajos. A brief excerpt from one historical account follows:

> In the fall the government, stockmen, farmers, and other employees go out into the back country with trucks and bring in the children to school. Many apparently came willingly and gladly; but the wild Navajos, far back in the mountains, hide their children at the sound of a truck. So stockmen, Indian police, and other mounted men are sent ahead to round them up. The children are caught, often roped like cattle, and taken away from their parents, many times never to return. They are transferred from school to school, given White people's names, forbidden to speak their own tongue, and when sent to distant schools are not taken home for three years.[53]

In 1928 Congress issued a report on the status of Indian education, the Meriam Report, named after Lewis Meriam, the chair of the committee entrusted with conducting the research and background study. After conducting an intensive investigation into myriad aspects of Indian life, the report focused on education; it found that conditions for the Indians were generally deplorable. The report recommended extensive educational reforms, the promotion of health, the nurturing of reservation economies, the preparation of the White communities for the entry of the Indians, adult education, and the preservation of family and community life. The report stressed the need to abandon the boarding school system and emphasized "[b]ringing education to the Indians rather than bringing the Indians to education."[54] The Meriam report was surprisingly modern in its attitude; it stressed that "[n]o course of study should remain static; it should be constantly revised in terms of children's needs and aptitudes; and no course of study should be made uniform in details over vast territory of widely differing conditions."[55]

Meriam, however, proved to be too modern. By 1940, the government had returned to its insistence on the boarding-school solution and complained that the "goal of Indian education should be to make the Indian child a better American rather than to equip him simply to be a better Indian."[56] The next decade saw a continued lack of support for the education of the Indians, with years in which federal money was not allotted to the on-reservation boarding schools which at least the Navajo and Hoi tribes endorsed. Instead, the government gambled that the tribes would begin leaving the reservations, and opted to not fund reservation schools. The gamble did not pay off – the Indians did not leave, and two-thirds of the Navajo children were left without schools; "[b]y 1969 there were still 4000 to 8000 Navajo children not attending school. Largely due to a lack of facilities."[57]

State public schools

As Indian education entered the modern era, the issues that emerged, different than earlier issues but still infected with the lack of respect and forced assimilation that marked the earlier eras, begin to look and sound yet more familiar to today's advocates of language-minority communities.

Beginning in the late nineteenth century, the federal government began providing funds to the states to educate Indian students in their state-operated public schools; since school financing is driven by property tax, and the reservations were nontaxable areas, the federal funds were intended to help particular state schools that might have found it financially difficult to provide for the education of the Indians. Despite specific requirements from the federal government that federal funds be used to retain Indian culture, the states accepted the money, mostly allocated under the Johnson-O'Malley Act (JOM), and taught Indian children only the culture, history and values of the dominant society, even going so far as to use textbooks that depicted Indians as savages.

In the 1950s with specific targeted funding for the education of the Indians in state-integrated schools, Indian enrollment in state schools did climb. While in 1930 53% of the Indian children were enrolled in state schools, by 1970 65% were attending state-run schools.[58] However, "it was common for school districts, particularly before the 1960s, to misuse Johnson-O'Malley funds that were designed to enhance Indian educational needs, by applying them to programs for the school at large, often benefitting non-Indian students more than Indian students."[59] The same complaint was made about the use of Title 1 funds, which were federal funds under the Elementary and Secondary Education Act targeted for poor and minority populations:

> [i]n theory, the remodeled JOM program and the innovative Title 1 program were geared to meet the needs of Indian students; in practice, a large portion of this funding was used for basic operating expenses ... in some cases non-Indian students benefitted more from [the funds] than Indian students.[60]

Despite the federal funding for local education, the federal government was generally unsuccessful in its attempt to improve public schooling for Indians. The JOM program for instance, suffered from many of the same weaknesses that plague the education of language-minority children generally: poor quality of teachers and administrators, hostile attitudes amongst the majority communities, the local schools' interest in funding for the children rather than in the children themselves, and the "difficult" relationship between the state and the federal administrators.[61] "All of this led to a type of education ill suited to the needs of Indian children."[62] From 1928–1973, "the lack of motivation, general deflation and semi-nomadic pattern of existence ... combined to make the Indian child feel there was no reason for attending or continuing school. Consequently, the Indian level of achievement remained well below the national average."[63]

THE PARTICULAR CASE OF LANGUAGE REPRESSION

The forerunner of English-only

From explicit English-only policies mandated at schools to the use of off-reservation boarding schools and the newest trend toward mainstreaming Indians off the reservations, the federal government has either purposely targeted Indian languages for extinction, or has taken careless steps that have led to native language loss.

Reviewing the federal government's rationale for imposing English on the Indians is instructive for today, for the reasoning resounds, chillingly, in the words of English-only advocates today. First, there was the assimilative nature of requiring the Indians to speak English: "through sameness of language is produced sameness of sentiment, and thought; customs and habits are molded and assimilated in the same way...."[64] The government also argued that it would be in the "best interests" of the Indians to learn English, and thereby increase their business dealings with Whites as well as make them better citizens. Only through English could the Indians "acquire a knowledge of the constitution of the country and their rights and duties there under."[65]

Finally, the English language was believed to be a morally superior language. English was considered "the language of the greatest, most powerful and enterprising nationalities beneath the sun."[66] The learning of English was supposed to "work a revolution in the Indian character and to lift them on to a higher plane of civilization." [67]

The war on the words and ways of the Native Americans, a war that used physical displacement, psychological pressure, corporal punishment and the threat of military intervention, achieved its goals – out of the hundreds of native languages that existed in US and Canada, only 211 are still being spoken and only 50 of these languages have more than 1,000 speakers; a few more are spoken by 50,000 speakers.[68] Since most languages are not spoken by children, the threat of yet more extinct languages is tragically real.

The loss of native languages is a loss of resources so fundamental to humanity that we can liken it to the loss of souls or minds. Anthropologist Robert Thomas has noted that language loss means that "'such people have surrendered their intellectual autonomy and independence to another society.' It also means that an entire group does not have an appropriate conceptual vehicle with which to examine, analyze, and talk about its own life."[69]

Bilingual education as an anecdote for mis-education: The Rough Rock Demonstration School and passage of the Native American Languages Act

A reaction to the mis-education of Indians was reflected in the founding of the Rough Rock Demonstration School in Rough Rock, Arizona, in 1966. The Rough Rock Navajo community was the first to elect an all-Indian governing board and the first Indian school to teach through and about the native language and culture. "Until the advent of the Rough Rock Demonstration School, no school had formally empowered parents or the community to have a significant say in the education of their children."[70] Within a decade of the school's founding, and after the passage of the Indian Self-Determination Act in 1975,[71] a dozen Indian schools had signed contracts with the federal Bureau of Indian Affairs to operate Indian-controlled schools.[72]

The Indian Self-Determination and Education Act was hailed even by jaundiced critics of the federal government as a hopeful attempt at Indian control of its own education. The Act essentially provided the legal basis for the regulation of the Indians' control of their own educational and community services paid for by the federal government. The rise of the Rough Rock school led to massive teacher-training and certification work, the development of high-quality Navajo materials, and a bicultural approach to curriculum. The impact of the bilingual/bicultural program on Rough Rock students has been decidedly positive: "[b]ilingual students who have the benefit of cumulative, uninterrupted initial literacy experiences in Navajo make the greatest gains on local and national measures of achievement."[73] The message of Rough Rock and the other bilingual/bicultural Indian-controlled schools was a "fundamental rejection of past educational practices and the reclamation of indigenous language rights and language education."[74] The goals of education for the Navajo students are clear, tribally-based and practical yet stringent:

(1)   fluency in both Navajo and English;
(2)   communicativeness;
(3)   ability to understand the speech, behaviors, values and attitudes of Navajo elders:
(4)   ability to demonstrate clan membership, privileges and protocols;
(5)   ability to discuss tribal government, current events and issues, tribal accomplishment and future.[75]

Various projects have been undertaken by the tribes themselves, without reliance on the notoriously unreliable federal government, to maintain and preserve native Indian languages. From the continued use of native languages in religious and ceremonial rites to the establishment of true developmental bilingual programs, the use of elders in schools to teach native languages to children and the development of home-based language-related teaching materials for the use of pre-schoolers, the Indian response to native-language loss had been multi-faceted, complex, home-based, and practical. In Wisconsin, the Oneida Language Project was created, which involves a two-step program for carrying out Oneida-as-a-Second Language programs in four schools. In the first step, young people are taught the language by fluent speakers on a particular subject. The youngsters then go into the classroom and teach the children what they themselves learned. The children then go home and repeat the lessons learned to the very elders who gave the original instruction and in that way the elders can check the instruction, and the benefits of their fluency is multiplied across the ages.

Whether the unique experiences and status of Native Americans can be used to advocate for a right to bilingual education not currently available to other linguistic minorities is an interesting issue that was given greater potency with the passage of the Native American Languages Act (NALA) in 1990, and then again in 1992. NALA established as the policy of the US: the preservation and promotion of "the rights and freedom of Native Americans to use, practice, and develop Native American languages."[76] The Act requires the President to "direct the procedures to assure that they are in compliance with this Act." That Act also requires that "by no later than the date that is one year after the date of enactment of this title, the President shall submit to the Congress a report containing recommendations for amendments to Federal laws that are needed to bring such laws into compliance with the provisions of this title."[77] Interestingly, *US English*, a neo-nativist group promoting the exclusive use of English by all levels of government, did not oppose the Act and noted "the unique relationship of native North American nations to our country" as a rationale for preserving languages that "otherwise would be in danger of extinction."[78] *US English* took the patronizing position that, if a language has been so victimized by restrictive language policies that it no longer presents a threat to national language homogeneity, then it can be the beneficiary of federal protection much like a cranky child being sent off to bed with a cup of warm but useless milk. Unfortunately, *US English* is probably not the only group that feels this way; preserving Native American languages is seen as a more palatable language policy than defending and nurturing the languages of recent immigrants, since neither Native Americans nor their almost-extinct languages are seen as a danger to the dominance of English.

Yet the existence of NALA has not dampened the desire of English-only advocates to see English established as the official language, and in fact their purposed legislation would not make an exception for the preservation and use of Native American languages. Perhaps *US English* was generous in its assessment of the law because it realized that NALA was no more than a statement of policy, with little funding and no rights or mandates actually attached to it.

The legislative "findings justifying the passage of NALA state that:

(1) the status of the cultures and languages of Native Americans is unique and the United States has the responsibility to act together with Native Americans to ensure the survival of these unique cultures and languages... (5) there is a lack of clear, comprehensive, and consistent Federal policy on the treatment of Native American languages which has often resulted in acts of suppression and extermination of Native American languages and cultures; (6) there is convincing evidence that student achievement and performance, community and school, pride, and educational opportunity is clearly and directly tied to respect for, and support of, the first language of the child or student... (8) acts of suppression and extermination directed against Native American languages and cultures are in conflict with the Untied States policy of self-determination for Native Americans; (9) languages are the means of communication for the full range of human experiences and are critical to the survival of cultural and political integrity of any people; and (10) language provides a direct and powerful means of promoting international communication by people who share languages.[79]

The Act then goes on to outline an official federal policy on Native American languages that includes the use of Native American languages as a medium of instruction in order to encourage and support:

(a)   Native American language survival;
(b)   educational opportunity;
(c)   increased student success and performance;
(d)   increased student awareness and knowledge of their culture and history; and
(e)   increased student and community pride....[80]

NALA embodies the most explicit and sweeping endorsement of native-language maintenance ever issued by the federal government. In sponsoring NALA, Senator Inouye stated that "[i]f native cultures are to survive and if Native Americans are to become full and productive participants in society ... then the United States must do all it can to protect and encourage cultural practices."[81]

Professor Dussias comments that with NALA the federal government:

signal[led] a clean break with the past as far as federal government policy toward Native American languages was concerned. The link between Native American languages and Native American culture was acknowledged not in connection with efforts to destroy tribal culture and assimilate Native Americans as had been the case in the nineteenth century, but rather in connection with recognition of Native Americans' cultural and political rights, including their right to maintain a separate identity.[82]

In 1992, through NALA, Congress established a grant program "to ensure the survival and continuing vitality of Native American languages."[83] The funding was supposed to complement the findings made in the original NALA and help to stem the flow of dying Native American languages. NALA money was given in one to three year grants for programs that would foster Native American languages. These programs included the establishment of community language projects to aid in the transmission of languages across generations, the training of native Americans as language teachers, interpreters or translators for the gathering of oral testimony, recording of Native American spoken languages, creation of dictionaries, etc. The impact of NALA funding, however, is greatly reduced by the requirement that grants awarded cannot exceed 80% of the cost of the project; this means that many under-resourced projects that would squarely fall under the aims of NALA can not be funded because of a lack of the required 20%. Further, funding under NALA has been limited: $5 million in the first year and then, amazingly, since languages were in more not less danger of extinction, only $2 million for the subsequent year.[84] So while the original NALA and the NALA re-adopted in 1992 were specific repudiations of past federal repression of Native American languages, the repudiation may be more symbolic than real.

One important issue that would indicate the sincerity of Congress in repudiating its past policies would be whether NALA can be used to mandate particular actions by school districts. In the one case that has presented this issue so far, *Office of Hawai'ian Affairs v. Department of Education*,[85] the court determined that there was no private right of action under NALA; essentially that the statements of policy contained in the Act were aspirational and rhetorical only, but that they did not give rise to substantive legal rights. In this case the Office of Hawai'ian Affairs had sought to use NALA to require the State Department of Education to create and support more Native Hawaiian language maintenance programs. The court found that there was neither an explicit nor an implied private cause of action: "though the statute does not expressly discuss whether it creates a private cause of action, there are otherwise no ambiguities in the statute from which one might infer an implied private cause of action, even if any ambiguities are construed in favor of Native Americans."[86] Indeed, when President Bush signed NALA into law, he specifically stated that he understood the Act "as a statement of general policy and ... [did] not understand it to confer a private right of action on any individual or group."[87] NALA, found the court, "consists largely of a statement of 'findings' that unique Native American languages and cultures have been suppressed in the past and should be fostered."[88]

The only provision of NALA that might be read to confer substantive enforceable rights would be §2904, which states that "the right of Native Americans to express themselves through the use of Native American languages shall not be restricted in any public proceeding, including publicly-supported education programs."[89] This provision, found the court, still does not rise to the level of requiring the operation of native language maintenance programs; "[r]ather assuming this provision applies to states [and not just to the federal government], at most it prevents the state from barring the use of Hawaiian languages in schools."[90]

Currently, *Office of Hawai'ian Affairs* is the only case construing the scope and meaning of NALA and, coming as it does only from a district court, advocates should not take it as the last word on NALA. Indeed, while NALA certainly does not seem to confer enforceable rights under a traditional legal analysis, it can still be a potent source of advocacy, and perhaps even inform a legal analysis on the rights of Native Americans to bilingual education.

With the existence of NALA, when a court is asked to construe "appropriate action" under the EEOA, it need not rely only on the three-prong test of *Castaneda*. Instead, the NALA explicitly states that what may be appropriate action for other language groups simply is not sufficient for Native Americans. "When Native American students are considered, the determination of whether the obligation to take 'appropriate action' has been met should be considered in light to NALA's findings and statement of rights regarding support for Native American students' first language."[91] Further:

> [i]n the face of NALA's policy favoring Native American language, it is unlikely that English immersion, or English transitional programs for one or two years will suffice for Native American students. Significant Native American language instruction is the preferred remedy or program to allow students to benefit from the objectives or public educational programs under the policy enunciated in NALA.[92]

Advocates for Native Americans have not yet used NALA to advocate for bilingual or bicultural education in a systemic way, so how far the Act can be stretched is not yet known. However, the applicability of anti-bilingual education legislation to Native American languages given the existence of NALA was recently the subject of a written opinion issued by the Office of the Arizona Attorney General. The Attorney General issued a statement that Arizona's newly passed anti-bilingual education law did *not* apply to federally or tribally operated schools, whether or not on a reservation, since the law applied only to Arizona's state schools.[93]

There are, however, many state-operated schools that educate Native Americans. In terms of off-reservation schools, the Attorney General relied on the interpretation of NALA provided by the Hawaiian district court in *Office of Hawai'ian Affairs*, to find that NALA did not pre-empt state law, but only prohibited states from restricting the right of Native Americans to express themselves through their native languages.[94] However, the Attorney General found that NALA's requirements do require that the state make some accommodations for native languages such that Navajo classes should be made available regardless of whether the Navajo children already know English.[95]

As to the applicability of Proposition 203 to state schools within reservations, the Attorney General ignored the expressed purpose of NALA and its acknowledgment of the connections between language and identity, a pre-requisite for legitimate self-government, to find that the new Arizona law did not necessarily conflict with NALA nor with the Navajo tribe's own right to self-government because it only "directs how students with limited English skills are taught to become proficient in that language."[96] Classes in Native American languages and culture could still be provided under Proposition 203, reasoned the Attorney General. Otherwise, Proposition 203 must yield to federal law wherever that law's focus on English language acquisition becomes incompatible with federal and tribal interests reflected in federal law."[97] The Attorney General would not speculate on those circumstances, but said that educators needed to be free to make good-faith efforts to comply with federal law, including the EEOA, without fear of incurring liability under Proposition 203 for failure to implement the new law's provisions.

CONCLUSION

All language-minority advocates and community members need to be aware of the history of discrimination and language repression suffered by Native Americans in the US. For this is a history that starkly demonstrates the results of contempt toward a racial group that is also a language-minority group. The results of this contempt were forcible attempts at acculturation that inevitably led to a denial, even persecution, of the minority language itself. Assimilation is usually seen as a benign concept urged on minority communities, presumably for their own best interests. Yet, the history of Native Americans belies this presumed innocence, and shows how the ugly face of racism can uncover the nationalistic and xenophobic nature of assimilation and convert it into an act of aggression. Advocates for language minorities need not look to far-off countries to find support for their arguments on the devastating consequences of repressive language policies; our own country has implemented these polices, and the tragic results are clear to all who are not wilfully blind.

That enforced assimilation was a failure for Native Americans, as it undoubtedly would be for any ethnic or racial group, does not mean that learning English is not valuable, or that language minorities ought to live in segregated ethnic enclaves. Rather, it means that the true identity of a people as reflected in its language, religion, culture, mores, and values, cannot be oppressed without ruinous consequences. The US government itself finally conceded to that lesson when it passed NALA – it was just too little, too late. We need not wait again for the government to learn its late lessons, we can struggle for identity-protecting policies for all now.

Although Native Americans have a distinct history in the US that is not shared by most language-minority groups immigrating to the US today, both sets of communities must share their histories and work for language rights together. A joint strategy for language rights should begin with reference to the US history of repressing Native American languages, and an understanding of the implications of those policies for language minorities today. Language-minority communities themselves must understand that the struggle for language rights preceded their arrival in this country, and must accept the political nature of that struggle. For instance, it is easy for recent immigrants to become caught up in the argument as it has been framed by the opponents of language rights – an argument couched in terms of patriotism toward their new country, and promises of economic advancement through assimilation. The Native American experience reveals the deceptive basis of those arguments. It is an experience that reveals that language policies are really about more than just pure language; they are reflections of the status of the language minority within the country itself, the attitude toward that minority by the majority, and the willingness of the majority to include the minority within the established power structures as they have been defined by the majority. The urge to re-make the Native Americans into the image of the Whites, which necessarily implicated language policies, went beyond a concern for their souls and was ultimately about land and power. Language-minority communities today need to analyze the present political context of the resurgence of linguistic intolerance and use that information to inform their struggle for language rights.

Native Americans, on the other hand, need to acknowledge that, while they have recently become the beneficiaries of more tolerant language polices as evinced by the passage of NALA, their linguistic rights are still fragile. Standing alone, Native Americans may be able to argue for limited exceptions to official English laws for their vulnerable languages. However, only the Arizona Attorney General has attempted to carve out an exception to Arizona's draconian anti-bilingual education law, and even that exception seems narrow indeed. It may be tempting to think that the US's attitude toward Native Americans has matured sufficiently so that Native Americans can enjoy some measure of hard-won tolerance, if not autonomy. However, I think that faith would be misplaced. For, it bears repeating, language policies are reflections of power struggles and as soon as tribes are seen as threatening to established power structures, as can very well happen with the current growing controversies concerning tribes' operation of gambling casinos, intolerance will emerge again. Rather, Native Americans and more recent arrivals need to work together to make respect the well spring from which language policies are formed. Once arguments are formed from the perspective of linguistic rights as moral rights, and not in terms of retribution, then policies of tolerance are a natural outgrowth, not a cheap compromise.

Notes

1. David H. DeJong, Promises of the Past: A History of Indian Education (American Press, Golden Colorado, 1993) at 200–01.
2. Alison McKinney Brown, *Native American Education: A System in Need of Reform*. 2 Kan.J. L. & Pub. Pol'y 105, 105 (1993).
3. Roy D. Folsom, *Equal Opportunity For Indian Children—The Legal Basis for Compelling Bilingual and Bicultural Education*, American Indian Law Review 3, 55.
4. *Id.* at 65. Actually, Folsom means to blame, not the integration of Indian culture, for that certainly did not happen in the Anglo school system, but the complete denial of Indian language, culture, indeed Indian life, in the school system.
5. *Supra*, note 3 at 58.
6. *Supra*, note 1 at 23.
7. Allison Dussias, *Waging War With Words: Native Americans' Continuing Struggle Against the Suppression of Their Languages*, 60 Ohio St L. J. 901, 909 (1999).
8. *Id.* at 908.
9. *Supra*, note. 1 at 5.

10. *Id.* at 15.
11. *Id.*
12. *Id.* at 6.
13. *Id.* at 15.
14. *Id.* at 10.
15. *Id.* at 4.
16. *Id.* at 5.
17. *Id.* at 4.
18. Charles A. Ferguson and Shirley Brice Heath, LANGUAGE IN THE USA (Cambridge University Press, Cambridge, MA, 1981) at 130.
19. *Supra,* note 7 at 921–22.
20. *Supra,* note 18 at 133.
21. *Id.* at 131.
22. *Supra,* note 7 at 923.
23. *Supra,* note 18 at 133.
24. *Supra,* note 1 at 34.
25. *Supra,* note 3 at 53.
26. *Supra,* note 1 at 35.
27. *See The Cherokee Nation v. Georgia,* 30 US 1, 17–18 (1831).
28. *Lone Wolf v. Hitchcock,* 187 US 553 (1903).
29. *Supra,* note 7 at 30.
30. *Supra,* note 1 at 57.
31. *Id.* at 58.
32. *Id.* at 65.
33. *Id.* at 26.
34. *Id.*
35. *Supra,* note 7 at 32.
36. *Supra,* note 1 at 58.
37. *Id.* at 58–59.
38. *See* Heather A. Weckbaugh, *Tenth Circuit Survey: Federal Indian Law.* 76 DENV. U.L. REV. 845, 846 (1999).
39. *Supra,* note 1 at 87.
40. *Id.* at 92.
41. *Id.* at 104.
42. *Id.* at 87.
43. *Id.* at 106. *See also supra,* note 3 at 55.
44. *Supra,* note 2 at 106.
45. *Supra,* note 1 at 110.
46. *Supra,* note 2 at 106.
47. *Supra,* note 1 at 115.
48. *Supra,* note 7 at 926.
49. *Id.* at 928.
50. *Id.* at 925.
51. *Id.* at 42.

52. *Id.* at 913–914.
53. *Supra,* note1 at 118.
54. *Id.* at 134.
55. *Id.* at 141.
56. *Id.* at 161.
57. *Id.* at 176.
58. *Id.* at 179.
59. *Id.*
60. *Id.* at 193.
61. *Id.* at 189.
62. *Id.*
63. *Id.* at 193–199.
64. *Supra,* note 7 at 914.
65. *Id.* at 915.
66. *Id.* at 916.
67. *Id.* at 917.
68. *Id.* at 973.
69. Scott Ellis Ferrin, *Reasserting Language Rights of Native American Students in the Face of Proposition 227 and other Language-based Referendum,* 28 J. L. & EDUC. 1 (1999) at 13.
70. Teresa L. McCarty, *Federal Language Policy and American Indian Education.* BILINGUAL RESEARCH JOURNAL, Winter/Spring. Vol. 17 No 1 & 2 (National Association for Bilingual Education, Washington DC, 1993) at 19.
71. Indian Self-Determination Act, PL 93-638 (1975).
72. *Supra,* note 70 at 20.
73. *Id.* at 26.
74. *Id.* at 24.
75. *Supra,* note 18 at 141.
76. Native American Languages Act, 25 USC §2903 (2001).
77. *Id.* at §2905.
78. *Supra,* note 69 at 4.
79. Native American Languages Act, 25 USC §2901 (2001).
80. *Id.* at §2903 (3).
81. *Supra,* note 7 at 942.
82. *Id.* at 944.
83. 42 USC §2991 b-3 (1995).
84. James Crawford notes that the Clinton Administration awarded only $1 million in grants for native language revitalization projects. *See* James Crawford, *Endangered Native Americans in Languages: What is to be Done and Why,* BILINGUAL RESEARCH JOURNAL, Winter Vol. 19 No 1 (National Association for Bilingual Education, Washington DC, 1995) at 31.
85. 951 FSupp 1484 (D Haw. 1996).
86. *Id.* at 1493.
87. *Office of Hawai'ian Affairs v. Department of Education* at 1493.
88. *Id.*
89. Native American Languages Act, 25 USC §2904 (2001).

90. *Id.* at 1495.
91. *Supra,* note 69 at 13.
92. *Id.* at 22.
93. 2001 Ariz. AG Lexis 8 (2001).
94. *Id.* at 12.
95. *Id.*
96. *Id.* at 13.
97. *Id.*

Chapter 8
Due Process and Governmental Benefits: When English-Only is Enough

INTRODUCTION

Due process is a flexible concept where the extent of procedural protections is determined by the interests at stake. For instance, due process protections are very high when personal freedom is at stake but can be much lower when monetary interests or privileges given at the government's discretion may be lost.

For language minorities in non-criminal settings, due process is implicated when governmental benefits may be lost, or homes in public housing units are threatened. Since so many language minorities in the US are also very poor, receiving adequate notice in those situations, and a chance to be heard when government services are at stake, are critically important. Central to providing due process for language minorities will be the language in which the notice of an adverse governmental action is made. This chapter will look at the extent to which due process is indeed adequately provided to language minorities and how courts have interpreted the Due Process Clause in these important, but not criminal proceedings.

Whether explicitly stated or not, the court cases reflect four arguments that are often used against providing translated documents and which advocates have not been very successful in addressing. For the most part, they reflect an entrenched belief system constructed around the US immigration experience, notions of self-help and the rigid civil rights law paradigm that allows for little expansion of group rights. They are:

(1) non-English dominance is a temporary problem, resting within the individual immigrant, but which all immigrants have faced and overcome;
(2) language minorities have no history of struggle or unfair treatment in the US so they can lay claim to no special protections;

(3)   language minorities are not necessarily members of ethnic or racial minority groups protected under the Equal Protection Clause;

(4)   the "slippery slope" problem: once special services (such as translations) are made for one group, then they must be given to all language groups because there is no fair way to distinguish between them, leading to an unmanageable, fiscally dangerous language policy.

Underlying all of this, of course, is the sense that in the US English is the "unofficial" official language and must ultimately be learned by all, sooner or later.

HOW MUCH "PROCESS IS DUE" IN EVICTION AND OTHER PROCEEDINGS?

The first case decided in this area reflects many of the underlying issues discussed above, which continue to re-surface. In *Carmona v. Sheffield*,[1] the plaintiffs, Spanish-speaking citizens, sued the California Department of Human Resources Development for operating its program of unemployment insurance benefits solely in the English language. The Department conducted interviews and hearings of appeals only in English, and used forms printed only in English. The specific plaintiffs here, Carmona and Venegas, were denied unemployment benefits and their appeal was dismissed. The plaintiffs claimed that their denial of benefits was the result of a lack of Spanish-speaking employees determining the validity of their claims and the failure of the Department to provide them with forms printed in Spanish. The plaintiffs claimed that the Department's action were violations of the Due Process and Equal Protection Clauses and of the Social Security Act.

The district court summarily dismissed plaintiffs' action without any real legal analysis but apparently found the plaintiffs' contentions too alarming to be taken seriously. The court re-characterized plaintiffs claims into an extreme scenario:

> In essence, plaintiffs' contentions would require the State of California and, presumably, all other States and the Federal government to provide forms and to conduct its affairs and proceedings in whatever language is spoken and understood by any person or group affected thereby. The breadth and scope of such a contention is so staggering as virtually to constitute its own refutation. If adopted in as cosmopolitan a society as ours, enriched as it has been by the immigration of persons from many lands with their distinctive linguistic and cultural heritages, it would virtually cause the processes of government to grind to a halt.[2]

What level of consideration should be accorded those who do not speak the majority language? That question ought to be decided by the legislatures, said the court.[3]

The plaintiffs did not fare much better on appeal to the Ninth Circuit. The district court's incredulity over the plaintiffs' claims had undoubtedly made its impression on the appeals court which issued an even shorter opinion than the court below.

Without more, the court found that there was no violation of the Due Process Clause because there was no "easy means of providing a more adequate form of notice."[4] Seen through this lens, California's approach was a "reasonable one."

As for the equal-protection claim, the court declined to decide whether any kind of suspect classification that would be protected by the Equal Protection Clause was created by the state. However, the court stated: "[e]ven if we assume that this case involves some classification by the state, the choice of California to deal only in English has a reasonable basis."[5] The court's real concern was expressed a little later in the opinion: "[w]e believe that the additional burdens imposed on California's finite resources and California's interest in having to deal in only one language with all its citizens support the conclusion of reasonableness."[6]

The legal analysis in this opinion took no more than three short paragraphs. The court disposed of the equal-protection argument in two sentences, declining to even apply the appropriate standards. This was a clear misapplication of equal-protection law. If there is a suspect classification at issue, then the government must do more than simply provide a "reasonable" explanation. Indeed, classic equal-protection analysis has shown that, once a group is specially protected, then the government must show a *compelling* reason for its actions.[7] Any arguments that plaintiffs may have made connecting language to ethnicity were clearly lost on a court far more concerned with the fiscal implications of the plaintiffs' claims than with evaluating the merits of their arguments.

While *Carmona* was being considered in California's federal courts, another similar case had been filed in the state court system. In *Guerrero v. Carleson*,[8] Spanish-speaking citizens sued California's Department of Public Social Services for attempting to terminate or reduce their welfare benefits when they received written notice of the termination/reduction of benefits only in English. The County of Los Angeles kept track of its Spanish-speaking clients, usually assigned them a Spanish-speaking case worker, and knew that a notice written in English sent to these plaintiffs would not be understood. Plaintiffs brought their claims under the Equal Protection and Due Process Clauses of the California Constitution.

In dismissing plaintiffs' claims, the court noted that the "US is an English-speaking country" and that the state has an interest in maintaining a single language system. The court did not address the equal protection claim but found that, since notice of the termination in benefits was sufficient under the Due Process Clause, then there was no harm to the plaintiffs. Indeed, plaintiffs had a duty to investigate further and have their notices translated for them when they realized they were of an official nature.

The dissent pointed out that the Due Process Clause is violated when the government knows its recipients speak only Spanish and send the notice in English anyway. To satisfy due process, notice must "be reasonably calculated under all the circumstances" to appraise the interested parties of the government's actions. Due process, said Judge Tobriner, is not black and white, but is composed of the relative importance of adequate notice balanced against the burden to the government in providing the notice.[9] Placing the burden on the recipient, however, does not make inadequate notice, adequate. As to the often-repeated concern that translated notices for some means translated notices for all, Judge Tobriner found that the majority of the court was engaging in a parade of horrors. Government need not grind to a halt to provide everyone perfect notice; due process requires a balancing that strikes in favor of the plaintiffs in this case because of the size of the Spanish-speaking population.[10]

In response to the *Guerrero* decision, the California legislature passed the Dymally-Alatorre Bilingual Services Act. The legislation, a model of its kind, provides that state and local agencies that furnish information or render services to the public must:

(1) employ sufficient numbers of bilingual persons to ensure access for non-English speaking persons;
(2) translate materials explaining there services into languages spoken by 5% or more of the populations they serve;
(3) offer translations or translation assistance in those languages spoken for any notices that may affect individual rights;
(4) conduct bi-annual surveys of local offices to determine the number of bilingual employees and the number and percentage of non-English-speaking persons served by each office, broken down by language.

In *Commonwealth v. Olivo*,[11] the Supreme Judicial Court of Massachusetts was asked to strike down the conviction of Puerto Rican defendants who spoke only a little English, were unable to read English at all, and had been served with eviction papers written in English only. The Housing Authority had declared the defendants' apartments unsafe. A Housing Authority inspector visited the apartments four times, and each time found the defendants still living in the apartments. The inspector attempted to explain the papers to the defendants in "broken English" and to suggest places where they might find alternative apartments. Defendants, however, were unable to read or understand the written orders to vacate. Defendants made no attempt to have the papers translated for them, and failed to vacate the premises. Defendants were charged with failing to comply with Housing Authority orders. A conviction is allowed under state law if the defendants acted in a willful, reckless, or intentional way. Defendants challenged their convictions as unconstitutional under the Due Process and Equal Protection Clauses. The state supreme court upheld that trial court's decision that the defendants acted recklessly by failing to have the papers translated when they were literally handed to them and Authority investigators kept visiting their apartment.

Turning to the due process claim, the court correctly noted that, for due process purposes, notice is sufficient if "the form of notice provided is 'reasonably calculated to give ... actual notice of the proceeding and an opportunity to be heard.'"[12] A person, however, cannot shut his eyes to "the means of knowledge which he knows are at hand, and thereby escape the consequences which would flow from the notice of [sic] it had actually been received."[13] The court then needed to address the limited English skills of the defendants: did their inability to understand the notice render them essentially unable to make the inquiries necessary to understand the notice? The court found that it did not. The court stated:

> we believe that in-hand service of an official notice by a constable was sufficient to put a reasonable person on notice that the order was important and, if not understood, required translation. Moreover, such translation would have provided the defendants with actual knowledge of the importance of the order and of their obligations thereunder.... Thus, we are of the opinion that the notice received by the defendants was constitutionally sufficient, and that bilingual notice was not constitutionally required.[14]

In its due process analysis, the court decided to put the burden on the recipients of the notice to translate, although it was clear that the state was well aware of the defendants' inability to understand the written notices. Cognizant of the path it could have taken, the court referred to the burden on defendants, stating in a footnote:

> Whether the agency sending the notice knows, or has reason to know, that the recipient is not literate in English does not alter the rule as stated above. The law does not place a burden on government agencies to ascertain whether the recipient is able to read English, nor does it require that they communicate with those not literate in English in anything but the *nation's official language*, not withstanding actual or constructive notice of the language deficiency. It might be appropriate and advisable for government agencies to give bilingual notice. It is our understanding that this is done in other contexts.... However, if such a burden on governmental functions is desirable, it should be done by legislative action and with carefully delineated rules and guidelines. It is not appropriate for this court to enter *so difficult and obscure an area* without legislative mandate.[15]

I have placed emphasis on two issues raised by the court that appear in many discussions about language rights, either explicitly stated, as here, or "shadowing" the public debate on services for language minorities. The first is the inaccurate portrayal of English as the official language of the nation. It is historically and currently inaccurate to state that English is the official language of the nation. English is certainly the common language, but the court seems to rely upon the invented "official" character of English to stop any further inquiry into the merits of the defendants' claims. The insistence that English is the official language also brands anyone not proficient in English as engaging in a kind of unsanctioned action that may not be criminal, but ought not to be countenanced by state governments – arbiters of "official" policy.

The second interesting issue raised by the court is its insistence that the judiciary is not equipped to handle claims that would take it into a "difficult and obscure area." This case, however was decided at one of the high points of civil rights litigation. The courts, especially the federal courts, but the judiciary generally, were closely involved in school-desegregation cases and in general systemic reform efforts. Conservatives, however, especially state officials, always argue that courts ought not to tread into policy-making roles and should defer to the legislature (usually ruled by the majority, who often have little interest in protecting minorities) rather than attempt reform themselves. Naturally, this kind of thinking finds its most receptive audiences with conservative judges. The *Olivo* court, however, attempted to hide its otherwise-clear biases behind an assertion that the issue before it was more "obscure" or "difficult" for it to navigate. This is certainly not the case – requiring state governments to provide translated or interpreted documents is not onerous, and can be easily tied to the size of the population at issue in order to determine the extent of protections. What appears to be truly "difficult" is the discovery of a judicial willingness to act.

As for the equal protection claim, the court found that, while people of Spanish descent may constitute a suspect classification, the English-only notice policy burdens not those of Spanish descent but "those unable to read English. This is not a suspect class."[16] Therefore, the policy will be upheld if the government has a reasonable basis for its actions. Given the language in the footnote quoted above, the court easily found that such a basis does exist:

> English is the language of this country. This conception is fundamental in the administration of all public affairs.... This is not an officially multilingual country, and notification of official matters in the *sole official language* of both this nation and this Commonwealth is patently reasonable.[17]

The idea that language status is not equivalent to racism, ethnicity, or national origin is an especially difficult one that has been discussed above in the context of *Hernandez v New York* in Chapter 5. The judicial unwillingness to recognize such connections occurs here as well as in *Soberal-Perez*, discussed below.[18]

In *Soberal-Perez v. Heckler*,[19] the Second Circuit also dismissed the equal protection, due process and civil rights statutory[20] claims brought by Spanish-dominant recipients of social security benefits and followed the reasoning of *Guerrero* closely. All plaintiffs in this case had received written notice of denial of their claims in English, and follow-up oral instructions in English. Consequently, plaintiffs either waived a right to a hearing or failed to file timely appeals.

In analyzing the equal-protection claim, the court found that, while Latinos do constitute a suspect class entitled to heightened constitutional protection, the failure of the Department of Social Services to provide forms and services in Spanish:

> does not on its face make any classification with respect to Hispanics as an ethnic group. A classification is implicitly made, but it is on the basis of language, i.e. English-speaking versus non-English-speaking individuals, and not on the basis of race, religion or national origin. *Language, by itself, does not identify members of a suspect class.*[21]

Further, plaintiffs cannot make out a discriminatory intent under equal protection, for here the legitimate purposes of the law cannot be missed: *"English is the national language of the United States."*[22] Again this is an unapologetic misconstruction of the status of English in the US. Although the court noted that three of the four plaintiffs were Puerto Rican and, therefore, did not have to pass English-proficiency exams before becoming citizens, the court made no other nod to the special status of Puerto Rico, to how the status of Spanish in Puerto Rico arrogates against the court's earlier statement on the "national" character of English in the US or to how Puerto Rican plaintiffs might have different, even enhanced, rights to translated services.

As to the due process claim, the court noted the fluidity with which due process claims are analyzed: the notice must be reasonable under the circumstances. Although the recipients could read only Spanish, the court found that "[n]otice in the English language to social security claimants residing in the United States is 'reasonably calculated' to appraise individuals of the proceedings."[23] The plaintiffs in this case, however, did have full evidentiary hearings with translators and counsel present. Perhaps it was this evidence of the government's assumption of some responsibility that emboldened the court to leave the door to possible future claims at least a crack open: "[w]hether due process would ever, under any circumstances, mandate particular documents or particular services in a language other than English is a question not before us."[24]

Since *Soberal-Perez* was decided, New York has re-asserted these due process principles in the context of notice provided to Spanish-speaking tenants of the New York City Housing Authority. In 1991, a district court found no violations of the Due Process Clause or of Title VI of the Civil Rights Act of 1964.[25] Echoing the consistent judicial fear of overburdening the government, the court stated:

> [to] accept plaintiff's contention that as a constitutional – rather than a legislative – matter, plaintiff has a right to have certain documents written in Spanish would place an insurmountable and unjustified burden on the Housing Authority. The Housing Authority, which singly administers the largest number of public apartments in this country, would have to keep track of what language each of its tenants speaks and send correspondence specially translated into each language. In each case, the Authority would have to ensure that each tenant understood the notices received, despite language disabilities, physical handicaps like blindness and mental handicaps.[26]

In an arguable extension of *Soberal-Perez*, the Second Circuit has applied the *Soberal-Perez* principles to the context of a criminal proceeding where property was forfeited. In *Salissou-Toure v. US*,[27] the plaintiff was a defendant in a criminal matter, spoke only French, and was incarcerated when he received an English-only notice of forfeiture. The case is an interesting blend of civil and criminal proceedings with the court deciding, the merits of the claims by relying on the analysis of *Soberal-Perez*. Here, Salissou-Toure pleaded guilty to heroin charges. When he was arrested on these charges, federal agents had seized personal property and $1,150 in cash. The personal property was returned, but the money was kept by the federal government as presumptively the proceeds of drug sales. Salissou-Toure was mailed a notice written in English-only of the seizure and his right to contest it. Salissou-Toure did not file a claim contesting the seizure, as he did not understand what the notice said. Ultimately, he filed a case in federal district court seeking the money taken from him. The trial court denied the claim, finding that the administrative forfeiture was not procedurally deficient. Salissou-Toure appealed.

On appeal the Second Circuit relied on *Soberal-Perez* to dismiss Salissou-Toure's claims. It stated that it saw no reason why the *Soberal-Perez* rationale should not be applied to forfeiture cases. The court went on:

> [t]here is no reason to preclude the application of the broadly stated and thoroughly sensible ruling in *Soberal-Perez* to this forfeiture proceeding. Toure attempts to distinguish *Soberal-Perez* on the basis that the plaintiffs in that case were at liberty when they received English-language notices, whereas he was confined and thereby limited in his ability to have the Notice translated. We are unpersuaded. A requirement that the government ascertain, and provide notice in, the preferred language of prison inmates or detainees would impose a patently unreasonable burden upon the government....[28]

DENIALS OF BENEFITS AND APPEALS

On the same day that *Olivo*, was decided, the Supreme Court of Massachusetts also heard the appeal of a Portuguese-dominant woman, Maria DaLomba, who had been denied unemployment compensation because she filed on untimely appeal of the original denial of benefits.[29] DaLomba had received the notice of the original determination in English-only. Although she brought the notice to be translated to a neighbor who had some knowledge of English, the neighbor told her only that it "wasn't anything." DaLomba only filed an appeal after she sought the assistance of a neighborhood legal workers group. The appeals to the Employment Security Board and for re-hearing before the entire Board were limited to the question of the timeliness of her appeal.

On appeal to the Supreme Court of Massachusetts, DaLomba argued that a Massachusetts statute, which requires that the appeal notice sent to claimant "shall state clearly" the place, manner, and time limits for appealing, would be frustrated by an English-only notice when the Division knows or has reason to know that the claimant does not speak English.

Relying squarely on *Olivo* and *Guerrero* the Court roundly rejected DaLomba's argument: "[w]e do not believe that a notice in English, clear on its face, is insufficient under the statute merely because, as to persons under a language disability it may not actually inform. English is the official language of this country and this Commonwealth."[30]

And again, the concern over resource-allocation was raised: "[w]ere we to adopt the petitioner's arguments in this cases, it might lead to a claim that a notice in English is insufficient as to illiterates and all non-English speaking persons."[31]

In *Hernandez v. Department of Labor*,[32] plaintiff Andomaro Hernandez filed for unemployment compensation with the assistance of an agency interpreter. The claims adjudicator denied Hernandez's claim, based on the employer's assertion that Hernandez was fired because of three consecutive unexplained absences. The letter informing Hernandez of the denial, and of his right to appeal, was written only in English. When the letter arrived, Hernandez brought it to a friend for translation. The friend completely mistranslated the letter. Three weeks after he received the letter, Hernandez went to the agency office to find out why he had not yet received benefits, and was then told of the denial. Hernandez filed an appeal the same day. After several appeals, each of which was dismissed because of the lateness of the first appeal, the Illinois appellate court finally decided that a hearing on the merits of the claim ought to be held. That decision, however, was appealed to the Illinois Supreme Court. The court reversed.

The court found that the case before it was essentially identical to the facts in *DaLomba*, and found that the reasoning of that case and of *Olivo* and *Guerrero* were persuasive. The court noted, however, that the Department of Labor did begin sending notices in Spanish to those claimants identified as Spanish-speakers and seemed to feel that such accommodations are best left to administrative and legislative policy makers.[33]

The preference for administrative solutions to the translation/interpretation issue was explicitly stated in *Alfonso v. Board of Review*,[34] which also relied on *DaLomba*, *Hernandez* and *Guerrero* for its denial of a untimely appeal. The Court stated:

> [t]he decision to provide translation, encompassing as it does the determination of when a translation should be provided, and to whom, and in what language, is one that is best left to those branches of government that can better assess the changing needs and demands of both the non-English speaking population and the government agencies that provide translation.[35]

The dissent in *Alfonso*, however, is a good one. In his opinion, Chief Justice Wilentz was not afraid to carefully evaluate the presumed burdens in the state, rather than summarily assume, as the majority often do, that linguistic diversity is too daunting for administrative agencies to accommodate. He stated:

> [t]he burden on the state to provide foreign language notice of appeal is composed of a number of factors. The state must determine what language the claimant speaks. This may involve training its personnel to elicit this information from applicants for benefits. It must acquire a translation of the salient materials – usually very little – into the claimant's language, and communicate this translated information to the applicant. These requirements amount to dollar expenditures and a degree of continuing vigilance on the part of state personnel to ensure that applicants are properly notified of their right to appeal adverse claims.[36]

On the other hand, the value of translation to Alfonso and to future non-English speaking claimants is great: not only an important monetary benefit but the "right to enjoy the same benefits to which her years of work entitle her, as do all other claimants who qualify for insurance."[37] For agencies there are a number of cost-effective ways to translate the documents used, including the use of "tag lines" in various languages alerting the recipient of the important and time-sensitive nature of the document received. For Justice Wilentz, *DaLomba* and *Hernandez* illuminate exactly what unjust results can occur even if claimants act quickly to have their notices translated.

Justice Wilentz was most courageous, however, when he expressed the growing role and in his words "quasi-official" status of Spanish in the nation:

> Spanish, unlike any other language, has quasi-official status in the United States because of our relationship to the commonwealth of Puerto Rico. Puerto Ricans are United States citizens withe the same responsibilities and benefits of other United States citizens, but schools in Puerto Rico are conducted in Spanish.... Spanish is thereby given special recognition as the native language of many United States citizens. While the majority may be correct that the United States may be characterized as "an English speaking country" ... neither the United States nor the State of New Jersey has established English as its official language. And when, implicitly and explicitly Spanish had achieved some measure of official recognition, the Spanish-speaking population may reasonably expect that information of great importance to their well-being will be conveyed to them in a manner that communicates the essential information required.[38]

In response to the oft-repeated mantra that prior waves of immigrants did without interpretation and translation assistance, Justice Wilentz was wonderful:

> [b]ut the fact that [prior immigrants] struggled is insufficient reason to require others to be penalized as well. Due process is an elastic concept, one that takes new form as our standards of fairness and compassion change with a changing society. Just as it would now be unthinkable for a judge to allow a *pro se* litigant to leave the courtroom without understanding his right to appeal and the time limit for action, so should it be incredible that an unemployment benefits claimant should be allowed to leave the claims office without being helped to understand those rights.[39]

CONCLUSION

Clearly, attempts to expand the traditional constitutional law paradigm to require governmental accommodations of language minorities within the context of administrative due process has not been terribly successful. Courts have allowed themselves to be stymied by the fiscal constraints often raised by local governments as a rationale for not requiring translation. At work, however, is undoubtedly the sense that less-than-fundamental rights and wrongs were at stake in these cases as well. The courts have apparently not been swayed that governmental benefits, even if they may indeed be the difference between eating or starving for many plaintiffs, are of sufficient constitutional import to warrant additional governmental burdens.

Related to this is the notion that, since what is at stake are benefits that no one has a greater interest in protecting than the plaintiffs themselves, then placing the burden on the plaintiffs is seen as legitimate.

Due process, however, is a flexible concept – not only are the rights at stake determinative of the amount of process actually required, but the size of the population affected may legitimately be considered when determining what steps governments ought to be required to take to accommodate linguistic diversity. The provision of translated forms and form letters into the five major languages that an agency serves would require minimal governmental expenditure, but would go a long way toward protecting the legitimate rights of language minorities to services and benefits. For smaller language groups, an indication that the enclosed notice is important or time-sensitive would help reduce the risk of erroneous claims determinations. Alternatively, agencies can make exceptions to time limits for claimants who can show that, because of their dominance in another language, they could not read or understand the letter sent to them. If agencies truly want to serve their communities and ensure that legitimate rights and claims are preserved, then there is much that can be done. None of these provisions would be unenforceable by a court, either.

Courts often proffer their unwillingness to become involved in the day-to-day operations of governmental agencies, and their unsuitability to making administrative decisions as rationales for doing nothing in the social service arena. Courts, however, are the ultimate arbiters of rights, and what is at stake is nothing less than the enunciation of rights – here, of language minorities. Rights determinations are not easy, nor are they prone to simple demarcation. This has always been the case, and that is why multiple factors are considered and why there are multi-part tests for determining not only due process rights but just about every other right that has ever ben enunciated by a court. Sloppiness is the nature of reality, and courts are involved in sifting through that reality to find legal norms. Advocates should not shy away from demanding that courts do in the language rights area what they have done in all other areas – develop factors to be considered, weigh rights at stake and the interests of the government, and always, always check their conclusions with reality. When judicial bias is checked in this way, the results can be not only impressive, but just.

Notes

1. 475 F2d 738 (9th Cir 1973).
2. *Carmona v. Sheffield*, 325 FSupp 1341, 1342 (ND Cal. 1971), *aff'd*, 475 F2d 738 (9th Cir 1973).
3. 325 FSupp at 1342.
4. *Supra*, note 1 at 739.
5. *Id.*
6. *Id.*
7. *See* Chapter 1, "Modern Equal Protection Analysis" section.

8. 109 Cal. Rptr 201, 512 P2d 833 (Cal. Sup. Ct 1973), *cert. den.*, 414 US 1137 (1974).

9. *Id.* at 208, (Tobriner, J., dissenting).

10. *Id.* at 209–210.

11. 369 Mass. 62 (Sup. Ct 1975).

12. *Id.* at 68 (cites omitted).

13. *Id.* at 69 (cites omitted).

14. *Id.* at 70.

15. *Id.* (emphasis added, cites to statutes omitted).

16. *Id.* at 72.

17. *Id.* at 73 (emphasis added, cites omitted).

18. But advocates should be aware of *Mendoza v. Lavine*, 412 FSupp 1105 (SDNY 1976) where plaintiffs brought a class action suit in federal court alleging violations of the Fifth and Fourteenth Amendments, Title VI, and the Social Security Act for the failure of New York City and State to provide adequate bilingual notices, forms, and assistance to Spanish-dominant public aid recipients. The court retained jurisdiction, noting the strength of the plaintiffs' claims while the federal Office of Civil Rights investigated the matter.

19. 717 F2d 36 (2nd Cir 1983).

20. Plaintiffs had brought a claim under Title VI of the Civil Rights Act of 1964, which prohibits discrimination by federally-assisted agencies. The claim was dismissed, however, on the grounds that Title VI was not meant to apply to programs directly administered by the federal government. The court did not engage in an extensive analysis of Title VI law. Title VI is discussed in greater depth in Appendix I.

21. *Supra,* note 19 at 41 (emphasis added).

22. *Id.* at 42 (emphasis added).

23. *Id.* at 43.

24. *Id.* at 44.

25. *See Vialez v. New York City Housing Authority,* 783 FSupp 109 (SDNY 1991).

26. *Id.* at 120. In New York, the issue of whether notice of eviction or dispossession must be provided in Spanish to tenants whom the Housing Authority knows understand only Spanish is winding its way up on appeal from local landlord-tenant court. *See 610 West 136th Street Tenants Association v. Romero,* L&T 01N 67967. *See also Metz v. Duenas,* 192 Misc. 2d 528 (Nass Co Dist 1999) where a local court held that an oral rent demand made in English to a tenant whom the landlord knew understood only Spanish was found to be insufficient notice as a matter of law.

27. 24 F3d 444 (2nd Cir 1994).

28. *Id.* at 446.

29. *DaLomba v. Director of the Division of Employment Security,* 369 Mass. 92 (Sup. Ct Mass. 1975).

30. *Id.* at 95–96.

31. *Id.* at 96.

32. 83 Ill. 2d 512 (Sup. Ct Ill.1981).

33. *See also Alonso v. Arabel,* 622 So 2d 187 (Dist. Ct App. Florida 1993).

34. 89 NJ 41 (Sup. Ct NJ 1982).

35. *Id.* at 46.

36. *Id.* at 49–50.

37. *Id.* at 50

38.   *Id.* at 58.

39.   *Id.* at 59. *See also Rivera v. Board of Review,* 127 NJ 578 (Sup. Ct NJ 1992) (Court ordered government agency to review the merits of an untimely appeal filed by a Puerto Rican migrant worker where the notice of a determination to repay the agency for overpayment of benefits was mailed in English-only. The Court cited to Wilentz's dissent in noting that "Puerto Ricans carry out most of their daily life and public business in the Spanish language.") *Id.* at 588.

Chapter 9

Commerce and Language Minorities: Remaking Old Laws for New Consumers

INTRODUCTION

If public sentiment in the US can be fairly characterized as wary of governmental regulation and mandates that restrain individual liberty, no arena reflects this bias better than the marketplace, the epitome of rugged individualism and restriction-free bargaining. Although there have been significant advances, the mantra of "buyer beware" reflects a persistent attitude in the consumer-protection arena. In the area of contracts, the basic assumption is that the contract is the product of two or more parties of relatively equal "bargaining power" and of similar intent. The burden is on the party attempting to invalidate the contract to show that either fraud or a misrepresentation or duress soiled the bargaining process such that no true "meeting of the minds" occurred and, therefore, no real contract exists.

This chapter will focus on consumer-protection issues as the critical area of the marketplace of particular importance to language-minority communities. There are two important reasons for this choice. First, this is also the commercial area in which there is a body of developing language rights law that must be analyzed and understood. Second, it is the consumer-protection arena that impacts commonplace commercial transactions that most of us handle every day without a second thought. Whether we are filling a prescription or buying a larger item such as a refrigerator, consumer protection laws ensure that documents are written intelligibly, warnings are advertised, and there is at least a modicum of fairness in transactions. The chapter is divided into two parts, commercial transactions and products liability.

Generalized national antipathy toward regulation leaves language minorities operating in the US economy at a special disadvantage. Contracts, whether in the formal sense of two parties negotiating a loan, for instance, or in the informal sense that is implicated between manufacturers and consumers (the manufacturer promises that, by paying certain sum, the product purchased will operate in such-and-such a manner; the consumer pays the sum and will be expected to use the product for the purposes for which it was created) form a daily part of life. Imagine how much more difficult life can become for the language minority when the basic paperwork for contracts to purchase a car, a home, even a refrigerator or a crib for a baby, is in a foreign language if. Even language minorities who are orally adept in English will find the task of reading through the "terms and conditions" of contracts daunting. Store lay-away plans and home delivery procedures alone can become too complicated for some language minorities to even avail themselves of those opportunities.

Relying on the oral representations made by salespeople is the customary route for even the English-proficient language-majority public who do not want to wade through complicated and monotonous paperwork. This path, though, is still fraught with dangers for language minorities. Merchants may transact business with language minorities only in English without the use of interpreters, they may use the threat of deportation on undocumented consumers who want to complain about unfair contracts, even misrepresent the content of documents written only in English.[1] According to Professor Bender, "[t]he Spanish-Only consumer has become a victim of choice for unscrupulous merchants in America. Current frauds cover the full spectrum of the consumer marketplace from telemarketing to home solicitation sales to the car lot."[2] Although Bender confined his remarks to the Spanish-dominant consumer, there is no reason to believe that these scenarios don't also take place with other language groups.

COMMERCIAL TRANSACTIONS

As in the other areas of law discussed so far, US federal law has not kept pace with the changing demographics of its consumer population. Consumer-protection legislation is scanty, generally speaking, but is virtually non-existent for language minorities specifically. For instance, the Truth in Lending Act passed in 1968, secures consumers' rights to make informed choices. The section on the informed use of credit reads:

> It is the purpose of this sub chapter to assure a meaningful disclosure of credit terms so that the consumer will be able to compare more readily the various credit terms available to him and avoid the uninformed use of credit, and to protect the consumer against inaccurate and unfair credit billing and credit card practices.[3]

The legislation, however, does not include any protections for language minorities specifically. In 1975, one New York court held that there was no requirement that disclosures under the Truth in Lending Act be made in Spanish to Spanish speakers.[4] Mora had argued that because of an inability to read, write or speak English, any disclosures made under the statute "were not meaningful." The court refused to read a translation requirement into the Act stating that such a requirement "should be based on legislative enactment, not judicial interpretation."[5]

State law, however, depending upon the diversity of the population and the tolerance of the state, provides some statutory protections. For instance, California's civil code requires that parties engaged in private commercial transactions furnish information in languages other than English in a variety of enumerated business contracts: in home solicitation contracts, in consumer credit contracts, in mortgage foreclosure consulting contracts, in notices of default under mortgage or deed of trust and in farm labor contracts.[6]

Additionally, there are two landmark contract interpretation cases that arose within the context of language-minority consumers and provide some measure of hope. In *Frostifresh Corp. v. Reynoso*,[7] defendants were a Spanish-dominant couple who needed to buy a refrigerator but had little money. The Spanish-speaking salesman ended up selling them a $900 refrigerator and adding an additional $245 credit charge. The salesman promised the Reynosos that it would cost them nothing, since they would end up making bonuses and commissions from the refrigerators sold by the salesman to their neighbors, friends, and family. A retail installment contract, written only in English, was signed. The appliance actually cost Frostifresh only $350.00. Although the Reynosos did not allege fraud, the court did find, on its own judgment, that the contract was unconscionable. A contract will be held unconscionable and voided if it is "shocking to the conscience." The court noted that the service charge, which was almost equal to the cost of the appliance, was in and of itself indicative of the oppression that was practiced on these defendants. "Defendants were handicapped by a lack of knowledge, both as to the commercial situation and the nature and terms of the contract which was submitted in a language foreign to them." [8]

The court ended up invalidating the purchase of the refrigerator, finding that the bargain was "too hard" and "the conscience of the court will not permit the enforcement of the contract as written."[9] On appeal, the court was reversed in terms of the actual price the Reynosos would have to pay, but the ruling that the contract was indeed unconscionable was not overturned.[10]

In *Albert Merrill School v. Godoy*,[11] a proprietary school offering a course in training to become a "data processing technician" sued a presumptive student for the balance of tuition fees due for the course. The defendant, a native of Puerto Rico, met the admission requirements, which included passing a dubious "aptitude" test. However, after completing 70% of the course and paying over $900.00 in fees, he informed the school that he would not complete the course. The student had taken four exams while at the school and never received a passing grade but, after the second exam, had been encouraged by the course instructor to continue and not be "chicken." [12]

The court began its analysis of the agreement at issue by stating that "[h]ad the contract been a normal business agreement between two parties on equal footing, probably at this stage there would be a judgment for the plaintiff."[13] However, in the present case there were enough indicators of unequal bargaining power between the parties to raise the possibility of an unconscionable contract. It is important, found the court, to determine whether "[e]ach party to the contract, considering his obvious education or lack of it, have a reasonable opportunity to understand the terms of the contract, or were the important terms hidden in a maze of fine print and minimized by deceptive sales practices." [14]

The disparity in education between the two parties, a student and the director of the school he wishes to attend, was apparent. The English language ability of Godoy, however, also played a significant part in the court's analysis:

> [i]t was apparent throughout the trial of this matter that the defendant had a reasonable though limited comprehension of day-to-day English language usage. On technical or legal issues, however, he demonstrated an uncertainty with various terms and difficulty in expressing himself often found in people in this city for whom English remains a second language.... In this case the issue of defendant's lack of facility in the English language is relevant to the question of equality of bargaining and the reasonableness of the contract." [15]

Finally, the court found the school's entire admission and assessment process deceptive; proprietary schools had a reputation for allowing almost any student into a school but appearing to be selective by using irrelevant and/or invalid tests for admission in the hopes of wooing students to pay for courses they may have no real hope of passing. The court invalidated the contract as of the date Godoy learned of the results of the second exam, and allowed him to recover the difference between the amount he actually paid and what he would have owed if had canceled earlier.

The lack of statutory protections, however, can lead to disastrous results if courts are not willing to step into the breach. For instance, in *Teran v. Citicorp Person-to-Person Financial Ctr.*,[16] the Terans borrowed almost $10,000 from Citicorp to make certain improvements on their home and pay off other debts. The loan was for 10 years and required monthly payments of $165, a smaller amount than what the Terans had been paying before they consolidated their debts. The improvement that the Terans wanted to make to their home was the addition of insulation. The company that carried out the installations actually had a Spanish-speaking employee who dealt with the Terans, directed them to Citicorp, and conveyed all of the necessary paperwork to Citicorp for them. The Terans went to Citicorp once with the Spanish-speaking representative of the insulation company to finalize the documents. Citicorp's representative spoke only English and made no attempt to translate the loan documents for the Terans.

Mr Teran was a miner and when the union went on strike he had no work and could no longer afford to make the payments to Citicorp. Mr Teran alleged that he called the bank and was told by a bank official that he did not have to make payments during the strike. In October 1980, Citicorp gave notice of default and of its election to sell the Teran's home under the deed of trust. In January 1981, the house was indeed sold to SMK Investments and the Katz family. Apparently, however, the notice of sale was given only in English. The Terans sued but lost twice at the trial court level. The Terans alleged defective notice, willful or negligent conduct, consumer fraud and violations of civil rights. The Terans argued that they were "Spanish-speaking and do not speak, read, or understand English" and did not realize they were giving their home as a security payment for the loan.[17] They argued that, had they realized that essentially a second mortgage was to be put on their home and that missed payments could result in a loss of their home and any equity they had in it, they would not have taken out the loan at all.

The appellate court analyzed the case before it under traditional contract law: one who signs a written document is presumed to know and consent to its provisions in the absence of fraud, misrepresentation or other wrongful acts. There was nothing in the record that permitted such inferences, since the Terans got exactly what they had bargained for. Further, the fact that the Terans may not have understood the documents at issue would have become relevant only if Citicorp had undertaken the responsibility to explain the documents to the Terans and, either intentionally or negligently, failed to adequately provide that interpretation.

Citicorp's representative, Larry May, testified in a deposition that "Alex," the salesman from the insulation company, accompanied the Terans to the meeting at the bank where the documents were signed. Mr May said he told "Alex" that he did not speak Spanish, and that it would be necessary for Alex to act as an interpreter for the Terans. Despite May's acknowledged ignorance of the Spanish language, his testimony that the complicated loan process that he was explaining to Alex was actually being translated to the Terans was not questioned. Instead, the court relied on "clear" Arizona law that the Terans' were obligated to secure interpretation of the document for themselves. The cases the court relied on were between thirty and seventy years old.[18]

Analyzed under traditional contract law, the Terans' claims, as factually compelling as they were, would not amount to much. The court stated:

> It is important to briefly state what this case is not. It is not a case of a finance company taking advantage of a poor non-English speaking couple. Although we may generally be predisposed to dislike the high interest rates charged to persons who must resort to such methods of financing –15.9% annual rate in this transaction – nothing suggests any illegality. Although we may also generally be predisposed to protect a consumer who cannot read, speak, or understand English, nothing suggests that a big, bad finance company took advantage of these consumers. Although we may be quick to protect a couple who, apparently because of a run of hard times, lost their home, there is again nothing to suggest any illegality in what occurred. There are no facts from which we can find or infer that the Terans should not be bound by the documents they signed.[19]

The Terans case is certainly a heartbreaking one, and we can imagine a different outcome had the court been willing to place minimal obligations on the lender to ensure that consumers, especially non-English-proficient ones, understand the documents they are about to sign. Requiring that the lender provide interpreters in situations where a lien is put on a house, usually a consumer's most valuable possession, certainly does not seem unreasonable. Courts could develop a standard that contracts with language minorities must be translated at the lender's expense or the contract will be presumed to have been obtained through a misrepresentation. This would place the burden on the lender, the institution that has the most resources and knowledge of the content of the documents, and would be consistent with the judicial assumption that true contracts exist only when there is a meeting of the minds.

Absent judicial courage in this area, however, legislatures can and should step into the breach. Illinois, for instance, does provide one model for protecting language minorities in an area rife with potential for abuse. The Illinois Notary Public Act attempts to address the cultural issues involved with the Spanish-dominant community's reliance on notaries in their home countries for many purposes, and the fact that the Spanish word for "notary" is the same as that used for "lawyer"–*abogado*. This can lead to abuse and fraud by unscrupulous notaries operating in Spanish-dominant communities who may misrepresent themselves as qualified and licensed to perform all sorts of legal work and charge fees for work they really cannot perform. The Illinois Act states:

> Every notary public who is not an attorney who advertises the services of notary public in a language other than English, whether by radio, television, signs, pamphlets, newspapers, or other written communication ... shall post or otherwise include with such advertisement a notice in English and the language in which the advertisement appears. This notice ... shall state: "I AM NOT AN ATTORNEY LICENSED TO PRACTICE LAW IN ILLINOIS AND MAY NOT GIVE LEGAL ADVICE OR ACCEPT FEES FOR LEGAL ADVICE." ...Literal translation of the phrase "Notary Public" into a language other than English is prohibited.... [20]

PRODUCTS LIABILITY

Products liability is an area of tort law that holds manufacturers and suppliers of defective products liable for harm that consumers, users, and even bystanders, experience because of the use of the product. Products are considered defective if they are manufactured defectively, designed defectively, or completely or inadequately fail to warn consumers about known risks or appropriate usage.[21]

The area of product safety within the context of language rights inevitably centers on the adequacy of written information and warnings about particular products. A manufacturer must warn of product risks when it knows or should know that a product, without warnings, is likely to be dangerous for its intended use. Manufacturers in particular are presumed to have "superior knowledge of the product and its potential hazards." Manufacturers are charged with knowledge of information obtainable from a reasonable inquiry of experts and reasonable search of scientific literature."[22]

A manufacturer's failure to warn, or its provision of an inadequate warning, may make it liable for harm that its product has caused under either a negligence or strict liability theory. When a plaintiff alleges that the manufacturer was negligent, the duty-to-warn inquiry centers on whether the injury was reasonably foreseeable by the manufacturer. Foreseeability has two aspects. Was the use to which the product was put foreseeable? And was the injury itself reasonably foreseeable? In strict liability cases, where the manufacturer can be held liable for the very fact of the injury without reference to its level of care, the manufacturer's knowledge of potential product dangers is presumed; plaintiffs do not have to show that the manufacturer knew of, or should have known of those potential dangers. Here again, however, foreseeability is an issue – the manufacturer will be held strictly liable if it could reasonably have foreseen dangers inherent in its product or in its anticipated use.[23] Within the context of language rights, the critical issue is whether the use of a product by a language minority is reasonably foreseeable. Given the growth of the language-minority population recently, some commentators urge that such use is always foreseeable and English-only warnings must, therefore, be found inadequate.[24] Some courts, however, will inquire into the marketing strategies of the manufacturer and/or supplier, i.e. did they purposely target their product or market their product to language-minority communities such that communities' use of their product was foreseeable?

Some courts have balanced a number of factors when evaluating the adequacy of a warning. For instance, a warning must:

(1) adequately indicate the scope of danger;
(2) reasonably communicate the extent of the harm;
(3) be physically adequate, e.g. large type, bold, capital letters, etc., to alert a reasonably prudent person to the danger;
(4) adequately indicate the possible consequences that can result from a failure to heed the warning; and
(5) use adequate means to convey the warning.[25]

The adequacy of warnings is usually a factual issue left for juries to decide. However, in some areas, such as drug products, there may be some or even extensive statutory requirements for labeling that help to set the standards for what is not only required but may be considered minimally adequate.

For instance, the Food and Drug Administration (FDA) has extensive regulations concerning the proper labeling of drugs. Over-the-counter drug companies must clearly label their products so that they are not in any way false or misleading. Labels must include among other things, directions for use, a statement of ingredients and indications for use or approved uses.[26] Non-prescription drugs warnings must be written so that they can be "read and understood by the ordinary individual, including individuals of low comprehension, under customary conditions of purchase and use."[27]

However, these regulations also specifically require that the labeling be in English:

> All words, statements, and other information required by or under authority of the act to appear on the label or labeling shall appear thereon in the English language: Provided, however, that in the case of articles distributed solely in the Commonwealth of Puerto Rico or in a Territory where the predominant language is one other than English, the predominant language may be substituted for English.... If the label contains any representation in a foreign language, all words, statements, and other information required by or under authority of the act to appear on the label shall appear thereon in the foreign language.... If the labeling contains any representation in a foreign language, all words statements, and other information required by or under authority of the act to appear on the label or labeling shall appear on the labeling in the foreign language.[28]

The FDA has a bit of history with regard to foreign-language labeling. For a period of time it required the provision of Spanish-language translation of patient package inserts on request to doctors and pharmacists. It noted that "the United States is too heterogeneous to enable manufacturers, at reasonable costs and with reasonable simplicity, to determine exactly where to provide alternative language inserts."[29] Even this rather weak requirement, however, was ultimately withdrawn as manufacturers complained of difficulty in obtaining accurate translations. In 1982, the patient package insert requirements for prescription drugs were abandoned.[30]

One devastating case arose in the context of an aspirin manufacturer's written warnings of the deadly Reye Syndrome.[31] Reye Syndrome was a disease characterized by severe vomiting, lethargy, or irritability that could progress to delirium or coma. It often occurred in young children or teenagers who were recovering from a viral illness. The mortality rate of the disease was high and permanent brain damage occurred in many cases. Several scientific studies conducted in the early 1980s began showing a link between the taking of aspirin and Reye Syndrome. In June 1986, the FDA required aspirin manufacturers to include in their packaging a warning about the syndrome. The FDA specifically mentioned the issue of foreign-language warnings. It stated:

> ...Although in the 50 states all required labeling must appear in English, the regulations do not preclude the distribution of labeling in a language other than English, in a special format, or in Braille along with the conventional English language labeling. FDA encourages the preparation of labeling to meet the needs of non-English speaking or special user populations so long as such labeling complies with agency regulations.[32]

Plough, Inc, the manufacturer of St Joseph's Aspirin for Children, included the following warning in its product:

WARNING: Reye syndrome is a rare but serious disease which can follow flu or chicken pox in children and teenagers. While the cause of Reye Syndrome is unknown, some reports claim aspirin may increase the risk of developing this disease. Consult doctor before use in children or teenagers with flu or chicken pox. The symptoms of Reye syndrome can include persistent vomiting, sleepiness and lethargy, violent headaches, unusual behavior, including disorientation, combativeness and delirium. If any of these symptoms occur, especially following chicken pox or flu, call your doctor immediately, even if your child has not taken any medication. REYE SYNDROME IS SERIOUS, SO EARLY DETECTION AND TREATMENT ARE VITAL.[33]

Rosa Rivera, the mother of four-month-old Jorge Ramirez, gave her son the aspirin without reading the directions or warnings appearing on the St Joseph's packaging; Jorge was suffering from a cold or upper respiratory infection. The packaging was only in English and Ms Rivera was literate only in Spanish. She did not seek to have the packaging translated for her, although there appear to have been members of her family who did read English. Jorge contracted Reye Syndrome and suffered devastating effects: quadriplegia, blindness, and severe mental retardation. In *Ramirez v. Plough, Inc.*,[34] Ms Ramirez sued Plough for failure to provide adequate warnings in Spanish of Reye Syndrome.

The trial court dismissed the case on a motion for summary judgment finding that "there is no duty to warn in a foreign language and there is no [causal] relationship between plaintiff's injury and defendant's activities." [35]

The appellate court, however, took a very different view. There was a triable issue of fact that ought to have been left for the jury to decide, namely whether Plough's "failure to warn in Spanish constitutes a failure to exercise ordinary care under the circumstances (because the injury is foreseeable) and whether the warning given was adequate."[36] That Plough was required under both federal and state law to provide the warnings of Reye Syndrome in English at least was clear. The question then is whether a reasonable manufacturer would have provided the warning in Spanish as well. A warning is considered "inadequate when it is not given in a manner likely to reach those to whom harm is reasonably foreseeable." [37]

Plough argued that, as a matter of law, it was not required to provide foreign-language warnings on products to be sold in the US. It also argued that requiring manufacturers to do so would violate public policy in so far as California had declared English to be its official language. The court, however, did not allow the public policy argument to go far. It stated that:

> [w]hile the constitutional, statutory, regulatory and judicial authorities relied on by respondent may reflect a public policy recognizing the status of English as an official language, nothing compels the conclusion that a manufacturer of a dangerous or defective product is immunized from liability when an English-only warning does not adequately inform non-English literate persons likely to use the product.[38]

Most compellingly, however, the court noted that, while there may be a public policy acknowledging English as an official language, there is another public policy at least as pressing: that of informing and protecting consumers. The court could discern no compelling reason to conclude that an "English as official language" policy should, in all circumstances, override consumer protection policies.[39]

The court was equally unconvinced that providing translated warnings was an impermissible burden on manufacturers. Instead, the court adopted a balancing test to help finders of fact determine what a reasonable manufacturer ought to do:

> [c]ertainly the burden and costs of giving foreign-language warnings is one factor for consideration in determining whether a manufacturer acted reasonably in using only English. The importance of that factor may vary from case to case depending upon the circumstances, such as the nature of the product, marketing efforts directed to segments of the population unlikely to be English-literate, and the actual and relative size of the consumer market which could reasonably be expected to speak or read only a certain foreign language.[40]

While Plough, Inc. presented no evidence by which the court could gauge the extent of its burden, Ramirez was able to show important factors: that Plough knew Latinos were an important part of the market for its St Joseph's aspirin, that Latinos were likely to, only or predominantly, use Spanish regularly and that, to exploit that market, Plough advertised the aspirin in the Spanish media. Given these facts, found the appellate court, the lower court should have let a jury decide on the foreseeability of a non-English-literate Latina purchasing its product and the reasonableness, within that context, of not providing Spanish-language warnings.

The appellate court in *Plough* seemed to be adopting a sensible middle-of-the-road course. It was neither afraid, as the lower court clearly was, of the unruliness of providing translated warnings, nor did it announce a new and extreme rule requiring foreign-language translations at all times, nor did it even require the automatic processing of translated warnings in all cases when the product at issue has been purposely advertised in foreign-language markets. Rather, it provided some guidelines but left the question of reasonableness up to a jury or other finder of fact.

The case, however, ultimately went up to the California Supreme Court, which did not agree with the appellate court's approach. Instead, it strove to provide uniform, non-challenging standards that would calm the jittery fears of pharmaceutical companies. The Supreme Court took issue with the appellate court's resolution of allowing the issue to be decided on a case-by-case basis:

> [a]s a practical matter, such an open-ended rule would likely compel manufacturers to package all their non-prescription drugs with inserts containing warnings in multiple foreign languages because, simply as a matter of foreseeability, it is foreseeable that eventually each non-prescription drug will be purchased by a non-English speaking resident or foreign tourist proficient only in one of these languages.[41]

The Supreme Court's reasoning is another example of alarmist arguments often touted by English-only advocates who find such a sympathetic hearing in many courts; namely that "if you do something for one language group, you must do it for all." The Court stated:

> [t]he burden of including warnings in so many different languages would be onerous, would add to the costs and environmental burdens of the packaging, and at some point might prove ineffective or even counterproductive if the warning inserts became so large and cumbersome that a user could not easily find the warning in his or her own language.[42]

The image the Court conjures is almost ridiculous: landfills over-filled with bulky drug packaging, yards of paper filled with indecipherable foreign languages, stuffed into non-prescription drug containers three or four times their pre-translation size. To avoid such harrowing scenes, the Court opted for what it saw as the prudent course: adopting the statutory schema, where English-language warnings suffice, as the standard of care for tort purposes.

The Court's panicked decision was certainly not a necessary one, and reflects again the judiciary's willingness to be alarmed by language issues much as courts in the past were alarmed by claims of race or ethnic discrimination. Nuanced and sensitive legal standards that balance the needs of language-minority consumers and manufacturers are possible, as the appellate court in *Plough* proved; there just needs to be an acknowledgment of their need and a willingness to fashion them. Both the acknowledgment and willingness, however, require an acceptance of a new reality in the US – one where language minorities can no longer be pushed to the sides of our consciousness – and a respect for that new reality that would inevitably lead to the willingness to accommodate.

One commentator, however, has noted that *Plough*'s analysis can and ought to be limited to apply to manufacturers of non-prescription drugs. Since these drugs are so extensively regulated by the FDA, the standard of care required by local tort law may already be met, making judicial inquiry irrelevant. Further, drug manufacturer's products transcend so many ethnic, cultural, and national boundaries that providing warnings in different languages may indeed be burdensome, especially when such warnings are not simple, and cannot be depicted symbolically.[43]

Regardless, fortunately, *Plough* represents neither the last nor the only word on how the claims of language minorities ought to be analyzed in products-liability cases. For instance, in *Hubbard-Hall Chemical Co. v. Silverman*,[44] Hubbard-Hall sold bags of insecticide called "Parathion" to Viveiros, a farmer in Taunton, Massachusetts. The bags were labeled explicitly, indicating the poisonous nature of the insecticide. However, the warnings were printed only in English and did not include the universally-accepted symbol for poison– a skull and cross bones. The label had been approved without substantial modification by the US Department of Agriculture.

Viveiros employed two natives of Puerto Rico as laborers or farm hands. One man could read some English, the other could not read any. During their employment they often used various chemicals for dusting and spraying. They had dusted with Parathion on several occasions and in one week used it four times. On August 14, 1959 the farm hands went to work dusting with Parathion, apparently never using the recommended masks or protective coats. After the day of work, both men were sick. After 6:00 p.m. they were taken in a semi-comatose condition to a hospital. They both died almost immediately after arrival. The evidence convinced the court that in each case the "cause of death was the effect upon them of having used Parathion in dusting operations on the Viveiros farm on the day of their death."[45]

After a trial, and despite judge's instructions that leaned heavily for the defendant, the jury found for the plaintiffs intestate. In dismissing the appeal, the First Circuit stated that the jury:

> could reasonably have believed that defendant should have foreseen that its admittedly dangerous products would be used, among others, by persons like plaintiffs intestate, who were farm laborers, of limited education and reading ability, and that a warning even if it were in the precise form of the label submitted to the Department of Agriculture would not, because of its lack of skull and bones or other comparable symbols or hieroglyphics, be adequate instructions of its (Parathion's) dangerous condition.[46]

Interestingly, this case, decided almost 30 years before *Plough*, did not allow the existence of federal law in this area to circumscribe its own analysis of the issues. On the question of the role of federal law, the court was clear:

> [t]he approval of the label given by the Department of Agriculture merely satisfied the conditions laid down by Congress for the shipment of the product in interstate commerce. Neither Congress nor the Department explicitly or implicitly provided that the Department's approval of the label carried with it as a corollary the proposition that defendant had met the possibly higher standard of due care imposed by the common law of torts applied under the local state law of Massachusetts in actions for tort for negligence.... Nor is it argued that in enacting the Federal Insecticide, Fungicide, and Rodenticide Act, Congress had occupied the whole field of civil liability between private parties in tort actions founded on negligence, so that federal rules of law governed such actions.... [47]

The plaintiff in *Campos v. Firestone Tire & Rubber Company*,[48] was born and raised in Portugal. He emigrated to the US in 1971 and shortly thereafter he was employed at Theurer Atlantic, Inc., a manufacturer of truck trailers. Theurer placed new truck tires on rims before installing them on the trailers. Campos' job was to assemble the tires, which involved placing a tire containing an inner tube on a three-piece rim assembly. He then put the assembled tire into a steel safety cage designed to prevent injuries in case the assembled parts separated under pressure; and then he would insert air into the tire by inflating the inner tube inside it. Until his accident in 1978, Campos had assembled thousands of tires in this way.

On November 1, 1978, Campos began to inflate a tire. He noticed, however, that a locking element on the rim components was opening. Fearing that there would be an accident if the pieces separated under pressure, he tried to disengage the hose. As he reached into the cage to do so the assembly exploded and Campos was severely injured.

Firestone had manufactured the rim assembly and Theurer had made the protective cage. Firestone had delivered manuals to Theurer describing the proper method of preparing tires and also a chart prepared by the National Highway Traffic Safety Administration which included the following advice:

> ALWAYS INFLATE TIRE IN SAFETY CAGE OR USE A PORTABLE LOCK RING GUARD. USE A CLIP-ON TYPE AIR CHUCK n2 WITH REMOTE VALVE SO THAT OPERATOR CAN STAND CLEAR DURING TIRE INFLATION.[49]

Although this chart was displayed by Theurer, it was of no use to Campos, who could neither read or write Portuguese or English.

Campos sued Firestone for, among other things, failure to adequately warn of the dangers involved in putting one's hand in the protective cage during the inflation process. A jury awarded him $225,000 in damages for the failure to warn. Campos had asserted that Firestone should have provided a graphic or symbolic warning against inserting a hand in the cage during the inflation process. Under cross examination, however, Campos' expert agreed that such a graphic probably would not have helped much after all.

The New Jersey Supreme Court, however, found that Firestone did indeed have a duty to warn against the danger of putting a hand in the cage during inflation of tires. Relevant questions included: whether the lack of warning was compatible with the duty to place in the "stream of commerce" products that are reasonably safe, suitable and fit; whether the absence of a duty to warn encourages manufacturers to eliminate warnings or to produce inadequate warnings; whether the danger is so basic to the purpose of the product (e.g. that a match will burn) that a warning would serve no useful purpose. The Court pointedly refused to weigh the additional cost of providing warnings.[50]

The Court concluded that Firestone did indeed have such a duty to warn:

> Moreover, there was evidence that written warnings were insufficient and that pictorial warnings should have been used .... In view of the unskilled or semiskilled nature of the work and the existence of many in the work force who do not read English, warnings in the form of symbols might have been appropriate, since the employee's 'ability to take care of himself was limited.'[51]

In *Stanley Industries v. Barr*,[52] two employees of Stanley Industries, doing-business-as Gallery Industries, were using Kleanstrip Boiled Linseed Oil to oil a cutting table on August 30, 1988. The oil can's label included warnings in English only of the flammable nature of the oil, the possibility of spontaneous combustion, and instructions for the proper disposal of rags. The label contained no graphics, symbols or pictographs alerting users to the oil's dangerous potential. The employees involved were two brothers from Nicaragua whose primary language was Spanish. One brother could not read or comprehend English, and the other was able to read words written in English on the label but had difficulty understanding their meaning. The rags that they were using soaked in the linseed oil spontaneously combusted and caused a fire at Gallery.

Prior to the fire, Barr and Home Depot, a distributer of the linseed oil and also a defendant, arranged to jointly advertise Home Depot's products, including Kleanstrip, in Home Depot's various markets including the Miami market. Home Depot specifically advertised on Latino television, on four different Latino radio stations, and in *Diario Las Americas*, a Spanish-language paper. Home Depot also employed a translator service to convert instructions to Spanish for several of its product lines, which it marketed with bilingual instructions.

Plaintiffs argued that since defendants had advertised its product extensively in the Spanish-language media, it was foreseeable that a Spanish-dominant person who could not read the English-only label would be using the product. Therefore, their failure to provide warnings in Spanish was negligence.

The court noted that the issue was one of first impression in that district. Relying on the reasoning in *Hubbard-Hull*, the court found that:

> [i]n light of the defendant's joint advertising in Miami's Hispanic media and the nature of the product, the court likewise finds that it's for the jury to decide whether the defendant could have reasonably foreseen that the boiled linseed oil would be used by persons such as Gallery's Nicaraguan, Spanish-speaking unskilled laborers.[53]

The court then denied defendant's motion of summary judgment and decided to let the jury decide on the adequacy of the warning.[54]

In a troubling echo of *Plough*, however, a case arising out of Puerto Rico was dismissed despite a forceful argument that warnings on products finding their way onto the island ought to contain Spanish-language warnings. In *Torres-Rios v. LPS Laboratories*,[55] Felix Martinez Diaz was severely burned by a flash fire that was triggered by sparks hitting CFC-Free Electro Contact Cleaner, a product manufactured by the defendant. Martinez was using the cleaner at a Bayamon, Puerto Rico company. Martinez was spraying the cleaner onto parts of a thermatool. A few feet away other employees were working with a welding torch. The sparks from the welding torch ignited the cleaner causing a flash fire that ultimately severely burned Martinez.

The cleaner's container bore warnings in English of the extreme flammability of the product and a warning to keep it away from heat, sparks, and open flames. The container also bore a symbol of flammability: a diamond-shaped warning containing a flame symbol and the words "FLAMMABLE LIQUID" written in white on a red background.[56]

The container's warning and labeling conformed to federal regulations under the Federal Hazardous Substances Act (FHSA), and other laws concerning workplace safety. These regulations, said the court formed a "[d]etailed scheme ... govern[ing] the handling and labeling of hazardous substances" meant to "'preempt any legal requirements of a state, or political subdivision of a state, pertaining to this subject."[57] The federal regulations, however, do not require that the warnings be provided in languages other than English. Subsection (f)(9) of the FHSA regulations, however, notes that, while the warnings must be in English, employers may add information in other languages as appropriate. Another provision provides that the material safety data sheet also required by federal law, "shall be in English (although the employer may maintain copies in other languages as well."[58] In order to prevail, reasoned the court, a plaintiff would have to show that the manufacturer did not meet the federal safety standards.

Under these standards, found the court, the label and warnings on LPS' cleaner container were adequate. Federal law left it up to the discretion of individual employers to add warnings in additional languages. Further, the symbol of the flame on a red background was a "universal symbol of flammability" which filled "any language gap."[59] The court concluded that:

> [a]lthough the pictorial did not fully explain the danger, it provided clear warning that, before working with the product, the user should either read the accompanying safety instruction or find someone to translate them. Absence of Spanish warnings, therefore, did not violate federal law and could not render the cleaner a defective product.[60]

The court cited to *Plough* for its last assertion.

Although *Torres-Rios* can clearly be distinguished from the other cases because it is more similar to *Plough* in the existence of comprehensive statutory protections that arguably set standards for labeling, it is still a troubling case – if only for the fact that it reflects an enormous gap in the creation of federal rules and their real-life impact on residents in Puerto Rico. The court's assertion that Martinez ought to have had the warnings translated assumes that there was someone present in what must have been a Spanish-dominant work site who could have translated the warnings. Although Martinez may have had a better claim against the employer given the federal statutory schema, we need to acknowledge the federal government's role and the responsibility of manufacturers who sell their products to US territories to protect these consumers and workers as well. Puerto Rico has been a US territory for more than 100 years; we should not still have to argue for its linguistic culture to be a consideration in federal rule-making.

CONCLUSION

It appears that, depending on the circumstances and the areas in which they distribute their products, manufacturers may have a duty to warn in languages other than English if the use of their product by non-English speakers is foreseeable. *Plough* and *Torres-Rios* appear to be exceptions to that very general rule where there exists substantial statutory provisions for labeling already. However, this area of law is very much in development and worthy cases ought not be thought of as "unlitigable" simply because of the existence of a regulatory framework. In *Torres-Rios*, a more understandable decision was reached than in *Plough* because of the explicit federal mandate that the federal law be considered controlling over state law. No such assertions were made in the *Plough* context. However, both *Plough* and *Torres-Rios* indicate the extent to which advocacy on federal regulations is needed. When manufacturers send or advertise their products in US territories where English is not the dominant language, expecting consumers and employees, even small employers, to find translators for complex warnings, is simply making safety the hand maiden of economics.

Notes

1. *See* Stephen W. Bender, *Consumer Protection for Latinos: Overcoming Language Fraud and English-only in The Marketplace"* 45 Am. U. L. Rev. 1027, 1034 (1996).
2. *Id.*
3. 15 USC §1601 (1994).
4. *County Trust Co. v. Mora*, 87 Misc. 2d 11 (1975).
5. *Id.* at 14. Other consumer-friendly legislation, such as the Magnuson-Moss Act (15 USC §57a *et seq.*, 1975) designed to protect consumers contemplating the purchase of durable goods from confusion as to the warranties of the manufacturer or seller, and the Consumer Leasing Act (15 USC §1667 et seq. 1976) designed to protect consumers considering entering into leases, simply have no provisions for language minorities and no court has yet interpreted them within the language rights context.
6. *See generally,* California Civil Code and California Labor Code.
7. 52 Misc. 2d 26, 274 NYS 2d 757 (1966).
8. *Id.* at 27.
9. *Id.* at 28.
10. *See Frostifresh Corp. v. Reynoso*, 54 Misc. 2d 119 (NY App. Term. 1967).
11. 78 Misc. 2d 647 (NY City Civ. Ct 1974).
12. *Id.* at 652.
13. *Id.* at 648.
14. *Id* at 649.
15. *Id.*
16. 146 Ariz. 370 (Ariz. App. 1985).
17. *Id.* at 371.
18. *See for example, Betancourt v. Logia Suprema De La Alianza Hispano-Americana* 53 Ariz. 151, 86 P2d 1026 (1939); *Condos v. United Benefit Life Insurance Co.,* 93 Ariz. 143, 379 P2d 129 (1963); *Sovereign Camp of the Woodmen of the World v. Daniel,* 48 Ariz. 479, 62 P2d 1144 (1936).
19. *Supra,* note 16 at 376.
20. 5 ILCS 312/3-103 (2000). In *Leyva v. Daley,* 1988 US Dist. LEXIS 10623 (1988) the Court explained that the Act evinced a concern that "aliens are particularly likely to be confused by the title 'notary public.'" *Id.* at 26.
21. *See* Linda M. Baldwin, *Ramirez v. Plough, Inc.: Should Manufacturers of Non-prescription Drugs Have a Duty to Warn in Spanish?* 29 USFL Rev. 837 (1995) for cases.
22. Douglas R. Richmond, *When Plain English Isn't: Manufacturers' Duty to Warn in a Second Language,* 29 Tort. & Ins. L. J. 588, 589 (1994).
23. *See Id.* at 591–592.

24. *Id.*

25. *See supra*, note 21 at 845.

26. *See* 21 CFR §§201.5; 201.10; 330.1(c)(2).

27. 21 CFR §330.10(a)(4)(v).

28. 21 CFR § 201.15(c)(1)-(3).

29. 45 Fed. Reg. 60754, 60770 (September 12, 1980).

30. 47 Fed. Reg. 39147 (September 7, 1982).

31. *Ramirez v. Plough*, 12 Cal. Rptr 2d 423 (Cal. App. 5th Dist. 1992), *rev'd* 863 P2d 167 (Cal. 1993).

32. 53 Fed. Reg. 21633 (June 9, 1988).

33. *Supra*, note 31, 12 Cal. Rptr at 426.

34. *See supra*, note 31.

35. *Supra*, note 31, 12 Cal. Rptr at 426.

36. *Id.*

37. *Id.* at 427.

38. *Id.* at 428.

39. *Id.* at 429.

40. *Id.* at 430.

41. *Plough v. Ramirez*, 25 Cal. Rptr 2d 97, 105 (Sup. Ct 1993).

42. *Id.* at 105–106.

43. *See supra*, note 22 at 601.

44. 340 F2d 402 (1st Cir 1965).

45. *Id.* at 404.

46. *Id.* at 407.

47. *Id.* at 407–408.

48. 98 NJ 198 (1984).

49. *Id.* at 203.

50. *Id.* at 207–208.

51. *Id.* at 208 (cites omitted).

52. 784 FSupp 1570 (Fla. 1992).

53. *Id.* at 1576.

54. The same result was obtained in *Arbaiza v. Delta Int'l Machinery Corp.*, 1998 US Dist. LEXIS 17886 (EDNY 1998), where a Spanish-dominant worker was severely injured by a table saw that was labeled with a small-print warning in English-only. The court denied defendant's motion for summary judgment, again finding that the adequacy of the warning was a question of fact for the jury. Arbaiza's failure to attempt to either read the warning or have it translated for him did not decide the case, however. Juries and courts must look to the "intensity of the warning language, and the prominence with which the language is displayed" to determine whether the adequacy or inadequacy of the warning was the actual cause of the injury, said the court. *Id.* at 19.

55. 152 F3d 11 (1st Cir 1998).

56. *Id.* at 13.

57. *Torres-Rios* at 13, *quoting*, 29 CFR §1910.1200(a)(2).

58. 29 CFR §1910 1200 (f)(9) and (g).

59. *Supra*, note 55 at 14.

60. *Id.* at 14.

Chapter 10

The Place of International Law in Promoting Linguistic Human Rights Within the United States

INTRODUCTION

As with US domestic law, the status of language rights within the context of international law is unsettled. Indeed, many of the domestic concerns about balancing the interests of language minorities against the greater society's interest in cohesion also dominate international law discussions on language rights.

This chapter will define international law, discuss its treatment in domestic courts and the extent of protections for language rights in international human rights documents and suggest a framework for a comprehensive declaration of linguistic rights.

THE DOMESTIC CONTEXT OF INTERNATIONAL LAW

Language minorities and the prohibition on discrimination on the basis of language are specifically mentioned in a number of human rights documents. Such recognition is in stark contrast to the almost complete absence of such wording in US domestic civil rights law. To have language specially recognized as a separate form of discrimination free from its relationship to race or ethnicity is important, for, as we have seen within the US, the absence of such explicit coverage leaves the burden on plaintiffs to explain and justify links between protected racial and ethnic groups and language discrimination; such links, however, have not always been recognized by US courts.

Still, the explicit recognition in international law extends only to prohibiting pro-active discrimination against language minorities. As with US domestic law, there are hard and fast distinctions between negative rights or non-discrimination rights, and affirmative or positive rights that require minority languages to be promoted or even extensively accommodated. The status of minorities and minority rights worldwide is so fragile, however, that it is a significant advancement in the international human rights area to have at least a clear international consensus that discrimination on the basis of language usage will not be tolerated.

Yet, despite this positive treatment and recognition, there is as much to be desired with respect to the status of language rights in the international context as there is within domestic law. For instance, there is no single human rights document dedicated solely to protecting language rights per se or even to defining either "language" or "language minority." Not surprisingly, there is a large gray area as to whether and to what extent language minorities actually have the right, either individually or collectively, to have their minority languages promoted or accommodated.

Further, the status of international law itself within domestic US courts is a major obstacle to the enforcement of whatever rights might actually be found in international law documents. In the United States, international law is generally treated as an unenforceable statement of goodwill – not binding law at all, but policy or political statements. International law or policies appear to have no place in domestic courts of law where issues of standing, harm, damages, ripeness of claims, mootness and causation – in short, very concrete, very "legal" issues – must be presented, briefed, argued, and hopefully won, before conservative judges or juries. In today's judicially conservative era, just having courts follow and accept traditional civil rights arguments based on domestic law can seem enough of a challenge. Asking courts to enforce international law documents that may appear vague, and where enforceability is questionable, is an even harder task. Judicial anathema to international law, however, need not be accepted by language-minority advocates.

First, it appears that it has been the judiciary itself rather than anything endemic to "international law" that has impeded many of the possibilities for aggressive domestic litigation of international law claims.[1] Such an arbitrary narrowing of avenues for redress of human rights violations ought not to go unchallenged. Rather, wherever there is an opportunity, the judiciary should be reminded that it indeed has the authority and the tools to adjudicate international law claims.

Second, a review of the major human rights documents and the rights they protect demonstrates that the periods of linguistic intolerance in the US (the World War I era, for instance) could and should have also been challenged as violations of international law. Finally, in the absence of enforceable domestic law that actually promotes linguistic diversity, recent legislative efforts to destroy or restrict immigrant-friendly programs such as bilingual education, or attempts to pass English-only laws, ought to be scrutinized under an international law paradigm if for no other reason than to contextualize our national struggle within the larger world struggles on behalf of minorities generally.

WHAT IS INTERNATIONAL LAW?

For the US, international law is the set of mandates and commitments reflected in treaties, charters and covenants between and among nations that the US has ratified or, arguably, to which it is at least a signatory even if full ratification has not taken place.

There are generally two types of international law: customary and statutory. Customary law reflects an international "norm," what is taken to be acceptable behavior by a nation toward its residents and others. Courts find the norms of international law by "consulting the works of jurists, writing professedly on public law; or by the general usage and practice of nations, or by judicial decisions recognizing and enforcing that law."[2] Norms that are called *"jus cogens"* norms enjoy the highest status within customary international law, are binding on all nations and cannot be preempted by treaty. Generally accepted *jus cogens* norms are torture, extrajudicial killing, genocide and slavery. However, US courts are wary of creating enforceable rights from *jus cogens* norms: "[o]nly 'where there is no treaty, and no controlling executive or legislative act or judicial decision,' will resort be made to customary international law."[3]

Non-customary or statutory law would be the rights and obligations found in written documents such as treaties and charters. A treaty is "a compact between two or more independent nations, with a view to the public welfare."[4] A charter is an instrument issued by a sovereign power to a nation or a portion of the people conferring certain rights, liberties, or powers.[5] US courts, however, have created artificial distinctions between types of treaties in order to limit the kind and number of claims that may be brought against the nation in domestic courts based on treaty obligations. So while the US Constitution states that treaties made under the authority of the US "shall be the supreme law of the land" and that "judges will be bound thereby," federal courts have created legalistic barriers to limit the enforceability of treaties to few circumstances.[6]

Not surprisingly perhaps, courts began creating these barriers in response to civil rights complaints about the treatment of African-Americans within the US. In the pre-civil-rights era, the National Association for the Advancement of Colored People filed an unsuccessful petition before the United Nations protesting the treatment of African-Americans; the Civil Rights Congress filed a similar petition charging the US with genocide against African-Americans. Meanwhile, other civil liberties groups filed suits in both state and federal courts challenging racial discrimination in education, transportation, employment, housing and land ownership as violations of the human rights provisions of the United Nations Charter and the Universal Declaration of Human Rights.

In order to staunch the flow of these claims, US courts created two doctrines that were meant to frustrate the wave of suits based on international law. The first is the distinction between "self-executing" and "non self-executing" treaties. A treaty will only be truly considered the "law of the land," despite the words of the Constitution, if it:

operates of itself, without aid of any legislative provision. But when the terms of the stipulation import a contract – when either of the parties engages to perform a particular act – the treaty addresses itself to the political, not the judicial department; and the legislature must execute the contract, before it can become a rule for the court.[7]

At least one commentator has decried this unjustified gate-keeping:

[a]voiding the sole relevant question – whether the plaintiff has stated a claim upon which relief can be granted – courts have fragmented the non-self-executing treaty doctrine into a series of preliminary obstacles that litigants must now overcome to enforce treaties through the courts.[8]

Only self-executing treaties will become part of US domestic law immediately upon ratification.

Whether a treaty is considered self-executing is obviously a judicial decision, since the distinction was judicially created. In making this determination, courts will look to whether the language of the treaty reflects a desire to confer rights or obligations on the residents of the contracting nations.[9] If the language is unclear, then courts will look to the circumstances surrounding the treaty's execution.[10]

In *In Re Alien Children Education Litigation*,[11] the district court in Texas found Texas legislation which denied undocumented immigrant children access to public education unconstitutional on equal protection grounds. However, the Court refused to find an enforceable right to education in Article 47 of the Charter of the Organization of American States, of which the US is a member. Article 47 provides in part that the member states would "exert the greatest efforts" to "insure the effective exercise of the right to education" at the elementary, middle, and higher levels. The Charter, found the court, was not self-executing since it did not include the:

kind of promissory language which confers rights in the absence of implementing legislation. The parties have engaged to perform a particular act, that is, to exert the greatest efforts to advance the cause of education. They have not contracted to provide free public education to all children of school age within the country.[12]

Of course, it could not have been lost on the court that had it found such a right in the Charter, then the Charter could have been the basis of other, perhaps more expansive rights, like one to a free public higher education. In any case, in affirming the lower court's decision, the Supreme Court, in consolidated cases challenging the Texas statute, did not rely on international documents at all, at least not explicitly. Instead, it relied exclusively on the Equal Protection Clause of the US Constitution to strike down the discriminatory legislation.

The International Covenant on Civil and Political Rights (ICCPR) is one of the few treaties signed and ratified by the US that has provisions protecting language minorities. Article 26 states:

> All persons are equal before the law and are entitled without any discrimination to the equal protection of the law. In this respect, the law shall prohibit any discrimination and guarantee to all persons equal and effective protection against discrimination on any ground such as race, color, sex, *language*, religion, political or other opinion, national or social origin, property, birth or other status.[13]

Article 27 states:

> In those States in which ethnic, religious or linguistic minorities exist, persons belonging to such minorities shall not be denied the right, in community with the other members of their group, to enjoy their own culture, to profess and practise [*sic*] their own religion, or *to use their own language*.[14]

The ICCPR was signed by President Carter in 1977 and ratified by Congress in 1992. When the Covenant was up for ratification, Senator Pell of the Foreign Relations Committee emphasized the need for the US to ratify the Covenant in order for the country to be able to continue its role as a moral arbiter of human rights. He stated that:

> [t]he United States plays a leading role in the international struggle to promote and protect human rights. However, failure to ratify the covenant has blemished our record and cast doubt, in some quarters, about the seriousness of our commitment to human rights. Ratification will reverse this situation. It will demonstrate that our commitment is serious and sincere and strengthen our voice as a champion of human rights.... The rights guaranteed by the covenant are the cornerstones of a democratic society. By ratifying the covenant now, we have an opportunity to promote democratic rights and freedoms and the rule of law in the former Soviet republics, Eastern Europe, and other areas where democracy is taking hold.[15]

The Covenant was indeed ratified, but with a package of "reservations, understandings and declarations" that limited the US's recognition of its obligations under the Covenant to rights already protected under domestic law. For instance, it imported domestic Equal Protection analysis to the non-discrimination provisions, noting that group distinctions are permitted "when such distinctions are, at minimum, rationally related to a legitimate governmental objective."[16] Further, the US "understands" that group distinctions in times of emergency may indeed be permissible, even if there is a disproportionate impact on persons of a particular group. This kind of language provides legal justifications for the kinds of human rights abuses documented against Japanese-Americans during World War II. Congress has never enacted implementing legislation and the ratification was subject to a declaration that expressly made it "not self-executing."

Besides creating the distinction between non-self-executing and self-executing treaties, the courts have also emphasized the need to maintain a "separation of powers" between the branches of government and its own judicial incompetence in foreign affairs to legitimize its unwillingness not to adjudicate cases under international law. In a watershed case in this area, *Banco Nacional de Cuba v. Sabbatino*,[17] a commercial case arising in the context of the nationalization of private companies by the Cuban government in violation of international law, the Supreme Court refused to apply international law to invalidate the Cuban expropriation decree. The Court set a precedent for federal court passivity in the face of international law claims emphasizing the importance of the judiciary to not undermine or embarrass the executive branch in foreign affairs. The Supreme Court insisted that the legality of foreign state actions are quasi-political questions best resolved by the executive or legislative branches and that courts have limited competence to "find" international law anyway. The Court insisted on a high level of clarity and international consensus on an issue before it would enforce rights. It stated:

> [i]t should be apparent that the greater the degree of codification or consensus concerning a particular area of international law, the more appropriate it is for the judiciary to render decisions regarding it, since the court can then focus on the application of an agreed principle to circumstances of fact rather than on the sensitive task of establishing a principle not inconsistent with national interest or with international justice.... There are few if any issues in international law today on which opinion seems to be so divided as the limitations on a State's power to expropriate the property of aliens.[18]

The effect of *Sabbatino*, however, went beyond the limited nature of its facts. In the opinion of one international law scholar, "*Sabbatino* undercut two of the most basic functions of an independent federal judiciary: to protect individuals against the power of the state and to ensure that government officials act in compliance with legal norms."[19]

As the 1970s closed, however, greater interest in using international law in the civil rights context grew despite the judiciary's hostility. Presumably this occurred for two reasons: (1) the growth of public law litigation generally with US courts being seen as effective forces for systemic social change; and (2) the growth in transnational commercial litigation in the US courts. The two areas, systemic or impact civil rights litigation and international commercial litigation, showcased the judiciary's ability to deal with sensitive, unsettled areas of public policy where public consensus had barely coalesced and its ability to interpret and apply international law in the commercial area. International human rights work would require the same kind of analysis, application and balancing of interests in areas that, while sensitive, were not considered immune to adjudication.

THE HISTORICAL USE OF INTERNATIONAL LAW IN DOMESTIC CIVIL RIGHTS CASES

Civil rights activists were not completely unaware of the potential power of using international law to try to convince, cajole or embarrass the federal courts into keeping the US in compliance with its international commitments. As noted above, it was the initial use of international law in domestic civil rights cases that ultimately gave rise to the backlash. Yet from 1946 to 1965 civil rights activists did at least include in their complaints, even if unsuccessfully, allegations of violations of international law, especially of the human rights provisions of the United Nations Charter (the "Charter") which essentially promotes equal treatment and respect for individuals regardless of their race, sex, language or religion and the Universal Declaration of Human Rights ("Universal Declaration") adopted in 1948.[20]

For instance, in *Oyama v. California*,[21] decided in 1948, a Japanese family was denied title to their land under California's discriminatory Alien Land Law. The state courts upheld the Alien Land Law and denied the Oyamas a right to their property. At the Supreme Court, the American Civil Liberties Union argued that the land law violated the Charter and noted that:

> [p]articularly in view of the forcible expulsion of persons of the Japanese race from California ... as a war measure, this Court's countenancing of war-time racial discriminations in the *Hirabayshi* and *Korematsu* cases, and the current attempts of the evacuees to regain their positions in the California community, is it [*sic*] the more imperative to hold the Alien Land Law as a gross deterrent to the promotion of "human rights and fundamental freedoms for all without distinction as to race."[22]

Although the Court did not rely upon the Charter provisions for its decision, it did strike down the land law for the way it was applied against the son of the "alien," who was an American citizen, as a violation of the Equal Protection Clause. Two Justices who wanted to see the Alien Land Law stricken down as unconstitutional in its entirety argued that the law was "inconsisten[t] with the Charter, which has been duly ratified and adopted by the United States, is but one more reason why the statute must be condemned."[23]

The Charter was raised twice more, in *Takahashi v. Fish & Game Commission*[24] and *Namba v. McCourt*,[25] both decided by 1949 and attacking west coast anti-alien provisions. Although in the second of these cases the Oregon Court felt constrained by the Supreme Court to uphold the constitutionality of alien land law legislation generally, it did discuss the timeliness for the overturning of the laws by the appropriate court. The court found that, in the years since the Supreme Court upheld the validity of the laws in 1923,[26] much had changed in the relations of the US with the rest of the world. Specifically, the Charter had been signed and ratified by the US. One commentator has said that "[t]he charter should be viewed as a constitutional document and a legal symbol that represents the changes in the American perspective of an altered world and our role in it."[27]

In more traditional civil rights cases like *Shelly v. Kramer*,[28] which was an attack on racially restrictive land covenants, the Charter was used by civil rights groups to stress the international condemnation of such restrictions. The US government argued before the Supreme Court for the unconstitutionality of the covenants, noting that international treaties and documents like the Charter comprised parts of public policy that also needed to be considered. The American Association for the United Nations was eloquent, stating that:

> unless assured equal access to housing and shelter, minority groups are discriminatorally deprived of liberty and property ... and the right to acquire and occupy property without discrimination because of race is one of the 'fundamental freedoms' protected by Articles 55(c) and 56 of the Charter.[29]

The brief argued that the language of Articles 55(c) and 56 of the Charter was a:

> solemn treaty obligation that required members of it to take separate action, but enabled them to carry out their responsibilities according to their respective political and economic institutions and processes. In the federal scheme this meant that the Supreme Court had the responsibility to assure that local governmental bodies, including state courts, did not violate the rights protected under the treaty.[30]

The Charter was also relied on by amicus in *Sweatt v. Painter*,[31] a case brought by African-Americans charging that a newly-created black law school in Texas violated the principle of *Plessy v. Ferguson*,[32] because it was not equal to the white school, as well as in *Bolling v. Sharpe*, a companion case to *Brown v. Board of Education*.[33] In *Sweatt*, the American Jewish Committee argued that the "separate but equal" provision of *Plessy* was anathema to the principles contained both in the Charter and in the Universal Declaration of Human Rights. Both the petitioners and the respondents in *Bolling* raised extensive arguments based on the Charter. The petitioners argued that the Charter provisions were self-executing and reflected public policy, stating in their memo of law:

> The objective of Article 55 of the Charter is to secure to all persons within a particular society the basic freedoms and rights of that society. Basic in any democratic society is public education. The petitioners see no necessity to belabor this point, for whether public education be regarded as a right or privilege it has been recognized throughout the United States as a basic element of government and in our interpretation of Article 55 and 56 it must be of necessity included within the terms "human rights and fundamental freedoms."[34]

Although the Supreme Court declined to use the Charter or other international documents to strike down discriminatory provisions, it could not have remained deaf to the moral force of the arguments embodied in those documents and the watchful eyes of the international community those documents represented. One commentator argued that the existence of the Charter and the Universal Declaration and their aggressive use by legal activists helped the judiciary to couch its, at times, revolutionary, decisions in traditional domestic language and helped shape US constitutional law "behind the scenes."[35]

In 1980, after years of federal courts either ignoring or not expressly acknowledging international law claims, the Second Circuit decided the case *Filartiga v.*

Pena-Irala,[36] which held that the Alien Tort Statute conferred jurisdiction over a lawsuit by Paraguayans against a Paraguayan official who had tortured their relative to death in Paraguay while acting under color of governmental authority. The case was noteworthy because it survived the usual judicial anxieties over separation of powers, and found that a consensus existed in international law regarding torture. The international community's condemnation of torture was clear and express, torture was illegal in Paraguay, so there was no fear of imposing a different standard of conduct. Further, the executive branch was not involved because the legal question was whether victims had a right to be free from torture which was actionable in federal court. Most probably, the fact that the case was indeed a torture case and not one involving less horrific circumstances was what propelled the court to take the case and reach a decision. Although *Filartiga* signaled a greater willingness on the part of the courts to adjudicate international law claims, these cases are still difficult if not impossible to win on international law grounds alone.[37]

Indeed, in a torture case decided in 1995, where the US was the accused torturer, the result was quite different. In *Hawkins v. Comparat Cassani,*[38] a federal district court noted that "there is no reported case of a court in the United States recognizing a cause of action under *jus cogens* norms of international law for acts committed by United States government officials against a citizen of the United States."[39] With that kind of preface, it is no surprise that this court did not find such a violation either. Instead, it used a multitude of arguments as to why relying on international law would not be appropriate.[40]

LANGUAGE RIGHTS WITHIN INTERNATIONAL LAW

International human rights documents contain a variety of statements from which generally-accepted linguistic rights can be affirmed. They include the right to the private use of minority languages, whether within the walls of a home, in correspondence, in private portions of marriage ceremonies or by private groups. Private broadcasting is to be allowed and so is the private publication of documents. The *public* use of minority languages is more problematic, and is generally governed by principles of non-discrimination rather than by specific mandates that minority languages be accommodated.[41]

Even these rights, which are overtly negative in that they do not necessarily require the state to promote minority languages, are open to interpretation and restriction depending on the size of the minority population at issue. Indeed, there is no unqualified right to use a minority language recognized in international law.[42] Within the context of negative rights, the prohibition on discrimination does:

> not imply that there may be no privileged use of recognition of the language of members of national minority, or for that matter of the official language. What is implied by the right of non-discrimination based on language is that, while it is quite legitimate to privilege the official or national minority language, there are situations where the end does not justify the means. It would be unreasonable

not to use other languages under certain conditions and where appropriate, if the numbers of speakers of such a language is high enough, and if the disadvantages these speakers face or the particular benefits they would be denied should the language not be used are sufficiently serious.[43]

The most important human rights document for language rights purposes is the UN Charter, which contains the first significant international prohibition on discrimination on the basis of language. Article 1(3) states that it is the aim of the United Nations:

> [t]o achieve international cooperation in solving international problems of an economic, social, or cultural, or humanitarian character, and in promoting and encouraging respect for human rights and for fundamental freedoms for all without distinction as to race, sex, *language*, or religion....[44]

The Charter was created in the aftermath of World War II with the horrors that humans in the name of states can visit upon one another fresh in the minds of the constituent nations. The human rights provisions of the Charter are considered the "culmination of a long period of preliminary planning by statesmen whose belief in human rights was part of the foundations of their international policies."[45] Indeed, the moral imperative to respond to the recently-witnessed atrocities of tyranny led President Roosevelt to declare his famous Four Freedoms – freedom of speech and expression, freedom of worship, freedom from want, and freedom from fear. He asserted that these freedoms were the "antithesis of the so-called new order of tyranny which dictators seek to create."[46]

Prior to the creation of the UN, the League of Nations had attempted to create explicit human rights protections during the Paris Peace Conference of 1919-1920. The Conference documents were generous on language rights, going beyond just ensuring freedom from discrimination. Primary schools with instruction in the mother tongue were to be established and facilities provided for the use of language minorities. Also, mother-tongue assistance was to be provided whenever minority-language members appeared in court. The provisions, however, were doomed by the failure to include a legal obligation to implement them and by a recurrent problem with establishing norms for positive language rights: a lack of enforceability.

One important language rights case that did arise prior to the creation of the UN, which laid out the paradigm for the understanding of language rights in international law, concerned schools for Albanian minority children. In *Minority Schools in Albania Case*,[47] the Permanent Court of International Justice noted that the minority treaties created at the Paris Peace Conference recognized two elements necessary to place language minorities on an equal footing with members of the language majority:

> The first is to ensure that nationals belonging to racial, religious, or *linguistic minorities* shall be placed in every respect on a footing of perfect equality with the other nationals of the State.... The second is to ensure for the minority elements, suitable means for the preservation of their racial peculiarities, their traditions and their national characteristics.[48]

Unlike the Peace Conference documents, the Charter did not attempt to declare positive rights for language minorities. However, it also did not protect negative rights adequately. One commentator noted that the:

> specific language of the [Charter] reveals the hesitance of the drafters to impose any positive obligation on the states with regard to the enforcement and implementation of language.... No positive duty to implement or enforce linguistic rights can be inferred from the language contained in the articles.[49]

The Universal Declaration of Human Rights adopted in 1948 reiterates the UN Charter's non-discrimination principles and specifically prohibits discrimination on the basis of language. Again, absolute recognition and protection of language rights were excluded from the Declaration. The Declaration, however, does contain guarantees of the right to freedom of thought, conscience, religion, and freedom of opinion and expression, the right to a fair trial and the right to education. All of these could arguably encompass language rights as the only way language minorities can enjoy these rights and freedoms to the same extent as others.

The freedom-of-expression guarantee contained in the Declaration in particular seems to be an appropriate vehicle for implying language rights. The interconnection between choice of language and the First Amendment right to freedom of speech was explicitly discussed by the Ninth Circuit in *Yniguez v. Arizonans for Official English*.[50] In Canada, where Quebec passed restrictive language legislation to protect the French language, the connections between expression and language were also made explicit and were the basis for the invalidation of many parts of the legislation. In *Ford v. Quebec*,[51] shopkeepers brought suit against the province for the legislation which required that they remove the English words from their store window displays even though the signs included the same words in French. In finding that the Charter of the French Language infringed on freedom of expression as guaranteed by the Canadian Charter and the Quebec Charter, the Supreme Court of Canada declared that:

> [l]anguage is so intimately related to the form and content of expression that there cannot be true freedom of expression by means of language if one is prohibited from using the language of one's choice. Language is not merely a means or medium of expression; it colours the content and meaning of expression. It is, as the preamble of the Charter of the French Language itself indicates, a means by which a people may express its cultural identity. It is also the means by which the individual expresses his or her personal identity and sense of individuality.[52]

The Canadian cases are ironic, for they present a governmental attempt to protect a minority language that Quebec felt was endangered by English, an economically and socially dominant language. The language-restrictive legislation that the US has experienced has been just the opposite – an attempt to homogenize by compelling the use of English, the language of the majority. The Attorney General of Quebec attempted to legitimize the legislation by citing to the vulnerable position of the French language because of declining birth rates among Quebec Francophones; the decline of the Francophone population outside Quebec as a result of assimilation; the greater rate of assimilation of immigrants to Quebec by the Anglophone community and:

> the continuing dominance of English at the higher levels of the economic sector.... It is strongly suggested to young and ambitious Francophones that the language of success was almost exclusively English. It confirmed to Anglophones that there was no great need to learn the majority language. And it suggested to immigrants that the prudent course lay in joining the Anglophone community.[53]

While the Court may have sympathized with the province's conundrum, it struck down the legislation as going too far to protect a French *"visage linguistique,"* and noted that the English-speaking community was also a part of the province and could not be eliminated from the visual image of Quebec. The Court, however, did indicate that requiring bilingualism as opposed to the exclusive use of French would be a constitutionally appropriate means to the end sought by the province.

Importantly, the Court also found that the Charter of the French Language violated the guarantee against discrimination based on language in the Quebec Charter of Human Rights and Freedoms. Analyzed under what we would call a disparate-impact rubric, because no language was specifically discriminated against, the Court found that the Charter has the effect "of impinging differentially on different classes of persons according to their language of use." The right impinged on, as discussed above, is the right to freedom of expression.[54]

In *Singer v. Quebec,*[55] the Court explained the freedom of expression more fully, pointing out that the freedom "[e]xtends to protect the freedom to express oneself in the language of one's choice but it does not extend to guarantee a right to express onself exclusively in one's own language."[56] Therefore, provisions of the Charter of the French Language that require bilingualism, while they may prove to be more onerous for non-bilingual anglophones to comply with, do not impair a recognized right.

International courts charged with interpreting the freedom of expression provisions in the Declaration and in the International Covenant on Civil and Political Rights, which also contains an "expression" clause, have not been as clear as the Canadian courts. In cases arising in France concerning the accommodation of Breton, the United National Human Rights Committee repeatedly rejected the complainants' charge that the government should have accommodated their preferences for Breton on official forms, despite the fact that they were also proficient in French.[57] Although these cases were brought as freedom-of-expression cases and dismissed on those grounds, they probably should have been decided as attempts to enforce unrecognized positive linguistic rights.[58]

In addition to the freedom-of-expression clause, the International Covenant on Civil and Political Rights also specifically set out minimal guarantees concerning the use of minority languages in the context of criminal prosecutions. Article 14(3) states in part:

> In the determination of any criminal charge against him, everyone shall be enti-
> tled to the following minimal guarantees, in full equality:
>
> (a)   To be informed promptly and in detail in a language which he under-
> stands of the nature and cause of the charge against him;
>
> ...
>
> (f)   To have the free assistance of an interpreter if he cannot understand or
> speak the language used in court.... [59]

No balancing tests or competing interests are allowed to restrict or limit these very basic rights. This is significant, as it appears to be the only situation in which language rights are so explicitly and completely protected in international law. Under all other circumstances, however, if positive rights exist at all, they are circumscribed by the size of the language-minority population and the costs to the state in the accommodation.

Article 27 of the Covenant, however, does contain interesting language that appears to recognize the right of established groups of linguistic minorities to use their language *collectively* or within *language minority groups*. Article 27 states that:

> [i]n those States in which ethnic, religious, or linguistic minorities exist, persons
> belonging to such minorities shall not be denied the right, in community with
> the other members of their groups, to enjoy their own culture, to profess and
> practice their own religion, or to use their own language. [60]

The use of the term "language minorities" in this context, however, appears to exclude immigrants to a nation or non-indigenous groups. Such a distinction does not appear to be justifiable from a human rights perspective and minimally would run afoul of Equal Protection guarantees in the US if enforcement for only certain ethnic groups was attempted.

In a study conducted by the UN's Sub-Commission on the Prevention of Discrimination and Protection of Minorities in 1967, the policies of nations towards their linguistic minorities were analyzed: four basic approaches to language rights were described that are probably valid today as well:

(1)   To declare all the languages spoken by the main linguistic groups, national languages. Examples of these countries were Switzerland, Belgium and Singapore.
(2)   The designation of some minority languages as official. Countries that followed this path included Finland, Israel, New Zealand, and Canada.
(3)   The granting of official status to some minority languages at the regional level only. These countries included Austria, Italy, Iraq, Ghana, and Nigeria.
(4)   The refusal to grant minority languages any official status while protecting their use by national laws, treaties or constitutions. The US, Sweden, Denmark,

Bulgaria, Poland, and Sri Lanka were examples of countries following this approach.

Importantly, but not surprisingly, the sub-commission study and report identified the use of the mother tongue in schools as the most important factor contributing to the continued vitality of mother tongues:

> According to the study, the capacity of a linguistic group to survive as a cultural group is critically dependent upon their use of the minority language in education. Thus, the study suggested an intrinsic connection between the right to an education and the right to use one's own language.[61]

Despite the report's findings, the use and support of mother tongue education varies widely from nation to nation – some states allow language minorities to establish their own private schools, others guarantee some level of mother tongue instruction in the primary levels. Others completely ignore or purposely oppress minority languages. Almost none provides mother-tongue instruction at the secondary levels.[62]

The study came to a sobering conclusion about language rights, however:

> ...violation of the principles of equality and non-discrimination ... are the only aspects of minority rights which can be remedied by the ordinary courts. No avenues of recourse of a judicial character are provided for violations of the rights of members of ethnic and linguistic groups to enjoy their own culture and use their mother tongue.[63]

Such a depressing, even if accurate, account of the state of international linguistic rights, however, ought not to be taken as all that can be achieved in the creation and enforcement of linguistic human rights. What is lacking is simple: the will to hold nations accountable. Creation of enforceable rights, even positive rights, is possible – as will be discussed below.

In addition to the charters and declarations discussed above, arguably language rights can be covered by other international documents that protect cultural rights and the rights of indigenous populations. For practical purposes, the US has not ratified these other minority rights documents.

Interestingly, language minorities are not included in two human rights documents that could have offered additional measures of protection – the Convention on the Prevention and Punishment of the Crime of Genocide adopted in 1956, and the International Convention on the Elimination of All Forms of Racial Discrimination adopted in 1966. Giving such short shrift to language minorities in these important documents is simply unacceptable, and seems inexplicable. However, the decision to eliminate language minorities was at least partly explained during the development of the Convention on Genocide: "linguistic minorities are not ordinarily in danger of physical extinction and that acts aimed at destroying the institutions should be dealt with in a separate treaty for the protection of minorities."[64] Of course, no such document on language rights has yet been created.

TOWARD A COMPREHENSIVE DECLARATION OF LINGUISTIC HUMAN RIGHTS

The legal scholar, Joseph Gromacki, created a draft declaration of linguistic rights that he felt would fill in the holes left by the existing international documents which did not fully, or even minimally, protect language minorities in their own right.[65] In doing so he attempted to balance the interests of individual language minorities, minority groups and the greater state while creating more concrete, enforceable rights. His proposed declaration is quite good and provides a wonderful starting point for re-imagining the directions in which international and domestic law can go to protect language rights.

Gromacki's declaration begins by noting that the international human rights documents in existence all "share a crucial linguistic dimension."[66] He then goes on to state that the need is clear for the provision of "explicit legal guarantees for linguistic rights to individuals and groups."[67] He delineates in some detail the rights that are to be protected, such as the right of an arrested person to be informed of the reasons for the arrest "in a language in which he or she understands,"[68] and the right to have a free interpreter in court.[69] The other rights are less specific in substance but are meant to ensure that language minorities are not subjected to differential treatment, discrimination or repression because of their language, nor can their use of a minority language be curtailed.[70] The provision on education states that:

> [a]ll persons have the right, either individually or collectively, to use their own language for the purpose of education to establish their own schools and, whenever possible, to receive teaching in their own language.[71]

Also, perhaps most generously and, consequently, most ambiguously, Gromacki defines the right to free expression as including the "freedoms of speech and expression in one's own language ... the right of all persons to seek, receive, and impart information and ideas of all kinds, through utilization of all forms of communication, in one's own language."[72] Yet Gromacki limits these basic human rights and places their enforcement within the context of national legislation. So, barring extreme violations of international norms (such as not providing interpretation services during criminal proceedings), Gromacki's declaration could not be the basis for greater domestic linguistic rights than those already recognized by nations. Specifically, his draft declaration states: "[t]hese freedoms shall be exercised in accordance with national legislation and all relevant international human rights instruments," which is unnecessarily limiting.[73]

The substance of Gromacki's declaration, however, is right. First with regard to negative rights, language minorities are not to be subject to discrimination based on their language, and they are to be treated, in all respects, the same as members of language majorities. With regard to defining discrimination, I would suggest the Canadian and US disparate-impact model: when a policy, practice or rule impacts more heavily on a language-minority group than on members of the language majority, then the practice is presumptively discriminatory. A nation, or a political subdivision of that nation, can overcome this presumption only by showing that there was a compelling governmental interest to be served which could not be met by any less discriminatory means.

Gromacki also correctly sets forth the substance with regard to positive rights. There is a right to translation assistance in criminal proceedings that no governmental interest should be allowed to overcome. When we leave the criminal context, however, his language becomes less certain. Substantive rights are spelled out within the context of freedom of speech and expression but they need be implemented only to the extent national legislation already provides for them. This does take some countries a long way – it defines minority language use as a right many countries already recognize at least for language majorities, as a part of freedom of speech. To the extent national legislation implementing such a right already exists, then we assume that it would apply to language minorities as well. The difficulty Gromacki tries to tackle, and which language rights advocates always face, is how to come up with a document that reflects enforceable and concrete rights, but which nations would be willing to ratify.

Minimally, other rights in addition to the right to translation assistance in criminal proceedings ought to be guaranteed without regard to the burdens on nations. Such rights include the right to vote and otherwise participate in the political processes of nations and their political sub-divisions. The right to access government should be made explicit as well. Here, "access" would mean the right to petition the government for redress of grievances with whatever translation/interpretation accommodations are necessary. When social services are involved, some line-drawing probably would be required. Minorities that make up a substantial part of a nation (this would vary depending upon the size of the nation) should expect to have governmental documents and services provided in their native language. Smaller groups should also be accommodated, but the accommodation may be less comprehensive if the nation or a political subdivision can show that it would be a burden to the government to provide more comprehensive services. By "comprehensive," I mean that actual bilingual people, not just documents, are available to assist members of the language-minority community. The government will not be excused from providing comprehensive services if the reason such services cannot be provided is that the government has engaged in such a pattern or practice of discrimination against the language-minority community at issue that there is a shortage of skilled speakers of the community's minority language. At all times the government should document its efforts, in the words of Gromacki: "to create favorable conditions for the full exercise of linguistic rights" and to allow language minorities to "participate fully on an equitable basis in the cultural, religious, social, economic, and political life of the state in which they reside."[74]

Schooling, one of the most difficult issues for language-rights activists to handle well, should be addressed explicitly. The research completed both domestically in the US and internationally by Capotorti indicates that, without native-language schooling, minority languages cannot retain their vitality. The continued survival of languages must be seen as a fundamental human rights concern that cannot be abrogated without a compelling governmental interest. Therefore, as in the social services realm, governments must provide free public native-language schooling, to the same extent it is provided to members of the language-majority groups, to members of substantial language minorities who would like such instruction. At no time is this to be used as an excuse to provide segregated inferior education to language minorities, or an excuse not to provide training in the majority language. Bilingualism, which ought to be a goal of all public education, can begin to be realized with language minorities. Smaller language-minority groups should receive instruction in the majority language and should be taught or have their native language reinforced in special native-language classes akin to foreign-language classes for majority students. Again, patterns or practices of discrimination that make it impossible to provide native-language instruction are not acceptable and nations must demonstrate what steps they take to ensure language minorities are given opportunities to participate equally in all aspects of national life.

This is just a framework for providing a more comprehensive international approach to linguistic rights than what is currently available, and may be flexible enough for nations to ratify. Strong international documents that protect language minorities can be useful in domestic US courts, even if our federal courts are loath to enforce international rights documents. With more anti-bilingual education legislation being passed and judicially upheld each year, it is critically important for language rights activists to have another tool in their struggle. International law, to the extent it shows that the US is out of step both politically and legally with international human rights norms, might be just that tool.

CONCLUSION

The world of international law is both inspiring and frustrating. The covenants on human, civic, and political rights seem to contain all those good things of which humans are possible made manifest in legally cognizable forms. On the other hand, those documents are so much more aspirational than realistic, more hopeful than practical. They seem almost to have been created with the intention that they will never actually be used to hold nations accountable. Unfortunately, as this chapter demonstrates, it is difficult to convince US domestic courts to enforce international human rights documents on behalf of national minorities. By erecting false barriers to enforcement, such as distinctions between kinds of treaties and needlessly limiting their remedial powers, domestic courts have effectively marginalized international law. This is truly regrettable since it not only deprives national minorities of another needed avenue for relief, but also limits public knowledge of international norms of behavior – a valuable tool for evaluating US domestic polices and for community education and empowerment.

For language rights, persuading courts to enforce international rights documents is just the first step toward the greater recognition of these rights in the international field. As discussed above, there is no single document recognizing language rights at all. The proposed declaration of linguistic rights is a nice first step toward ensuring that language rights be enumerated and specifically protected, both worldwide and domestically. Agitating for the creation of such a document may have great educational implications. To discuss language rights within our own borders beyond the narrow, parochial battle of bilingual education is sorely needed and would shed necessary light on worldwide approaches to language and bilingual public schooling. Much work needs to be done to popularize the concept of language rights, even within minority communities, before they can be realized on paper. Discussing a potential human rights document on language and even discussing how the courts have generally reacted to human rights complaints is a extremely worthwhile if for no other reason than for language-minority communities to know that they are not alone and that the world holds a stake in the resolution of these issues.

Notes

1. *See generally,* Harold Hongjun Koh, *Transnational Public Law Litigation*, 100 YALE L J 2347 (1991).
2. *United States v. Smith*, 18 US 153, 160–61 (1820).
3. *Matter of Extradition of Cheung*, 968 FSupp 791 (Conn. DC 1997), *quoting The Paquete Habana*, 175 US 677, 700 (1900).
4. Henry Campbell Black, BLACK'S LAW DICTIONARY 5th edn (West Pub. Co. St Paul, MN, 1979).
5. *Id.*
6. *See* US CONSTITUTION Article VI. Since treaties may be modified by subsequent statutes or other executive agreements, they do not pre-empt federal law or the Constitution. *See Hawkins v. Comparet-Cassani* 73 FSupp 2nd 1244 (CD Cal. 1995).
7. *Foster v. Nielson*, 27 US 253, 314 (1829).
8. *See supra*, note 1 at 2361. One federal trial court did note that "federal courts have the authority to imply the existence of a private right of action for violations of *jus cogens* norms of international law in the absence of self-execution of a treaty. *See also White v. Paulsen*, 997 FSupp 1380, 1383 (ED Wash. 1998). Yet even the *White* court did not sustain an international law claim.
9. *See People v. Saipan v. US Department of Interior,* 502 F2d 90, 101 (9th Cir 1974). The Ninth Circuit developed a four-part test to determine whether a treaty is self-executing. The test requires an analysis of:
   (1) the purposes of the treaty;
   (2) the existence of domestic alternatives;
   (3) the availability and feasability of alternative enforcement methods;
   (4) the immediate and long range social impact of self- or non-execution.
10. *See Sei Fuji v. State*, 38 Cal. 2d 718, 721–22 (1952).
11. 501 FSupp 544 (Texas DC 1980), *aff'd, Plyler v. Doe*, 457 US 202 (1982).
12. *Id.* at 590.
13. INTERNATIONAL COVENANT ON CIVIL AND POLITICAL RIGHTS (hereafter ICCPR) 1977, Article 26, 999 UNTS 17 (emphasis added).
14. ICCPR Article 27 (emphasis added).

15.   138 Cong. Rec. S4781-01 (1992).

16.   *Id.*

17.   376 US 398 (1964).

18.   *Id.* at 428–429.

19.   *Supra,* note 1 at 2363.

20.   *Supra,* note 13 at Art. 1(3), Art. 15, Art. 55, Art. 76 of the UN Charter.

21.   332 US 633 (1948).

22.   Brief for the American Civil Liberties Union as *amicus curiae* on the *writ of certiorari* at 13–14.

23.   *Supra,* note 21 at 673.

24.   334 US 410 (1948).

25.   185 Ore. 579, 204 P2d 569 (Sup. Ct 1949).

26.   *Terrace v. Thompson,* 263 US 197 (1923).

27.   Bert B. Lockwood, *The United Nations Charter and the United States Civil Rights Litigation.* 69 Iowa L. Rev. 901, 948 (1984).

28.   245 US 60 (1917).

29.   Brief for the American Association for the United Nations as *amicus curiae.*

30.   *Supra,* at 934.

31.   339 US 629 (1950).

32.   163 US537 (1896).

33.   347 US 483 (1954).

34.   *Memorandum of Law for Petitioners at 57–58.*

35.   *See supra,* note 27 generally.

36.   630 F2d 876 (2nd Cir 1980).

37.   *See for example Sanchez-Espinoza,* 770 F2d 202 (DC Cir 1985) (challenging alleged support of armed forces against the government of Nicaragua); *Ramirez de Arellano v. Weinberger,* 724 F2d 143 (DC Cir 1983), *rev'd,* 745 F2d 1500 (DC Cir 1984) (*en banc*), *vacated and remanded for reconsideration in light of subsequent litigations,* 471 US 1113 (1985) (challenging alleged occupation of plaintiff's Honduran land for use as a training facility).

38.   *Supra,* note 6.

39.   *Id. at 1255.*

40.   *Id. at 1255–1256.*

41.   Fernand DeVarenness, *The Existing Rights of Minority in International Law* in Language: A Right and A Resource, Miklos Kontra, Robert Phillipson, Tove Skutnabb-Kangas, and Varady Tove (eds) (Central European University Press Budapest, Hungary, 1992) at 118–127.

42.   *Id.* at 124.

43.   *Id.*

44.   UN Charter Article 1(3).

45.   Arthur N. Holcombe, Human Rights in The Modern World. (New York University Press, New York, 1948) at 4.

46.   Henry S. Commager (ed.), Documents of American History, 7th edn (Prentice Hall, 1963) at 446.

47.   *Minority Schools in Albania* (advisory Opinion). 1235 PCIJ 64 (1935) at 17.

48.   *Id.* at 17 (emphasis added).

49. Joseph P. Gromacki, *The Protection of Language Rights in International Human Rights Law: A Proposed Draft Declaration of Linguistic Rights*, 32 VA. J. INT'L. L. 515 (1992) at 532.

50. 119 F3d 795 (Ariz. 1997).

51. *Ford. v. Quebec* [1988] 2SCR 712.

52. *Id.* at 716.

53. *Id.* at 778.

54. *Id.* at 787.

55. [1988] SCR 790.

56. *Id.* at 818.

57. *See Guesdon v. France*, UN Doc. A/45/40 (1990); *TK v. France*, UN Doc. A/45/40 (1990).

58. *See generally* Fernand De Varennes. *Language and Freedom of Expression in International Law*, 16 HUM. RTS Q. 163 (The Johns Hopkins University Press, 1993).

59. ICCPR, December 16, 1966 Article 14(3).

60. *Supra*, note 14.

61. *See supra*, note 49 at 544.

62. *See* Tove Skutnabb-Kangas, BILINGUALISM OR NOT: THE EDUCATION OF MINORITIES (Multilingual Matters, Clevedon, 1981) at 291.

63. Francesco Capotorti, *Study on the Rights of Persons Belonging to Ethnic, Religious and Linguistic Minorities*, UN Doc. E/CN. 4/Sub.2/384/Rev.1 (1979). at 102.

64. *See supra*, note 49 at 526, *quoting* Mala Tabory, *Language Rights as Human Rights*, 10 Isr Y. B. HUM. RTS 167, 174–175 (1980).

65. *Supra*, note 49.

66. *Id.* at 76.

67. *Id.* at 77.

68. *Id.* at 78.

69. *Id.*

70. *Id.* at 78–79.

71. *Id.*

72. *Id.* at 578.

73. *Id.*

74. *Id.*

Appendix

Title VI of the Civil Rights Act of 1964

Along with Title VII, Title VI of the Civil Rights Act of 1964 was passed during the height of the civil rights movement. Title VI has come to be an important vehicle for vindicating the rights of language minorities in almost every context of public life, from education to social services and even prisoners' rights. The life of Title VI, however, is in grave jeopardy given a Supreme Court decision issued in 2001 that severely undercut its usefulness as a tool for civil rights enforcement.

HISTORY AND SCOPE OF TITLE VI

The Civil Rights Act was passed because Congress felt that the piecemeal and slow pace of civil rights enforcement through the courts alone was insufficient and not necessarily effective. In submitting the proposed Act to Congress in 1963 President Kennedy stated:

> Simple justice requires that public funds, to which all taxpayers of all races contribute, not be spent in any fashion which encourages, entrenches, subsidizes, or results in racial discrimination. Direct discrimination by Federal, State, or local governments is prohibited by the Constitution. But indirect discrimination, through the use of Federal funds, is just as invidious; and it should not be necessary to resort to the courts to prevent each violation.[1]

It was President Johnson, however, who would sign the bill into law in 1964. The final Act provides that "[n]o person in the United States shall, on the ground of race, color, or national origin, be excluded from participation in, be denied benefits of, or be subjected to discrimination under any program or activity receiving Federal financial assistance."[2]

This is sweeping language, especially when the term "federal financial assistance" is read broadly; and it has been. Such assistance does not only cover monetary funds in the form of grants, loans, and advancements as well as simple funding, but also indirect assistance such as Medicaid reimbursements, financial aid to students at private schools, the grant or donation of federal property, the use of federal personnel, the lease of federal property or the acquisition of federal property at reduced or nominal fees.[3] The Act expressly exempts from coverage federal assistance in the form of contracts of insurance or guarantees as well as individuals who are the ultimate beneficiaries of the funds.[4]

Title VI prohibits discrimination in any "program or activity" of a recipient of federal funds. Again, the terms "program or activity" have been defined broadly to include "all operations of the institution or governmental entity receiving or distributing federal funds, rather than the narrower range of activities directly associated with the particular federal funding stream."[5] Congress explicitly recommitted itself to this broad interpretation in 1988 when it passed the Civil Rights Restoration Act, which expressly overturned a much more limited definition of the terminology adopted by the Supreme Court in *Grove City College v. Bell*,[6] which dealt with Title VI's sister legislation, Title IX, prohibiting gender discrimination.

In terms of employment, Title VI has a limited role, since Congress passed Title VII to deal specifically with employment discrimination, discussed in Chapter 4. When an entity receives federal funds primarily to provide employment, however, Title VI does have a role. If the entity receives federal funds for other purposes, the employment Title VII would apply.[7]

The Act requires that federal agencies, such as the Department of Transportation, Department of Education or the Department of Labor, for instance, enforce the policy through the issuance of rules, regulations or orders establishing the standards for recipient compliance with Title VI. Agencies can enforce the law primarily through a withholding of federal funds for violations through their respective Offices of Civil Rights (OCR). No funds may be withheld unless an express finding of non-compliance has been made on the record and the recipient given an opportunity to be heard and attempts at voluntary compliance have failed. In order to give recipients fair notice of their obligations under Title VI, Congress mandated that agencies promulgate standards in the form of rules, regulations and orders, governing the administration of Title VI.

For instance, the Department of Health and Human Service's regulations provide, among other things, that a recipient may not:

[p]rovide any service, financial aid, or other benefit to an individual which is different, or is provided in a different manner, from that provided to others under the program; ... [r]estrict an individual in any way in the enjoyment of any advantage or privilege enjoyed by others receiving any service, financial aid, or other benefit under the program; ... [t]reat an individual differently from others in determining whether he satisfies any admission, enrollment, quota, eligibility, membership or other requirement or condition which individuals must meet in order to be provided any service, financial aid, or other benefit provided under the program....[8]

Further, agency regulations have specifically prohibited recipients from:

directly or through contractual or other arrangements, utiliz[ing] criteria or methods of administration which have the *effect* of subjecting individuals to discrimination because of their race, color, or national origin, or have the *effect* of defeating or substantially impairing accomplishment of the objectives of the programs as respect individuals of a particular race, color, or national origin.[9]

By prohibiting policies or practices that have a discriminatory *effect*, federal agencies turned Title VI into a real weapon in the civil rights struggle. Every Cabinet department and approximately 40 agencies adopted Title VI regulations prohibiting "effects" discrimination. In *Guardians Association v. Civil Service Commission of the City of New York*,[10] seven members of the Supreme Court decided that §601 of Title VI prohibits intentional discrimination – a scope no wider than that provided by the Equal Protection Clause. Five members, however, joined in the additional decision that federal agencies may adopt regulations under §602 that "effectuate" §601 by banning policies and practices that have discriminatory effects. This holding was re-affirmed in an opinion by Justice Marshall in *Alexander v. Choate*,[11] when he wrote that "actions having an unjustifiable disparate impact on minorities [can] be redressed through agency regulations designed to implement the purposes of Title VI."[12]

Victims of discrimination need not jump the substantial hurdles of proving discriminatory intent under the Equal Protection Clause analysis erected by the Supreme Court. Since *Guardians* was decided, policy decisions (for instance on where to site a hospital or a garbage dump) that had a negative effect on minorities could be subject to a searching legal analysis in a court of law. The effects standard codified as federal regulations was arguably the single largest contribution made by the federal government to the continued vitality of civil rights enforcement. It is no wonder then that their legality is under heated attack. Making out a claim under the effects standard, or a "disparate impact" case, is discussed below.

ADMINISTRATIVE ENFORCEMENT

The Office of Civil Rights (OCR) of each federal agency has a process through which individuals or groups who feel that they have been the victims of discrimination can file a complaint with the appropriate office; either on a form provided by OCR or through an informal letter. The complaint process is designed to be community-friendly, and the complainant needs few resources to start the investigative process. Further, unlike formal litigation, there are no standing requirements, so community groups and civil rights activists who believe others are being subjected to discrimination can file a complaint. Complaints should be filed within 180 days of the date of the challenged discriminatory action.

Once a complaint has been filed with OCR, there is little formal role for the complainant. OCR will decide whether to investigate and will conduct its own investigation with little input from the complainant. However, legal analysis of the issues presented, statistical data, even significant anecdotal information, ought to be provided to OCR. Further, complainants should attempt to be a part of the resolution of the complaint, and should diligently keep track of any progress being made by OCR. OCR has the power to terminate funds to recalcitrant recipients but that is a rarely-used power employed as a last resort after much negotiation for more amicable resolutions has failed and only after the recipient has been given explicit notice of the probable fund-termination. In *Grove City College*,[13] the Supreme Court affirmed the withholding of federal funds from a college that refused to execute an assurance that it would comply with Title IX prohibiting gender discrimination; the Court relied on the language of Title VI authorizing fund-termination in reaching its decision on this sister statute. The Court also expressly found that funds could be terminated without a finding of actual discrimination by the college.

However, relief specific to the individual complainant, such as injunctive relief or damages of any kind, is not available under this administrative process.

Although OCR clearly has a significant role to play in enforcing Title VI, it is still a governmental agency whose agenda is often driven by politics. When conservatives are governing the nation, civil rights enforcement under Title VI is often quite limited, only to increase again when Democrats are in office. Jenkins notes that:

> [t]he statute's early years saw relatively strong federal enforcement, particularly by the Department of Health, Education and Welfare (HEW).... During the Nixon Administration, however, HEW's commitment to desegregation in education declined.... After a brief resurgence under the Carter Administration, Title VI agency enforcement lay dormant for over a decade. With the exception of attacks on affirmative action, the Regan and Bush Administrations' approach to Title VI enforcement ranged from benign neglect to open hostility.[14]

Also, as a political entity trying to enforce the law against other political entities, the record of the federal agencies has been weak: few resources are actually devoted to Title VI enforcement, the process of investigation, fact finding and negotiation can take years, and politically unpalatable complaints are left to linger without definitive action. Although the Title VI administrative enforcement scheme can provide real relief from discrimination without the need for complainants to have significant resources for legal help, the enforceability of Title VI in the courts is of critical importance.

PROVING INTENTIONAL DISCRIMINATION

Claims of intentional discrimination may be brought under §601 of Title VI. In these cases the level of protection afforded by the statute is no greater than that afforded by the Equal

Protection Clause. However, unlike claims made under the Constitution, successful plaintiffs may be able to collect monetary damages for violations of §601. In order to prove a *prima facie* case, a potential plaintiff who does not have direct evidence of discrimination must demonstrate that:

(1) she is a member of a class protected under the Act;
(2) she was denied an opportunity or benefit for which she was qualified or she was otherwise treated negatively;
(3) a person or persons of other racial or ethnic groups received the denied benefit or were spared the negative treatment or that the opportunity which the potential plaintiff was denied remained available.

This framework emulates that developed in employment discrimination cases decided by the Supreme Court such as in *McDonnel Douglas Corp. v. Green*,[15] *Texas Department of Community Affairs v. Burdine*,[16] and their progeny.

If the defendant rebuts the plaintiff's *prima facie* case, then the plaintiff must show that the rationale offered by the defendant is really a pretext for discrimination. The plaintiff bears the burden of persuasion throughout the case. Here, the plaintiff must really prove more than that the proffered reason was simply untrue; she must prove that, were it not for her race or ethnicity, the defendant would have acted differently.[17] Further, it is generally not enough for plaintiffs to show that defendant took an action even though it knew or should have known that the action would have a racially discriminatory impact. Intentional discrimination will be proven only by a showing that the defendant took the action *because of*, not in spite of, the discriminatory effect.[18] However, circumstantial evidence of intent may be drawn from statistical evidence of discriminatory impact, of historical evidence of past discrimination, of departures from established practices in defendant's treatment of plaintiff, and of the legislative history of a governmental action or policy.[19]

Should the plaintiff have *direct* evidence of discrimination, such as statements attributable to the defendant showing discriminatory animus towards plaintiff, the plaintiff need not go through the burden-shifting analysis. Also, if the challenged policy is discriminatory on its face, then the plaintiff need not go through this analysis. For instance, a policy that simply treats individuals differently based on their age or gender or race/ethnicity would be subject to challenge as facially discriminatory. In *Los Angles Department of Water & Power v. Manhart*,[20] an employer's policy requiring female employees to make larger contributions than males to a pension fund was found to be discriminatory on its face. Policies that are discriminatory on their face are quite rare in today's more sophisticated society. This is a particularly difficult framework to fulfill if the plaintiff is challenging broad governmental actions having a discriminatory effect on a particular racial group. Then the plaintiff would have to show that the governmental entity involved took the challenged action purposely to discriminate against a group. Rarely will a court, without damning direct evidence, find that the government acted in such a manner. Yet, our society is replete with situations in which the needs or interests of minorities are ignored or neglected as governmental entities take one action after another that have devastating consequences for minority communities. In such situations, the government is seldom acting in a purposely discriminatory manner as recognized by the law. It is here, in these much more common but less clear-cut legal situations, that the regulations under §602 of Title VI can play such a crucial role for civil rights enforcement.

CONSTRUCTING A DISPARATE-IMPACT CASE

The courts have consistently found that agency regulations that prohibit practices and policies that have a discriminatory effect are, in essence, prohibiting practices that have disparate, negative impacts on racial/ethnic groups.[21] The elements for constructing such a claim are borrowed from the analysis established in the Title VII employment discrimination context, discussed in Chapter 4, by the Supreme Court in *Griggs v. Duke Power Co.*[22]

In order to prove such a negative impact, the plaintiff must first establish a *prima facie* case of discrimination through statistical evidence that the challenged practice has a disproportionate negative impact on members of a particular racial group. The burden then shifts to the recipient to show that the challenged practice has a "manifest relationship" to the mission of the recipient, or that there is a "substantial legitimate justification" for the challenged practice.[23] In the educational context, the relationship should be one of "educational necessity."[24] Even if the defendant meets this burden, however, plaintiffs can still win under the disparate-impact standard if they can show that another less-discriminatory alternative is available to defendants.

Although the disparate-impact avenue is a more generous framework for plaintiffs than proving intentional discrimination, there are still significant hurdles a plaintiff must overcome in order to establish a *prima facie* case. Alan Jenkins has grouped those issues together into three broad categories characterized as "baseline," "magnitude," and "causation."[25] Under baseline considerations, the primary question that the plaintiff must address if there is a disparate negative impact is: who is being compared to establish the disproportionality? Under certain circumstances, the question can be fairly simple to answer. For instance, if an entrance exam to a college is being challenged, the pass rate of the complaining group is compared to the pass rate of all others. In *Sharif v. New York State Education Department*,[26] a *prima facie* case under Title IX was established against the continued use of the SAT exam to award merit scholarships where the difference in scores between males and females was 10 points. Consequently, more males were receiving the awards than females.

In the land use context, one commentator notes that:

> the comparative inquiry for Title VI purposes is the racial composition of persons being displaced or otherwise harmed by a development compared with the larger population that could potentially be affected. Absent discrimination, one would expect that the persons negatively affected by any given project would roughly reflect the racial composition of the county or service area at large.[27]

So in *Coalition of Concerned Citizens Against I-670 v. Damian*,[28] a *prima facie* case under Title VI regulations was established where 75% of those displaced by a highway project were racial minorities compared with a majority-white service area. In *Bryan v. Koch*,[29] a 30% statistical disparity was found to be sufficient to establish a *prima facie* case.

Under the issue of "magnitude," Jenkins has found that "[a] plaintiff may be reasonably certain that a cognizable discriminatory effect exists where the proportion of her racial group that is adversely affected by the challenged action is greater than two to three standard deviations from that of the baseline population as a whole."[30] Such statistical specificity, however, is rarely needed; what is necessary is that the disparity be "significant," or at least "definite, measurable."[31]

A more complex issue for plaintiffs is showing causation: that the practice complained of is actually the cause of the negative effect. The complexities of this issue are best presented with an anecdote from the education context. For instance, the high Latino drop-out rate in the US has been the source of national taskforces and a multitude of reports. In cities like New York, easily 30% of the school system's Latino students do not graduate; this is by far the highest drop-out rate of any racial or ethnic group. Community members feel with good reason that the school system is failing their children. A disparate negative effect of *something* is clear. Of *what* is the question that is still unanswered. Although a multitude of sins can be laid at the door of the City's Board of Education, identifying the one or two practices which, if changed, would address the drop-out problem has proved to be impossible so far. The challenge to would-be plaintiffs is to identify the wrong specifically and trace it back to its particular cause. On the other side, once a recipient has shown that the practice complained of is not the cause of the grievance, it need not show that there is legitimate relationship between the practice and the mission of the agency; a *prima facie* case has not been shown.

PRIVATE RIGHT OF ACTION

Since Title VI was enacted 37 years ago, it has been considered enforceable in the courts. There is nothing, however, that expressly states that potential plaintiffs have that right and courts have either assumed the right exists or applied an analysis developed by the Supreme Court in *Cort v. Ash*,[32] which inferred a private right of action. In *Cannon v. University of Chicago*,[33] the Supreme Court found that there was a private right of action to enforce §901 of Title IX which was patterned after §601 of Title VI. Indeed, the Court stated that "[w]e have no doubt that Congress intended to create Title IX remedies comparable to those available under Title VI and that it understood Title VI as authorizing an implied private cause of action for victims of the prohibited discrimination."[34]

Since the decisions in *Cannon* and *Alexander, supra*, most lower federal courts assumed the existence of private right of action under Title VI for enforcing both §601 and the regulations under §602.[35]

In *Chester Residents Concerned For Quality Living v. Seif*,[36] the Third Circuit became the first federal appellate court to analyze in depth the existence of a private right of action to enforce the Title VI disparate-impact regulations. That case involved the disparate-impact regulations passed by the Environmental Protection Agency (EPA) to enforce Title VI and the siting of a waste processing facility in a high-minority area. Finding that the holdings in both *Guardians* and *Alexander* were ambiguous on this point, the court found an implied private right of action under the Third Circuit's own case law as supported by the Supreme Court's decision in *Cort v. Ash*. The factors that courts must look to *Cort* for determining whether a private right of action actually exists despite an explicit grant of authority are:

(1) whether the plaintiff is one for whose benefit the statute was enacted;
(2) whether the cause of action is one traditionally relegated to state law so that inferring a federal cause of action would be inappropriate;
(3) indications of legislative intent, either implicit or explicit, to create or deny a private right of action;
(4) whether inferring a private right of action is consistent with the underlying purposes of legislative scheme.[37]

Evaluating each of these factors, the Third Circuit did find such a private right of action but its decision was ultimately vacated as moot on appeal.

The Third Circuit was again called upon to evaluate the availability of a private right of action under the disparate impact regulations of Title VI in *Powell v. Ridge*,[38] a case challenging Pennsylvania's school funding formula as racially discriminatory. In deciding this issue, the court needed to answer whether "the agency rule is properly within the scope of the enabling statute" and whether "implying a private right of action will further the purposes of the enabling statute."[39] Relying upon the Supreme Court's ruling in *Alexander v. Choate*, the *Powell* court easily found that the §602 regulations were properly within the scope of Title VI itself. It also was able to quickly conclude that the purpose of Title VI, to combat discrimination in federally funded programs, was furthered by private rights action –"a private right of action will increase enforcement."[40]

The court, however, also needed to evaluate the other factors under *Cort* as interpreted by the Third Circuit in *Angelastro v. Prudential-Bache Securities, Inc.*[41] In *Angelastro*, it was held that courts should allow for private rights action under agency rules:

[w]here the enabling statute authorizes an implied right of action ... if doing so is not at variance with the purposes of the statue.... [I]f Congress intended to permit private actions for violations of the statute, "it would be anomalous to preclude private parties from suing under the rules that impart meaning to the statute."[42]

Relying on the Supreme Court's twin pronouncements in *Guardians* and *Alexander*, the court determined that the regulations did indeed meet the *Cort/Angelastro* tests. Further, the fact that the regulations prohibit more activities than the statute alone was not significant, for the courts have often found in other situations that more prohibitive regulations are valid; indeed, the breadth of the regulations was the very reason why the courts needed to engage in the *Cort* analysis at all. With its decision, the *Powell* Court definitely joined the Third Circuit and at least eight other circuits that had implicitly or explicitly found a private right of action under the disparate-impact regulations.[43]

These decades of progress for private enforcement of the Title VI regulations, however, were completely undone by the Supreme Court in *Alexander v. Sandoval*,[44] a language rights case challenging Alabama's English-only law. The details of the trial and the facts of the case are discussed in detail in Chapter 2. However, after the Spanish-dominant plaintiffs won at the trial and appellate levels, the case was appealed to the US Supreme Court.

The Supreme Court reviewed only the technical issue as to whether there was a private right of action that would allow private individuals to sue to enforce the disparate impact regulations of Title VI. In a five-to-four decision, the Court held that there was not. The Court found that neither its holdings in *Cannon* nor in *Guardians* expressly found that such a private right of action existed. *Canon*, the Court said, was decided under the structure of Title IX, and assumed intentional discrimination. Further, among the splintered decisions of *Guardians* could only be found a willingness to reconsider in the future whether there was a private right of action under the regulations.[45]

Congress creates a private right of action, said the Court, and there is no "rights creating" language in Title VI under §602 of the Act. Rather, §602 appears only to implement the right to be free of intentional discrimination already created by §601, and §602 is to be enforced through the federal agencies themselves through the termination of funding or other "means authorized by law."[46]

Justice Stevens, in his dissent, tried to provide advocates with a brief reprieve. He suggested that private litigants could challenge public policies with a disparate-impact under §1983 of the Civil Rights Act.[47] That route has already met with some disappointment, however. Ironically, it was the Third Circuit that decided in 2001 that the §602 regulations do not create an interest enforceable under §1983 because the interest in being free of disparate impact policies is not implicit within the body of Title VI itself.[48]

This case arose within the South Camden section of New Jersey, a high minority area considered environmentally disadvantaged. The Waterfront South area in particular contained two Superfund sites, several contaminated and abandoned industrial sites, and many operating facilities including chemical companies, waste facilities, food-processing companies, automotive shops and a petroleum coke transfer station. The Waterfront South area "hosts 20% of Camden's contaminated sites and, on average, more than twice the number of facilities with permits to emit air pollution than exist in the area encompassed within a typical New Jersey zip code."[49]

Residents sued under the disparate-impact regulations of Title VI to try to stop completion of a granulated blast furnace slag grinding facility that had implications for the air quality in the Waterfront area. The New Jersey Department of Environmental Protection (NJDEP) had allowed the construction of the facility, saying that a company-provided analysis met its specifications for air quality control. The residents complained that the NJDEP had not considered the racially disparate impact that the facility would have on the neighborhood.

The residents filed an action in court which began successfully. Soon after the trial court granted the residents' request for a preliminary injunction, however, the Supreme Court decided *Sandoval*, striking down the disparate-impact regulations that the residents had relied on. The trial court allowed the residents to amend their complaint by adding a claim to enforce the disparate-impact regulations under §1983. Relying on prior Third Circuit precedent and undoubtedly taking courage from Justice Stevens' dissent, the trial court allowed the injunction to stand, notwithstanding the decision in *Sandoval*, under a §1983 analysis.[50]

In reversing the district court, the Third Circuit engaged in an analysis that followed the reasoning in *Sandoval*, i.e. whether the statute of Title VI could be read as containing a private right of action. The court found that:

> [i]nasmuch as the court found previously that the only right conferred by section 601 was to be free of intentional discrimination, it does not follow that the right to be free from disparate impact discrimination can be located in section 602. In fact, it cannot. In sum, the regulations, though assumedly [*sic*] valid, are not based on any federal right present in the statute.... the regulations do more than define or flesh out the content of a specific right conferred upon the plaintiffs by Title VI. Instead, the regulations implement Title VI to give the statute a scope beyond that Congress contemplated, as Title VI does not establish a right to be free of disparate impact discrimination. Thus, the regulations are "too far removed from Congressional intent to constitute a 'federal right' enforceable under §1983."[51]

How each individual district court and Circuit court will actually handle the *Sandoval* decision remains to be seen.[52] That *Sandoval* has sent a shudder through the civil rights world cannot be overstated. For decades, the civil rights community has relied upon the *Guardians* holding and the other Circuit courts to confidently move against public agencies for disparate-impact violations. The plaintiff residents of South Camden, however, are now leading the way through a new civil right terrain – making out intentional discrimination within a legal context that defined intentional discrimination narrowly under the Equal Protection Clause.

For language rights activists, *Sandoval* was a particularly harsh blow since there is no express proscription against linguistic discrimination; disparate-impact is the foremost way that language rights claims can be litigated with any hope of success.

Notes

1. HR Doc. No 124, 88th Cong. 1st Sess. (1963), *reprinted in* 110 USCCAN 2392.
2. 42 USC §2000d.
3. *See* Jenkins, Alan, *Title VI of the Civil Rights Act of 1964: Racial Discrimination in Federally Funded Programs* in CIVIL RIGHTS LITIGATION AND ATTORNEYS FEES ANNUAL HANDBOOK (1995) at 174.
4. *Id.*
5. *Id.*
6. 465 US 555 (1984).
7. *See* 42 USC §2000d-3.
8. 45 CFR §80.3(b).
9. 45 CFR §80.3(b)(2) (emphasis added).
10. 463 US 582 (1983).
11. 469 US 287 (1985).
12. *Id.* at 293.
13. *Supra,* note 6.
14. *Supra,* note 3 at 175–76.
15. 411 US 792 (1973).
16. 450 US 248 (1981).
17. *St Mary's Honor Center v. Hicks,* 509 US 502 (1993).
18. *Personnel Administrator of Massachusetts v. Feeney,* 446 US 256 (1979).
19. *See Village of Arlington Heights v. Metropolitan Housing Development Cor.,* 429 US 2525 (1977).

20. 435 US 702 (1978).

21. *See, Georgia State Conference of Branches of NAACP v. State of Georgia*, 775 F2d 1403 (11th Cir 1985); *Meek v. Martinez*, 724 FSupp 888 (SD Fla. 1987).

22. 401 US 424 (1971).

23. *See Elston v. Talladega County Board of Education*, 997 F2d 1394 (11th Cir 1993); *New York Urban League, Inc. v. New York*, 71 F3d 1031 (2nd Cir 1995).

24. *See Larry P. v. Riles*, 793 F2d 969 (9th Cir 1984).

25. *Supra* note 3 at 186.

26. 709 FSupp 345 (SDNY 1989).

27. *Supra*, note 2 at 186.

28. 608 FSupp 110 (SD Ohio 1984).

29. 627 F2d 612 (2nd Cir 1983).

30. *Supra*, note 3 at 187, *citing*, *Guardians Association v. Civil Service Commission of City of New York*, 630 F2d 79 (2nd Cir 1980).

31. *Scelsa v. City University of New York*, 806 FSupp 1126, 1140 (SDNY 1992).

32. 422 US 66 (1975).

33. 441 US 677 (1977).

34. *Id.* at 703.

35. *See Burton v. City of Belle Glade*, 178 F3d 1175 (11th Cir 1999); *New York Urban League, Inc. v. New York*, 71 F3d 1031 (2nd Cir 1995); *City of Chicago v. Lindley*, 66 F3d 819 (7th Cir 1995); *Larry P. v Riles, supra*, note 23, *US v. LULAC*, 793 F2d 636 (5th Cir 1986); *Bryan v. Koch*, 627 F2d 612 (2d Cir 1980). However, some courts have remained skeptical. *See dicta in New York City Environmental Justice Alliance v. Giuliani*, 50 FSupp 2d 250, 253 (SDNY 1999), *aff'd*, 184 F3d 206 (2nd Cir 1999); *South Bronx Clean Air Coalition v. Conroy*, 20 FSupp 2d 565, 572 (SDNY 1998).

36. 132 F3d 925 (3rd Cir 1997), *vacated as moot, Seif v. Chester Residents Concerned For Quality Living*, 524 US 974 (1998).

37. *Supra*, note 32 at 78.

38. 189 F3d 387 (3rd Cir 1999).

39. *Id.* at 398

40. *Id.*

41. 764 F2d 939 (3rd Cir 1985).

42. *Supra*, note 38 at 398–99.

43. *See, Buchanan v. City of Bolivar, Tenn.*, 99 F3d 1352 (6th Cir 1996); *Villanueva v. Carere*, 85 F3d 481 (10th Cir 1996); *New York Urban League, supra*, (2nd Cir); *David K. v. Lane*, 839 F2d 1265 (7th Cir 1988); *Castaneda v. Pickard*, 781 F2d 465 (5th Cir 1986); *Latino Unidos de Chelsea v. Secretary of Housing & Dev*, 799 F2d 774 (1st Cir 1986); *Larry P. Riles, supra*, note 24.

44. *Alexander v. Sandoval*, 532 US 275 (2001).

45. *Id.* at 283.

46. 42 USC §2000d-1

47. Justice Stevens stated: "I thought then as I do now, that a violation of regulations adopted pursuant to Title VI may be established by proof of discriminatory impact in a §1983 action against state actors and also in an implied action against private parties." *Id.* at n.6. And:

   "[t]o the extent that the majority denies relief to the respondents merely because they neglected to mention 42 USC. §1983 in framing their Title VI claim, this case is something of a sport. Litigants who in the future wish to enforce the Title VI regulations against state actors in all likelihood must only reference §1983 to obtain relief; indeed, the plaintiffs in this case ... presumably retain the option of re-challenging Alabama's English-policy in a complaint that invokes §1983 even after today's decision." *Id.* at 299–300.

48. *South Camden Citizens In Action v. New Jersey Department of Environmental Protection*, 274 F3d 771 (3rd Cir 2001).

49. *Id.* at 775.

50. *See, South Camden Citizens in Action v. New Jersey Department of Environmental Protection*, 145 FSupp 2d 505 (DNJ 2001).

51. *Supra*, note 46 at 789–790.

52. In 2002, a New York district court followed the reasoning in *Sandoval* and *South Camden* to dismiss a disparate-impact claim brought under §1983. *See Ceaser v. Pataki*, 2002 WL 472271 (SDNY 2002).

Printed in the United States
68247LVS00002B/49-88